THEIR FATHERS' WORK

THEIR **FATHERS' WORK**

Casting Nets with the World's Fishermen

William McCloskey

INTERNATIONAL MARINE/McGRAW-HILL

Camden, Maine • New York • San Francisco • Washington, D.C.
Auckland • Bogotá • Caracas • Lisbon • London
Madrid • Mexico City • Milan • Montreal • New Delhi
San Juan • Singapore • Sydney • Tokyo • Toronto

Also by William McCloskey

The Mallore Affair, a novel of India

Highliners, a novel of the fishermen of Alaska

Breakers, a sequel to *Highliners*

Fish Decks, a nonfiction account of the fishermen of New England, Newfoundland/Labrador, Norway, and the Chesapeake

International Marine

A Division of The McGraw-Hill Companies

DOC   10   9   8   7   6   5   4   3   2   1

Text and photographs copyright © 1998, 2000 William McCloskey.

All rights reserved. The name "International Marine" and the International Marine logo are trademarks of The McGraw-Hill Companies. Printed in the United States of America.

The Library of Congress has cataloged the cloth edition as follows:

Library of Congress Cataloging-in-Publication Data
McCloskey, William B., 1928–
   Their fathers' work : casting nets with the world's fishermen /
William McCloskey.
      p.   cm.
   Includes index.
   ISBN 0-07-045347-0 (alk. paper)
      1. Fisheries—Anecdotes.   2. Fishers Anecdotes.   3. McCloskey,
William B., 1928–   . I. Title.
   SH331.M335   1998
   639.2—dc21   97-49595
                                         CIP

Paperback ISBN 0-07-135820-X

Design by Paul Uhl, Design Associates, updated by Shannon Thomas
Production and page layout by Janet Robbins and Shannon Thomas
Edited by Jonathan Eaton, Tom McCarthy, Pamela Benner, Margaret E. Cook
Maps by Tech Graphics Corp.
All photographs by the author

To Wynn
my son and fellow adventurer

Contents

Acknowledgments

A pleasure after the grind of years it takes to write a book is the opportunity to thank the people whose help made it possible. The list is very long. So many gave hospitality on land and sea, shared information, and became friends along the way.

Those who offered a roof over the head of a grateful writer usually traveling on a shoestring, along with their insights: In Newfoundland Jim and Sharon Winter of St. John's and Jack and Florence Troake of Twillingate, with open doors over so many years ("but leave yer boots in the pantry, b'y") that I've watched their children grow to adults. In New Zealand, Tom Fishburn of Greymouth. In Chile, Hans Schmidt and Pepe Montt, bold young men working to extend the fortunes of local fishermen through new grounds and new equipment. And in Alaska—Tom Casey, Hank and Jan Pennington, Harold and Marcie Jones, and Chris and Jim Blackburn of Kodiak; Jeff Bailey and Ken Adams of Cordova; in Bristol Bay Harold Brindle, head of Red Salmon Cannery, and Chuck Bundrant, founder of Trident Seafoods; Rich and Joanie Abbott in Chignik.

And those who provided decks under my feet. Besides those in Chile and New Zealand mentioned above: In Japan, Shikahiro Sumida, owner of the driftnet vessel *Sumiho Maru No. 75* that carried me for nearly a month. In Norway, the brothers Oddmund and Tor-Eirik Bye aboard their *Myrefisk* trawlers. In Indonesia, Bali village headman Embli Astara and his barefoot crew. In Newfoundland, Pat Antle of the trawler *Zamora* on Grand Bank. In New England, Joey Testaverde out of Gloucester and Pete Jacobsen out of Fairhaven/New Bedford.

In Alaska the list always starts with Thorvold Olsen, one of Kodiak's highliner skippers, now of the *Viking Star,* aboard whose *Polar Star* I first stacked a seine and crewed a king crab pot. In Bristol Bay, Magne Nes, who hired me aboard the *Gail T,* John Crivello of the *Manhattan Kid,* and Guy Piercey of the *Katherine B.* In Chignik, Ernie Carlson of the *Desperado,* Dave Anderson of the *Gypsy Queen,* and Clem Grunnert of the *Adventuress.* In the Bering Sea, Leiv Loklingholm of the *American Beauty.* In Cordova, Kenny Carlson of the *Tarah Rose* and Virgil Carroll of the *Miss Carroll.*

Those who patiently read parts of the manuscript within their expertise include John Crivello, forty-nine years a Bristol Bay gillnetter and still counting; Peter Schmidt, CEO of Marco and respected pioneer of the new Chilean fisheries; Harold Brindle, second-generation manager of the Red Salmon Cannery in Bristol Bay; Ernie Carlson and Mori Jones, Chignik salmon men, witness to near disaster; Marilyn Leland and Ken Adams, driving Cordova participants in protecting fisheries from the sludge of the *EXXON Valdez* oil spill; Jay Hastings, Japan fisheries representative; Josephine Brennan, my hometown guardian of syntax and vocabulary; Bill Shires, rough-seas rescuer of two Oregon fishermen trapped in an overturned boat; Moritaka Hiyashi and Andre Tahindro at the United Nations.

Those paving the way with contacts I otherwise could never have made without immense time expenditure include Alan MacNow, representing the Japan Fisheries and Whaling Associations; Peter and Hans Schmidt in Chile; Jim Campbell, late New Zealand fishery commissioner; Bart Eaton, fisherman, council member, and practical visionary of the fishing industry, ready both with insights and exuberant anecdotes.

And those who fit no category above. Cathy Harig and Eleanor Krell of the Enoch Pratt Library in Baltimore, always willing to research a source. Jack O'Dell at U.S. Coast Guard headquarters. Leo Strobridge and Wayne Evans of Canadian Fisheries at Newfoundland headquarters in St. John's. Wilson Kettle, Canadian Fisheries inspector now retired, bright presence throughout nearly two decades of trips to Newfoundland. Ian Strutt and Peter Hjul, the helpful and always supportive editors of *Fishing News International* in London, and Jonathan Fisher, editor of *International Wildlife Magazine.* Thanks also to editors at *Atlantic, Smithsonian, New York Times Magazine, National Fisherman, Pacific Fishing, Oceans, Alaska, Audubon, Johns Hopkins Technical Digest and Magazine, National Wildlife,* and *Alaska Fisherman's Journal,* in whose pages versions of the material in this book appeared. At International Marine, to Jon Eaton, editorial director, who quickly left an imprint with encouragement and imaginative new approaches, and Tom McCarthy, managing editor, whose enthusiasm reinforced my work.

The book is dedicated to my son, Wynn, fellow-adventurer aboard Alaskan fishing boats and in seat-of-the pants travels from Great Barrier Reef to the Red Sea to the Amazon to the Algarve. The precious family support group includes also my daughter, Karin, physician and healer of children; my parents, Bill and Evelyn, remaining always there in spirit; and above all my wife, Ann, who sets the standard.

Introduction

NOW. . . FISH CAN'T HIDE! It's an ad for the newest electronic fish-finding device. The manufacturer is Japanese, the potential customer American, the implication worldwide. Yet another new addition to wheelhouse equipment, both expensive and efficient, to torment the fishing skipper. "If I don't buy it," he'll reason over the account book in one of a dozen languages, "I'll lose my edge to the others. But if I do invest, I'll have to push my guys that much harder to pay for the cursed thing."

Too bad for him. The times catch up with every occupation. The result should be at least more fish available in the markets from New York to Santiago to Taipei. Except that Nature's supply is not infinite. Sea creatures reproduce in commercial quantity only on continental shelves (or, in a few places, on dropoff coasts with extreme upwelling), where relatively shallow water combines sunlight with nutrients to create the conditions for life. Of the nine largest shelf areas in the world, the United Nations Food and Agriculture Organization (FAO) reports that seven are in serious decline, and classifies four of these as "commercially depleted." The national and international custodians of these precious food grounds are slowly awakening to the danger. Will they react in time?

No major new forces have entered the picture since the first edition of this book went to press in early 1998. Yet the elements of the saga do not pause for long. The ocean's resources are dynamic, reacting to fluxes in climate, chemistry, and predators, while humans, the main predator, find opportunity where they can.

China continues to expand its fishing fleets around the world. Spain continues to jockey for larger quotas within the European Union. The fishing fortunes of Chile have diminished at least temporarily with a dropoff of jack mackerel off its central coast. Toothfish in the Indian and South Atlantic Oceans continue to be overfished; by seven times an informally agreed-upon quota by several nations, according to one report, with Spain, Norway, Chile, Argentina, and China being the worst offenders. (Only Norway appears to have taken official steps to stop its negative role.) A United Nations agreement on certain international controls of the world's "Straddling Stocks" of sea resources continues to await the ratification of at least thirty nations to become sea law, and remains a few signatures short.

Threats to the fishing life continue. With greater regard for opportunity than for truth or fairness, some animal groups guided by emotion still push to protect all marine mammals (even individual creatures) at the expense of whole fisheries, and some sport groups work to ban all near-shore commercial nets (in the name of conservation) in order to have it all for themselves.

Fishing dates further back in man's food-gathering evolution than farming. It ranges these days from those who leave home each morning in an open skiff to those who sign for a several-month voyage to far seas. Boys still follow their fathers and grandfathers to the boats. As I traveled the Pacific and Atlantic, pulling nets and lines from Alaska and Japan to Chile and New Zealand to Newfoundland and Norway, sharing the heavy wet work—along with occasional danger and frequent raucous spirits—I could never believe that all this gut vitality would ever be ground under by mere shortages, mismanagement, and greed. But some of it has. And more will come.

"Joey don't know any more," the wife of a New England fisherman friend tells me, "whether to go try make a living on the boat or go to council meetings to fight for his rights."

Meanwhile the changes roll in like heavy surf. Surely some fishermen will survive them, so that this account of their labor, aspirations, and perils will remain an account of the living rather than the disappeared. I can only tell my tales, outline the issues, and hope for the best. If I've delivered nothing but a lament for those of a dying culture, we'll be the poorer for it.

WILLIAM MCCLOSKEY
March 2000

THEIR FATHERS' WORK

"And Jesus, walking by the Sea of Galilee, saw two brethren, Simon called Peter, and Andrew his brother, casting a net into the sea, for they were fishermen. . . . And going from thence, he saw other two brethren, James the son of Zebedee, and John his brother, in a ship with Zebedee their father, mending their nets."

—Matthew 4:18, 21

"We, the twelve disciples of the Lord, wept and mourned, and each one, very grieved for what had come to pass, went to his own home. But I, Simon Peter, and my brother Andrew, took our nets and went to the sea."

—Apocrypha the Lost Gospel According to Peter

CHAPTER ONE

Asking for It

Bering Sea

November 1976

"You're unloaded," says the canneryman. The snow on his parka melts quickly in the heat of the boat's galley. It is three in the morning. The poker and drinks and guitar playing began at eight last night, after the boat arrived from a week on the Bering Sea with a hold full of crab.

"Ve go," says Leiv, the skipper, and, to a lady friend bunked with one of the bachelors: "Get your ass on the dock."

Minutes later the crew has fitted the hatch cover back into the deck, battened gear, and cast off lines from the ice-slick pier. To starboard the domes of Unalaska's little Russian Orthodox church slip by, dark against the blue glow of the snow-covered mountains. Leiv turns the *American Beauty* at a right angle to the church and heads toward the mouth of the bay, past Dutch Harbor. A snow squall hazes the lights on the steaming processor ships scattered alongshore, finally obliterating them. The close white mountains are dim and shardlike. Leaving their lee the boat plunges head on into the seas of a forty-knot northwester. Within an hour of the final poker chip on the galley table, we have left all traces of even the tenuous Aleutian civilization. Protected only by the deck beneath our feet, we're on our own.

It is a long 150 miles to the grounds where the crab pots lie. The boat pitches, thuds into troughs, takes crashing tons of water over the pilothouse. The crew stands watches in turn, and sleep. I lie in my bunk, seasick from too much drink (I thought we'd spend the night calmly in port), listening to a monotonous groaning creak overhead. In the forepeak locker just beyond, cans fall from the shelves and tumble back and forth with each roll. An inch from my face, on the other side of a few steel plates, the raw sea gurgles.

A new night begins when Leiv homes in with loran to locate the first string of pots. He shouts and slows the engines. Everyone pulls on oilskins and silently goes into it. Hail splatters like glass in our faces, black waves swell higher than our heads, the wind roars and whines, and sea foams across the deck.

The deck lights pick up the two pink marker buoys of the first pot, dipping in the troughs. Frank throws a hook and grapples the buoys aboard. He bends the pot line through the hydraulic crab block and starts to coil it as Dale operates the controls to reel it in. Frank's hands fly like pistons, dropping three hundred feet of line by his boots in even rings. I bait, chopping frozen herring and fish heads. My knees dig into the wooden tub for support. Up comes the heavy, square, swaying seven-foot steel-and-mesh pot. Terry and Steve grab the sides as it bangs against the rail, and guide it crashing into place on the launcher rack.

The pot—essentially a big box trap—holds dozens of six- to eight-pound purple king crabs that crawl sluggishly against each other. The spikes on their shells will tear our hands without heavy rubber gloves. The door of the pot opens like a hamper: a picker pot. We lean in to pull crabs out, hand over hand, sorting on the run, flinging back females and undersized, splashing obvious keepers into the circulating water that fills the hold, piling doubtfuls to be measured. (Minimum size for this Bering Sea opening is six-and-a-half inches across the carapace. The farthest spike point on the carapace does it.) In the rush we still take care not to smash or dismember the creatures, since busted crabs die and benefit no one.

I unhook the perforated bait can that has been soaking for days and dump the rotted remains of old herring over the side. Hundreds of seabirds screech and dive to retrieve the pieces while I retch from the whiff. Always pushing it, we re-bait, mend a tear in the pot's web, secure the lid, stack the line to uncoil properly, and at a shout from Leiv lift the pot, followed by line and buoys, back into the sea.

It takes seventeen hours to work one hundred pots: six an hour. In just a few years, by the 1980s, hydraulic pot lifters will have speeded up and be able to coil automatically, and hard drivers like Leiv Loklingholm will expect to work twice as many pots per hour. Yet, only two decades ago, the technology for this fishery was still so experimental that the lifter, the big square pots, and the very design of the boat under our feet were all in the future. Stability had been the major concern: Boats that could buck rough water with a net on deck capsized routinely under a load of heavy pots that raised the center of gravity. And wooden boats proved inadequate because the crabs needed to be kept alive in steel tanks of circulating seawater.

The steel 108-foot *American Beauty,* engineered by Marco Marine Construction in Seattle, has a raised fo'c'sle and other adjustments to elevate its freeboard, and a centered fish hold—all to keep the vessel trim, even with pots aboard, when the bow plunges into heavy seas.

Suddenly, a big wave sweeps over the side and drenches us, hitting with such force that we grab for support. Frigid water trickles down my neck through the raingear and fills one of my boots. Leiv thrusts his bearded face from the pilothouse and assesses anxiously, then roars a Norwegian *har har* against the wind. "Hey, dot'll vake you bastards, eh?" We yell casual obscenities and throw things at the quickly closed wheelhouse door. His apology will show in honed alertness so it won't happen again. He'll mind even more tensely—every second, every hour—the relation between rolling sea, careening steel pots, and fragile deck.

Some fishermen have nine or ten lives, some barely one, no matter their caution. One chilly January day another year I arrived late in Kodiak and bunked with a friendly crew who had delivered their catch, then moored for the night. We were joined by the men of another crabber whose skipper planned to put to sea in a few hours. His crew included two brothers, Jim and Clint, shaggy-haired, quiet young guys shipping out together. They had fished enough years to be experienced but were still, somebody joked, just ol' country boys. They grinned, but didn't contradict.

Next afternoon at sea the country brothers were working together on deck. The boat had already run a string of crab pots. A wave no worse than many others washed over the rail. "Clint! . . ." Jim called quietly. Clint looked up in time to see his brother disappear over the side in a blur of orange raingear. No one saw more of the cause than this. As the boat circled back wildly, with the men throwing life rings from deck, they saw Jim's bearded face in the orange hood bob up twice among the waves. And that was it.

The crabber made it back to the Kodiak pier at 2 A.M. In the dark and cold I watched the surviving brother stumble off carrying duffel bags for two. Nobody spoke. A part-owner of the boat took the youth home, to wait for the early Anchorage flight and connection to the lower states. The Kodiak paper withheld names in reporting the accident so Clint could make it home first to tell their parents. The crabber, with its stunned skipper and remaining crew, was a top-of-the line boat, with more safety equipment than any law required. It hadn't helped.

Aboard Bering Sea crabbers, the square pots (six-and-a-half to eight feet square by three feet high), at 650 to 800 pounds empty, are monsters, and with sea life added their weight rises quickly beyond a ton. When the deck rolls and pitches, the pot becomes a wrecking ball with sharp edges as it clears the rail and swings aboard. A hand or leg in the way can be smashed. Maverick seas have swept pots overboard with a man leaning inside to mend or bait, taking him to his death as if hitched to an anchor.

When the pots begin coming aboard *American Beauty* with only a crab or two, Leiv decides it is time to chase the migrating creatures elsewhere. He gives the word to start stacking. As each pot comes aboard we empty it but, instead of returning it to the water, stuff the coils of line and marker buoys inside, then horse the heavy pots across deck to tie them frame to frame from the rails. Soon, little maneuvering room remains. We work backed against a wall of shifting steel frames, booming a second and third layer of pots on top of the first, cautiously handling the dangerous weight.

Terry, assigned to secure the top stack, scampers up and down like a monkey, tie-ropes slung over his shoulder, boot toes slipping on the frames, fingers clutching web. Later, I will try this on another boat, and I will make the mistake of crouching atop an unsecured pot as I tie it to the others. A sea hits and the pot lurches. As the others cry warnings, I scramble off the swaying structure that likely would have taken me with it, into water rough and cold enough to keep whatever it received. One crab skipper I know hires nobody over twenty-two, because young reflexes are so important.

Open-sea crabbing in Alaska is dangerous in other ways. The fishery occurs when gales and ice descend, because king crabs fill their shells fullest in fall and early winter, and tanner crab fullness starts in January. In late winter, boats in the Bering Sea battle icebergs as well as the weather. During my first week on a crabber, in November with the worst weather to come, a man on one boat lost a finger, a man on another lost the bridge of his nose when a heavy hook flew out of control, and seas smashed the windows of two pilothouses. A vacancy had been created when two converging hydraulic bars crushed a man's thigh. A few months later, another crab boat I'd ridden briefly from Dutch Harbor to Akutan took a trick sea near the Pribilofs, capsized, and sank within five minutes—incredibly with no loss of life thanks to survival suits and nearby boats.

Sometimes the sun shines on the Bering, glittering on whitecaps. At other times, within minutes of the sun, fogs roll in and stick to the waters. Occasionally the sea turns glassy calm, but it is always cold. Gusts up to ninety knots cut through oilskins and thermals, chilling the sweat inside. Regardless of care in the wheelhouse, waves sometimes roll straight over like a mule-kick. The workday lasts up to twenty hours, steadily, for a week or so until the hold fills enough to deliver. Working thirty or forty hours straight is not uncommon under a driving skipper with an experienced crew: pay is based on a share of the catch, the catch might not always be there, and the season is limited.

When the boat cruises between strings, steered by a coffee-strung skipper who gives himself no rest (these boats cost over a million dollars, shared often with a partner, but with plenty of mortgage to pay), we peel oilskins to our boots, flop on an inside deck, and sleep instantly. When the engine slows at the approach of a new string we rise automatically—near agony if not done fast—and stumble back on deck, bones aching until the work lubricates them again. Meals become sporadic, taken as snacks stuffed in passing until Frank, the man designated as cook (everyone has an ancillary job), can find time away from deck. And thirst! We consume gallons of "bug juice," flavored water. Life turns primitive, a simple push against fatigue and against the pain of muscles pushed strenuously, over and over. It is exhausting merely to stay balanced on the heaving deck. Terry keeps going by clocking his share of each keeper: "That's a quarter . . . a buck . . . two bucks. . . ." Some fishermen, at the worst of it, bite their lips and cry, but they continue to work. You have to be there to understand.

Terry is the bright presence aboard *American Beauty.* He has a natural bounce however much the deck pitches. Inches shorter than the others and a bit rounded, he looks unsuited for the work but handles loads as heavy as anyone's. Even under fatigue he spouts a quip or joke. Terry regards me, the novice, protectively. If I slack or err he offers a hand. We banter above the noises of ocean and machinery. This crew is young and unsuperstitious enough that my tendency to whistle while I work bothers nobody, while I find it a comfort. (I check carefully first, man by man. This is no casual matter aboard a fishing boat.) After one day of storm and rotten bait, I'm seasick despite all the fresh air and facefuls of clean salt water. At table I stare at Frank's Norwegian fish balls without eating. Terry pauses from wolfing his food. "The Baltimore warbler is silent tonight," he says gently.

A steamletting with Terry can turn explosive. Once, a rotten sea blob comes up in the pot. Terry slings it at Frank, a generally quiet Norwegian, who flings it back full force. Within seconds a wild game of catch erupts. When the original sea-ball disintegrates, Terry leaps to the storage deck, cuts loose a spare inflated buoy, and throws it down. Only when the buoy shreds does the game end. Another time, during about the fifteenth hour of steady work, we're returning stacked pots to the water from both sides of the boat. Terry grabs one of the seven-hundred-pound monsters and, pushing with the roll of the boat, hefts it across deck single-handedly to the starboard rail. Not to be outdone, Frank shoves the next pot by himself. The others join. I run back and forth pulling out the heavy coils and baiting as everyone competes to have pots ready to heave overboard the instant Leiv calls the command. When it is over we're all panting, sweating, grinning, and reinvigorated.

On another typical night around 1 A.M., as hail slashes in streaks across the deck lights, I brace by the rail to hook a pot, balancing on ice underfoot. Beyond the boat, white patches of foam and gulls move rhythmically in a darkness that is otherwise a void. Mountainous swells tower above the little deck. Suddenly I am pressing my knees into the steel side for the protection of something solid. "Well, stupid, you got yourself into this," I mutter. But if a *deus ex machina* were to swoop from above as in a Greek drama to take me back to warm, safe comfort, I'd refuse. Then the pot surfaces, leaving no further time to be awed by vulnerability.

How indeed did I get into this? It started boldly, though not with the facing of primal forces.

In the 1950s, I served on a Coast Guard ship in Alaska, plying coasts of wondrous scenic wildness. The imprint was indelible, and in the 1970s, with two children raised and a career duly pursued, Alaska and seafaring remained in my system. Atavism, self-indulgence, whatever, at the mid-forty mark I craved my dreams and had the luck of an understanding wife and employer.

In 1975, I found my way back to Kodiak briefly while researching an article for the *New York Times Magazine* on foreigners fishing American waters. With an extra day to kill, I asked my way aboard a fishing boat netting salmon. We pulled up fish. I felt them in the net, and slapping around my legs. Freighters, military ships, passenger liners, sailboats—all had figured in my previous seafaring, and they all offered experiences with the sea, but they had dealt only with the surface. The fishing boat interacted with life in the unseen depths, a different dimension altogether. I couldn't forget it.

There was also the passage of progress to consider. Small-scale fishermen with their own boats might soon be a thing of the past, like the vanishing family farmer or the iceman who once delivered pearly, dripping blocks on his back to my grandmother's icebox. Plenty of woeful opinion supported this. If I wanted to see, I'd better look before fishermen became a memory.

In Kodiak, the main town of a hundred-mile island off the central Alaskan mainland facing the open Pacific Ocean, where I had pranced as a young Coast Guard officer knowing everything, I found myself walking boat to boat with hearty facade, asking crewmen half my age if they needed an extra hand. Nobody was unkind, but nobody said come aboard. I followed the expedient course of many greenhorns and hired onto a cannery line for money to keep going. And the best way to persuade some fishing skipper to hire me, I reasoned, was on scene in oilskins, when boats delivered, showing I could work.

The Kodiak salmon season had not yet begun, although seiners were gearing up. But other boats were trawling for shrimp and bringing in big loads. (A few seasons later, the shrimp would simply disappear, as would the king crab—a story for later in the book.) At the canneries, men waist-deep in shrimp shoveled them into hoppers, to start the creatures' course from livestock to food. I fancied myself behind a shovel deep in some hold, ultimately seabound after calling up merrily, "Hey guys, need a crewman?"

Instead, the foreman assigned me to a conveyor belt deep inside a big, gloomy building. Surrounded by odors of disinfectant, I stood picking small white candlefish and wisps of seaweed from among the passing tons of pink shrimp. My partner, a sullen, pimpled teenager, lacked even a hello. The grating we stood on, as water rushed beneath our boots, had devilish protrusions that interfered with comfortable stance. The shift each day lasted twelve to fourteen hours. Half-hour lunch break, fifteen-minute coffee breaks, no time to rush the near-mile to the docks for another go at the salmon seiners in harbor.

Candlefish picking was closer to the real world than the romance of a fishing boat, the truth of life's work at the bottom rung, the lot of millions. My eyes followed the foreman each time he rushed past. When finally I grabbed his attention I tried to make it sound offhand and amusing: "Hey, going crazy here! I'm good with a shovel." He stopped for the seconds it took to absorb the information over the hiss of water and clang of machinery. "You've got a very important job. Keep at it." And he was off. My last chance for hours.

Suddenly one day the foreman grabbed my arm and hustled me to a new location. Instead of descending to a boat hold we clanged up metal stairs to the steamy ceiling. With the heat and concentrated odors of cooking shrimp it felt like the inside of the cooker itself. Within minutes I had on long rubber gloves (which leaked), and a Japanese was instructing me in the distribution of shrimp that sluiced by the thousands from huge shining vats into a battery of peeler machines.

At least I could move in a twenty-foot area. And my fellow peelermen, all Asian, would nod back and take time to show me the tricks of the machinery. My trough had a trap door to each peeler, and these metal plates required frequent adjustment for an even flow. Sometimes the trough clogged, calling for swift measures. After the candlefish, here was action and intellectual involvement. Soon I became king of the trough, orchestrating the trap doors, playing games to see how long I could withhold shrimps from one chute without emptying it, how much I could stuff another without clogging it.

The candlefish shift had started at 5:30 A.M., confirmed on my time card. At about 7 P.M. I glanced from my new height to see the sullen teenager and his newest assistant hose the belt, pick out bits of seaweed, and punch out. Theirs was an initial step in the cannery process, while the product of my new post still poured from the cookers.

Two hours later the cookers stopped steaming. I hosed and scrubbed with the others, pushing more vigorously than they. Time still to walk the docks and perhaps find guys aboard their boats. Viewed from above, the peelers were clean. I waved and started to leave. The others laughed and beckoned me back. When they lifted the baffles, a jungle of antennas, eyes, and slivers lay matted in every crevice. They took a coffee break first. We punched out around midnight after hosing, picking, scrubbing, hosing, dislodging, and disinfecting. The boats in the harbor, as I walked past, lay dark, their masts black against a sky with remaining vestiges of northern latitude light.

I was not destitute in Kodiak. During the quick visit the previous year I had met Tom Casey, head of the local Fishermen's Marketing

Association. Casey, a bear of a man with a foghorn bellow and a knack for writing narrative poetry, had befriended me to the point of offering me a room. Nor, now, was I lonely. My son Wynn, age fifteen, had followed, finding it inconceivable that I should have all the adventure. We bunked with generous Tom. Wynn worked at a different cannery, his own man. (We said nothing about the husky kid's age.) In Tom's living room where he slept, Wynn roused enough to mumble as I tiptoed in to general snores, and we exchanged whispered notes of our day. "Mom and Karin phoned, said hi and be careful. And Da: Happy Father's Day."

The salmon season was about to start. A hill of seine nets and corks rose on the decks at the town floats. Each net, when passed through the suspended power block, spread with the grandeur of a sail as the men inspected and mended. The boats themselves were saucy, scuffed, businesslike, the essence of contact with the sea. The more I watched, the more I yearned to be aboard.

Next morning at coffee break I forwent free cookies to patrol the cannery dock, staring at shrimp boats that came to deliver. Crewmen aboard had little interest in chatting with an obvious cannery hand, betrayed by lightweight oilskins (laundered, disinfected, and reissued daily) of a kind that would have ripped under heavy deck use. Beyond the canneries toward town, two seiners glided from the harbor and pointed north, the route around the island toward Cape Igvak, of the first salmon run. The fleet was leaving.

At lunch break I ran the unpaved road to the town docks, gulping bits of sandwich. The full harbor of last night now had empty slips like missing teeth. The air was charged with whoops and high-keyed shouts. Two weeks before, shoulders and carts had carried boxes down the ramps containing nets, machine parts, paint, canned food. Now the boxes held fresh groceries and frozen meats, signs of imminent departure. Engines turned, puffing blue smoke astern. On decks, crewmen once willing to chat barely nodded as they hustled. The boat rails separated us like a wall, as if the men had already put to sea.

On one boat a skipper who had been remotely sympathetic, arousing my hopes, called: "Wanna throw me those lines?" I unmoored his boat. It backed smoothly from the slip, its graceful hull suddenly a thing of heart-stopping beauty. I watched it glide toward the breakwater as the men on deck tied down. The sinuously stacked corks of its seine caught a gleam of sun through the clouds. At the breakwater the boat responded to the sea and began a gentle rock. A minute later it pitched. Mast and booms swooped. To those fortunates aboard, the boat came alive.

I raced back to the cannery, the sandwich a lump in my stomach. The foreman—usually scarce given his far-ranging duties—passed and frowned as I punched in late. The yellow oilskins of my fellow-peelermen in the loft already moved in patches through the steam. I geared up, sweating from the run, hastened to my post pulling on soggy gloves, and with a tight smile relieved the man who had kindly filled my place and his own. The heat of cooked shrimp stuck in my throat like brass. I worked madly without games, and reviewed the realities.

Coffee break. Go for broke. I shucked oilskins to race for a pay phone down the road. The foreman passed and cautioned: "Don't be late again."

I phoned Tom Casey at his harbor office. During one of his meetings with seiner skippers as head of the marketing association, I had stood up to introduce myself and ask for a berth, winging it about my ability to cook, to learn, to do anything. (Polite, sympathetic indifference—I was, after all, forty-five and green.) One skipper had at least smiled. Tom identified him later as a highliner, respected throughout the fleet. In harbor I had seen many boats and would have signed aboard the scummiest, but the 58-foot *Polar Star* of the man who smiled looked particularly groomed and able. "Tom! Do you think Thorvold Olsen would take me along just for the ride? I'll pay for my food."

"Thor's probably left, Bill. He doesn't wait around. No, I can see the boat. Want me to call his house?"

"Please!"

I waited as the minutes of the coffee break ticked away. When someone tried to use the phone I begged him off. Coffee break over. In the distance down the road (where twenty-six years ago I had strolled critically among fishing boats as a Coast Guard officer on a sturdy ship) I could see masts moving toward open water.

The phone rang. "OK," said Tom. "Thor'll take you. He leaves in an hour. I'll come get you to pack. Be outside."

I raced through the cannery to find the foreman, now scarce again. "Look, this isn't my way, but I'm quitting. Sorry. Thanks. OK?"

"Don't come back."

An hour later, giddy with good fortune—having sent Wynn a message to stay with Tom and hang tough—I stood on the deck of the

Polar Star holding boots and a thrown-together seabag, backed against the cabin to be out of the way as the four crewmen made final stowage. The rocks of the breakwater glided past and the scrubbed deck began to roll. Fittings on the tightly battened boom clicked with the motion. The roofs of cannery row became mere buildings like all the others of Kodiak nestled on flats and hills beneath the green slope of Pillar Mountain.

Between protective islands the open Pacific Ocean swelled in. Spray shot back from the bow. The stern rose and slammed into water. "You going to be seasick?" asked one of the men, Corky, pleasantly.

"Nope," I grinned, feeling queasy. I had gulped a pill. It helped.

The *Polar Star* passed wooded coastline beyond which rose peaks still snowed in June. Eagles flew. A sea lion's whiskered snout poked from the water, then flipped away. In a corridor between islands the water curled in whirlpools. Corky, who had turned chatty, volunteered that this was Whale Pass, to be navigated with caution and best at slack tide. In the wheelhouse where everyone settled, Thor Olsen unrolled a chart, plunked a coin beside it, and beckoned me over with his slight smile. "A quarter if you can find our position." (I did.)

By light next morning we had crossed forty-mile Shelikof Strait, which separates Kodiak Island from the jagged snowy peaks of the mainland south of Anchorage. The high granite Bird Bluffs of Cape Igvak rose above us, white from guano, cawing with birds. Two dozen other seiners maneuvered in the same area, waiting. Thor took position and held it, scanning as did everyone for signs of sockeyes. There was life beneath the choppy water. Glint of silver and a splash. "Jumper to starboard three o'clock," muttered someone, adding to me: "Don't point, Bill, let other boats find their own." Thor eased us toward the splash.

When Fish and Game announced by radio that the season had opened, Thor snapped "Go!" and the skiff clanged away. We towed, then hauled back in a series of steps. Everyone knew his part. I stood aside, watching. How had I ever expected someone to hire me green? At last the boom raised a netful of big silver fish. Their muscular thrashing thumped the deck before they tumbled into the hold.

By the second or third set I had identified some little piece of work to do—a strap or a line stowed or provided—without intruding into the general rush. By week's end I had been accepted with good humor into the process, coiling purse line, stacking web, lining with the others to pull large catches over the rail, pitching the stiffened fish from the hold at delivery time to a tender. Even the dead salmon, each a slippery six-pound handful grabbed from sloshing, bloody gurry, felt good.

Thor ran it all, from the wheelhouse or with a leap to deck during haul, barely raising his voice. (Other skippers, I was to learn, become shouters and screamers in the heat of a set.) Appropriately, his men called him "Boss." He was the boat's presence, quietly easygoing but driven, all business, confident, the master of every gear and part aboard his boat (most installed by himself). I had chosen wisely.

By summer's end I was crewing with a share aboard another, smaller boat. Indeed by then Wynn had joined me on the water and we crewed together. I had settled in enough to be a short-tempered cook (doing this in addition to deck work), loud and salty when the boat lurched and pancake batter spilled over my stove's two burners.

My son and I returned to Kodiak and the boats the next year, and the next. By then the glow had frayed for Wynn, thanks to a seiner skipper from hell and another slightly less so, plus a stint trawling the Bering Sea with a Korean joint venture that barely made expenses. He decided that fishing would be part of his résumé, not his life, and now satisfies his sea urges making sophisticated deepwater mixed-gas dives on sunken wrecks. I, though, had swallowed the bait, taking ever longer leaves from the office in Baltimore to be a fisherman.

I'm back in Alaskan crabbing water in early winter, aboard a different boat with different crewmates, glad to be here, but not that certain at the moment. The boat thuds to the clack of tight-stowed dishes as we hit a sea. Outside, water bubbles over the deck, and white scud flecks and smokes on the crests rising beyond the rail. It is the rail I watch from the warmth of the galley, or rather the gleam on the rail visible through a back window while bracing my mug on the table. Although painted no more than two months before, part of the rail has been abraded back to gray metal by the scrape of gear, while brown rust nudges through a nick in the paint. In the seconds between seas, wind ripples the wet surfaces of metal and rust, and even blows patches dry enough to lose their sheen. Suddenly the gleam stays glassy.

Fifteen minutes later, brown rust and gray metal have turned milky under an unwavering gleam. The heavy wire stays have begun to thicken. Tight-lashed ropes that always retain a small amount of sway now jerk rigid until a thud of the boat dislodges particles like broken glass. Our big square crab pots are stacked astern three high to the height of a man and a half. With each roll their steel frames shift as always a fraction against the lashings, no more than a cough. The webbing looks clear, a lacework of mesh beyond which moves the sight of pointed seas.

I climb to the wheelhouse. Cautiously: "Might be icing."

"Tell me." Jack, the skipper, crouches over the wheel with his head thrust forward like a turtle, his beard nearly touching the window. Cloudy mountains of water roll beyond. The wiper labors. Each stroke pushes a thin sheet of ice.

I keep my voice casual. "Just a little around the edges. No trouble that I can see with the pots." I wait for shrugged reassurance, but Jack only plies ahead.

Another boat is thrashing a quarter-mile to starboard. She crests high enough to seem on air, then troughs to her mast-top. Both boats simply jog to keep the best heading possible through the storm. The nearest haven at Dutch Harbor lies a hundred miles away. Dutch, a raw spot that people usually wish to leave, seems now the heart of warmth.

Is it my imagination, or have we started to roll more slowly? I know the crab yarns, how boats stacked with pots become top-heavy with ice and capsize with all hands. Alaska crabbing is a fishery young enough—developed after World War II—that this was the lore of trial and error before the advent of wide-beamed boats like ours, built specifically for the work. But capsizing still happens.

The others remain calmly asleep in their bunks, a reassurance. Hours before, while we emptied pots and stacked them on deck to try a new location, three straps in a row snapped in the surging water and Jack shouted down to halt fishing. We had been working at least a dozen hours after four hours' sleep. The others secured gear, peeled boots and oilskins, and went straight to their bunks. With danger Jack would have kept them awake, I told myself. Yet, although I have the watch, he chose to keep the helm as the wind increased, waves rolled higher, and the temperature dropped.

Jack turns to look through the back wheelhouse window, but ice has nubbled it opaque. "Down in the galley, check the pots outside," he says. "Don't go on deck."

On the way I touch the thick orange bag with my initials on it, stuffed in an open closet along with the other survival suits. Mine is on the bottom. Should I tug it out and push it on top for quicker grabbing? No, nothing's wrong, I tell myself, and hurry on.

The web lacework of the pots has thickened. I can now barely see the waves through it. The steel frames have turned white. So have the rail and the ropes I had been watching. When Jack hears the news he blasts the horn used to wake all hands for deck. The others appear from below within seconds, pulling coveralls over their thermal underwear.

"Maybe have to dump the goddamn pots," says Jack. "First get out and break ice around them." To me, the least experienced: "Stay off the pots. Tie yourself in somewhere."

Nobody speaks. My hands tremble as I pull on layered clothes, trying to balance protection from cold against bulk. Anybody who slips overboard in this can expect no retrieval. My boots, rolled back by the stove to dry, remain damp from taking seas hours before. They pull on slowly. Suited against weather, gloved hand clutching a mallet, I follow the others to deck wondering if I'm going to die.

Action diminishes fear. Wherever I slam the mallet, ice clatters down or flies to sea in the wind. My eyes water, the hairs in my nose frost, and soon fingers and toes feel as breakable as the ice. I hear rather than take time to see the others chop at the wall of ice covering the pots. Death becomes incidental to the importance of banging on layers of white frozen water.

And then, unseen forces take control. The wind eases and shifts to lose its sting. Great swells of water continue to roll, but surfaces banged free of ice stay free. At last Jack shouts us back inside.

We tumble against each other back into the galley and dog the back door tight. Tim and Moss laugh mindlessly, unable to stop. Ralph, quiet in a corner, appears to be in prayer. We can't stop shivering. Despite the galley heat, ice feels lodged in my marrow. Jack, haggard, cries jokes to us from the wheelhouse.

The storm passes. The crew rotates thirty-minute watches, allowing Jack to crash some rest. After each watch I barely crawl into my bag before falling asleep again. Four hours later Jack appears back in the wheelhouse, red-eyed and silent, the last of cold bitter coffee in his mug. He examines our position, cruises for half an hour, then sounds the horn. "Move it. Goddamn pots on deck don't catch crabs." Nobody objects.

CHAPTER TWO

It's a Livin'

Georges Bank

November 1979

"You makin' any money up there?" asks a heavy voice over the wheelhouse radio. These New England accents are a continent removed from those of the Bering Sea

"Nope," says our skipper glumly. "Nope, nope, nope." We hear him from deck as we slice cod bellies and strip guts at high speed to ice the set and have a breather before the next set comes aboard. "I'm losin' my shirt every haul," mourns our skipper. "Shoulda quit the other day. Just give me two decent sets, I'd be happy. All day got forty-five fish, that's all we got."

We're working too hard even to pause as we laugh. The game of hard luck talk (except to one's buddy in some prearranged code) is as old as fishing itself, an act probably pulled two thousand years ago by Norsemen and Chinese and Galileans. The truth is, until a day and a half ago, we were indeed bringing up little but torn nets and "water hauls" (empty nets) for fully seventy-two hours. Now, finally, we've found the fish off Nantucket Shoals. Announce it and bring a fleet of other boats to pick the site clean? Ha.

The deck lights gleam on our yellow oilskins as we bring up the next drag with its dangerously clanking otter boards, empty the bag, shoot the trawl back over the side, then wade into the mounded catch to sort it. There are cod weighing ten to fifty pounds, thin flounders—both white and yellowtail—mackerel, and lobsters, all of which we keep, plus an array of other sea creatures—squid, sandpaper-skinned dogfish, scallops, great flapping skates—that go back over the side either because the buyers back in New Bedford aren't interested or because we catch too few to make a market.

After we sort, our four-man watch dresses the cod. Chris and Dave do the cutting, keeping their steels handy for frequent blade hones as they stand in sloshing blood and gurry. Jake and I slide hands into the opened bellies to eviscerate them. Icing below follows. The water in November, and a month yet from winter, is immensely cold. So are the fish intestines. But our fingers must be free, so we wear only tight cotton gloves through which the slime and blood seep. You can tell a northern fisherman by the puffiness of his fingers and the apparent flaccidity of his grip—hands grown waterlogged and stiff from exposure. Out over the water a nor'easter blows twenty knots, enough to kick up a routine-size sea that coughs into the scuppers and bubbles around our ankles. With night the temperature has dropped from cold to bitter, and some of the water on deck turns ice-white and slippery. The crew of this dragger keep the nets working clockaround by staggering watches. My present watch has five more hours to go, followed by four hours to eat and sleep before the next eight-hour trick, on and on for a week or until we fill the hold. There's less pressure here, or bull labor, than with crabbing on the Bering Sea. Also less stimulation, and less fun.

"It's a livin', b'y, but ain't much of a life now, is it?" said a Newfoundland trawlerman on another boat at another time, as we gutted cod. A man of the sea, this one, a type who would wither in the confines of an inland factory. Fishermen take comfort in griping.

Snagging fish to survive may be the second occupation man taught himself, after scavenging saber-toothed kill but before using a stick to furrow for seeds. (Prostitution may still have been the first *profession*, as people claim.) The number who fish for a living in coastal nations seems limited only by the area of fish-producing continental shelves available or by the nation's interest in eating fish. According to latest statistics of the United Nations Food and Agriculture Organization (FAO) and the U.S. National Marine Fisheries Service (1997: always a couple of years behind by the time all numbers are crunched), Asia catches more seafood than any other area of the world—69 million metric tons landed (a metric ton equals 2,200 pounds) compared with 14.4 million in Europe, 17.7 million in South America, 8.6 million in North America, and 5.8 million landed in Africa. The greatest consumers among nations are Iceland (202 pounds annually per capita), Japan (148 pounds), Portugal (129 pounds), South Korea (105 pounds), and Norway (101 pounds). In contrast, the United States consumes 48 pounds per capita, Canada 50 pounds. (Remember, these statistics include farm-belt inhabitants and infants—the total population.) Several of the world's top fishing nations catch more, or less, seafood in comparative years depending on Nature and politics. Throughout the 1990s China has consistently harvested more fish than any other nation, much of it in aquaculture, a centuries-old Chinese activity only recently become a force in other fisheries. China's reported 1997 catch was 35 million tons. Peru, in second place, reported 7.8 million tons (most of it low-value, but still nearly as much as all of North America combined!). Japan, now in third place as international restrictions deplete its fleets, held the premier position throughout the 1970s and 1980s. Back then the Soviet Union followed as number two but now, as Russia, has diminished to seventh place. Peru and Chile vie these days for top places depending on how El Niño and upwelled Pacific currents deliver meal fish to their coasts. Back in 1975, when Peru was number four, Chile held only fifteenth place, dramatic demonstration of how Chile has recently developed its fisheries. Throughout these years, the United States, with five to six million metric tons, has usually occupied fifth place, give or take one position. (Within the United States, Alaska lands five times the volume and value of its closest competitor state, Louisiana, and nine times more than all of New England combined.) Others of the top nations delivering at least two million metric tons, in order, are India (number six, with its harvest rising steadily through fish farming), Russia, Indonesia, Thailand, Norway, South Korea, Iceland, and the Philippines. Among other players of legend or influence in the fishing world, Denmark is number fourteen, Vietnam fifteen, Mexico sixteen, Spain nineteen, Taiwan twenty, the United Kingdom twenty-two, Canada twenty-one, and Portugal fifty-one.

Fisheries cannot be cataloged under one heading. No single instance tells it all. Men (and some women, hereinafter assumed) fish by themselves and collectively; with nets, pots, lines, dredges, and spears; in warm and cold waters during all seasons, in all manageable sea states, aboard vessels ranging from log catamarans and open dories to factory ships, wherever the waters support edible marine life. Some return home every night, and never leave the sight of land; many stay out a few days to a couple of weeks and travel to the edges of their local continental shelves; and some, in the distant-water fleets, leave home for two to eight months at a time.

How can you characterize these thousands who cast their lot aboard fishing boats? Some live in grass-and-sod huts and some in sturdy houses, few in mansions. Within these conditions many are well off at least by the standards of their society, although thousands remain at scratch level. Along the village beaches of Asia and Africa and South America—indeed any place in the world including parts of the United States—some fishermen in the leakingest old wood skiffs hand-pull gear within sight and earshot of steel fishing ships where clanking winches haul huge nets. Which of the two groups is the more successful and content depends on one's preference and definition.

In most occupations, there are those who have stumbled into the work, those who headed there on purpose, and those who were born to it. Among fishermen throughout the world, most come from the latter category: fishermen by birth, perhaps stuck with it—especially in low-income coastal societies where options are few. Fishermen in third world countries are traditionally among the poor. (The assumption in the tale of the greedy fisherman's wife who mishandled three wishes was that she lived in poverty.) But working in cold and slime is a powerful alternative to going hungry. Life at the nets may have lacked prestige in the big world—Newfoundland teachers a generation ago threatened kids with: "If you don't study, you'll end up on the boats!"—but in sea-blown communities where everybody's daddy, brothers, and uncles fish, it is considered a man's proper occupation. In this narrow milieu, the best fishermen become the most respected citizens.

Traditional village fishermen train in a university of life that farm kids would recognize. Their families expect them to pitch in as soon as they can lift and haul. In Newfoundland outports, boys of nine and ten are already small men in pint-size "oilers" and rubber boots, standing on a crate to reach the gutting table, hopping-to aboard the boat when it comes alongside the pier. In Norwegian coastal villages, boys the same age converge at any time of afternoon or night that cod boats arrive. They set up boxes that look like shoeshine kits on which they spear the hundreds of fish heads that flop to the floor, and deftly slice out the part known as "cod tongues," a regional delicacy. Many lads of the world's fishing villages want nothing better than to grow to the age when they can match their fathers' work, probably first as a "boy" on a fractional share, working into a full share as they prove able. I have seen kids in Kushiro, Bali, Lofoten, Madras, the Algarve, Labrador, and Oregon give reverent touch to the nets their dads are mending.

In the same communities I have seen old men, no longer able to go themselves, caress the outgoing boats with their eyes. Often by then, a lifetime of pulling gear from cold water has caught up, and their twisted hands are so arthritic they can barely hold a needle to mend the web ashore and still be part of the work. Do the kids ever notice this, and project their own fate as they equate manhood with hauling a full share of the nets and lines?

From a warm room it still sounds romantic. But what happens in these traditional fishing communities when the options increase? It happened for coastal Norwegians after oil was discovered in the late 1960s on grounds that formerly yielded only fish, and for Newfoundlanders when they became a province of Canada in 1949 and the new government built roads to end the isolation of the outports. In both places—where the waters are rough and cold—many sons left the boats and never returned. Why doom yourself to longer hours and chancier pay than most have to endure, to heavier and messier labor, greater danger, and more discomfort? The wonder is that any stayed except those too old to change. In Newfoundland Joey Smallwood, the first premier after the confederation with Canada, announced the dawn of a new era not dependent on the sea and advised triumphantly, "Burn your boats, men!" Factories built with funds from a generous new government would liberate outporters from their harsh life facing cruel water. It turned out that this was not an assembly line workforce despite the repetition of gutting fish. Newly liberated young fishermen indeed followed the roads out to cities—Toronto in particular but also Boston and points between. Since a fisherman needs more skills than most to survive, many were equipped to enter the economy at such levels as carpenter, welder, and ship's officer, so some made good money. But the boat-filled outports did not empty after all. (Nor have Norwegian coastal villages.) Enough sons returned to the boats after having tasted the hectic, grubby, confined city life that the fishing generations continue. "'Tis in me blood, must be," mused a young Fogo Islander who had left and returned, as he dangled his newborn lad within sight of both his boat and the grave markers of his grandparents and great-grandparents.

There is a satisfaction to being your own person. "Don't answer to nobody but yourself," I've heard in a multitude of languages and dialects. This even from crewmen who forget for the moment how an easygoing skipper can become a screamer on the grounds, and from skippers who forget the coffee-knotted pressures that can accompany their search for fish.

Not all traditional fishermen stay in home port, especially the energetic ones when local abundance wanes, or those cast adrift by political circumstance. Many net haulers who set out to Georges Bank from New England ports speak Italian, Portuguese, and Norwegian at home; some fishermen in Texas and Louisiana speak Vietnamese or Mexican Spanish; and others on boats from Oregon to Alaska pull gear to shouts in Norwegian, Japanese, Serbo-Croatian, Aleut, even Bostonese. In the waters of Alaska's Bristol Bay, where fishermen converge from all over for a single month each July, the radio frequencies carry a linguistic smorgasbord.

Then there are those from other backgrounds—generally young and sturdy—who gravitate to the famous fishing ports of the world to seek adventure and maybe get rich. In the United States they come in greatest numbers to New England—Spencer Tracy in *Captains Courageous* still shows on late-night TV—and to Alaska, which has the reputation for seafood abundance and bonanza.

The would-be fishermen include farm kids and city kids, many these days with a degree or at least a year or two of college. They pound the docks looking for a berth, or, in New England, a "site." Eventually some skipper might take one aboard as an "inbreaker," as the Norwegians say, probably to work for a fractional share or nothing since they are essentially unskilled labor in an occupation requiring specific skills. If a fellow can stick it out, he'll shape up and learn quickly while probably working harder than ever before. The dilettantes drown or leave.

From the graduated greenhorns with dogged motivation, and from the younger generation of the traditional core, have come some of the hardest-driving and most successful modern fishermen, as well as some of the most innovative: those willing to try new methods, gear, species, and markets. Such men are the bedrock of fisheries quite different from the old ones. Manufacturers of electronics sell them pinpoint navigation devices, sonars that display schools of fish in rainbow colors, and monitors that tell what has entered the nets. The new breed of fisherman pays dearly for the electronic gear, then masters it for a sophisticated pursuit of fish surpassing the dreams of only a generation ago.

The equipment increases their production—but of course they must catch more fish to pay for the equipment. This is one of the sneakers of modern fishing. The pressures increase also, because more efficient gear catches more fish, and the stocks of the world have proved finite. In some fisheries the search for a catch has become as strenuous as the harvest. "It's not as much fun as it used to be," one Alaskan fisherman told me after he had switched from a small wooden boat with nothing more than radio and a radar to a sleek fiberglass craft equipped with the latest. And, from an upwardly mobile young skipper in Norway who had hocked himself for a boat that is the showpiece of his village: "I now am stressed."

A fisherman has always needed to be proficiently skilled, but a modern fisherman must be a walking vocational school. Although the advent of the small marine engine relieved him of sail and oar, it meant he had to become at least a seat-of-the-pants mechanic. Nothing has ever replaced his need to reweave torn nets on the double with needle and twine, or to repair any number of things in wood and metal. Welding? Wiring? How can a man with a family and a moderate-size boat afford to hire a professional every time something breaks? Hydraulics brought relief from the heaviest pulling but opened a new set of systems to understand. Now with fishfinders and instant navigators he must be at least a patch-up electronics technician besides.

Add to this for skippers a growing literature of nonseafaring requirements—licenses, area closures, all kinds of new government reports that must be kept and filed. And insurance. The American enchantment with litigation, if it continues unchecked, may by itself put American fishermen out of the competition. Other governments place sensible limits on compensation for fishing boat mishaps.

The work of pulling creatures from the sea for a living is often dangerous, nearly always uncomfortable. Why do men do it? Most would answer honestly: money, like any other work. Some of the adventurers in each generation come to the wild waters of the world, like those off Alaska, drawn by the promise of an open-sky calling difficult to define in justifiable terms. Many, many more throughout the world grow up in closed communities where they learn their fathers' work on boats and then continue, using the skills they know. Of these, how many are simply stuck without other options? The romance of the sea is mainly for those not pitching and slaving in it with little sleep, those not perpetually wet with salt sores on their lips. And yet. . . .

CHAPTER THREE

Rollers

Chignik, Alaska, 1986

Though it is June, here in coastal Alaska it is chilly enough in the high, dark net loft to smoke the breath. Double long johns and sweaters help as we stand for hours mending nets, repairing gear, insulting friends from other boats. Rain thunders on the roof. When someone opens the big doors to back in a truckful of gear we can see, through a curtain of water, rivulets cutting between the small houses of Chignik Bay. Lakelike puddles accumulate on the concrete pier outside the cannery, and people in oilskins shuffle through them up to their boot tops. We're all waiting. While fishermen putter with their nets, the manager of the Aleutian Dragon cannery frets with forty college kids all ready to work, eating his food, and dispiritedly watching the rain from bunkhouse doors while his machinery lies ready but idle. Nobody likes the sight of those wind-kicked whitecaps just beyond the harbor entrance.

The reds—some of the world's prime sockeye salmon—are reported milling at the Chignik River weir. The Alaska Fish and Game guys up there have already counted half the escapement they need to open the season, but someone hears that the weir has just been washed out from all the heavy rainwater pouring from the lake, bringing the count to a halt. Nobody knows anything for sure, so we just keep busy. Crews began to assemble and gear-up their boats in icy, bare winter just three weeks ago, but now spring explodes everywhere. Each time the rain stops and the mists open, the mountains are topped with less snow. Long white fingers from the weathered peaks have become flashing waterfalls. Day by day the vegetation greens. On June 8 the scrubby bushes on the lower slopes are twigs. By June 10 they have sprouted buds and little leaves. Odors of wet growth reach straight to the blood and bone, making our muscles ache to start our own springtime rite of pulling big fish.

Chignik is a family place, isolated by mountains and water, where fathers and grandfathers have pulled nets before, and where brothers and old schoolmates compete on the fishing grounds. The crew of the *Desperado* have prepared the seine, which lies stacked aboard the boat moored to the cannery pier. Now, with time to kill, Ernie Carlson, the skipper, decides to hang a new deepwater seine for use later in the season. The tedious job requires lashing web to line, and weaving panels of web together, moving inch by inch down each section of net stretched taut.

Mori Jones, skipper of our buddy-boat the *Protector,* saunters in with his crew. They remove dripping oilskins and since their own nets are all finished, fall in alongside us with wide flat twine needles. Mori is wiry and soft-spoken. As he disparages the ability of the *Desperado's* skipper to hang a net much less catch fish, he appears small—despite padded coveralls—beside Ernie, a man with robust natural padding. Ernie grunts an appropriate retort. Elwyn, the oldest member of the *Desperado's* crew at forty-five, and the cutup, crouches delicately to tie one end of twine to a post and the other end to a flap on Mori's coverall. Then he strolls outside and yells suddenly: "Mori, that your boat broke her lines?" Mori leaps into a run, and the leashlike jerk that brings him down fuels jokes for the next hour.

On the map of Alaska, Chignik lies about halfway between Kodiak Island and the first of the Aleutian Islands, a coastal pip in the great mountainous spine of western Alaska that pulls from the mainland like taffy to become the thousand-mile Aleutian Chain. Mountains isolate Chignik to make it a place far away and alone. No road connects across volcano-studded wilderness to Anchorage, about 450 air miles away, nor even between the three mostly native communities: the Bay with piers for two canneries and houses built on slopes to the harbor; the Flats facing the Lagoon where low tide leaves boats so grounded that men can walk to their houses; and a traditional Aleut village by the Lake. Residents converge at a large store on one side of the Lagoon, reached by boat when the tide is high enough to avoid shoaling.

The *Desperado* stays moored to the cannery pier and we sleep aboard. Only Ernie lives in Chignik. An imposing man in his late thirties, with a drooping handlebar moustache and a rounded face typical of his partial Aleut heritage, he is a mainstay of a prosperous Chignik generation in its prime. Old enough to have seen an evolution in the fishing ways of the community, Ernie still has the youthful drive to fish hard and to be a fisherman's spokesman when negotiating prices with the canneries. His home overlooking the harbor has comforts not always associated with remote fishing villages.

The Carlson living room is a friendly place, a carpeted and warm sanctuary from the chilly rain beating outside. At night Janis Carlson feeds us big meals of spaghetti, black cod, curried shrimp, or moose. The two Carlson kids romp over Elwyn and his own son, Ron, both also Carlsons although they now live in California. Barry Northcutt, the *Desperado*'s other crewman, has no native blood, but he has fished with the others for enough seasons to be considered part of the family. Mori Jones often comes up from his boat for dessert and the usual discussions of gear and prices. Part native also, at forty-two he is a veteran of twenty-five years fishing in Chignik although he lives with his family in Washington, where he runs a small shipyard.

At last, Fish and Game announces the first opening of the season: twenty-four hours starting at 6 P.M. Barry and I take the skiff to buy last-minute supplies. We tie up at a pier among two dozen other craft bouncing together, all here for the same purpose. Inside a small store, a shack surrounded by mud, fishermen crowd the aisles, their boots splashing through puddles that collect from holes in the roof. We buy potatoes, Pepto, canned corn, frozen sirloin, felt-lined rubber gloves, toothpaste, candy, and grease. The checkout girl wishes each customer a good harvest. Outside, rain blows across the pier at a slant. We shoulder our boxes, climb down a long slippery ladder, leap to the surging deck of the first boat, then balance across slick rails. Barry stops on nearly every deck to exchange handshakes. "See you out there, man, take care," call other young men, many with beards, whose shoulders fill their oilskin jackets. Even those standing stationary have legs on springs, legs too pulsed with anticipation to be still.

Back on board the *Desperado* we shout final insults and good wishes to the *Protector*'s crew—Mori, his brother-in-law Rex, Dave, and Gary—and head out with other seiners for the Lagoon, where fish are reported running strong. After several stormy days the wind has slacked to a ten-knot easterly. The rain dumps. It makes no difference to men in oilskins ready to start fishing. Graceful seabirds wing against the wind. They remain with us, suspended practically motionless, strips of white against the crags of rock with tops lost in fog. The wind blows salty, a clean odor interspersed with whiffs of wet young greenery. Alive, all of it. "Yah-hoo!" we yell.

Ernie steers from the flying bridge, scowling into the wet wind through his bush of moustache, the rest of us around him. Rain splashes into our coffee. "Jumpers, jumpers!" somebody shouts. "The fish are here!" Ernie jaunts the *Desperado* ahead of the others, especially the *Protector*. Not exactly a race, but he pushes the throttle whenever we might lose the lead.

The Chignik estuary includes shifting gravel bars that in one place funnel the sea's tidal flow into a tricky current. We must hug close to high rock bluffs where known deep water lies, and can trust to no more than twenty feet of channel. Despite the appearance of wide water (since the bars lie submerged), this allows practically no room for maneuvering. Today the wind generates rough water here. Steady swells build across the shallows and sweep along behind us, hitting our stern and pushing us so that sometimes we surf ahead. It makes for a circus ride, requiring a constant bend and sway of legs planted firmly apart to maintain balance. Each time we take a roller-coaster dip we cheer.

The other boats a quarter mile behind us form a line to pass through the narrows. Ernie glances back at the *Protector*. "Look at that ride Mori's taking," he says exuberantly, and then more seriously: "Look out, Mori!"

The *Protector* has suddenly stopped pitching ahead. It has turned and is rolling, stuck in a trough. "Man, he'll broach, he'd better. . . ." We glimpse through rainy haze: the bright oilskins of two figures on the bridge, bracing to stay vertical, and the other two on deck near the stern clutching a rail as the boat rolls so far their faces nearly touch the water. The *Protector's* mast arcs across the horizon to the other side, and continues, into the water. She capsizes. In seconds we gasp at the boat's rounded maroon bottom.

Ernie cries out like a creature stabbed. Then, his voice rising, he grabs the radio microphone and shouts "Mayday! Mayday! *Protector's* down!"

Other boats are closer. The rain blurs them all. Ernie guns the engine for maximum power, and turns our boat in a violent tight circle as we hold on. The turn is quick enough to make it between swells—Ernie knows how to handle his boat even when his hands beat the wheel in a frenzy. We suddenly feel the terrible coldness of the water on our faces, cold ignored moments ago. Men last only minutes in such water.

"Oh shit, all the skiffs," mutters someone with a tight throat. A skiff is the only possible means of rescue and the skiffs visible, including our own, are all tied securely aboard for the rough passage.

"Get lines for a halter, strap me in a survival suit, I'll swim to 'em," says Barry, and leaps down the ladder to deck. He yanks a foam rubber coverall from its bag and starts pulling into the clumsy garment as Elwyn and Ron begin unlashing coils of rope. Ernie heads the *Desperado* straight toward the cluster. As we approach, we strain for signs of life in the choppy water. Three other pitching boats keep as close a distance to the overturned hull as they dare. Waves splash over the top and swells often obscure it altogether. No men cling to it, no one bobs in the water.

A skiff weaves through the waves from among the boats. Somebody has managed to launch one, but it's leaving the scene empty. As it approaches us, hidden sometimes by swells, we see only the dark figures of a coxswain braced astern at the controls and another at the bow. Then, as the open boat plunges closer we see dark figures huddled in the bottom, too much a mass even to count heads.

"Did you get 'em, did you get 'em?" we cry. "All? ALL?" Our voices are hoarse, near to screaming. No answers. The skiff comes closer as it heads up the channel toward calmer water. Ernie turns our boat to run with it. "Mori, Mori, you there man?" A huddled figure glances up—we can't recognize the face—and gives half a wave. "Gary? Dave? Rex?" Others at the bottom of the skiff stir. The man standing at the wheel is too absorbed in safe maneuvering through the turbulent water, but finally the man in the bow nods and waves a quick gesture of affirmation.

We cry, silently, each to ourselves.

The swells are subsiding enough that the convoy now speeds through the narrows without the same danger existing a half hour before. When we reach calmer water the rescue skiff puts the men on a tender (a larger and better-equipped boat than any of ours), then returns to the *Scorpion,* its own boat. By a miracle of luck the *Scorpion*'s skiff had been too big to bring aboard, thus leaving it in tow and ready to go when the *Protector* capsized.

The *Scorpion*'s skiff man, Glen Stepanov, had leapt into his dangerously bouncing little open craft and started the engine. Another crewman, Alan Kelmakof, jumped in and started bailing. They cast off the tow line and bucked through rough water that could have swamped them. At first only two of the *Protector*'s crewmen clung to a ridge on the upturned hull. By the time the skiff reached the wreck the other two had appeared, gasping, from under the hull. While Stepanov maneuvered to keep from crushing the men, Kelmakof pulled them one by one over the furiously bucking side, limp as dolls and double their body weight in heavy wet clothing.

Aboard the *Desperado* we heat food and rummage spare clothing from seabags, talking compulsively about how it had happened, then fall silent. We tie alongside the tender. Ernie leaps over the rail and we follow. What do you say to buddies who have nearly died just minutes ago, whose odds as corpses were greater than ever walking a deck again? The four subdued figures have the great mystery about them. We hug them. They hug back. Men from other boats tie alongside and do the same. Plenty of choking up.

One by one the rescued friends step over the rail to our deck. Then there's an explosion of activity, and talk in short phrases, endless "You OK?" followed by quiet spooked "Yeahs." Their hands shake too much to grip anything, so we light cigarettes and put them in their mouths, hold mugs of coffee as they drink, spoon in hot soup. They can't stop shivering. We peel off soaked clothing—the deck becomes so slippery we shuffle to keep balance—and strip blankets from the bunks to wrap around their shoulders. Someone brings a big bag of clothing collected from the other boats to augment our own extra shirts, coveralls, jackets. We remove their boots and soggy thick wool socks, rub their feet, find warm footwear. We make the cabin stuffy-hot, but they still shiver as we add blankets on top of blankets.

"Cold bones, never had such fuckin' cold bones," one of the survivors chuckles apologetically.

"Thought you were gone there for a while, partner," mutters Mori quietly to Rex.

"Yeah. Wondering myself."

Details of their incredible survival emerge. A maverick wave had swept up the *Protector*'s stern and plunged its bow under the water while pushing the boat broadside to the waves. A second freakish wave followed close and rolled the boat over. Mori and Rex had been standing together on the bridge. When the boat broached and capsized it swept them under. With luck they continued around in an arc and grabbed up to the other side.

Dave and Gary had been on deck near the stern when the first big wave overtook them. The stern rose, the boat jolted as the bow plunged into water, and then with the second wave the deck churned into the water like a paddle and carried them under. The surface where their feet had stood seconds before became an overhead cage with floating lines and hoses. Frigid water rushed through their clothing. Fortunately both were swimmers, and they had gulped air when they saw they were going under. As the capsized boat rolled in the water, the deck that trapped them tilted upward and Dave saw a patch of light through one of the inverted scuppers. He swam toward it, tearing away debris. Gary followed. They emerged clutching the side of the hull, close to Mori and Rex.

The slick hull rose and tumbled in the water with only a single narrow guard strip to grasp. Although strong men in good shape, their wet heavy clothing and the cold drained their strength like air from a punctured tire. One boat approached close enough to pitch a line, but they had no energy to grab and the line kept falling short in the waves. Swim a foot or two to reach it? "Guys get lost when they leave their boat," says Mori. Gary adds: "That's the only thing I could think of, man. I'll stay with the fuckin' boat, I ain't leaving, no way, man!" When the crewman in the rescue skiff picked them off one by one they were barely able to help themselves.

Ron ventures that, rescued and riding all wet and windy at the bottom of the open skiff, their asses must have been frozen solid. "No," muses Dave, thinking about it. "We felt warm and great after the water."

With chains of smokes and pots of coffee in the warm cabin the experience tumbles out, over and over. "Pulled back on the throttle, we were digging in, not going anywhere, thought we were going too fast—but I fuckin' wasn't too close to the bar—"

"—started goin' over on that fuckin' bridge, man, looking down at that water coming at you? Fuck!"

"—I looked up one time, you were gone."

"—Yeah, went down, thought fuck, I ain't going to die here, man, I'm goin' up."

Everybody laughs and laughs.

"You was on the down side, last to come up."

"But I did come up!"

"I knew you'd fuckin' make it."

"I was swimmin' like a sonofabitch!" The collective laughs increase with each statement. "—fuckin' daylight, I seen them scuppers, saw light."

The laughter dies in a sudden silence. Elwyn breaks it with: "Anybody see his breath down in that cold?" and it all starts again. No one wants a silence.

The normally quiet Mori turns hyper. "I wasn't going to let you go, you sonofabitch," he says with an excited laugh to brother-in-law Rex. His eyes widen. "No way, no way. Hear about that from my sister for the rest of my fuckin' life? No way, man, no fuckin' way."

Rex, shivering to himself, acknowledges quietly, "Fingers couldn't hold any more. They just wouldn't hold."

"Grabbed around your fuckin' neck, crooked around like a stranglehold, said 'you sonofabitch I ain't'. . . ." Mori starts laughing, and cries out: "If you'd a' died I'd have killed you!" He buries his face in the sleeve of the greasy coveralls he now wears, then looks up and laughs again.

We ferry the men to a bunkhouse ashore. En route we pass one of the large tenders to which we all delivered. It gives us a toot and we toot back. Mori runs on deck and shouts exuberantly, "I ain't dead yet, you fat sonofabitch!" Everybody yells between the two boats as whistles blast.

At dock, Ernie rummages in a compartment by the wheel and finds a ring of keys that he gives to Mori. They're for his truck, and for his second boat that he had just rigged for the season to tender rather than fish. "Put back the power block, she's ready to fish."

Mori studies him blankly. The loss of his own boat has not really sunk in. He looks at his three crewmen. One avoids his glance. "We'll talk it over, yeah . . . only I guess . . . only if we all decide to fish together."

"Yeah, if we fish, not with fuckin' strangers. . . ."

By the time we put the four survivors ashore they can walk casually up the hill, carrying the wet mess of their own clothing in plastic bags. As for us, the opening is now only a half hour away. We head full speed to the gravel bar where Ernie wants to set.

CHAPTER FOUR

Atavism

Chignik, Alaska, 1986

June

Aboard the *Desperado* Ernie jockeys for position to make our first set. A fleet of other boats crowds the water around us while two polite, business-like enforcement officers in orange flotation suits cruise among the boats checking crew licenses. We maneuver near the bar, a gravel spit that intrudes into the water like a finger pointing to the high rock bluff under which the *Protector* had foundered. The bar might compress the current to make a hellish passage for boats riding swells, but in doing so it also funnels the fish. We're keyed up and agreeably tense. The *Protector* guys are safe, and the rain has stopped, though the sky and choppy water stay slate gray.

Sockeye salmon—also called reds for the throbbing color of their meat—enter Chignik waters in two great surges. This is the early one of mid-June. Nature mysteriously programs all Pacific salmon to travel back to the waterway where they hatched, to lay and fertilize eggs before dying. The Chignik reds have lived four to six years, spending the first two in the lake above Chignik, and the rest in the Pacific Ocean. Then they ran their programmed gauntlet from salt water back to the fresh water of their birth, passing Cape Igvak to the north or Sand Point to the south en route to the Chignik estuary. Their final course took them through the gravel-bar narrows (the ones that destroyed the *Protector*), through the Lagoon past the Flats, around little islands, and finally upriver to the Lake.

State Fish and Game biologists must ensure that enough salmon escape nets (and hungry bears as eager as fishermen) to propagate the year-class before opening the season. They have done this by counting fish that passed safely upriver through a weir. The salmon come in surges, and escapement must be allowed from each surge. We now await the season's first opening.

Not everyone can fish in Chignik, where the salmon have reached their maximum weight (that is, they are heavier than at Cape Igvak). In 1974 Alaska passed the Limited Entry law, which restricts the number of salmon seining licenses to prevent overfishing. Chignik licenses went to boatowners with a documented history in the area, making it essentially a native fishery, since most residents come from Aleut stock. No rule prevents nonnative outsiders from working as crewmen. Only Barry aboard the *Desperado* comes from outside altogether. The joke-loving Elwyn, a cousin of Ernie's, grew up in Chignik. Elwyn's ancestry includes a Swedish grandfather on his paternal side and an Italian grandfather on the other, both of whom married Aleuts.

Seiners themselves are relatively new to Chignik. Within Elwyn's memory of fishing with his father, the canneries set huge traps to scoop out captured salmon as needed. In those days, which lasted into the 1950s, Chignik fishermen had a limited choice: work traps for the cannery, or, daring to buck the system, set nets from the beach and pick them from open skiffs. The canneries thought they owned the fish, and used all the pressure at their disposal (considerable those days in an isolated native community) to discourage individuals from intercepting "Company" salmon. The balance changed decisively when Alaska gained statehood in 1959 and the new state government outlawed deadly efficient salmon traps.

Aboard the *Desperado* we're ready. On deck Elwyn holds a mallet poised to hit the spring that will release the skiff. In the skiff astern, now bouncing and shifting in tow with the engine puffing smoke in neutral, Barry braces himself, ready to be cut loose. Skipper Ernie stands on the bridge at the wheel. All of us peer over the water for a shape that will betray a school of sockeyes below the surface. "Jumper there," mutters Ron, jerking his head toward a telltale dark shape and splash. Ernie turns the wheel to include the splash in the circle of our seine.

Off goes the flare from a Fish and Game boat. It rises in a distant, dim, pink-red fireball, confirmed by radio voices. Ernie signals and guns the boat forward. Elwyn hits the release and it clatters to deck. "Eee-hah!" whoops Barry as his skiff breaks free, carrying its end of the net. Corks thump across the stern, and the attached web and leaded line zip off alongside. The skiff and boat move apart, stretching out the net between them. All around us other boats are doing the same.

In purse seining, two boats work the ends of a net to encircle a school of fish swimming near the surface. (Only those species that school at the top of the water column can be caught this way.) Floats hold the top of the net on the surface, and weights pull down the bottom, stretching out a wall of web. After the encirclement, the larger boat takes aboard the smaller one's end of the net to close the circle, then draws together the net bottom through rings like an old-fashioned draw purse. The fish, which remain near the surface, are thus trapped in a bag. The control boat then gradually hauls in the floats and the attached web, crowding the fish into a smaller and smaller bag, until the catch is concentrated enough to bring it aboard.

With arm signals from Ernie on the *Desperado*'s bridge, Barry in the skiff positions the net in an arc across the current. Other lines of beaded white or yellow floats, curving with the current, bob everywhere from boats around us. Ron, as junior crewman, takes first turn plunging on deck while the rest of us watch for jumpers. In the skiff, Barry plunges also. The plunger, a wide metal cup on a long pole, makes a cracking pop when banged into the water, then continues down in a white cloud of bubbles. The disturbance it creates at each end of the net scares fish from their easiest escape. (Some skippers say that only the bubbles count, while the noise makes the guy plunging think he's accomplished something.)

After half an hour Ernie waves to the skiff in a wide enough motion to be seen from a distance, and Barry brings his end of the net back in a circle to the boat. We catch his heaving-line and haul in. The process of bringing the net aboard takes another half hour. We can see blue streaks when a fish swims close to the surface of the enclosure (which is why sockeyes/reds are also called bluebacks). As we haul, the circle tightens continuously until most of the net lies stacked aboard. Inside the circle fish tails flap at the surface.

We line the rail, lock fingers into web, and with a collective grunt pull the bag aboard. The dripping weight hits our legs, and three dozen fish thump on deck. A small catch compared to our expectations, but at least now our hands have the right smell and touch. Some of the fish buckle and then straighten with such energy that they shoot into the air. The silver of their bodies and the line of blue glints even under clouds. We grip them by the tail one by one to toss into the hold, and they still flap with enough strength that their seven-pound weights seem double. We handle such fish with respect while blanking our minds to their death throes, as must anyone in the business of providing food from fellow creatures.

Ernie's radio conversations reveal that the *Protector*'s skiff has floated free of the overturned wreckage. Later someone sights it, swamped, riding toward the beach. Once it grounds, waves will soon batter it to pieces. Around ten in the evening, with the gray sky still amply light, we stop fishing and go to the skiff's rescue. By the time the skiff floats, the cold rain has started again, and Ernie and Barry have bailed enough water in surf that they empty their hip boots like vases.

At 11:30 P.M. we anchor. Wet socks and underwear soon weigh down a line over the oven, from which a lovely odor of sizzling meat emerges. Barry, his oilskins shucked and boots traded for slippers, soon dishes out his traditional opening day steak dinner, having done the basics step by step on the run between sets and the skiff rescue. (During work we smeared crackers with peanut butter and jam.) Down in a chain of gulps go the big steaks running with juice, along with baked potatoes, canned corn, and prefrozen apple pie. An hour after anchoring, even the dishes have been washed, and the cabin is dark except for a flicker from the stove pilot.

Rain splatters on the outside housing. And, in the bunk built against the mere inch-thick skin of the bow, waves knock close to my head. Their proximity echoes the fragility of the fishing life. During the days before the capsizing, we had hung nets alongside the *Protector*'s crew, eaten with them and grab-assed. If we aboard the *Desperado* had hit a series of freak waves, would we still be alive? I surely wondered for myself. Had wondered it only in passing all day in the heat of action, but now. . . .

Past 1 A.M. I wander topside, bone-tired but sleepless. Rain has turned to misty drizzle. The white corks of our seine glisten under the masthead light. Snowy mountains blur across the dark sky. Anchor lights on other boats around us reflect in the choppy water. All is quiet, suspended. The breeze blows chilly sea-odors. I raise my oilskin hood and shiver—this life that responds so briskly to cold and wet could die in seconds. Predawn morning is a time when dreams have logic. The brush with deadly forces from the sea makes me feel an atavistic partner to others who have worked the waters for food over the centuries, both the survivors and the drowned. The primal danger remains despite engines and steel hulls, and I am taking my chances with the rest.

My earliest ancestor, still half ape, had probably puzzled out ways to catch slippery critters from the water long before he began dragging a stick through the earth to cultivate plants. Danger became a part of it soon enough. The hunt-survival instincts that had him stalking food ashore, from carrion to mastodons, eventually led him to hollowing logs into boats so he could chase fish into water over his head: drowning water. He was probably more careless of tomorrow than we, since bare survival gave less leisure to brood about. Maybe I had been there, chasing salmon over these very killer Chignik currents without a thought except for dinner.

Atavism in the spooky hours can go on and on. Suppose fishing had been my lot through the ages and this was my attraction to nets and boats? (My excuse!) Might I have once grunted up web beside a fellow on the Sea of Galilee who left the boat for an impractical calling the rest of us could never fathom? When I travel in this life I haunt museums, and sometimes see evidences of other possibilities. What of those aborigines who carved the wooden fish hooks lying now in a dusty undated case of the little Iquique museum on the north Chilean coast? Or, in Cairo on a painted chest from the fourteenth-century B.C. tomb of Egypt's pharaoh Tutankhamen: the king himself in a boat spearing a variety of big fish with bow and arrow. His queen sits below with spare arrows in hand, while a servant holds the already-impaled catch. Fishing had already filtered up from humble spearmen putting food on the table to a sport of kings. Less likely that I had been the pharaoh— fewer such berths to go around—than the hunkered guy holding the fish and perhaps cautiously coaching on spear technique. Viking artifacts in Oslo, circa A.D. 800, include metal fishhooks that would be at home on baited lines today. A temple rubbing on my study wall, taken from tenth-century A.D. carvings at Angkor in Cambodia, depicts a barefooted fisherman straddling a bow as he hauls a wide net from the great fish-filled Tonle Sap. And, half a world from there on a tusk at the Mayan ruins of Tikal in Guatemala, carved before Europeans claimed discovery of the New World, grotesque stylized figures pull goggle-eyed fish into a boat. Before Columbus, Basque fishermen nearly as careless of their safety as aborigines had followed the currents across the uncharted Atlantic from a sunny homeland to pull cod from the cold, foggy Grand Banks off Newfoundland. Men close to my heart. I feel the rawness of their lives as I shiver on the Chignik deck.

Back to my bunk aboard the *Desperado*. In the tight-fitted space Elwyn's rumbling snore begins close to my ear, then gains momentum. I'm awake for the rest of the night, I think in the moment before I fall asleep.

Next morning at four Ernie starts the engine with a turn of the dashboard key. The grind and then steady chug send our feet to deck automatically. The thick socks on the stove line are mostly dry. We've slept in our long johns, but, as everybody moves at once, the sluggish pull into pants and shirts still leads to bumped elbows in the small space. Water kept hot all night on the stove soon becomes coffee. By chilly gray light at 4:30, the release clatters to deck under Elwyn's hammer, and off goes Barry in his skiff, pulling a swath of corks and web for the first set of the day.

By eight, three sets are aboard as the sky begins to clear. In the brightness after the rain, sun sparkles on the remaining snow of the upper peaks. Mori radios out. His guys have decided to keep fishing, and they'll start right away converting Ernie's extra seiner offered them. (They decide, however, to fish on the ocean beach, an area close to the open sea that does not require passing again through the narrows.) On deck the fish remain big firm ones, a joy to handle, and each set brings in fifty to a hundred more. Suddenly everything has turned OK.

We fish steadily, beating against the clock, since the twenty-four-hour opening will close at 6:30 that evening. Then Fish and Game announces an extension as the escapement count continues to mount satisfactorily. In all, with continued extensions, the opening continues ninety hours, nearly four days. June sunlight lasts twenty hours each day. We fish all of it, and push the twilight besides. Time enough to rest when the biologists call it quits.

We deliver daily to one of the tenders buying for the processor to which Ernie has contracted. To offload we jump down the hold into the fish. In a few hours they are transformed from sparkling silver creatures to dull ones, awash in a gurry of slime and blood that gives off a metallic odor. The tender crewmen boom over their brailer, a heavy-mesh bag pursed shut at the bottom, which Ernie maneuvers from deck. (Skippers don't pitch fish.) Each of us tosses thirty fish into each brail, counting as we go, then however many more the bag can hold. The fish are slippery, gripped best by the tail. It is messy work, sweating in hip boots and oilskins, faces plastered with gurry, but *fishing* is messy. Our hands hold the abundance of the catch. We compete to see who can reach his count first.

Competitiveness is the essence of fishing in Alaska, where frontier stimulus (some call it greed) still lies close to the surface. In Chignik, where families live near their boats, brother sometimes tries to beat brother in rival boats with only occasional good humor. But when we're forced to stop fishing after the *Desperado's* power block breaks, and the spare hydraulic motor has the wrong-size shaft, a radio call from Ernie brings one of his rivals at once with a replacement. A dozen skippers sometimes find themselves fishing the same spot, especially the channel off the bar where the fish are sure to pass. They need to take turns. Boats wait with their bows pushed into the gravel to save fuel, while crews visit and banter rail to rail. They compare notes on the identical weather that everyone watches together, and discuss the relative merits of different engines and hydraulic pumps. CB radios drone with the same subjects, and others more immediate. "If you ain't going to fish, Joe, get out of the way," growls a voice from a nearby boat waiting its turn, to a boat that has gone into the water but delayed setting.

"I'm fishin' man, just caught a snag, hold the fuck on for a minute there."

A voice with a strong Aleut inflection tells somebody at length in another area how his boat's stove caught fire and how they put it out. "That was seven o'clock it happened, like that," he concludes.

Everyone especially deplores and denounces the predations of thieving Kodiak boats that intercept the very fish we are waiting to snare, at points like Cape Igvak that "our fish" pass en route to home waters. Rich Kodiak should catch its own goddamned fish.

The system of "turn-hauling" gives boats the luck of the draw. We're lined up, with our turn close enough that Ernie keeps the engine going after he adjusts position on the bar. We watch the *Gypsy Queen,* skippered by Dave Anderson, a highliner from the Flats, lay his net with the current and then hold it. Fog rolls over the water so that we see the surface in patches. A jumper splashes ahead of the net. Then "Bang, there goes another one!" says Ron wistfully. Watching from deck, we practically lean toward the *Gypsy Queen's* net in our empathy, while Ernie mutters: "Tow him wide open, that's the way . . ." As Anderson purses we can see fish beating down the corks. "Oh man, wish we was next," continues Ron, "Look how that net's plugged!"

When the *Gypsy Queen* begins to close her net—has therefore stopped fishing and relinquished the water—the boat beside us, next in line, backs off the gravel to take position. Suddenly a different boat moves from the line and the corks of its net begin to stretch out from its moving skiff. *"Motherfucker!"* bellows the skipper of the boat with rights, an easygoing man with whom we had just shared coffee. "You jumped your turn, *jumped your turn!*" Whistles blow as men on other boats take up the outraged cry.

By now the maverick boat has its net taut in the water, and the fish beating against the corks show a spectacular haul. But, as we watch, the silhouetted skipper on the bridge waves a signal to his skiff man, who throws off his end of the net to float slack in the water. The action releases all the fish. On deck the crewmen start hauling back the dead net over the power block as the rightful boat takes its place and sets around the area where the fish had appeared.

The rightful boat roundhauls—its skiff quickly encircles the fish and returns to the boat immediately rather than holding the net for a period. The boat that had jumped its turn is next, but since it will take half an hour to restack her seine, the *Desperado* goes out instead. There are still jumpers in the water. We roundhaul also in our turn. The big, beautiful silver bluebacks thrash a spray across the whole surface of the enclosed seine, throwing salt and slime in our faces. "Hot today man, hot too-day," cries Ron as he unlashes the brailer from the side of the housing.

We thrust the aluminum rim of the brailer—a smaller, long-handled version of the one used by the tender when we delivered—down into the mass of fish and scoop up a bagful. Their fat bellies press against the mesh as the boom raises the bag enough for us to pull it across deck to the hatch. The brail-load weighs about three hundred pounds. When we have it positioned, Barry pulls loose the drawcord and fish thump into the hold. Their tails flap like drumbeats against the glazed insulation. We can feel their power when we grab spillovers by the tails to pitch them into the hold and their muscular thrash almost tears them from our grip. Such work calls for whooping and shouting.

The maverick boat follows us into the water where the fish had milled, taking its turn at last. But the fish are gone. Their bag comes aboard with twenty, no more.

I have fished salmon in other Alaskan waters where the crewmen on a boat with its nets into a moneybag of fish would have jumped rails and bare-knuckled it rather than empty their net. Certainly in Bristol Bay. I've seen it happen.

"Chignik's the only gentleman fishery left in Alaska," a local old-timer tells me later.

Eleven years later, Ernie Carlson is still fishing the *Desperado,* and Elwyn, vowing each year will be his last, remains in the crew. The gutsy men of the *Protector* who kept on fishing after a glimpse at death have dispersed to other grounds and occupations—except for skipper Mori Jones. Mori, who continues to run a hundred-year-old family boatyard started by his grandfather, still stalks the Chignik sockeyes every year aboard his forty-seven-foot *Islander.* The crew now includes his son and oldest daughter. "I'm very fortunate that my children like to fish," he declares.

Bering Sea, Alaska, 1976: Lonely at the top. Skipper Leiv Loklingholm watches deck work from his wheelhouse rail. Everyone's safety depends on his boat-handling.

Bering Sea, Alaska, 1976: A crewman throws a hook to retrieve a crab pot buoy as water crashes over the rail. Rubber bands around the legs help keep out seas.

Ernie Carlson, skipper-owner of the *Desperado*,
Seattle, 1997.

Chignik, Alaska, 1986: The *Desperado* hauls its seine aboard over the power block as the skiff
man holds the boat off the net.

CHAPTER FIVE

Encroachments

Those pirates, they're pickin' off our fish," cried Chignik fishermen with the bitter conviction of men hit in the pocket. By "pirates" they meant crews from other parts of Alaska, principally those from Kodiak like my friend Thorvold Olsen, fishing off Cape Igvak to intercept sockeyes swimming to their Chignik home waters. But at Cape Igvak with Thorvold the water was never calm. Currents could be vicious. Wind sometimes filled the net like a sail as we stacked, pulling our arms until they never stopped aching. If anyone thought of the fellows at Chignik a hundred twenty miles down the coast in their sheltered lagoon, it was to declare them spoiled by good fortune to have the fish that escaped our nets come swimming into their very laps as they lazed in sheltered waters.

Can migratory creatures be owned? The answer in isolated Chignik differs from that in a place with wider expectations. Chignik fishermen trace family ties from house to house, existence depends on one species in a single season, and a malefactor will still withdraw like a gentleman. During winter little but the *vrooom* of snowmobiles breaks the silence. Kodiak society is more fluid, rules less rigid, opportunities greater, a hopping place that draws ambitious fishermen from all over. Boats fish multiple species at different times of the year, trucks honk throughout the winter as they carry gear to the harbor, and the beat of rock thunders from the bars. At Igvak a Kodiak boat might be less inclined to bow out gracefully from an error.

Kodiak fishing traditions barely form before someone shatters them with a new method or target. It makes the town vital, but encroachment-prone beyond the worst Chignik nightmare. In 1988, Kodiak clashed full blast with fishing interests other than its own. By then, much of the local fishing scene had changed in the twelve years since I'd picked over shrimp before Thorvold rescued me. (Or indeed since I'd first seen the town in 1952, a mere waystation of small boats before the great potential of its waters had been discovered.) The money crops in 1976 were salmon, shrimp, and king crab, while a very traditional halibut fishery supported in particular some hundred Norwegian Americans based in Seattle. By 1988 both the shrimp and crab stocks had crashed, through either overfishing or changes in water temperature. (No one has proved either conclusively.) And halibut fishing had lost its hard-nosed Norwegian mystique as stocks flourished and other fishermen gave them a try. But with the crustacean decline—or because of it when the predator cycle reversed—finfish such as cod and pollock reached commercial numbers as never before. The abundance spurred a domestic fleet of trawlers and trawler-processors that had not existed in 1976. The plant where I maneuvered sluicefuls of shrimp now converts locally caught pollock into a fish paste called *surimi*.

In March 1988 several of the new big trawler-processors, all based in Seattle though they caught their entire product in Alaska, were headed north to the Bering Sea. As they passed a halfway point off Kodiak they discovered a windfall. It happened to be spawning season for local pollock, and a biomass of these half-pound fish filled the water. The Seattle transients set their nets on the same stocks that smaller Kodiak draggers were harvesting for delivery ashore over a period of months, and in nine days scooped up the entire annual Gulf of Alaska pollock quota. The incident left Kodiak shore plants without the fish they needed to remain in full operation for the rest of the year, and left local trawlers without their projected livelihood throughout the autumn.

The larger Seattle boats compounded the outrage. They kept only the roe—for which Japan paid inflated prices—and dumped the rest of the fish over the side. Some of the Kodiak plants roe-stripped ashore on a smaller scale (the practice was not illegal) but used the rest of the pollock for fish paste and meal. The concentrated stripping at sea not only wasted food, but also covered the seafloor with rotting fish that plugged the nets of local boats trying to make up their losses fishing for other species.

While it made no difference to the outraged victims in Kodiak, some of the big-boat skippers had been driven as much by desperation as by greed. The American trawler-processor fleet of approximately fifty ships at the time had kept growing with success, and the increasing number of ships competed for a quota that remained constant. Owners could expect fewer fish per vessel, while they still had to meet the same pay-rolls and mortgages. The trawlers needed to feed as constantly as hummingbirds.

In Kodiak, the shore plants had felt squeezed even before they lost half their annual fish projection, because the local catch had diminished. Ironically the local small draggers had themselves, in previous years, fished out once-abundant pollock stocks in Shelikof Strait between Kodiak Island and the Alaskan mainland. The Shelikof depletion had been a turf battle among fishermen of the same community, in which "fixed" gear fishermen had lost to those with "mobile" gear. Mobile gear—trawls—pull a net across the seafloor or through part of the water column. Fixed gear—pots, baited hooks, small anchored nets—stay put and are thus more selective. Biologists' warnings in the Shelikof had gone unheeded, and the disaster brought down a shower of local hostility. Dispossessed fixed-gear fishermen blamed politics and self-interest. It might have been "trawl-bashing," as claimed by Al Burch, a respected trawlerman from shrimp days and president of the local Alaska Draggers Association, but nets dragging the seafloor, unless closely tuned (as Burch claimed was done), *could* sweep all in their wake.

Thus tensions among neighbors and countrymen driven by economic realities. But fish swimming in the wild may cover many venues, even those of different nations. Some of the stakes are too high to be settled with a shrug as happens between Igvak and Chignik, or with new domestic regulations as happened after the Shelikof depletion and the roe stripping off Kodiak. Back in the late 1950s there were "cod wars" when Iceland sent gunboats to force British trawlers off cod stocks within fifty miles of its shores. During the same period, to the indignation of Americans, Peru and Ecuador impounded California-based tuna boats within their 200-mile waters, long before the United States and the rest of the world recognized a nation's right to sovereignty this far from shore.

Two-hundred-mile national jurisdiction over marine resources, which by 1977 the United States, Canada, and most other coastal nations had claimed (Japan did not declare until 1996), is now the norm. But this has created its own turf clashes. In the spring of 1995 Canada, to curb overfishing of desperately endangered stocks, cut the nets of one Spanish trawler fishing just outside the international 200-mile line on its adjacent Grand Banks, and impounded another. The Spanish proved indeed to be breaking the agreed rules, and Canada's showdown led to a more enforceable arrangement. Halfway around the world a boxing match continues round by round, with no referee except ultimately the United Nations, over rights in the waters off an otherwise insignificant cluster of islands called Spratlys in the South China Sea. The islands fall outside 200-mile lines but are surrounded by Vietnam, Brunei, Philippines, Malaysia, and Indonesia, all of which claim fishing rights, as do more-distant Taiwan and China, both of whom have fished here.

The opportunities of 200-mile rights have too much potential for nations in possession to give them up. France holds St. Pierre and Miquelon, twelve miles off Newfoundland's west coast, and makes sure that the two small islands remain a full province linked directly to Paris. Russia continues to hold the Japanese-speaking Kuril Islands in sight of the north Japan coast, a war booty taken over fifty years ago, despite Japan's refusal to sign a peace treaty and resume full diplomatic relations until receiving them back. (At this writing in 1998 there may at last be an accommodation here, although as recently as August 1997 Russians fired on a Japanese fishing boat lost in fog near the Kurils, wounding two.) When in 1982 the British risked war to keep its Falkland Islands protectorate, located some thirty times closer to Argentina than to the United Kingdom, its several strategic reasons included fishing presence. International incidents keep occurring over occupation of Quemoy and Matsu, islands within sight of the Chinese mainland but a hundred miles from Taiwan, that the Taiwan-based Republic of China claims essential to its defenses. The drive here is military, but the Formosa/Taiwan Strait that separates the two powers is prime fishing water.

Canada and the United States might be expected to share a common interest, like Siamese twins. But if fishermen ran the two offices there would probably be shooting. On the Pacific coast, salmon that spawn in U.S. and Canadian rivers migrate home past both coasts to be intercepted by fisherman of both countries. Canada accuses the U.S. of taking more than its share, while Americans accuse Canadians of disrupting the spawners by fishing other species at crucial parts of their cycle. The anger reverberates in Ottawa (less in D.C. since Americans don't consider it a matter of national honor), and a fishery treaty between the sister nations has remained unsigned since 1992. In the summer of 1997 incensed Canadian salmon fishermen boat-blockaded the Alaska ferry that had stopped at Prince Rupert en route from Seattle to Ketchikan to dramatize their anger over the lack of settlement.

The chagrin between American and Canadian fishermen is polite stuff compared with a brush I had in Taiwan. At the time (1993), the U.S. government was nearing an agreement with Russia that would close off the "Donut Hole," an enclave of international water enclosed within the two nations' 200-mile lines in the Bering Sea. Taiwanese boats fishing the "Hole" were destined to be among the losers. One afternoon in Kaohsiung, Taiwan's main southern port, I visited an unloading quay with my interpreter, Mr. Liang. A cargo net transferred loads of frozen albacore from a ship's hold to the loading dock. Men and women hooked individual fish from the frost-steaming pile and thumped them into trucks or stacked them like cordwood. The women were faceless behind cloths wrapped from nose to chin (typical dress for laboring women on the Taiwan docks), but several of the men watched me grimly. One man lumbered over, a cargo hook in one hand and a beer can in the other. "Who's that?" he asked Liang in Chinese. American? Americans didn't care if they put Taiwanese fishermen out of business to starve, he snarled bitterly, without looking at me. "Americans don't even eat fish! You treat us like thief!" Liang translated worriedly. He added in a murmur: "Let us go. They might beat you," and relaxed only when we reached the street.

Taiwan does seem to be in the thick of territorial disputes, with its immense Western-backed prosperity that allows heavy boat investment, but with only limited fishing grounds under direct control. From a recent cull of news publications:

- "Argentine Gunfire Wounds Taiwan Fishermen off Falkland Islands." (AP wire)
- "Island Dispute Sparks Ire Against Japan. Taiwan and China also claim territory." *(Christian Science Monitor)*
- "Eight fishermen from Kaohsiung released from an Indonesian jail where they said 30 more Taiwan fishermen were being held." *(Free China Journal)*
- "A U.S. Coast Guard cutter mounted a .50–caliber machine gun in a show of force that persuaded a fleeing Taiwanese squid-fishing vessel to stop for a search after a three-day, 600-mile chase." *(Seattle Post-Intelligencer)*
- "Taipei is considering retaliation against the Manila government for refusing to return seven Taiwan fishing boats out of Kaohsiung impounded by the Philippine Navy." *(Free China Journal)*

Nor is Taiwan alone. The restless fishermen of two other countries with more boats than marine resources—Thailand and Spain—seem unable to stop regarding the oceans as commons despite this generation's increasing rules of national and international ownership: "It is estimated that some 200 Thai fishing vessels have been arrested by Myanmar, Malaysia, India, Indonesia, and Vietnam this year [1996] and about 600 fishermen remain in jail." *(Fishing News International)*

Incidentally, Thai fishermen ignore also unspoken rules, as they proved two decades ago to the permanent shame of the fishing occupation the world over, when they plundered and coldly murdered at sea hundreds of helpless refugee Vietnamese boat people.

The Spanish have their own enduring reputation. William Warner, riding aboard a Spanish trawler in the early 1980s, reports in his book *Distant Water* that its officers were concerned for their national reputation due to routine lying about the size of catches—at least by other Spanish trawlermen off North America. Crewmen had watched those on ships of other countries shake fists in passing. Reported the *Wall Street Journal* of May 29, 1986: "In the three years up to last January, 3,645 Spanish freebooters were waylaid by the French" fishing illegally in French waters. The *Journal* wrote this on the eve of Spain's entry into the European Union, but predicted that EU fishing controls would "trim the sails" of Spanish (especially Basque) fishermen. Curbed indeed has been the massive level of encroachments, because the Spanish fishing fleet itself has diminished through lack of places allowing them to fish, while the Spanish government appears trying to clean the image of its fishermen by punishing those caught. Yet as reported by *Fishing News International* in two successive 1997 issues: the Spanish trawler *Hermanos Gandon IV* was cited on the Nose of the Grand Banks for misreporting its catch—33.8 tons during five days on grounds, but reported only 14.8 tons. And "An 'ingeniously concealed' secret hold aboard a United Kingdom–registered Spanish vessel arrested recently by Ireland has been described as 'a work of art.' A boarding party took three hours to find the hold as it was in a secret compartment and disguised as a fuel tank. The hold was complete with freezing equipment and a lighting system."

Nor do only a few nations have the monopoly on territorial disputes or encroachments. Fishing crews often fall victim. From recent reports, taken from *Fishing News International* except as noted:

- "Growing Russian irritation at Norwegian fishing policy, especially over arrest of several Murmansk-based trawlers."
- "Dutch warn the European Union, which has failed to take action, that the Danish industrial herring and sprat fleets are taking stocks

of Dutch fish for food. 'They're slowly taking our future away from us. We may be forced to take action ourselves.'"

• "Somalia catches French tuna catamaran *Viking Explorer* fishing illegally 80 miles offshore."

• "Illegal seizures of fishing vessels are increasing and pirates are demanding growing ransoms to free fishing vessels and their crews. Ships from the former Soviet Union—particularly those operating off the African coasts where civil wars continue—face a high risk of being hijacked."

• In April 1997 "India and Pakistan held peace talks, and agreed in a goodwill gesture to free several hundred fishermen held by the two countries." (AP)

• "The United Nations' Food and Agriculture Organization (FAO) reports that illegal fishing off certain Arab countries with under-developed domestic fisheries equals the reported negotiated catches. This is especially the case in east central Atlantic off Morocco and Mauritania, but also in the northwest Indian Ocean off Somalia and Yemen."

• "New Zealand seizes all five Russian vessels of a fleet for misreporting hoki catches, and refuses bond to release them."

• "According to a South African spokesman: 'Action must be taken to stop illegal fishing of Patagonian toothfish in the Southern Ocean.' Scientists and legal vessel owners in South Africa and other countries are now angry at the high level of what they allege is illegally catching toothfish, also known as seabass or black hake. 'The reason some Argentinean and Chilean vessels are here is testimony that their own toothfish industry has collapsed.'"

And, an ultimate international arrest reported by Reuters: "A Kenyan-registered vessel accused of illegal fishing in Somali waters has been held by a Somali faction. The Italian-owned *Bahari Hindi* was intercepted on 22 April [1997] by militiamen aboard speedboats and she was forced to dock. The 34 crew included Italians, Kenyans, Poles, Senegalese, Romanians, and four Somalis. Abdi Said Ali, chairman of Jarriban district, central Somalia, said that the crew is being well treated pending trial."

It is unlikely that any of the world's superabundant fishing waters will in our time be free of competitors for their marine wealth, since with exploding populations and efficient catching technologies there is no longer enough to go around.

Not all waters teem with sea life. Except for migratory fish like tunas and salmon, fishing abundance occurs where oceanographic conditions produce rich nutrients, since it takes food to attract fish. Single-celled phytoplankton, the primary food of other sea creatures, grow through photosynthesis: exposure to light. It is only in areas where water keeps gyrating from depths to the surface to give that gulp of light to plankton by the billions that growth explodes. Only the cooler waters of temperate latitudes, however, produce the very productive grounds. In warm tropical waters the growth cycle accelerates too quickly so that plankton use up the nutrients and die as quickly as they generate. Cold surface waters sink in season, which generates a steady upwelling that boils up bottom minerals that phytoplankton need. In warm waters, on the other hand, thermal stratification seals the mineral nutrients to the seafloor.

Thus the great seafood grounds occur in the relative shallows of chilly continental shelves like those off Alaska and Newfoundland, or where deep, cold, circular currents upwell as do those off Peru and Chile and off southern Africa. Here an endless supply of food sustains a huge population. Big fish and crustaceans eat their smaller counterparts, but every creature flourishes.

The hard fact is that not enough seafood lies in the world's limited productive waters to fill the nets and hooks of all the world's fishing vessels. Some lose. Lucky the fishermen of Kodiak, Chignik, and other Alaskan ports. The salmon they catch, under sensible state management not bound by other state or international claims, as well as most fish and crustaceans in federal 200-mile waters off their coasts, are abundant enough to go around, whether they believe it or not.

CHAPTER SIX

Knee-Deep in Crude and Bullshit

The *EXXON Valdez* Disaster

Seining at Cape Igvak introduced me to the sheer joy of catching fish. Seining in Chignik duplicated that basic experience and added the sometime danger. Encroachments were another reality of fishing, from competitions for a single stock within local waters to those of nations each taking whatever rights and expectations it could enforce.

Another essence of fishing is the man-made event, accidental and not, that affects whole communities. There are short-term events that send boats scurrying temporarily: French nuclear tests in the South Pacific or China's rattlesword firings across the Formosa Strait. Of longer duration: In the Black Sea, jellyfish that apparently migrated in the ballast water of freighters from distant ports have flourished to destroy anchovy on which area fishermen depend. In Canada, Norway, and Japan, pressure by other nations with citizens of high moral purpose and nothing to lose have closed the hunts for harp seals and for minke whales, fisheries of unendangered species depended on by entire communities. In Cambodia, to help subjugate a society that lives on rice and fish, the despicable Khmer Rouge systematically destroyed the nets, traps, and boats of its countrymen.

Elsewhere beyond a fisherman's control, just after midnight on March 24, 1989, the supertanker *EXXON Valdez* grounded on Bligh Reef in Prince William Sound and gurgled out 11.2 million gallons of crude oil. Before the oil—a black, stinking plug several feet deep— had run its course through prime fishing waters, it had thrown the Alaskan fisheries in its path into devastation. At least one fishery, herring, has yet to recover.

The spill, which occurred just twenty-five Good Fridays after the 1964 earthquake destroyed part of the same region, came at the worst possible time. It was the area's season of greatest biological activity, the primary reproductive period for most mammals, birds, fish, and marine invertebrates. In early April, herring would start to pour into Prince William Sound from the sea for an annual spawning that would soon see billions of the fish depositing eggs and cloudy sperm along the coasts. Two weeks later, fry from the Sound's famous salmon hatcheries would start to migrate seaward, directly through the oiled waters at the time when a spring bloom of zooplankton provided them feed, following a natural schedule that could not be altered. By late May, mature salmon would begin a summer-long return from the sea to spawn in the rivers of their birth throughout the Sound and along the coast.

The insidious oil moved along the length of Prince William Sound as a swath, choking beaches on numerous islands in its wake. At the outset in calm weather, proper equipment might have contained the oil. (This was the fault of the oil consortium Alyeska and of lax state agencies, not Exxon, incidentally.) Storms soon broke the plug into ungovernable patches moving in thick fingers that stuck to the land without seeming to diminish. Traveling a few miles a day on the currents, the oil left Prince William Sound on Day Six to enter the Gulf of Alaska, slowly clogging harbors down the coast. By Day Fifty it had surrounded both sides of Kodiak Island. The remaining slick continued along the coast, into Chignik and beyond, coating beaches up to 600 miles from the spill site.

In my youthful Coast Guard days as a junior officer, I had piloted the CGC *Sweetbrier* past Bligh Reef without a thought of hitting it, so far was it from the channel. Beautiful, precious country. In Baltimore, after reading of the spill, I choked up. Within three weeks I was there. By this time, thirteen years after picking candlefish in Kodiak, I had pulled enough nets and written enough about fishermen that I could talk my way out on patrols to see for myself.

On Smith Island in the direct path of the spill, my boots suck into the oil and hold me almost anchored. Pressured, Exxon has flown crews out to scrub rocks, and now ferries reporters to observe them. (Scrubbing is effective for cameras, but each tide brings in more stuff. Eventually eleven thousand workers will hose beaches with water and steam.) Workers pass with their yellow or orange slicker pants dripping opaque brown glop. Hell comes to mind over and over. Figures move through the steam like the damned in the Gustav Dore *Inferno*. Oil forms a thick slimy mat over every rock. I waddle to keep from falling. To wipe sweat from your eyes means oiling your face. Out on the water, where boats tow floating barriers called booms to capture pockets of oil and deliver it to barges that skim it aboard, sludge coats hulls and clogs propellers. Life is smothered. Dead fish of a potential harvest float like dirty cobblestones, and birds pulled from the mess could be bundles of sticks. The sulfurous stench lodges so deeply in my nose that I seem to be eating it. When standing in the middle of such a beach I want to break and run—but where?

Tough people weep freely. A large, once-white bird stands unsteadily at a distance. Its wide wings, built for soaring in search of food, are coated black. They flap helplessly. When the befuddled creature tries to fly as always before, the weighted wings lift it only a few inches in the air. Wherever it hops, its clawed legs disappear into thick brown mousse, a pudding formed by waves churning crude oil and seawater together. The bird has retreated beyond rescue to shoal rocks, too dangerous for a boat, too deep for a man on foot. Oiled feathers lose their insulation and buoyancy, so the creature will eventually freeze or drown. No one has a gun handy to help it to an easier death.

Next day I fly over Prince William Sound, an expanse 90 miles wide and forty miles north–south. We can see only parts at a time, but our height gives an inkling of the great bay's size, beauty, and complexity. There are forested islands, rocky peninsulas, and mountains packed with snow as thick as ice cream. Glaciers snake down from the north.

We first cross western parts of the Sound that the spill has mercifully bypassed. Then, sinister black streaks and sheens begin covering the water. A long tanker heading toward Hinchinbrook Entrance and the sea cuts a triangular swath of wake straight through the oil. (The Coast Guard closed Valdez harbor just after the spill, but now, three weeks later, the petroleum crude of Prudhoe Bay is moving again.) The greatness of surrounding nature dwarfs the tanker, but the huge engine-powered ship still stretches as long as a pencil on a table. In some coves lie instant communities of boats and barges nestled together. On blackened beaches nearby, clusters of workers in bright oilskins move about cleaning rocks. We fly over bays laced in a helter-skelter of orange, yellow, and white booms like yarn tangled by cats. Man and his objects intrude everywhere.

The three towns most affected by the spill are Valdez and Cordova, the respective oil and fishing centers of Prince William Sound, and the larger fishing center of Kodiak 250 miles away facing the Pacific Ocean. (Plenty of other communities are also affected, especially small native villages that live mainly by fishing.) The atmosphere in fish-dependent Cordova is driven, heartsick, and angry. In Valdez, permanent residents might be as heartsick as anyone else over polluted wilderness, but the disaster jeopardizes fewer people's work and the atmosphere is more typically hopping and opportunistic. In Kodiak during the first weeks before the spill descends, people watch warily as they would a hurricane that might or might not hit.

On the day I arrive in Valdez, the small airport is as busy as Chicago's O'Hare. Built to handle a dozen flights a day, it's averaging three to four hundred. Crates with gear ranging from parts to big pumps litter the waiting room. Notices both scrawled and printed cover the doors. One: "Notice all pilots and crews. Report all sightings of unattended boom that appears to be adrift. Several 100 ft. of boom broke free and is thought to be in the outboard tanker lanes near Rocky Bay Montague Island." Cars outside the airport whisk off suited businessmen with briefcases, pickup trucks collect men in stiff orange flotation suits, and a ramshackle bus takes aboard people—not all of them kids—with knapsacks and bedrolls.

Valdez, relocated and newly built after a tidal wave from the 1964 earthquake destroyed the old town and killed thirty-two people, has wide roads and low buildings. Snowbanks rise above most roofs even in April, so traveling the two main streets seems walking a labyrinth. Nestled between snowbanks stands a supermarket, a large drugstore, the two-story Petroleum Building, motels, and other evidences of civilization, including an A-frame church.

Oil companies and media crews have booked accommodations indefinitely. Motels all have NO VACANCY signs, as do an assortment of trailers on side roads and even a tent-covered pickup truck. At night the legs of sleepers stick from the windows of parked cars and trucks. Jeff Gard, the on-site head of the Cordova fishermen's organization, red-eyed from lack of sleep as he coordinates the protection of salmon hatcheries with cleanup officials, rescues me from a sleeping bag on a floor to provide a bunk in an oil rig trailer reached by planks over mud.

Hundreds of men and women have poured into Valdez from Anchorage—a bumpy seven-hour drive—expecting immediate jobs at oil-company wages. One kid I meet has driven his truck from North Carolina up the Alcan Highway. Most wait for days at the employment office. When the big hiring begins at last, the pay starts at $16.95 an hour, and with dawn-to-dusk days on overtime the average paycheck reaches about $1,800 a week. Meanwhile the crime rate rises precipitously, trash and broken bottles pile high, and human waste accumulates in dark corners and bushes. Residents watch with chilled shock.

In the warmth of a noisy Valdez bar I meet two red-eyed fishermen whose very woolens smell of oil. They have trouble suppressing grins as they shovel Tex-Mex enchiladas, order seconds, and gulp beer straight from the pitcher. "Oh man, you'd like to puke from the stink," Joe says appreciatively. They've been pushing their boat into the worst of the sludge to dip the stuff into gallon bait buckets, then deliver it to a collection barge. Exxon is buying back its salty oil at $5 a bucket. "Last two days we scooped and sold 'em what? Seventeen hundred fuckin' buckets of bounty, one thousand seven hundred times *five*. Gotta be back out first light tomorrow. Pass that pitcher, buddy!" Eventually Exxon's reported bounty price rose to $20 a gallon for oil thus rescued. Even so, knowledgeable observers claimed that Exxon got more cleanup per buck from such fishermen-entrepreneurs than from any other project it funded. No wonder, as the cleanup progressed and the employment ranks swelled, that the carpetbaggers in Valdez bars raised their glasses to toast Joe Hazelwood, the *EXXON Valdez*'s skipper with an alcohol problem whose tanker had unleashed the bonanza.

An extensive disaster force has mobilized in Valdez within a remarkably short time. Three weeks after the spill the American Legion Hall is such a warren of command posts that a guard directs people with credentials and shoos others away. Carpenters nail partitions around groups of people intensely phoning. Bulletin boards display layer upon layer of announcements. Weary men stomp through in boots and black-spattered orange float suits—uniform of anyone flying to the beaches.

Across the road in the old town hall the State of Alaska churns out piles of documents and directives. Elsewhere instructors conduct classes in beach cleaning for would-be workers. In the Petroleum Building on the main street, Exxon public relations people produce daily press releases showing how much Exxon cares, while putting a brave face to reporters and photographers clamoring for a place on one of the helicopters ferrying cleanup equipment to the ruined beaches.

Up on a hill the high school gymnasium has become the otter rescue center, while a classroom building two blocks downhill houses the bird rescue center. Both, organized spontaneously, soon became funded open-end by Exxon. In the converted gym, curtained makeshift cubicles shelter volunteers in raingear who struggle to clean and save little oil-coated otters flown and trucked in from the beaches. (Before long the volunteers enter the Exxon payroll circuit, but most did not come for this.) Scattered canvas protects only parts of the polished basketball floor from sharp-edged cages and heavy boots. The place smells of wet animal hair, feces, and soap. The animals, some so encased in thick crude that their eyes cannot open, and with their immune systems utterly disrupted, need to be cleaned in stages at controlled temperatures. Common detergents prove effective, applied with tools that include Q-tips (for oiled ears and nostrils), towels, and absorbent sheets.

Survival rates are poor, although they have improved with trial and error. Of the 399 otters pulled from the muck at this point, only 46 remain alive. The count at the bird rescue center is even sadder, with 150 birds alive of 2,292 collected. An aura of horror hovers over both places. They are grimly quiet, broken only by tight-voiced instructions from people emotionally shaken. Everyone tries to speak softly so as not to agitate their charges further.

Outside the gym, rows of cages shelter the lovely dispirited otters that have been cleaned. A rope barrier around the cages and KEEP OFF signs protect the weakened animals while they recuperate. Gentle-voiced attendants, hosing the little aquatic creatures regularly with water to keep them cool while feeding them strips of geoduck (a chewy mollusk from their home waters), need to minister cautiously. Otters are charming but also ill-tempered, and nature built their teeth to crack clam shells.

A busload of dignitaries arrives with entourage. The delegation features Interior Secretary Manuel Lujan. Everyone wears appropriate checked shirts. Scheduled to the minute to see a snatch of everything before flying back to Anchorage for dinner, the group storms in a cheerful pack to the otter cages. A public relations person detaches the rope barrier, and the leaders gather close to the otters, lost from view among photographers straining to record the event. Minutes later everyone bustles back aboard the bus, first posing gaily by the blue sky and creamy white alps. Some have never seen Alaska. Soon they'll be back in Washington, time enough for long faces. Fortunately they leave. Minutes later a truck from the harbor brings boxes of dying creatures, and things become tense.

The Coast Guard has been assigned to coordinate the cleanup. Every afternoon at the Valdez Legion Hall, in a conference room packed to the doors, it holds a public assemblage of all the commands involved. On this day the admiral in charge, Edward Nelson, a broad-shouldered, agreeably authoritative man who would be a reassuring sight on any ship's bridge, keeps the meeting low-keyed and informal. The exchanges indicate the tentativeness of a situation where forces can be mustered but Nature calls the shots. He summarizes: 319 vessels now employed, twenty-five aircraft in the air today. The Coast Guard cutter *Sweetbrier* (my ship in Alaska thirty-eight years before) is rigging a gate boom, and the cutter *Rush* has resumed air traffic control duties.

The admiral next describes a beach seen earlier in the day that was not on the list for cleaning, and passes around a sample of oil he has gathered. The thick black-green crude clings sluggishly to the sides of the jar. It stinks. "I want to see some rear ends and elbows cleaning up that stuff soon." He notes that some one thousand people are waiting in town to be hired. "Exxon, do you know when you'll start your next hiring and get these people off the street?" Soon, assures an Exxon rep. Someone reports that the residents of a small native village along the potential path of the spill can get no booms and have stretched logs across their harbor entrance. "We need to find some booms to release to those people, to relieve their minds."

In the months that follow the spill becomes a self-generating industry. The Valdez population swells from 3,700 to an estimated 12,000. Besides reporters, cleanup experts, and cleanup workers, there descends a predictable crew of lawyers and prostitutes as well as marine biologists, environmentalists, equipment salesmen (some with useful ideas, some with near-scams), social workers (to assure the populace that they have a right to be shocked—as many are indeed, and deeply—and then to counsel them), social scientists (to observe the shock on the populace), and all manner of other experts.

Many of Valdez's 3,700 inhabitants at the time of the spill have Texas drawls and count Valdez a temporary residence. Residents of Cordova, population 2,500, fiercely consider Cordova their home. So isolated that it can be approached only by air or from the sea, the town resists attempts by the state to connect it by road to Valdez and Anchorage. People warn not to leave a car unlocked in Valdez, but in Cordova they leave keys in ignitions. Cordova has the old-clapboard look of a frontier town, just as it did when I first saw it in 1952. The main street dips from a hill, and houses overlook the boat harbor. A two-block string of shops, eateries, and bars constitutes downtown. On all sides rise majestic mountains. Most business concerns fish.

The town's flags all fly at half mast, "due to the death of the environment" according to a sign in the Reluctant Fisherman, the town's main lodging, where fishermen gather for morning coffee. Voices choke, and there is anger. For years the Cordova District Fishermen United, CDFU, has been beating on oil company doors and in the state legislature for stronger government oversight, and for better facilities and equipment to contain both the terminal's daily effluent and an inevitable major spill. They have received little attention.

The crisis quickly hits Cordova's economy. The Alaska Department of Fish and Game cancels the Sound's herring fishery, a major source of income just poised to begin, since herring on their way into the Sound might encounter oil. Worse, oil threatens three salmon hatcheries, the core of Cordova's fishing. The facilities were developed laboriously over fifteen years, supported by a two percent levy on fish sales from every boat and by cost recovery from hatchery harvest. The nonprofit co-op, Prince William Sound Aquaculture Corporation (locally abbreviated "Pizwak"), is recognized internationally as a model of salmon aquaculture—ranching, not farming. Each spring the hatcheries release millions of salmon fry that travel through the Sound to the sea and faithfully return fifteen months later as mature two-year-old adults. Release time is near, and cannot be postponed.

The fishermen of Cordova mobilize like a garrison to protect the hatcheries. Volunteer skippers and crews race across the Sound carrying whatever barriers they can find to seal the entrances of hatchery harbors against floating oil. (At first, according to CDFU's executive director Marilyn Leland, Exxon refuses the services of volunteers, stating: "We can't afford the liability of using amateurs." By Day Two, as the spill moves out of control, they change their minds.)

When I arrive three weeks after the spill, lines of fishermen are signing up their boats at the CDFU office. In a rear office volunteers as well as the organization's president, fisherman Gerry McCune, race from phones to marine radios, supplying and coordinating boats already stationed at the hatcheries. The same tension drives those in the adjacent office of the aquaculture corporation. A report dated April 11 notes that the Cordova fishing fleet on the scene numbers 118 boats and three hundred persons. By now, Exxon has announced it will pay for the boats, materials, and men needed to check the oil. McCune refuses scornfully to go on Exxon's "guilt payroll," as do other CDFU board members, including Ken Adams, Michele O'Leary, Jack Lamb, and Rikki Ott (who ironically warned a Valdez group about potential cleanup inadequacies by conference phone just three hours before the tanker grounded). They remain angry volunteers working eighteen-hour days.

Papers plaster the walls: prayerful schoolchild letters from California to New York, emotional local statements (a sprawling child's hand declared "Tanker captains should drink milk"), phone numbers for volunteers, times of boom-setting classes (required of anyone hired for the cleanup), and instructions for picking up live and dead creatures from the water. A scrawl over an Exxon form releasing the company from further claims for a sum received warns: "Don't sign."

The Exxon representatives flown in to process claims keep coffee and cookies in their office to soothe the outspoken Cordovans, but manage to do little soothing. "I'm not a spokesman," says one of the men tersely. "Never been to Alaska before." He won't comment on a rejected laundromat's submission, based on its losses, claiming that the canceled fishing season eliminated the usual out-of-town influx of cannery workers and crewmen who used its machines. (Exxon eventually gives in, wisely, since until then Cordovans use it to show how little the oil company gives a damn.) "But I'll tell you," volunteers the Exxon man sturdily, "I think Exxon's doin' a wonderful job here." He and the others keep their Texas accents and opinions close to the guarded office or in their rooms at the Reluctant. This is not oil-oriented Valdez.

The flurry on the day I arrive centers around the shipment of a new heavy-duty boom from Norway. It was ordered just three days ago (paid for by Exxon, undoubtedly at fantastic expense), in desperation over the inadequacy of the materials being provided by the oil companies. Huge crates of the deflated boom are now being loaded aboard the salmon tender *Max,* its engines throbbing to start immediately for the overnight run to the hatchery at Sawmill Bay. Another boat, the *New Era,* is already headed for Sawmill with a small advance load. An expert just arrived from Norway plans to fly out next day to supervise the boom's deployment.

The Norwegian agrees to take me with him, and in preparation I attend a two-hour training class in boom setting and beach cleaning. Thirty men squeeze into a corner of the Masonic Hall that evening as environmental workers continue writing the day's reports on makeshift desks. "I'll start," says the instructor, a man with muscular wrists who looks as if he could handle heavy equipment, "by saying that what can go wrong *will* go wrong. OK. Nature's going to do what it pleases. But there's ways of getting along with Nature." He diagrams booms, long floating tubes used to encircle a spill and keep it from spreading: how to set a boom in relation to currents, how to tow it without losing oil underneath or over the top ("oil builds a head wave if you tow too fast"), when to lay multiple barriers, since a single boom cannot control the concentration. The fishermen, accustomed to improvising with tools, ask practical, work-oriented questions.

Next morning, in gray drizzle as whitecaps lap around the pontoons of our small plane, we lift from Cordova harbor for Sawmill Bay. We know we're approaching the hatchery, seventy-five air miles away, before we see it. The concentration of boats increases, and booms stretch from island to island like orange and yellow spaghetti. The San Juan/Armand F. Koerning Hatchery itself is an isolated cluster of long buildings and piers built on pilings at the back of a narrow bay. Floating ramps lead into a maze of fish-holding pens. From the air, forested hilly islands surround the complex as far as the eye can see. We land by the pier. The pilot in hip boots stands on a pontoon to hand out boxes of parts and a bag of mail, then flies off again at once. With the spill, his every flight hour is booked. Under a hard rain, we pull oilskins over our float suits. The air smells of spruce. Nearby, a stream roars downhill.

We head out on a boat with Eric Prestgard, the hatchery manager. A colony of boats mills around us. Eric passes out the mail from the plane. Most of the oilskinned crewmen stand on deck despite the rain, chatting between boats. "Guys don't have much else to do, they fish and hunt together other times," says Eric. In a normal year they'd now be in the thick of blood-pounding herring hauls. Many have not touched land during the three weeks since the spill. After the initial push their duty has become that of mere watchmen, ready for action but marking time.

A complex of booms blocks the harbor entrance. First to seaward lie absorbent booms, light puffy material with black oil smudged along its white and yellow surfaces. Inside the rings of absorbent floats is the heavier barrier boom, its thick orange surfaces glistening in the rain. "We've got to keep inflating that barrier crap," says someone. "It's eight years old and leaks. We pump out seawater every day but it's sinking lower." Radio chatter rises over the engine noise. The cabin has a CB tuned to boats in sight and a VHF tuned to a standard monitoring/emergency frequency.

"Reporting twenty-five hundred, maybe three thousand gallons of new product south side of Smith Island," drones a voice on the VHF. "That's Exxon. They call their spilled stuff product. We call it shit."

The *New Era* arrives with the first load of Norwegian boom. Each of two big crates holds 650 feet of material weighing four thousand pounds. It comes in sections the length of the deck, with heavy metal plates at each end. It takes six men to pull the flattened layers of thick rubber from the crates and haul them to the after rail for bolting. An air compressor inflates the sections as they drop into the water, and the boom pops into a two-foot black snake. In contrast the leaky, aging orange boom seems the stuff of a child's pool. One of the boats attaches a line to the end of the inflated boom to pay it out smoothly, even though the thick material guides itself. "You don't need those guys," says the Norwegian. Eric shrugs. "Let 'em think they're doing something. Everybody's bored."

Next day I return to Cordova aboard the *New Era*. At 5 A.M. the sun bathes a pink light over the snowy peaks. The skipper, fifty-nine-year-old Gerry Thorne, strides his wheelhouse barefoot in overalls and a T-shirt. He likes to talk. I soon know he's fished Cordova waters for more than half a century, from age eight with his dad "in a skiff with one shackle of gear" back in 1938. "I've always, no exceptions, reported any discharge I see from tankers. They hate me, the oil companies. Look at those mountains. Beautiful? Makes your heart stop. You're fuckin' right I ride the oil companies' ass. They don't understand honesty, they'll lie, they'll do anything to get you off their backs. If I ever lied like that my father'd turn over in his grave and rub off his arms."

By 9 A.M. drizzle and gray clouds have replaced the sun. Our boat's VHF radio sputters transmissions from other vessels. My ears prick up at a calm voice that begins: "This is Coast Guard cutter *Sweetbrier*. . . " A few minutes later she emerges from the mist, my old ship. Her hull is still black, the housing white, the booms and masts tan, fresh-painted under good maintenance but honorably scraped here and there from the buffets of work. I grab binoculars, and watch for the minute before the hull disappears back into the rainy mist. "They're good boys aboard her," says Gerry. "I've seen 'em screw up ashore, but they do their duty."

As duty called during the cleanup the 180-foot *Sweetbrier* worked any job that its size and presence required. So did its sister ships *Ironwood, Sedge, Iris,* and *Planetree,* the medium cutters *Storis* and *Yocona,* and the high-endurance cutters *Rush* (designated lead ship), *Morgen-*

thau, and *Midgett.* Later the *Sweetbrier's* captain, Commander John Cook, told me: "We worked around the clock to keep even with our regular work and still do all the rest." Regular duties centered on servicing navigational aids in Prince William Sound. The ship also variously transported heavy equipment for fishermen working to save the hatcheries, served as an air traffic control center, performed security work, maintained a safety zone around the grounded *EXXON Valdez* for several days, conducted beach surveys, shuttled supplies and dignitaries, deployed beach monitors, and set oil booms along with massive concrete anchors to hold them in place. Cook did not need to add that the extra hours earned the Coasties no Exxon workers' high hourly pay and overtime.

We detour to Outside Cove on Naked Island. Here, towed about twenty-five sea miles from Bligh Reef, lies the ruptured 932-foot tanker *EXXON Valdez.* The ship's black hugeness can be appreciated only by comparing it to the toylike size of the boats alongside, many of which must be large to judge from the heavy equipment visible on their decks. The remaining crude aboard her has been pumped off (the spill might have been nearly five times what it was, since the hole released 11,200,000 gallons of the 53,094,510-gallon cargo) and divers work from surrounding boats to repair the hull enough for safe passage to an Oregon shipyard. "It took 'em three days to start mopping that shit," mutters Gerry. "Too late then. Three days! Every one of those oil bastards, we ought to drag 'em naked through the oil, then put 'em on a beach with a toothbrush and say 'Clean it all, every rock, before we let you go.'" As we approach closer to the disabled tanker a boat heads out to shoo us away.

Kodiak town, while like Cordova approachable only by air or sea and only a short hike or boat ride in any direction from howling wilderness, is less insular, more driving and driven. The place always has energy. Kodiak fishermen travel farther in their quest for harvest, fish year-round, swagger more pronouncedly, spend heavier. Many Kodiak boats make thousand-mile trips to the Bering Sea, and some owners commute from Oregon and Washington, which gives them outside perspectives. Downtown Kodiak (rebuilt around its boat harbor after the 1964 earthquake/tidal wave) has more stores, lodgings, eateries, and processing plants than either Valdez or Cordova, and during normal times noisier bars.

The waters around Kodiak Island and adjoining Afognak Island remain clean three weeks after the spill, but currents bring the oil daily closer. Harassed state and Exxon officials release statements declaring that the oil will disperse before it reaches the islands while ignoring requests for boom materials that by now have become desperately scarce. In the crowded harbor crews begin to gear up for the season on herring, to be followed by halibut and salmon, while other boats have been fishing all winter for cod and pollock.

The Kodiak United Fishermen's Marketing Association headed by Jeff Stephan begins to organize some of these vessels in case the officials prove wrong. Volunteer crews, lacking commercial booms, begin to lash logs together as do fishermen in native villages like Ouzinkie and Karluk around the island. A headline in the April 12 issue of the *Kodiak Daily Mirror* states: "Oil slick appears to be breaking up; Kodiak safe." Three days later Debbie Nielsen, a small, brightly intense young woman who skippers her own seiner with a mixed crew of men and women ("If a guy asks me for a berth, I figure he's made up his mind to take orders from a woman") finds black oil lapping onto the beach by her cabin on northern Afognak. She radios the alarm. The next *Daily Mirror* headlines: "It's thick, it's gooey—it's definitely here!"

No communal hatcheries focus energies as in Cordova. Some have the impulse (and emotional need) to rush out and start cleaning beaches with anything at hand. However, Exxon, faced with liabilities of a scope it is just beginning to understand, blocks volunteers in favor of workers not yet hired. People stew helplessly. They hold a march to let off steam. Eventually Exxon agrees to pay and the hiring begins. Workers sign on for jobs they tried to start as volunteers. Suddenly they are not alone in readiness to help. The politics of choosing boats for the hired cleanup (not all can be chosen) grows so hot that Stephan resigns his emergency role. The hurly-burly has begun that will leave Kodiak the most damaged of the major towns affected by the spill.

As oil coats the beaches—most of it mousse, even more difficult to handle and impossible to burn—and as petroleum odors foul the air: "We went through a grieving process," Kodiak city manager Gordon Gould will later recall. Thorvold Olsen, my highliner skipper friend who has spent his life fishing the salmon, crab, and bottomfish around Kodiak Island, adds: "Pulling dead animals out of the oil, it kept you depressed." Thor leaves after three weeks working his boat *Viking Star* at high pay. Debbie Nielsen's beach faces the onflow of oil like the prow of a ship. Each new volley of the foul stuff hits her first. While clearing beach herself she raises enough noise that eventually overworked Exxon officials give her calls priority. At last helicopters bring cleanup crews at her demand. They work clockaround some days. "Like being in a war," she will later remember. After a month of the pressure she collapses and requires medical evacuation. A year later, with her turf more-or-less restored by cleanup and scouring by winter storms, Nielsen can declare quietly over a beer in Kodiak: "I still get depressed and angry whenever I think of all the dead things, the violation of my home."

Kodiak's problems increase week by week. A newspaper cartoon from the lower states illustrates Alaskans' fear, from bureaucrats to fishermen: The punch line declares that the blackened fish on a restaurant menu is not Cajun but dipped-in-crude Alaskan. In the early 1980s a similar disaster of perception—the discovery of botulism in three cans of Alaska salmon—plummeted the price of pink salmon to fishermen from forty-five cents a pound to seventeen cents. The price took three years to recover. To head off any similar hint of contamination the state closes every fishing ground where even a sheen appears on the water. The insidious oiled water creeps into each of the Kodiak bays where salmon have returned to spawn. Fish and Game cancels each salmon opening, one by one. Crews geared for the excitement of salmon runs deal instead with desolated beaches or they wander idle. Fights and domestic violence nearly triple over the summer. Public meetings become shouting matches.

Picking Up the Pieces

Exxon might have shown corporate responsibility in accepting blame, but by many accounts the Texas-based giant appears to have been clumsy with local concerns. "They tossed money at us to keep us quiet," declared Kodiak Mayor Bob Brodie, still bitter a year later. "But they only accomplished what we forced them to do." Brodie became president of the Oiled Mayors Association, formed when the heads of the twenty-six communities most affected by the oil spill decided while comparing notes that Exxon was dealing with each separately, using different standards. "Maybe what they didn't realize," said Jeff Bailey, a post-Vietnam Cordova fisherman with a degree, "was the number of college-educated fishermen they were dealing with—people who would challenge what they said and refuse to swallow corporate bullshit."

As the summer wore on, Cordova fishermen found that, unlike the salmon-closing disaster in Kodiak, oil had bypassed a few of their salmon grounds. On occasion Fish and Game allowed them to fish selectively. But they received only thirty-five cents a pound for fish that the year before had brought eighty-five cents. Not only did buyers take advantage of their being caught in "oiled" waters (they were not), but so many buyer vessels had hired out to clean oil that the shoreside processors felt no need to compete. The Japanese also capitalized on the notion of "tainted product." They immediately cut by more than half the price they paid fishermen for herring in Bristol Bay, an area not remotely touched by the oil, and used the spill as leverage for setting later salmon prices.

The spill affected the civilized order of things. With everyone gone to clean beaches for vastly more than the prevailing wage, including teenagers on their first summer jobs, communities felt a sudden dearth of service functions from beanery cook and potwasher to garbage collector. Some businesses closed altogether.

A year later, a bruised feeling remained in the way people talked, even as boats geared for a new salmon season that promised to be bountiful. I flew back to Smith Island near Cordova with an assessment team that went from beach to beach identifying places that still required cleaning. Any realist had to be impressed. Smooth, clean rock stretched for hundreds of feet in both directions, dark at the waterline, gray where it dried. An Exxon representative pointed out scattered patches where oil lingered. I would have missed them.

In Kodiak some fishermen turned wary, even sheepish. Those new boats in harbor with the latest in wheelhouse electronics, those others with new engines and new hydraulic systems? Many had been a dream before spill money made them possible. Skipper-owners hired by Exxon to clean oil often earned more than in their best fishing seasons, sometimes $4,000 a day. Now their boats and gear were in better shape to fish the dangerous Kodiak waters than their competitors who lost out on working for Exxon or had scorned doing it. Nor had shadows and resentments dispersed from the way some skippers maneuvered to keep their boats on the work list over others, and how some skippers and plant owners chose not to share with their crews the compensation money for lost fishing or processing. "It held up a mirror to us," says

Hank Pennington, the Sea Grant marine advisory agent in Kodiak. "A lot of people were not real happy with what they saw when they finally looked." Said a respected Kodiak fisherman, bashful of being named, "Exxon really unequaled things." In Kodiak, though, the salmon resumed their normal cycles.

The first Cordova fishery to be closed in the wake of the spill had been that for roe herring in Prince William Sound—the roe a major Japanese market. A year later, the state of the herring was considered a harbinger of the cleanup's effectiveness.

I joined Virgil Carroll's crew aboard his fifty-foot seiner *Miss Carroll:*

We anchor in Galena Bay, less than ten miles in back of Bligh Reef. Everything is keyed for action. Men shout. Boats seem to vibrate even at anchor. Spotter planes buzz overhead. Even the sun throbs on the snowy mountains around us. I recognize some of the same boats and men that moved together last year, tending boom around the hatchery water of Sawmill Bay. Herring have begun to pour into the bay by the millions, to judge by the dark fish masses that sometimes glint just under the clear surface. In spawning, the males will release clouds of milky sperm near shore, and then the females will rush in to deposit ten-thousand-egg sacs of roe on any available surface within the cloud. We must intercept the females before they drop their roe. The seagulls keep us posted. They screech all night long under the nervous flicker of northern lights while they fight for roe accumulating on the rocks. We itch to fish, feel it in our bones.

On April 12, 1990, Fish and Game judges that enough eggs have been fertilized to assure the next generation. It announces two-hour standby and then, at 10 A.M., says that it will declare the opening within five minutes on either side of 1 P.M. The time allowed for the roe catch has always been short, usually two hours, to protect spawners from being overfished. But the official's steady voice drops a bombshell. "The opening will last twenty minutes, repeat twenty minutes." Shouts of disbelief bounce across the water from boat to boat. The dictum means that all the boats, crowded and jostling in only a handful of small bays, have no more than twenty minutes to lay their seine in the water and close its circle. Scant chance to reset a net that comes in empty. Any seine not closed completely at the end of twenty minutes, moreover, will have to be opened to release all its fish. Easygoing Virgil starts chewing antacid pills like candy.

The bay begins to roar with the engines of boats and planes. "This is *Blue Angel*," our spotter pilot announces from overhead on our selected radio band, "Calling Gray Boat. Head down past Ellamar Bay." As we move I count sixty other boats in the space of a mile. By the time we reach Ellamar Bay only a half hour remains. Other boats crowd so closely we hear conversations on their decks, and Virgil must maneuver to keep from bumping other rails. We gather in the wheelhouse. At about countdown-minus-twenty minutes, everyone pulls on boots and raingear, then takes position in the skiff or on deck. The pilot gives readings to maneuver us close to a plug of fish he can see from the sky.

Over the main radio, Fish and Game declares: "The sac roe fishery is now open." *Slam* goes the spring lock, and the skiff moves off with one end of the seine. The net pays out astern. Other boats and their skiffs crowd ours in zigzags. From a control bucket on the mast Virgil mutters radio commands to his son Doug in the skiff as he maneuvers around competition while listening to his pilot. He must roundhaul, given so little time. Quickly Doug circles the skiff back with his end of the net.

"The sac roe fishery is now closed." Too late for a second chance.

As we begin the steps of pursing, the water in our circle of corks stays so placid it looks empty. Then, slowly, it begins to stir. Little eddies appear like the first action of water being heated in a pot. More and more eddies splash beads that sparkle in the sun. Suddenly near the boat a dark mass of fish swirls like streamers in the wind. Then the fish in the net start to surge everywhere, and the water begins to boil. Boil!

We've caught millions of herring, 212 tons of them it turns out, a column of fish about twenty feet across on the surface and eighteen feet straight to the bottom. Nearly another hundred tons escape over the corks as Doug in his skiff and the pilots, now landed and balancing on the plane's pontoons, try to hold up the far edges of the seine. By midnight, eleven hours after making the set, enough tenders have come alongside with suction hoses to take the last of our fish, and we eat dinner. (Nobody has thought to eat anything all evening except for candy bars on the run.) Overhead the northern lights flicker in great ribbons across the entire sky. We stretch and shout. The first fishery after the big spill has made it.

But, three years later, 1993, only a quarter of the expected herring returned to the Sound, and most of these carried VHS, a viral disease.

Fish and Game closed the fishery. By the following year the stressed herring stocks had also developed a fungus. Resident Fish and Game biologist Evelyn Brown, who had monitored the herring for years before the spill, surmised in 1995 that the trouble began when spilled oil attached to subsurface plankton that the herring ingested. "It may have been a combination of oil, low plankton, and high fish density, with VHS—a virus turned on by oil. Younger fish seem to be recovering." Only in the spring of 1997 did there appear to be enough healthy herring for Fish and Game to allow the return of a limited fishery. But the catch was very poor and has continued so.

The Great Spill affected the sockeye salmon migrations in an ironic reverse. So many fish had escaped to spawn, with no nets to cull them, that, for years later, overpopulation strained the food chain.

A disaster can sometimes yield information on situations impractical to simulate. The spill sites became great laboratories. No wildlife of such number and variety had ever been so affected in an area where they could be recovered quickly and studied, and biologists converged. Cleanup techniques brought in other experts ready to advance their experience and knowledge. Unfortunately the companies and agencies that commissioned scientific research, presumably to prevent future spills or handle them, held their data as close to the chest as poker hands. Lawsuit stakes were too high to share information that might be used to advantage. According to Cordova biologist Brown in 1998: "Although Exxon had full access to government-collected data by 1992, Exxon's reciprocal data sharing took several more years. Nor did the Exxon data ever come in a form readily comparable to government results. The whole litigation process impeded the publication of scientific results and data sharing on both sides."

In 1992 Exxon settled Alaska's claims with a $900 million grant to be used as the state saw fit to rebuild the damaged area. By early 2000, however, some court-ordered reimbursements to fishermen from a class-action suit remained unpaid as Exxon continued to contest a $5 billion punitive judgment.

In 1997 when I last visited some of the sites, all had returned to normal, at least visually. Oil, however, remained deep in some rocks and gravels. That same summer, eight years after the spill, a team of twenty workers loosened enough still-fresh crude on Latouche Island in Prince William Sound to contain it with booms in the water. After more than a month using "air knives" that injected air and solvent beneath the surface to bring up the oil, they reported that more remained. As for wildlife, in the restored areas I saw, eagles flew, and otters floated lazily, cracking clams that rested on their bellies. Darker information came in reports from the *EXXON Valdez* Oil Spill Trustee Council, created by the state independent of Exxon (but with Exxon penalty money) to oversee the claims funds. A 1992 report noted immediate damage to the reproductive abilities of salmon and other creatures that had been exposed to the oil, none of which would affect their edibility to humans. Of the Sawmill Bay hatchery where I had helped set boom: "Survival to adulthood of salmon fry released from the . . . hatchery, located in the middle of a heavily oiled area of the spill zone, was half that of Esther Hatchery located outside the spill area." A 1994 report noted that in the oiled areas pink salmon survival had begun to reach normal levels again, but concluded from further research: "It now appears there is an inheritable difference in egg mortality for fish from oiled versus unoiled streams."

The 1999 report listed both pink and sockeye salmon among the recovering. Also in the "Recovering" category were mussels, archaeological sites, common murres, and herring. Under "Not Recovering" were harbor seals, three species of cormorants, harlequin ducks, a specific pod of killer whales, and pigeon guillemots. The only species fully "Recovered" were bald eagles and river otters. Countered Exxon in a statement the same year: "The dispute over which species have recovered is largely a technical argument over the precise definition of recovery."

Although Exxon took the heat and paid the damages, the blame in retrospect lay also with three other organizations. Exxon should, of course, have paid closer attention to the shortcomings of personnel with strategic jobs, from a skipper with an alcohol problem to an unlicensed mate and a timid helmsman. But the Coast Guard was not keeping watch that night on a ship strayed from course, a monitoring duty the underfunded agency had been forced to cancel under budgetary constraints, but apparently had not reported adequately to mariners. Alaska's environmental agencies had maintained an inadequate overview of the Alyeska Pipeline Service Company. And Alyeska, the consortium of seven petroleum giants who shared the cost and profits of the famed pipeline and was committed to clean up any spill that occurred, did not have adequate spill equipment in working order.

The complacency is flabbergasting. As an example of Alaska's laxness, the legislature of the wealthy oil state had in just the previous year denied $252 *thousand* (not million) for activities that included terminal and tanker inspections, a review of Alyeska's oil spill contingency plan, and more aggressive enforcement. Oil revenues had serenaded Alaskans (still do), who pay no state income tax because oil money covers most of the state's budget. They in fact receive a check each year for their share of oil profits. The gift received a few months before the 1989 spill bestowed $826.93 on each adult and child. No wonder people were slow to challenge benevolent oil.

British Petroleum owned just over half (the controlling share) of Alyeska, Exxon and ARCO about twenty percent each. Mobil, Amerada Hess, Unocal, and Phillips held the remaining smaller shares. As part of its commitment, Alyeska guaranteed—with a reported $17 million earmarked for the purpose—to respond immediately to an oil spill of any size with the equipment and skilled personnel to contain and collect it. Some time in 1981, four years after the pipeline had opened and run safely, according to congressional testimony following the Bligh Reef grounding, Alyeska disbanded its twenty-man professional spill team and assigned the duties as secondary ones to other workers. Echoing the builders of the *Titanic,* Alyeska declared in writing that a large-scale disaster was impossible given the quality of its system.

Dennis Kelso, commissioner of the Alaska Department of Environmental Conservation, testified with a damning statement: "The industry's response during the first, critical seventy-two hours of the spill was ineffective, in part because of Alyeska Pipeline Service Company's decade-long efforts to scuttle any meaningful oil spill contingency plan." Thus, despite assurances all along, Alyeska possessed neither adequate equipment nor a battle plan to use it when the unthinkable happened.

The *EXXON Valdez* on Bligh Reef will retain a significant place in the history of oil spills because it generated more than momentary awareness and outrage. In August 1990 President George Bush signed the Oil Pollution Act requiring greater safety precautions in transporting oil within U.S. waters, legislation that had meandered for fifteen years through seven House committees and three Senate committees. Without public revulsion over pictures of the nation's wilderness smothered in black crude, congressmen would still be hearing the rationalizations of petroleum lobbyists. Domestic spills have indeed decreased.

Long before the bill passed, as I saw firsthand a year after the spill, Alyeska with new religion had begun to escort each tanker leaving Valdez. It continues to do so with both a seagoing tug and a state-of-the-art escort/response vessel carrying boom and skimmers. The consortium now allows members of a citizens advisory council to observe operations in the Valdez terminal whenever they wish (previously denied), and pledges to listen to what they have to say. It also hires some one hundred local fishing boats to train for several days a year as a standby spill disaster fleet.

"The time to get upset again," declares Ken Adams, a Cordova fisherman and a veteran of the oil wars, as he straightens hooks on miles of halibut longline aboard his boat *Martie,* "will be the day you read how expensive, redundant, overkilled, downright unnecessary all these new precautions are since nothing bad has happened recently. And then we'll be starting all over."

Ten Years Later, Anchorage, Alaska, 24 March 1999

As scientists, politicians, fishermen, and others gathered for a symposium to mark the tenth anniversary of the spill, Ken Adams, his hair now whiter but his weathered face more vigorous than a decade before, stood up at the end of a biologist's graph-heavy presentation to ask, "How are you focusing all this knowledge to help the injured fisheries of Prince William Sound?" The grave reply was a masterful non-answer. From a fisherman's viewpoint, effects of the runaway oil collapsed the herring fishery which has only feebly recovered, while the value of local pink salmon has declined so disastrously that Prince William Sound seine permits now bring roughly fifteen percent of their pre-spill value. How much of this is spill cause-and-effect and how much that of other forces can be debated on and on, as it apparently is. Certainly an increased world supply of farmed salmon has cut the price of some wild salmons.

In truth, nature can be affected by the consequence of a man's few seconds' bad judgment, but it cannot so easily be maneuvered back. Nor, as natural forces evolve, can everything continue to be blamed on the spill's disruption. Exxon declared in a position paper dated late 1999, "The environment of Prince William Sound is healthy, robust and thriving. That's evident to anyone who's been there, and it is also the conclusion of many scientists who have done extensive studies of the PWS ecosystem."

Biologists at the tenth anniversary symposium reached an unexpected consensus regarding oil that remained in the substrate of several oiled beaches, as stated in a NOAA brochure: "Oil is more persistent in the environment [of Prince William Sound] and up to 100 times more toxic to developing fish than previously thought."

Meanwhile, into the new millennium, Exxon, having settled state and federal claims, continues to fight a 1994 court class-action award of $5 billion in punitive damages and $287 million in compensatory damages. In truth, no civil punitive penalty of similar size has ever been granted. Of the compensatory claim, Exxon contends (and the court has agreed at least in part) that all but $19 million has been paid through other settlements, including its own voluntary program and payments made by the Alyeska Pipeline Company. But: "We won't be healed until Exxon settles completely," declared one fisherman at the symposium, to which social psychologist J. Steven Picou agreed from the lectern.

For another perspective, the extent to which Exxon did accept responsibility and make restitution could be compared to that concerning a smaller but disastrous spill of high-grade fuel oil in December 1999 off Brittany, France. Although losses are still being assessed, lobster and oyster fishermen along the coast report a total loss of their season's catch, while scientists fear that the stocks may suffer long-term damage. But, to quote *National Fisherman*: "As a result of the complex consortium of international interests involved in ownership of the tanker, local press in France say it is nearly impossible to find anyone to hold accountable."

This is often the history of blame and compensation following inevitable oil spills. The world sea harvest remains hostage to the overpopulated world's demand for affordable oil, which is routinely delivered so expediently and in such quantity that accidents happen.

CHAPTER SEVEN

Turbot Warriors

The Grand Banks

On no other fishing grounds of the world do the ghosts of drowned fishermen speak more ancient and current languages than on legendary Grand Bank off Newfoundland, Canada's easternmost province. Basques from Spain rode Atlantic currents here possibly before the Norsemen of A.D. 1000 briefly colonized part of Newfoundland, although the Basques stayed at sea and so left no trace. All this happened when men sailed on the North Star and a prayer, before invention of the compass, and centuries before Columbus "discovered" the New World.

After the English explorer John Cabot reported in 1497 that his men scooped up cod in baskets, fishermen from France, England, Portugal, and non-Basque Spain converged on the Bank. It was a raw, foggy place for men from the Mediterranean where the sun beat hot and bright, but the stocks of cod were immense and Catholic Europe bought fish. Salted and dried cod kept virtually forever, and could feed armies. The English and French colonized the coasts of Newfoundland, Nova Scotia, and Labrador to be closer to cod.

Fishermen from the American colonies began venturing to the Bank by the early seventeenth century. Captain John Smith wrote in 1614 (off Maine in the same geologic system): "He is a very bad fisher who cannot kill in one day with his hooke and line, one, two, or three hundred cod." By the nineteenth century the great-great-great-grandsons of these Americans from Gloucester and other New England ports spent May into autumn on the Bank so routinely that they called themselves "bankers." There came Icelanders, Greenlanders, Norwegians, and Faeroese, and, jumping centuries to the 1950s and the advent of far-seas trawler fleets, also Russians, Poles, Germans, Japanese, Bulgarians, Estonians, Latvians, Italians, Romanians, Cubans, and Koreans.

Grand Bank is a vast undersea plateau larger than Newfoundland island itself. Its depths range from seventeen to fifty fathoms. (A fathom is six feet.) It is the largest by far of a congeries of sea plateaus that follow the coast from Newfoundland and Nova Scotia in Canada to Maine and Massachusetts in the States. Only gullies separate Green and St. Pierre Banks from Grand, while a one-hundred-fathom curve encloses the three, and the mass combined is often called by the collective plural Grand Banks. Other major banks along the coastal curve include Banquereau, Sable, La Have, Browns, and Georges. The banks end in walls that plunge more than a mile to the Atlantic Ocean bottom. In a sea drained of water they would appear from below as high mesas, green as jungle from all the nutrients, their flat tops lost in the sky.

The Gulf Stream from the south and the Labrador Current from the north converge on Grand Bank's relative shallows. A resulting turbulence boils endless plankton to the surface, long enough for them to absorb the light they need to grow, thus generating steady feed for a tempest of sea life. The meeting of warm Gulf Stream and cold Labrador water also produces fogs and cruel weather.

Death waits impartially on all the banks. One mid-April I flew over Grand Bank with the U.S. Coast Guard and the Titanic Society to help perform an annual ritual on an anniversary of that "unsinkable" liner's 1912 fatal collision in fog with an iceberg. (This flight occurred in the late 1970s, when the Coast Guard still helped maintain an international ice patrol begun as a result of the *Titanic* disaster. Now satellites keep the watch.) The plane flew to the exact latitude and longitude of the sunken liner's grave, passing colonies of fishing boats with nets in the water, and then circled to find the nearest iceberg. The berg glistened, a white ship-killer of jags and blue crevasses. We strapped into halters to lean safely from the opened rear bay of the aircraft, practice-dropped a dye canister, then with prayers flung a wreath that slid down the berg's peak and settled.

Once on the Bank in a forty-foot sloop I sailed for three days in fog thick enough to hide the bow from the stern. We had no radar—no more than had any vessel here in the centuries before about 1950. Without a compass—as none had before the twelfth century—we would have circled without orientation. It was iceberg season, when calved chunks of glaciers from Baffin Bay had drifted the Labrador Current this far south. Our foghorn mooed, sometimes bouncing an echo that might be a wall of ice. An occasional horn mooed back from some craft that passed invisibly, but we felt alone. Half the four-person crew listened and peered constantly, standing continuous watches two-on two-off through dark and light in the chilly damp. Sound itself played tricks. Once we heard the bullish bellow of a major foghorn coming from starboard. Suddenly the terrible wall of a freighter swished by the port bow, leaving us to pitch in its wake.

If we were that vulnerable, what had it been like for men who rowed open dories, handhauling cod two miles from their mothership, when fog rolled in and sounds played games with direction? Two 1885 paintings by American artist Winslow Homer show dorymen in such fogs. *Lost on the Grand Banks* depicts two men who clutch the side of a dory that rides unstable, peering into a flat gray wall from horizon to sky as whitecapping seas roll underneath. *The Fog Warning* shows a fisherman in his dory, with fish and gear underfoot. Hands on oars, he regards a sinister streaking smudge of dense slate moving in the sky above his distant ship. It's easy to like the style and draftsmanship, but some of us can also feel the painting in our gut. The doryman may be doomed. In few places have hardship, fogs, storms, and accidents claimed so many.

From a New England newspaper's account in 1880 entitled "At the Mercy of the Seas":

> "John Whitlaw and Samuel Orgrove, two of the crew of the fishing schooner *Edward A. Horton* out of Gloucester, left that vessel on Grand Bank, Thursday, July 1, 1880, for the purpose of hauling their trawls. After loading their dory they found themselves unable to return to their vessel, on account of a heavy fog having shut in, and rowed aimlessly away in the hope of finding succor. After undergoing great exposure and hard-ships, on the following Tuesday they effected a landing upon the coast of Newfoundland, greatly reduced and almost in a dying condition from their enforced abstinence from food and drink. They were kindly treated."

More typically Whitlaw and Orgrove would have become a statistic, names on a cenotaph mourned by those back home, two strikes of a bell at an annual service for those lost that year at sea. An 1882 Gloucester publication entitled *The Fishermen's Own Book,* reports 2,249 fishermen and 419 boats lost at sea from that town alone in the fifty years previous.

The compilation for 1880 listed ten names under Capsized in Dories "all on the Bank fisheries," and then reported under Lost in Dories in the Fog: "Matthew McDonald and Joseph Merchant from schooner *David A. Story,* on the Banks, in February; John Higgins and David McDonald from schooner *Marion,* on Western Bank, March 28; Joseph Coffee and Charles E. Seebloom from schooner *Epes Tarr,* on Western Bank, April 18; William Geary and John Landry from schooner *Schuyler Colfax,* on the Banks, August 21." Let these few names be memorial to thousands.

Banks men first fished from their main vessel with baited lines over the rail. Eventually they developed dory fishing, with gear called "trawls," lines that we now generally call longlines. ("Trawl" now applies—except in some isolated communities—to the quite different gear of nets dragged through the water like an open bag.) In dory trawl-lining, according to an 1882 account, the men of a schooner baited hundreds of hooks all attached to tarred cotton lines that when connected stretched a mile and a half. The gear went into two-man dories that, when launched from the mothership, were rowed in different directions. The men anchored their lines on the seafloor in a collective pattern like wheel spokes radiating from the ship. After tying flagged buoys to the anchors, they left the lines to soak overnight and returned to the ship.

The 1882 account, apparently by a Banks fisherman, continued: "At daylight all hands are called out to breakfast, immediately after which the dories are hoisted out, and they row to the end of their trawls, being guided by the flags when it is clear; but when it is thick and foggy, which most frequently happens, finding the outer buoy is difficult and the dories frequently lose themselves."

After working the lines all day the dorymen, with any luck now knee-deep in cod, rowed back to the schooner and pitched the fish aboard. Then they lined up into the night, splitting and salting their catch. The thousands of hooks for the next day also needed to be baited. The account notes: "There is some rivalry between dories as to which shall bring in the most fish or get done first." Nothing has changed in the competition department. Fishermen—especially in traditional communities where everyone knows each other—still play out rivalries like kids at soccer. It adds purpose to the labor.

And labor! Hauling-in was done hand over hand: at forty fathoms deep that meant pulling up 240 feet of line weighted with multiple fish, some of which reached fifty pounds. Fishermen still set longlines, and in some communities still haul them by hand. I've helped pull a laden gillnet into a skiff, quickly hurting and exhausted (while my Labrador professionals kept a steady grunting pace). Salt water might lighten the fish-weights, but it still feels like leaning over a slippery cliff and pulling up big rocks with all your back, for hours.

The 1882 account concludes: "When the bait gets exhausted, or becomes too stale for the fish to relish it, we proceed to Newfoundland to procure another supply. On such occasions we sometimes have many leisure days, and to beguile time we arrange a dance on shore, which is kept up from dark till daylight." In the 1970s in St. John's, long after dory days on the Banks but still in the time of foreign fishermen, I looked in after midnight on a Portuguese shore-leave dance, attracted by the noise in a town otherwise asleep. It was no place to enter sober, nor to pick a scrap without being prepared to back it all the way.

The old Gloucester book is a mine of dangers passed. From a local newspaper:

"Washed Out of a Dory: On a breezy day in November 1880, the crew of the schooner *Grace L. Fears* started out to haul their trawls. Although it was rough, the waves frequently breaking and the wind blowing in gusty puffs, it was not considered especially dangerous since the tide, which ran quite strong to windward, would materially assist them in again reaching the vessel.

"In one of the dories were William T. Lee and Jack Devine. When these two had safely hauled the larger part of their trawl, and the boat, which had on board several halibut, lay hawsed up in such a manner that her side was exposed to the sea, a huge curling wave came tearing along, striking with full force that threw the men overboard and nearly filled the dory with water. Fortunately for Devine he went over near enough to grasp the gunwale of the dory and climb into her. The wave threw Lee a dozen feet from the boat. He was so much encumbered with heavy clothing and sea-boots that he could not prevent himself from sinking. In the meantime his dory mate fastened the trawl to the bow of the boat so as to keep her as nearly head to the sea as possible, and, frightened for his own safety made desperate attempts to bail out the nearly filled dory.

"As good fortune would have it, the slacking of the trawl allowed the dory to drop slowly to leeward, while the tide swept the struggling man to windward. As he sank for the second, and as he thought last time, his hand felt the trawl under water. He at once began to haul himself toward the dory, hand over hand along the line. One of the stout hooks caught his forefinger and passed completely through it. He reached the other hand as far up the trawl as he could and, with a desperate pull, tore the hook completely through and out of his finger. Then, just as Lee got his head above water, with his hand clutching the gunwale of the boat, a second hook caught in the leg of his trousers."

The article describes more effort before Lee pulled himself over the side of the boat "and fell senseless to the bottom." Despite shock and the mutilated finger, Lee recovered enough to finish hauling the trawl before returning to the ship.

The Portuguese "white fleet" still fished the Banks until 1952 from open dories that fanned out from a mothership. By then their dories had compasses aboard, and small motors, although men still capsized or vanished in fog. A 1950s account noted that these practical men did not spend the cold day on the ocean in rubber boots, but rather in leather boots with thick wooden soles that insulated better. They still pulled nets bare-handed. No method so romantic—to those contemplating it safe from high odors of old fish and unbathed sweat—harvests now from the Banks.

By the early 1950s, centuries of hands-on hooks and nets were swiftly superseded on major fishing grounds by huge nets aboard ships with enough crew to tow around the clock. Some form of dragging a net had been practiced on a small scale for centuries. Documented in Great Britain as early as 1640 under sail, trawling by steam power began in the late 1880s. Up through the mid-twentieth century British trawlers dominated Atlantic waters (and became effective minesweepers during both world wars). Factory trawlers—new creatures of the seas—were first designed by an Englishman, although Soviets and West Germans soon copied them in quantity. Their powerful engines and hydraulic haulers could handle nets larger and tougher than ever before, and they had an industrial-scale capacity to process and freeze. All this had only become possible using advanced technologies developed during World War II.

In the mid-1950s the first such factory giants appeared on the Grand Banks, and by the 1960s huge fleets from elsewhere camped off any coast with an abundance of seafood regardless of local rights, to fish and process around the clock. Back then, the resources of the sea still seemed infinite, since such strain had never been put on them before: common property available to anyone strong enough to take it. The main factory fishing nations gave no thought to stewardship. The Soviets in particular fished stocks to depletion, then moved on to others. The Spanish gained a reputation for targeting a species that schooled with a dozen others that they wasted. No nation fished conservatively, despite the warnings of marine biologists, especially on stocks located off other nations' coasts.

In North America, eastern coastal residents from Labrador to Nova Scotia to New Jersey, and on the West Coast from California to British Columbia to Alaska, could see the lights and illuminated skies of foreign factory fleets fishing around the clock just off their shores. Local fishermen's pots and gear were simply overrun at the foreigners' convenience. Soviet ships in particular had a reputation for bullying—and also quite accurately for outfitting trawlers to spy. Grand Banks had always been international. It now became a near-Soviet fiefdom, with vassal states from everywhere but Canada, off whose shores the Banks lay.

At the height of the foreign presence I boarded fishing ships of the Soviet Union, Japan, Spain, South Korea, and other nations off the U.S. coasts, courtesy of the U.S. Coast Guard. By treaty they received us reluctantly but cordially, hoping to hurry the inspection (although the Coast Guard and National Marine Fisheries Service—NMFS— officers took their time). But for the high flapping Jacob's ladders that waited on deck to carry us down to our ship's skiff in choppy water, we might have in politeness drunk their toasts "to friendship" rather than their tea. The ships ranged from smelly third world rustbuckets to scrubbed floating hotels. All had a level of efficiency, from huge bags of fish dragged up the stern ramp and dumped impersonally like grain through a hatch into holding bins, to rows of set-faced people below decks cutting, dressing, and freezing the product. It was a quite different kind of fishing from that I had known in Alaska, working on a deck at eye level with the sea.

Only a stopgap U.S. law protecting "creatures of the continental shelf" like lobster permitted an arrest for illegal species found aboard. One NMFS inspector circa 1975 judged the ships of a Soviet fleet we boarded to be fishing triple the entire negotiated mackerel quota for the Soviet presence that included two other fleets. He duly reported. Typically the report moved up through NMFS channels to the parent Commerce Department—which lacked authority to act—and passed on to the State Department, where at best it figured in a mild low-level diplomatic rebuke.

I rode my first fishing trip on Grand Bank in 1979, two years after Canada and the United States had declared 200-mile control, when their own vessels on grounds off their coasts had begun to take some of the catch the foreigners once thought they owned. The fishing life I had observed aboard large foreign trawlers remained much the same on this Canadian vessel, except that the crew left home for a week or two rather than months.

September, 1979

It's all business on the Canadian 152-foot trawler *Zamora* as it prepares to leave Catalina, Newfoundland's most northerly winter port. The crew walks aboard with their gear shortly before departure, then batten for sea as we head out. Squall spray soon hazes the low buildings of Catalina. We pass a lighthouse on the rocky coast, push into water with whitecaps, and settle into a steady roll.

In the wheelhouse Captain Pat Antle sets his course, then braces himself in a raised swivel chair and starts a series of sideband calls to sister ships on the grounds. With radio distortion their thick Newfie brogues—an amalgam of ancestries from Ireland, Cornwall, and Devon—are such foreign tongues to my American ears that I lose both the exchanges of information and the easy jokes. The ocean is giving us a knockabout night. Below on the messdeck Bill the cook, a lean bald man with a usual grin, serves up a chow of salt meat, potatoes, and boiled greens—the sort of meal with which to meet seasickness head on, win or lose. The men shovel in their food glumly.

The ship carries thirteen crew, about the size of that on the old Yankee dory schooners. A deck watch consists of five or six, with the schedules staggered so that each man works eight hours on, four off. The officers—captain, mate, chief engineer, and second engineer—follow a six-on six-off pattern. Only the captain stays immune from turning-to in the factory. The men come from the outports and have been raised to the fishing life. Some broke away for a time. Cities like Toronto seemed the place to go. Bill worked in construction there, Sean as a welder, Jack as a laborer. But forces drew them back—seagoing tradition, communities where their fathers and grandfathers are buried, rocky barrens less confining than the rude and congested cities.

On the grounds next morning the wheelhouse siren sounds for the first set. The men of the watch "rubber up" in their foul weather clothing and go business-like into slanting rain on the rolling open deck. The cod end of the net eases down the stern ramp along with its protective multicolored chafing gear. "Hole, b'y," calls someone. The boatswain and the mate pounce on a tear in the thick web, their needles working furiously. Soon chains and metal balls scrape down the steel deck along with the last of the net. The floats that raised the net while the balls weighted it stay briefly on the choppy surface like a V of orange beads, then submerge. The men shackle the mouth of the net to "doors," heavy flats that, underwater, hold open the net's mouth as the boat pulls them.

With all gear in the water the deck clears except for the two warps (the cables holding the net) unrolling from drums. On the bridge I note from the echo sounder that we're trawling a 60-fathom bottom. Captain Pat says that for this depth he lays 275 fathoms of cable in the water—three times the depth, plus fifty fathoms extra for shoal and some more for heavy weather.

Nothing remains to be done for the three to four hours of the tow. The watch settles around a messtable to read, doze, or play cards. Monotony is a truth of fishing, whether killing time or repeating the same tasks. Trawler duty requires spurts of effort rather than the steady push of, say, purse seining, handlining, or pot hauling.

At length the siren gives its rasping whirr, and the watch (now other individuals) dresses for deck. The bag emerges up the stern ramp with flounder heads poking from the green mesh like guns in an arsenal. An OK haul, says Pat: about four thousand pounds. The men empty the bag directly below through a slide, shoot the trawl again at once, then go below to dress the catch.

Gutting fish on the run is messy, whether it be little flounder or big cod. (Give me the latter, for the satisfaction of a good handful.) Flounder intestines nestle in a small "poke" that can be cleared with a flick of the knife. Massive cod intestines need to be swept from the slit belly with a strong hand. A fish every few seconds, on and on through thousands. We stand on a wood platform, stooping over the bins. Wash water sloshes around our calves, sometimes higher by a foot when the ship rolls. From my notebook:

"Soon covered with guts—oilskins, face, down the neck . . ."

A conveyor takes the dressed fish to the holds to be laid between layers of shoveled ice. (Within a few years, stacked plastic boxes will replace layering. Fish compressed for a few days in bottom layers do not meet a growing customer demand for better quality.) By the time we finish and wash down, an hour has passed. There is less time now to be bored before the next haul-in.

The hauls increase as the weather calms. The biggest—fifteen thousand pounds—arrives in the middle of the second day. All hands from both watches turn-to, except the captain holding the bridge, with those of the off-watch losing their sleep time. I stand next to Pardy, the mate. We joke and talk a bit over the engine noise.

My notes record:

"Endless! Each time I gut through a pile, another is kicked into place from the mountain of fish stuffed down the trapdoor. Water sloshes into boots and through rubber bands around rainpants. Hands cramp after first hour, hard to grasp fish by heads, while taking care the quick sharp knife doesn't lop a finger. Monotonous beyond any back buster that never seemed to stop on Alaskan boats for salmon, shrimp, or king crab."

Toward the end, Bill the cook leaves the line to start chow. It's time for fancy stuff—thick pork chops. We hose ourselves and stuff on the run, with the siren already sounding for the next set coming aboard. So it goes for days.

A ship's steel walls and engines with backup do not guarantee all protection. One night we have just shot the net. In the wheelhouse the radio crackles with voices. Suddenly the captain jumps from his raised watch chair and hurries to find locations on the chart. A fire has started in the engine room of a sister ship, *Zelia*. He sounds the siren and shouts to the watch, who appear on deck to haul in the net. Fire is akin to sinking for a seafarer, because it leaves no place to go. Everyone turns alert and tense. The *Zelia* men are *Zamora* men's neighbors, some with familial ties. By the time the end of the net reaches the ramp we're nosing into seas at high speed. The men lash the deck gear for a rough run, then gather on the bridge to listen to the radio. The bow pitches and dark seas slam against the windows. A half hour later the *Zelia's* captain announces that they have contained the fire. The men joke off their relief and disappear below. We retrace our course, and resume the fishing routine.

Since this fishing experience on Grand Bank the wheels have rotated a cycle or two. In 1979, Canadians and Americans had, only two years before, gained control of fishing grounds within 200 miles of their coasts. The stocks remained shaky from foreign overfishing—we targeted flounder rather than the traditional cod because cod was still depleted. But expectations for great harvests soared. Both the Canadian and U.S. governments had passed measures that would encourage fishermen to update their fleets, with the goal of developing domestic fisheries to tap the great protein harvests the foreigners had usurped.

Unfortunately, development became its own monster. It led to government-assisted overcapitalization to build modern fleets quickly, and subsequent pressure from the overcommitted (who needed to make a living while paying off the easy loans) to harvest beyond prudent biological limits. Canadian fishery policy is dictated directly from Ottawa, U.S. policy indirectly through regional councils that advise the Commerce Department. Both Ottawa and the New England Council bowed to fishermen desperate for full holds to pay new debts even as stocks decreased from heavy fishing by too many boats. In fairness, the Maritimes and New England are areas of tradition, where grandfathers had fished the same grounds, and fishermen felt deeply entitled to all they could catch. But in practice the excesses of the "greedy foreigners" simply passed to flags of the neighborhood.

So successful were narrow interests in the short term that within some dozen years staples like cod and flounder virtually disappeared along the entire eastern North Atlantic coast through overfishing. By 1993 alarmed Canadian regulators had closed virtually everything off Newfoundland, including Grand Bank. Two years later Americans followed suit off New England. Some overcapitalized fishermen lost everything.

Canada's closure of its banks might have appeared to give cod and flounder stocks all the breather possible. Grand Bank, however, extends into international waters beyond Canadian jurisdiction. It protrudes in a fifty-mile knob at the south called the Tail and a twenty-mile nub to the east called the Nose, as well as in a separate eastern mount called Flemish Cap. Predictably, displaced foreign ships with nowhere else to go descended there to fish for all the payloads they could bring aboard. These non-Canadian grounds, however, are part of the Grand Banks ecosystem that Canada needs to manage if it expects its own stocks to recover, since fish spawn and migrate within the whole system. Guilty of allowing overfishing themselves, the Canadians now manage the Banks as best they can, by fiat in home waters, through negotiation and international pressure beyond national boundaries.

For years Canada's negotiating conduit has been the North Atlantic Fisheries Organization (NAFO), formed in 1978 by nations with fishing interests in the area. Historically the organization has been ineffective, since members who disagree with decisions can file a protest and continue fishing as they please. The European Union exercises stronger control of its members—Spain's fishing behavior has been a problem—but these do not include all of NAFO. Norway and Iceland have declined to join the EU. Others of NAFO but not of EU include Canada, the United States, Cuba, Russia and former Soviet bloc countries, Japan, and South Korea.

By the early 1990s cod and flounder had become so depleted that even the nations fishing the Tail and Nose of Grand Bank agreed to leave them alone. Only turbot, or Greenland halibut, survived in any commercial quantity, because it schooled in canyons five hundred and more fathoms deep and thus escaped conventional fifty-fathom drags. The Spanish found the species worth coming the distance to catch, and developed the technique for catching them at that depth. Their large fishing fleet from Galicia province had idled boats and unemployed crews after losing grounds off southwest Africa, when Namibia declared independence in 1990 and established its own fisheries. Some Portuguese came also. NAFO imposed no regulation. Turbot was one of the few remaining species of the world available for the taking—as virtually all had been just a mere two decades before.

By 1992 some thirty to forty Iberian trawlers, mostly Spanish but a few Portuguese, converged annually off the Banks to fish the turbot. Canada suspected them of using the new fishery as an excuse to catch more than the relatively large turbots—catching fish that the Canadians had sacrificed some 50,000 jobs of its own people to preserve—but they found it difficult to prove.

Recalls Wilson Kettle, a longtime Canadian fisheries enforcement officer, during rides on Canadian patrol ships acting for NAFO: "We'd come in sight of a Spanish ship and all of a sudden there's his net started aboard, water shooting like spray off the warps they'd come in so fast. We'd follow procedure, radio we desired to board for an inspection, and no answer. Then after the net was on deck a good while: oh, all at once their radio worked. Gave them time to remove any sock [fine-mesh liner] and hide it, you see. Probably in some crewman's quarters where we'd never find it. Then we'd say 'Why didn't you answer us?' and they'd say 'Oh, we were so busy with the net,' or 'Too dangerous for you to come alongside and us hauling gear.'"

Spain was catching an estimated annual 40,000 tons of turbot. In late 1994 Canada persuaded NAFO to set a 27,000-ton quota. Early the following year it maneuvered a NAFO vote that assigned 18,000 tons of this to Canada and only 2,000 tons to EU, to be allocated among Spain and any other member nation that applied. Under

NAFO rules members can object to a decision and refuse to abide by it. EU objected and set its own higher quota. EU's Iberian members proceeded to fish the high quota, ignoring the NAFO decision.

In fairness, Spain had pioneered the turbot fishery, and its fishermen felt cheated. The turbot ruling came as one more indignity in a line that started with the 1976 penstroke that pushed them from 200-mile grounds they had fished—and felt that they owned—for the generations of four centuries. No other fishing nation seems to have adapted so poorly to new realities, even Portugal, which could claim an equal history on Grand Bank.

Meanwhile, Canada fretted, certain that Spanish boats continued to take more than turbot. Ottawa decided to force a showdown. In early 1995 it amended an existing domestic law to prohibit Spanish and Portuguese ships from fishing turbot in NAFO waters. Could one nation make its own international law? If the outcome had been different the objections might have been stronger. In the Canadian fisheries enforcement community, leaves were canceled. Canadian fisheries officer Aubrey Anderson remembers the tense preparations for action as the patrol ships—whose crews routinely practiced armed boarding drills—cruised the turbot grounds.

The Spanish persisted in fishing, and Spain sent a patrol ship of its own to protect them. Ottawa gave the word. As Canadian patrols hovered close, a workship with equipment on deck to cut thick steel cables moved in on the fishing vessel *Pesca Maro Uno* towing its net through the water. Said one gruff radio voice to another in Spanish that a Canadian interpreted: "They don't have the balls *(cujones)* to cut our warps." The Canadians did. The net they recovered did indeed contain a small-mesh liner, illegal by NAFO rules, designed to capture immature fish protected by the entire international community.

Two days later the Canadians encountered the 256-foot *Estai* fishing in defiance of the new law. Anderson was in the armed boarding party lowered from the patrol ship *Cape Roger* to board her. The *Estai* cut its tow and steamed off, calling by radio for help from the rest of the Spanish fleet. She refused to lower a ladder for the boarding skiffs racing alongside, and tossed off a ladder thrown up by the Canadians. Sometimes in such a case, Anderson said, you could just jump aboard if they wouldn't lower a ladder. "If weather conditions are right, get the right roll on the boat, you can go right over the rail, got no problem. But not when the boat's running away from you at eight or ten knots." The patrol ship *Cowley* joined the chase until another Spanish trawler cut across its bow to slow it. At length the *Cape Roger* fired tracer shots across the *Estai*'s bow and the fishing ship hove to.

Anderson among the five sidearmed fishery enforcement officers climbed aboard along with five trained crew to make the arrest. Following a drill they had practiced exhaustively, the senior officers proceeded directly to the bridge to confront the captain, clear out all others, and check for weapons (even for sharp instruments like calipers). Some members of the party stayed to guard the boarding ladder, while others guarded the way between the two groups. During the impounded *Estai*'s trip to port the arresting party stayed on the bridge. The patrol ships in escort sent over sleeping bags and all their food.

In St. John's, ten thousand cheering Newfoundlanders crowded the capital city's quays. Their government had finally taken action. (A few years before this, angry unemployed Newfoundland fishermen whose own grounds had been closed took their boats out to confront the foreign ships still fishing, but Ottawa had not supported them. Prime ministers had changed since then, from Brian Mulroney to Jean Chretien.) The *Estai* might have been arrested by chance rather than another, but it turned out to be the prize. Not only was it the queen of the Spanish trawler fleet—the newest and best-outfitted—but its recovered net contained an illegal liner, eighty-one percent of the turbot in its hold was undersized by NAFO rules, and a secret hold hidden by nets stacked on a wooden trestle contained twenty-five tons of illegal catch. The Canadians had proved their point.

Popular opinion supported Canada. Outrage followed in predictable places. In Vigo, Spain's major fishing port, they burned Canadian effigies, while at the United Nations the European Union's fishery commissioner Emma Bonino denounced Canada's "piracy." The Canadian showdown appeared to be timed, since fishery officials from some one hundred nations were convened at UN headquarters for a session of the Conference on Straddling Stocks to draft a code for international far-seas fishing. The startled international community pressured the involved nations to settle their differences. Within the month the parties had signed the Canada-European Union Conservation Agreement. Under its terms Canada relinquished a portion of its turbot quota to the EU and received in return a commitment to effective enforcement measures in the NAFO area. Foremost among these was a pilot program for one hundred percent observer coverage, advocated by Canada for years but resisted strongly by a few nations, including Spain and Iceland. NAFO adopted the same measures later that year.

After the Canada-Spain showdown the Spanish reduced their presence for the rest of the year. The twenty-seven vessels of late June 1994 became fourteen during the same period in 1995, just after the *Estai* arrest. The European Union, overriding Spain, agreed to place observers on all vessels beginning in 1996. The Spanish fleet in June 1996 numbered seven, a reflection both of the reduced quotas, and the reality of now being able to take only legal-size fish.

In May 1996, fourteen months after the fracas now known as the Turbot War, things had settled enough that Ottawa consented to let me ride a fisheries patrol in the international portions of Grand Bank. Before I reported aboard the ship I called on the enforcement people at Fisheries and Oceans in St. John's (nerve center for Banks activities), and flew a Fisheries patrol surveillance flight over the area.

The Iberian turbot fleet, now much diminished from its unregulated days, was not the only fishing presence. On and around Flemish Cap, a roughly circular knob of continental shelf detached from the eastern Grand Bank shelf, finger-size *Pandalis borealis* shrimp had in the recent past multiplied in such abundance—probably due to the shortage of predator finfish—that since 1993 they have drawn fleets of high-seas trawlers for a new international fishery.

The patrol flight covered that day a limited southern portion of the shrimping fleet on Flemish Cap. We overflew twenty-nine trawlers (pilot Ed Simms banking low like a dive-bomber for swift identifying passes), and made radar contact with twenty-five others. Below us red-hulled Icelanders, white-hulled Canadians and Norwegians, rusty Estonians and Russians, and others, pitched in water that looked barely rougher than glass from above except for whitecaps. All were trawling shrimp within agreed areas.

Later air patrols during the time I rode the patrol ship at sea reported an Icelander and then a Greenlander fishing in prohibited zones. With the accuracy now available from the Global Positioning System (GPS) the plane's recorded observation provided sufficient evidence to issue the offenders a citation next time they were boarded. At the Fisheries office Wayne Evans, regional supervisor for offshore enforcement, confided: "Some ships out there, not the majority, still play the margins, still play the tolerances to the limit."

The old doryman's humble man-to-fish method kept him inefficiently close to the killer sea, but however passionately he competed he never took more cod than the sea could regenerate.

No more.

CHAPTER EIGHT

Myre Remembered

Norwegians

Flemish Cap, May 1996

The 235-foot Canadian patrol vessel *Leonard J. Cowley* is a comfortable ship, maintained close to spotless, as easy a rider as possible in thrashing Grand Bank waters. This makes life no less wet in the rubber-sided boarding skiff after the ship's davits have thumped us into the ocean. We're wearing water-repellent float suits, but the spray that cascades over the blunt bow still hits like a gunful of ice. Frigid water smacks in at my neck and trickles through thermal underwear even though I turn to take it from the rear. The coxswain, ship's chief mate Joe Squires, stands faced into it, as do the two enforcement officers from Fisheries and Oceans, Wilson Kettle and Aubrey Anderson.

We head for a Norwegian trawler working the shrimp on Flemish Cap. From skiff level its long black hull disappears beneath rolls of water that had seemed mere swells from ship level. I was too busy suiting up to pay attention to the Norwegian's name. As we pitch past the trawler's stern with its mouthlike open ramp, I glance through water dripping from my cap to note the name on the high steel side. *Myrefisk Two*. Nine years before, I had traveled the Barents Sea cod grounds north of Norway aboard *Myrefisk Two*.

The first order of business is to negotiate the Jacob's ladder, a dangling twenty feet of wooden treads joined by thick rope. Joe Squires brings our skiff expertly to the ladder, but the surge against the hull raises and plunges us a dozen feet. One moment the treads clack at eye level, next we look up from a trough with the ladder's bottom out of reach. I haven't jumped to one of these for years. The trick is to leap and commit at the instant the ladder faces you, then climb like hell as the boat swoops into the trough so that it doesn't slam your legs on the upsurge. It's all in the timing. When I first did this as a young Coast Guard boarding officer forty-five years ago, the skiff's gunwales were wood and a leg could truly be crushed. Now, rubber sides threaten mainly a bruising. But you still need the reflexes.

Aubrey, a limber Newfoundlander in his twenties, politely offers me first leap, and I just as politely gesture him first. If the damn thing breaks, let him enjoy the swim. Aubrey does it as easily as crossing the street. I watch his figure in its bulky orange float suit ascend hand over hand and disappear up over the rail.

"Take your time, Billy b'y," says Wilson firmly. I've known Wilse Kettle, a sunny man in his late fifties, for nearly twenty years, since first we met on the Newfoundland sealing ice. Wilson apparently plans to stay in the swooping skiff to pull me from the water if something goes wrong. I leap and scramble. At one point the ship rolls toward us, leaving the ladder suspended in air. I clutch the rope sides until the counter-roll bumps me against the slippery steel hull and then go vigorously. Why, safe on deck, should I be panting from just a half-minute's climb? Wilson follows with the ease of a lizard on a wall.

"You have not so changed," says a calm voice.

The same curly hair and serious, friendly manner, the broad face marginally older. "Tor-Eirik." I grin, we shake hands, and I venture "Hvordan gar det?" from Norwegian I haven't tried to speak for nearly a decade. We last shook hands on a dark November morning in 1987, in wintering seas so far north that the pale sun gave only two hours of light, when I transferred in a wet skiff from this very deck of *Myrefisk Two* to the newer *Myrefisk One* captained by Tor-Eirik Bye's brother Oddmund. So many faces have passed before each of us since then that I'm amazed he remembers me. "Even the same hat," he notes. It's true: the same brown wool cap has covered my head on fishing boats since the first salmon seiner in Alaska and the king crabbing. Fishermen are entitled to their luck tokens.

Officer Wilson Kettle introduces himself with business-like cordiality and shows his and Officer Aubrey Anderson's credentials as Northwest Atlantic Fisheries Organization (NAFO) inspectors, authorized to carry out boardings according to NAFO procedures. We walk to the wheelhouse, past taut steel cables towing a net on the seafloor, and up stairs through scrubbed corridors. The fishing log lies ready. More than a year has passed since the turbot war and subsequent agreements, and inspections are now routine.

In the warm orderly wheelhouse the two fishery officers remove their stiff float suits. Officer Anderson sets to work over the chart table to copy the past month's catches by species and volume. The mate on watch offers cups of strong coffee. Tor-Eirik, the captain, stripped to a sweatshirt worded SKILLED EARTHLY TRACKERS that hugs his solid frame (exercise bike in a corner), alternates between glances at his log being invaded by a stranger, catch-ups with me, and informal answers to Officer Kettle about his ship's fishing. A haul will come aboard within the hour, so we can see for ourselves.

I ask about friends remembered back in Myre. The town in northern Norway, several degrees above the Arctic Circle, is home to the Bye brothers and the ships they captain. Tor-Eirik updates me. Asbjorn Wolden, the trawler's former deck boss, "has worked now on a shrimp vessel in Labrador for two year." Kaare Hagerup, a respected local fishing industry pioneer who during the German Occupation of World War II had routinely tricked the enemy out of fish quotas to feed his countrymen, "is not so active any more." Oddmund is busy on a new vessel jointly owned with Tor-Eirik and another brother.

Our talk brings back the harsh, lovely coast of northern Norway with its islands, low, often misted mountains, and coves where chimneys and masts rise behind sheltering boulders. The area, except for the major city of Tromsø, is a congeries of remote towns and villages tucked into coves close to the fish. Buildings are relatively new. The Germans burned all they could when they retreated in 1945 from the detested five-year occupation. The Norwegian government rebuilt—adding new roads to connect island hamlets—when it realized a strategic purpose in keeping the coast inhabited given its Soviet neighbor's cold war ambition.

Myre is the center of the north region called the Vesterålen that leads into some of Europe's richest fishing grounds in the Barents and Norwegian Seas. The town has emerged in importance with its trawler fleet and a major fish plant built to process the fleet's catches. Villages among the islands, once deeply poor and reached only by boat, are now connected by a network of roads and bridges that give traditional daytrip gillnet and longline fishermen access to the Myre plant. Myre has grown since 1954 from a population of 350 to more than 3,000, with attendant prosperity. Stores flanking its paved main street include two florist shops. Other paved roads lead to compact modern houses below the surrounding mountains. In late October when I visited, warm amber lights illuminated the snow beneath windows framed by lace curtains. With abundant local power the lights glowed in a show of affluence throughout the long winter darkness.

In March 1980 I traveled from Tromsø to the outermost coast some thirty miles away. Bleak was the word for the day and the landscape, yet the snow-gray mountains and the fjords they lined had a solemn beauty. This was fishermen's country all the way to the ocean. Each occasional lonely but new-looking house had a fishing boat tied to an adjacent pier. On the way we called at a new concrete seafood plant with a half-dozen employees, built and run briskly as a co-op by eight fishermen. In an inlet farther on we met a bearded young man who operated a plant that consisted of a single shrimp-peeling machine. He was buying from a placid, pipe-smoking, unshaven fisherman in torn oilskins aboard a small wooden cabin boat. The man had steamed his own shrimp in a pot on deck, thus realizing a fifty percent higher price than he would have made by delivering live. The seawater in the pot looked sludgy enough to have been glue, but the shrimp came out a clean, glistening pink and their fresh taste put frozen packet shrimp to shame.

We reached the rocky coast's end at Sommerøy, and the raw sea winds let us know it. Slick ice coated hilly paths through the snow where people walked huddled between their neat houses, the general store, and the piers of two small fish plants. By 3 P.M. the slow, cold twilight had darkened everything, and lights began to blink in windows.

Just beyond the breakwater crashing waves broke into spray as a boat pitched toward shelter. Ice glazed its gillnets on deck. Crewmen unloaded cod and redfish into a shelter away from the wind, then lined along gutting bins to clean them. Orange and yellow oilskins glowed under a bare bulb. In the unheated shed, the damp air smelled heavily of fish, particularly intestines. The chill seemed to make little difference to men who had worked on a winter sea all day. They joked as the words smoked from their mouths in the frosty air.

I felt at home here. These were like crewmates in Alaska and New England from Norwegian backgrounds, seeming never happier than when the air was cold and the water rough as long as it yielded fish. Hard times at home in past generations had sent hundreds of Norwegian fishermen to the States, to settle and ship out especially from Fairhaven/New Bedford on the East Coast and from Ballard/Seattle out West. "Squareheads," they were called, probably for doggedness. Some, like first-generation Leiv, my Bering Sea crab skipper, born in Karmøy, had grown heartier than any fisherman I met in Norway. Most stayed quietly to the job without complaint, whatever the hardship.

At another pierside shed, men from a longliner had already cleaned and delivered. Their work continued as they straightened hooks, replaced frayed sections of line, and baited for the following day. The convivial time at the bins had passed—the time sparked by slapdash mess and the abundance it implied—and now everyone bent to the dreary business of kinks and twists. Before anyone had finished, a blue twilight outside had turned to dark, and a cutting wind tore along the packed ice of the village's main road. The lighted houses waited like warm oases. This was a different fishing life than that aboard trawlers like the *Myrefisk One* and *Two* that stayed at sea for more than a month at a time.

Before the big-trawler fishing culture, coastal Norwegians worked the land and water as both fishermen and farmers in season. They took to their boats in late winter when great schools of cod migrated down from the far north to spawn, passing within a few miles of land. While braving brutal conditions on the water the men did not sail far to sea. By late spring the fish had run their course, and the men turned to their fields to plant and harvest during the long daylight of northern summer.

The *skrei* (spawning cod) follow a course south past Myre and the Vesterålen to the next series of glacier-cut islands, the Lofotens. At the southern tip of the Lofotens (still far above the Arctic Circle) the skrei U-turn into a wide cul-de-sac of water facing the mainland. Lofoten fishing is a hardship saga in itself, the stuff of legends. Men have sailed that forty miles from mainland to Lofoten, across raw February seas in open wooden boats, since Viking times a thousand years ago. Artifacts prove it. Norway's small-boat fishermen still go to Lofoten to meet the migrating skrei, but they do it now with engines. Often they bring wives (or girlfriends) and set up housekeeping in dormlike *rorbus* for the season. The water remains rough, the transient life rustic.

The social change began after World War II. Seeing the advances of its Russian neighbor in Central Europe, Norway in 1949 decided that neutrality had become unrealistic and joined the North Atlantic Treaty Organization. The NATO alliance gave the nation a new source of income through Allied military expenditures. Then in the late 1960s came the discovery of oil in the North Sea. Commercial drilling began in 1971 and suddenly there was wealth, which the socialist monarchy found ways to distribute so the entire nation felt the benefit. Men in a village economy could take "cheap" government loans to mechanize their boats and farms and to deliver themselves from oxenlike labor. But to meet their payments, the new equipment had to earn its keep all year. Few could afford to maintain in partial idleness both a hydraulic net hauler and a combine/thresher. It forced most to choose between fishing and farming.

Most younger fishermen now stay with the boats full time, since the modernized fleets can follow the cod and other fish a hundred and more miles away from shore and catch them the year around. Such is the case with the trawlermen from Myre. Their fishing life is greatly different from that of their fathers and grandfathers, in less time spent at home but greater prosperity.

When, in November 1987, I rode Tôr-Eirik's *Myrefisk Two* and his brother Oddmund's ship, each crew spent a month or more at sea defined by six-hour watches on and off, day after day. Despite a living area as comfortable as a bucking workship could provide—individual cabins and baths—there was plenty of boredom. The total videotape repertoire consisted of a few American movies with Norwegian subtitles which, for lack of greater occupation, received repeat screenings that chattered even at three in the morning.

The men's banter flowed with yawning predictability. You called home and nobody answered? Ahh, what must your wife be off doing, with you not there? General chuckles, with no evidence of real concern from men who had all grown up together and continued to live in the same communities. The day's posting of catch volume, and the fish prices back home, drew the closest attention. This represented crew share money, the reason for being there. "My dad, a carpenter," observed one crewman, "he's glad when he makes half as much as I do."

I soon was pitching in. Most of the work proved anything but exciting. After a bag of fish came aboard (which could indeed sometimes be a sight to pump the blood) a boom raised the net, showing a slimy underside from flaps of chafing gear, and the bag spilled its contents through the hatch to the factory holding tank below. The "fabrik," located directly under the fishing deck, stretched as a wide-open area the length of the ship. It was a chilly, clean place of stainless steel troughs and conveyor belts that smelled of scrubbed metal and, faintly, of fish. As the men entered they pressed buttons to start the machinery, and to the clanks of belts and choppers got to it.

Things were more mechanized than on the smaller Canadian Grand Banks trawler I had ridden in 1979, a decade before, although hands still gripped fish. At the pull of a lever, the fish poured onto a belt— a slippery mass, cod and occasional other species as well as grainy black seafloor rocks—and moved to the cutting machines. The machines still relied on human input. The operator placed the cod head-up and belly-out in clamps affixed to a rotating drum, fitting them by the gill fin against the top of the clamp. He needed unflagging dexterity to feed the machine fast enough to fill each space as he slapped fish after fish in place by the hundreds.

The drum carried the fish around to unseen knives. With a steady screech of blade against bone that kept the operator wearing sound-proof earmuffs, the knives headed the fish, slit open their bellies, and scooped out most of the intestines. (If the operator, his hands working by rote with perhaps his mind on a sunny Canary Islands' beach as he sang to himself, snagged a sleeve on the inexorable machine, he could push a safety panel to cut off power at once.)

The work of converting living creatures to food is always messy. Pink and gray offal dripped from the drums and splattered everywhere. An organic odor pervaded the area. As I fed one of the machines, a fleck of intestine flew into my mouth. It was startlingly bitter, and the taste remained for more than an hour.

Another series of belts took the carcasses to tanks of clean water where computer-timed jets washed them a minimum of seventeen minutes. Then they moved the length of the room to a chute that dropped them into a hold the next deck below. The hold was another world altogether, reached through a gear locker by climbing over stacks of clattering metal trays. A frosty place, it contained a mountain of crushed ice. To enter it we threw down shovels and slid after. As the fish carcasses flopped from the chute we arranged them in trays along with shoveled ice. We stacked the trays like bricks, which the ice cemented, row after row all the way to the ceiling. The cementing was fortunate. Once, the ship took a violent roll that sent loose trays crashing around us. The empty steel trays were heavy enough, but what if the ice lock had broken on the full trays that towered above us twice our height, each weighing nearly a hundred pounds?

Once on Oddmund's ship I listened to him argue seriously for over an hour—plenty of time to kill—with two juniors who had complained of a trawlerman's hard life after hauling a set on the cold deck and icing it below. They sat in a carpeted lounge on padded chairs weighted to grip the deck, as the ship rolled steadily through conventional rough weather. Oddmund, erect and confident, set them straight in good humor. As he told me later, "Many times we are talking about this. The young men speak of how hard a life. They don't know history, that for fishermen hard life is normal. How tough it is to shovel the ice, they say. In early day, ice came in blocks and had to be chopped first. Nowadays a machine at the plant chops it for them. Many little things like this, on and on. It's OK."

Two of six brothers and six sisters, Oddmund and Tor-Eirik come from a fishing tradition. Their father began at age twelve aboard his own father's boat, and all the Bye brothers have remained fishermen as have most of their sons. Oddmund started from Myre at age fourteen aboard his father's longline boat, following traditional routes from Lofoten to Finnmark. In the process: "My father learn me the right feeling for fish."

Aboard the parental longliner in 1949 conditions were normal for a medium-size inshore boat. "We were a crew of seven or eight, all fished at the same time. One six-day trip we had seven hours' sleep altogether. No special cook; crew must cook for self. Everybody in bunks together, wash hands and face from a basin." Indeed conditions on inshore boats have changed only partially in the interim, given a limit to the comforts that can be crowded into a small space, and lack of manpower to divide work into shifts.

Big trawlers have altered the fishing life for those who choose it. Bye left his father's boat to work awhile aboard larger boats, trawlers, that fished farther from shore. After that, he stated frankly: "I couldn't like small fishing boats anymore." Aboard those first trawlers they slept a mere two to four in a cabin and had an entire two bathrooms to share. He has been a trawlerman ever since.

In Myre one night I talked with some fishermen who had not converted from the inshore life. Smoke drifted around the tables in a large second-floor room of the Fishermen's Hall. Low-key men in the rough clothing of the boats chatted, read, killed time, before going home for the night. Outside, shops were dark. The deserted sidewalks had slush on top and ice underneath. The only other public life appeared to be at the other end of the main street in the Grand Hotel Myre, where the first beat had begun thumping through the one-story building from a rock group in the basement called "Pinocchio."

Those around one table at the Fishermen's Hall (gathered for my benefit by a friend who also helped with my shaky Norwegian for those who didn't speak English) included Ottar Heimly, who skippered a net boat; young Geir Roeman, who fished aboard his father's net boat; Harold Antonsen, who crewed aboard a longline boat; and Tormond Kroknes, a fisherman for fifty years who now taught fishery methods at a local school. Together they represented a cross section of Myre's inshore fishing scene—crewmen and skippers, youth, age with its long perspective, different fishing gear. There was an easy interaction. The teacher Mr. Kroknes, for example, now several comfortable pounds heavier than most working fishermen, had been a crewman for Ottar's father during ten of his fifty years on the boats.

Geir, a rosy, muscular man in his late twenties wearing jeans and a denim jacket, volunteered at once—as if afraid the point might be missed—that he considered the local small boat fleet to be dying. Young men sought jobs in the offshore trawler fleet, he said, while hardly any inshore fishermen were younger than forty-five. Look at his fifty-year-old father, for whom he fished, and the three other crewmen beside himself, older yet. An old men's boat. He said it cheerfully, without unkindness, but he was plainly restless.

Wasn't that right? Geir asked Ottar Heimly, the gillnet skipper. Ottar, a man with hair still black and the contained manner of a businessman or a carpenter, conceded that he himself had turned forty-five, an approximate age shared by three of his crew. Of the others, one was sixty-seven, and only one could be called still young.

Young guys knew a better life on trawlers when they saw it, said Geir, wistfully. Maybe they worked long hours, but they spent much of this time sitting around between hauls. "They don't wish to work so hard as we do." Trawler life each day was nothing like taking the sea in your face on a small open deck. When you left the deck you went to clean quarters, and ate good meals prepared by a cook. And, if the fish disappeared as they had now off Myre for the gillnetters like himself, the union made fishing companies promise a guaranteed income. Nothing like that on a small inshore boat.

Inshore fishing was still a better, more independent life, said Ottar the gillnet skipper, and Harold Antonsen the longline man agreed. As for trawlers, Ottar added, Myre probably needed the ones she had to keep the fish plant busy at all times of the year but: "Most of us coast fishermen, we are afraid of trawlers." Added Antonsen: "Before they came the cod were bigger." Young Geir was silent, apparently torn by conflicting opinions. His father wanted him to stay on the family boat, and so far had prevailed.

Inshore men needed no further problems, but seals now poured into coastal waters. Thin, hungry seals, from too big a population. As they chewed fish voraciously they drove the cod offshore into strong currents that made it harder to set nets and lines. Last winter local gillnets had come up with some fifty thousand seals tangled in them. Such nets caught no fish, were usually damaged and often destroyed, and took hours to untangle. "In fifty years I have fished," said Tormond Kroknes, the fisheries teacher, "there was never seals into the nets. But now the Greenpeace people have stopped us hunting seals, and they come too many of them, hungry." The seal harvest had been part of a fisherman's living, and had also kept the population in check.

A woman in the kitchen of the Fishermen's Hall served us coffee and cold pancakes with a creamy filling. It marked the end of the meeting. "Guess you'll have your own boat one of these days soon," I said to Geir, making conversation. He shrugged, mildly. "I think not until my father dies."

A few minutes later back at the hotel I saw Geir sitting with friends, engulfed in the blare of Pinocchio. He leaned back, smiling, at ease, his jacket stretched under the bulge of thick chest muscles. Whatever compromise he had made, between following the others of his generation to the easier trawler money and staying with the inshore tradition that he judged to be moribund, he remained a fisherman in a society that respected his work.

Back aboard *Myrefisk Two* off the Grand Banks, Canadian officers Kettle and Anderson, acting as NAFO inspectors, have copied the logbook record of catches. It remains to inspect the hold to ascertain that the catch has been reported correctly. We proceed down through corridors to a factory space, then through a hatch and down a frosty ladder. The hairs on my nose freeze in the suddenly claustrophobic −38° Celsius cold. The officers have examined the ship's specs to determine the number and location of compartments. They stretch a tape to check the hold's dimensions, and count rows and tiers of bags to estimate the total number in storage. Back in the wheelhouse they extrapolate logbook figures to compare declared and actual catch. All appears in order. During another Norwegian boarding this year, Kettle had calculated a discrepancy between containers and capacity. He returned to the freezer to be shown, under bags of shrimp, a large protrusion from machinery on the other side.

Enough time has passed that the tow is ready to come back aboard. "Haul up five minutes," announces skipper Bye over the PA system. In the changing room the men on watch step into boots and thermal flotation coveralls, slip on inflatable life vests, and fit hard hats over their caps. Within the allotted five minutes they have appeared on deck. Bye has already activated the two forward drums to start reeling in the net.

A trawling net and its attendant tackle have a basic design whatever the size. Small and large trawlers alike carry a net that culminates in a conical bag to trap the catch, held open by flat vanes called doors or otter boards. On a little Gulf of Mexico shrimp boat the doors might be wooden and easy to handle, but aboard trawlers like *Myrefisk Two* the doors are steel monsters that, flying wild, could crush the entire gang on deck. While baited lines and gillnets stay passive in the water and rely on the initiative of the fish, the trawling process requires a net kept in forward motion to corral the fish. When the boat pulls the net through the water, this forward motion planes the doors outward so that, attached at either wing, they keep the bag an open-mouthed trap.

A headline attached to the upper mouth of the net carries hollow plastic floats the size of a basketball, of a bright color like orange so they can be seen far out on the water. A footrope attached to the lower mouth carries heavy bobbins, gray steel balls with the diameter of an arm. In the water the combined upward pull of floats and downward pull of bobbins keeps the net vertically taut like a wall.

Myrefisk Two's warps continue in and the doors, still dragging the seafloor a third of a mile away, will have begun to move toward each other as they close the mouth of the net. When the doors surface they rise heavily, one to each side of the ship. They make a thundering bang as the men maneuver them flat against the hull and chain them secure while the sea smacks water in their faces. Water makes every surface glisten under the deck lights. The warps continue in, and the big bobbins scrape up across the steel deck. Off in the water the net surfaces. Its orange floats dip and reappear among the whitecaps. The bag containing the catch—the "cod end"—wallows beneath the floats, a sausage mass of green web. Seabirds attack the bag and dive in its wake to snatch broken scraps of shrimp.

Since the net cannot be wound around a drum like the cables, it must be brought aboard a length at a time. A crewman wraps a line around the web of the net, now compressed like a tube by coming up the ramp, and attaches the line to a cable that winches a section of net up the length of the deck. He repeats the strapping process to pull aboard another length, and so until the bag itself comes entirely on board.

A sturdy grill like that for an outsized barbecue bulges at a forty-five-degree angle within the narrow tube. By NAFO agreement all shrimpers on Flemish Cap must use these bar separator grates (termed "Nordmore grates") to filter out species larger than the shrimp. And indeed, when the bag itself comes aboard, it contains virtually no by-catch.

A full trawlerbag of sea life snaking up a ramp never loses its eerie fascination. Imagine the fattest gourd, multiply by a thousand, and picture it pulsing with live creatures that strain against its outer walls. Sinister in its mass, the bag is also (except to the fish inside) joyously abundant.

The green mesh of this bag encloses bright pink shrimp. A crewman climbs over the bulging meshes and grabs a rope dangling from the tight rounded bottom. With a grunt he yanks hard. A shackle clacks, releasing the drawrope that holds shut the bottom of the bag. The bag opens. Shrimps gush out like molasses, pouring layer onto layer around the man's legs before he jumps away. Beneath the regurgence a hydraulically powered steel hatch opens, controlled from the bridge. A boom raises the net, and the bag spills its contents through the hatch to the holding tank in the factory below. The men shovel down stray piles of shrimp as they might shovel grain. The big hatch closes. Trawler *Myrefisk Two* has harvested.

With the haul safely stowed, Wilson Kettle and Aubrey Anderson step into the empty net on deck. Kettle inserts a flat triangular scale into the web. He measures out twenty consecutive meshes, which Anderson records. He then measures several openings in the Nordmore grate. The widths are all within agreed limits, 40mm (1.56 inches) for web, 22mm (0.85 inch) for the grate.

The net is ready to be set again. At Tor-Eirik's signal the crew pushes the cod end of the net down the ramp, and the friction of the water as the boat reaches an approximate four knots' towing speed drags out the remainder with its floats. The floats drift astern in a bright-colored V. The steel doors are attached. The whole apparatus sinks from view, to unfold deep in the water as a moving trap for the next school of shrimp in its path.

During our hour and a half aboard *Myrefisk Two* the wind has mounted steadily. It shows in the breadth of the whitecaps kicking beyond the rail. Wilson radios the *Cowley,* dimmed by a sudden curtain of hard rain. The skiff starts toward us, bouncing higher and cutting deeper into troughs than before. Tor-Eirik sees us off in our watertight float suits without bothering to wear a raincoat. I send greetings to friends back in Norway, while noting sinister waves that slam the lowered Jacob's ladder against the hull. Jumping onto that ladder safely was a trick. Worse is jumping off. The skiff swoops up and down, and you have to leap aboard decisively on the upsurge or risk tumbling far.

Wilson climbs down first. In a moment he's standing upright in the skiff, urging me to take my time. It's important to commit all the way. A laggard foot stuck on a rung when the rest of you has jumped can be a leg-breaker. I wait my chance on the dangling ladder, leap, make it. For pride's sake I force myself to stay upright for a moment to wave to Tor-Eirik (Wilson may be helping) before the skiff's slippery bounce lands me in a heap. Aubrey scampers down and off we go. Tor-Eirik and I continue to wave to each other until the rain curtain blends him into the graying shape of his ship.

Prince William Sound, April 1989: Acting independently before Exxon officially started funding the spill cleanup, Cordova fishermen lay heavy booms to halt oil flow into their cooperatively owned salmon hatchery at Sawmill Bay. An air compressor inflates the boom.

Prince William Sound, April 1990: One year after the *EXXON Valdez* disgorged oil a half-dozen miles away, the seiner *Miss Carroll* purses 212 tons of herring from a single twenty-minute set. The abundance was short-lived, though—later herring generations became susceptible to disease caused in part by oil-related stress. Stopped in 1993, the fishery by 2000 had still seen only partial recovery.

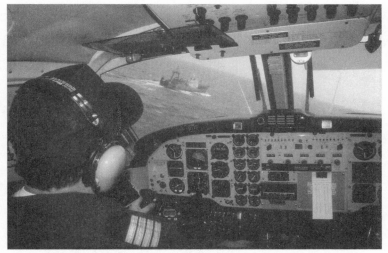

Grand Banks International Zone, 1996: An Estonian trawler is sighted and logged during a routine Canadian fishery air patrol. Violations are enforced by patrol ship.

Stamsund, Lofoten Islands, Norway, 1980: After a day's fishing that started at about 3 A.M., fishermen visit while awaiting their turns to deliver cod at the gutting bays. The convergence of small boats from the mainland for the late winter run of spawning cod is a tradition dating back to the Vikings.

CHAPTER NINE

Russians and Spaniards

Flemish Cap, 1996

May

The Canadian patrol ship *Cowley* has a wide, modern wheelhouse from which to ponder sunsets and fog. Or, this afternoon, to brace against a rail and watch the bow rise, pivot, then smash into the water to wallow, roll, right itself, and swoop high again. Twin ten-foot geysers shoot up as the bow cleaves a wave. Beads from the geysers pause suspended, gleaming like fireworks in the late sun, and the next instant splatter against the windows, obliterating the view. It's a good time for yarns, since west and then northwest winds up to forty-five knots, with swells over thirty feet and whitecapped seas, have kept us from boarding inspection.

Mate Joe Squires has the watch, assisted by seamen Dominick Sutton and Don Williams. Both fishery officers, Wilson Kettle and Aubrey Anderson, are checking the chart against positions of the fishing fleet reported from yesterday's air patrol over the area. And a professional fisheries observer, John Martin, paces the deck between rolls as he kills time until we reach the Norwegian trawler he is assigned to ride. All aboard are Newfoundlanders, though from areas with different brogues, sometimes talking so rapidly that an outsider loses the words. Subjects range from boats, engines, and weather, to wives and girl-friends (bachelor Aubrey), to additions on houses (these men do their own construction), and though it is only May, to hunting in the fall.

Radios sputter with laconic transmissions. A trawler pitches into sight. First its bow shoots up as the stern disappears under a swell, and then the bow plunges and the stern rises high. "Bit rusty, looks like," Wilson notes through binoculars. "Probably our Russian." We close enough to confirm that it is the Russian we've been seeking and Wilson calls on the radio. No answer. He switches to a different channel. "*Yunaya Smena, Yunaya Smena,* this is the *Leonard J. Cowley.* Do you read me?" He tries a third channel. A heavy voice acknowledges in furry English. Wilson's voice is crisp, cheerful, business-like. "*Yes* sir, we're Canadian NAFO inspectors on board *Leonard J. Cowley.* We'd like to come aboard your vessel if the weather clears, tomorrow morning."

"Yes. Tomorrow. OK."

"Could we speak to your observer, please?"

"Observer. Yes. You wait."

The observer is Vikki Hammond, who had previously radioed a request that the *Cowley,* when on the grounds, send over some "painkiller." Wilson talks lightly but guardedly, concerned that she might be having a problem. She assures him things are fine. It's just that the cook had an abscessed tooth, and she gave up her reserve aspirin to help relieve him. The *Yunaya Smena* had been scheduled to fish for only a month, but now had extended its stay for another month, leaving her in short supply. Might there also be some vitamin C, newspapers, and dental floss? "Oh, and a couple rolls of nice toilet paper?"

"I'm thinkin'," continues Wilson, talking Newfoundlander to Newfoundlander. "What about if now, if tomorrow morning the weather's permittable, maybe you'd like to come over for some good Canadian cooking while we do our boarding?"

"Sounds like a day from heaven."

The sun has sunk low enough that the waves cast shadows, and orange light colors the spray. The wheelhouse talk rambles again. Mate Joe Squires, a large and deliberate man of thirty-seven, has just earned his master's papers. He lets others do the talking although, when asked, admits he wonders when if ever he'll get a command. Canada will soon combine Fisheries and Oceans at sea with the RCMP—Royal Canadian Mounted Police—and with the latter more heavily funded they are likely to take precedence. Dominick and Don, young men with families and plans, join in wondering what will happen to the informality of Fisheries under the possible shipboard dominance of military-minded policemen.

"Yu'll wear yer bright uniforms every day, foine and dandy," quips Aubrey with his Burgio spin. Nobody on the bridge wears anything like a uniform, although indeed the officers dress up when going to board a foreign ship.

"There was this fella," starts Wilson, and pauses to chuckle. At dinner the radio in the wardroom had picked up a station in St. John's with a popular local comedian. In thickest dialect the man told of attaching a car engine to a snowmobile, and his wild ride over the snow under immense power. In a run of mishaps he hits a rock that rams his buddy in the crotch, on and on for twenty minutes, finally ending underwater with the buddy trying to restart the engine with a whip-cord. Wilson and Aubrey had been so doubled with laughter they'd stopped eating, and as Wilson retells it he needs to stop now and then.

Wilson, fifty-nine, is perpetually sunny when relaxed, reassuring but firm when inspecting foreign ships, so solid in the shoulders that one would not mess with him. He has the profile of a Roman emperor, softened by sandy hair and an easy lilt. This is one of his final trips before retirement, after a career with Fisheries and Oceans spent on the water (except for annual leave, always during fall hunting season). I first met Wilson in 1979, when he served as fishery officer aboard a sealing ship that took me aboard. He taught me to move on the ice without "gettin' a wettin'," to "copy" from pan to pan as he had done since boyhood. His movement over flats of dipping ice had been free and gleeful. Back in Wilson's hometown, Port aux Basques on Newfoundland's west coast, his boat and house are self-built, complete with the welds, plumbing, and wiring. Retirement? Not to idleness but to work on a bigger house, enjoy more time with his wife, Viola, "do things" for his sons. The Kettles are long-lived. Grandfather Kettle died at 103.

A mellow outlook has not affected Wilson's commitment to the laws he is hired to enforce. Just a month previous with a different partner, he was forced to arrest a Canadian scalloper caught fishing without a proper license within the country's 200-mile waters. (Skippers with licenses reported the offender. In 1996 scallops and lobsters were the only two fisheries the Canadians allowed on their part of the Grand Banks.) The man's boat and catch were confiscated. The situation saddened Kettle. He remembered the skipper, who in prosperous cod days ten years ago had owned a "fine big boat" but had been reduced to hard times when the cod fishery collapsed. The eighteen-man crew accepted the arrest philosophically. One man had been aboard three other boats caught by Kettle fishing illegally in the past five years.

Aubrey Anderson, thirty, is equally authoritative on the job, and tenacious, but so merry with staccato comment that he seems born for comedy alone. He keeps trim, eats little meat, and uses no gravy "except on me French froies." Most of his siblings from isolated Burgio on the south coast remain there to work in the local fish plant. He owns some houses, is building one himself, thinks of selling mail-order jewelry on the side, and generally crackles with plans and anecdotes. Like Wilson Kettle, he brightens a room or a wheelhouse merely by entering.

To pass time I tell of past visits to Russian trawlers, in Soviet Union days when I rode with the U.S. Coast Guard in U.S. waters on both Georges Bank off Massachusetts and the Bering Sea off Alaska, before 200-mile jurisdictions began in 1977. Those were bigger ships than the ones today, heavily manned, at a time when there was plenty of product to grab and the state could distribute manpower without regard to profit. The Soviets had always been cordial despite the dour, important political officer in coat and tie who watched while the captain showed his papers. The crews had included women. All that I saw were hefty but cheerful "Katrinkas," and despite the Soviet claim to equality between the sexes they all worked in front of a sink or behind a mop.

Hospitality at a table was part of the ceremony. The captain always offered tea mixed with strawberry jam, then vodka even if we protested. How could toasts to U.S.–Soviet friendship be refused altogether? I had grown adept at pretense since the Jacob's ladder waited, drinking to universal fraternity with locked lips and a hand covering the glass to mask its level, then slipping the vodka unobtrusively into the mug where I'd saved enough tea to give color. My account earns a laugh in the Cowley wheelhouse.

Although back then the United States had no arresting authority in its fishing waters unless we found lobsters or other "creatures of the continental shelf" aboard, ships let us aboard: The time of control was ominously close and foreign nations had become cooperative negotiators. Now, again, boardings are accepted without question in these different waters under the NAFO agreement of 1995. "They play along now, the Russians," confirms Wilson. "So do even the Spaniards, mostly."

"Yeah, b'y. Mostly."

"A while back," continues Wilson, "they did what they wanted. It stuck in my craw, how I'd see violations and could do nothing."

The Spaniards. Is it fair to single one nation from all the others? In Asia the Thais have similar repute for encroachments beyond a usual fishermen's competitiveness. Recorded deeds are the proof. As noted before, Spanish fishermen seem to feel an entitlement on grounds they have worked for centuries, but little stewardship for the stocks on them.

With Wilson and Aubrey, as with other Canadian enforcement officers who have spent time in the field, the mention of Spain opens the
anecdotes. Spanish far-seas fishermen have the reputation both for
agreeable hospitality and for ingenious cheating.

Aubrey starts off. It was 1994, in the fall before the turbot war,
aboard the Spanish boat *Dorneda* on Sackville Spur just off Grand
Bank—"a mozy ol' day, foggy and wet," he calls it. He'd gone aboard
7 A.M. with fishery officer Judy Dwyer for a brief routine boarding, and
ended up staying forty-one hours. First they inspected the hold, a
process limited along with logbook work to three hours unless waiting
for the net to come in. "I asked captain when he'd take back the net,
he said in six hours. So we stayed." Six hours later, with no movement
on deck, the captain when asked said another six hours. "A normal
tow aboard a single stern trawler is six to eight hours, no more. I knew,
after the first six hours, there was something in that trawl he didn't want
us to see. So we stayed." Hours later, with still no activity: "Asked
captain again. Finally he said OK, we'll take back the trawl."

The Spaniards brought the net in as far as the otter boards. "Once
they got the trawl doors back, everything stopped. Captain said the
winch is broke. Very convenient. And the engineer—at least he's
dressed like the engineer—comes to the bridge with a little motor not
much bigger than you could hold in two hands no problem a'tall—
and showed me it was burned out. So it was. But I don't believe at all
that it came from the winch. Too small. So anyway, skipper said the
winch was broke beyond repair and he had to wait for another part to
come from another Spanish vessel."

Anderson called his supervisor at the Fisheries office in St. John's,
who consulted Ottawa and returned with: "It's your call if you think
you've got something." They settled in the wheelhouse. "No sleeping
bags or anything, because we weren't planning to stay. I didn't go to
sleep at all, I sat up in a chair all night. Judy had a little nap. Food sent
over. By next morning twenty-four hours had passed. The boat with the
part didn't show. Didn't come and didn't come. So about noon dinner
time I said: 'Captain, the boat is not comin'.' He said 'Oh I don't know.'
Anyway, he still wasn't goin' to give in."

About two in the afternoon the captain seemed to yield. They started
taking back the net very slowly with a pulley rigged to one of the
smaller winches. "I suppose he wanted to try to save face. Didn't want
to all of a sudden fix the winch. So anyway we stayed and waited, six
o'clock in the evening. He said: 'The crew must rest, must eat.' So the

crew went below for supper. After an hour and a half, the crew must have eaten by now, 7:30, I said 'Captain, when will the crew come back to take back the trawl?' He said: 'Oh no, not until mañana.' So I said foine and dandy, and I got on the radio and called over to the *Cowley*, said we'll need sleeping bags, going to stay a little while." This was the second night.

About eight the *Cowley*'s smallboat delivered the sleeping bags. "The skipper looked, said what are you doing? I said we're going camping. We'll stay for two weeks if we got to. So I rolled into my sleeping bag in the middle of the bridge at eight-thirty in the evening. Said it's toime for a nap, you know? When I did that he put his arms up, called the crew back up and started taking back the trawl again. And about four hours later around midnight the whole net came about."

The fish inside, largely undersized, were rotten and stank from long immersion. "Sure enough, the net carried a liner net of around 68 millimeters, and legal size is 130. Just a little more than half what it should have been." Following NAFO procedure the inspectors removed the liner and locked it to a rail, out of the way with a numbered NAFO seal, for action by agreement when the ship returned to its home port in Vigo.

"Big penalty that got 'em, likely."

"Well," said Wilson, "One boat I reported onto since the turbot war, Spanish, it came back with a different skipper. Maybe some of the boys in Vigo are trying."

"If you'd had observers aboard back then," notes John Martin, the professional observer headed to a Norwegian ship, "you'd not have seen that happen." Since then, as a result of NAFO agreements made after the turbot war, a trained fishery observer rides aboard each vessel fishing the international Grand Banks.

Carry a spy aboard each fishing ship, paid by the ship? Fishing boat inspections have been part of the scene since at least the postwar surge of high-tech fishing, either through fiat in home waters or negotiation beyond national boundaries. Observers are a newer concept, but one established by Canada since 1978 aboard some of its own vessels fishing Grand Banks, and since the early 1980s on foreign ships within its 200-mile waters. American groundfish trawlers in Alaska now all carry observers following accusations of wasteful overfishing. So do the tuna vessels of all nations working the eastern Pacific, accused of setting on dolphins. Fishery observing has become an occupation, handled through organizations that train candidates and broker their hiring (thus making them not beholden to the ships they ride that pay their bill).

The job has been cast to include data collection, which modifies the spying stigma. Data from the eastern Pacific tuna fleet has led to changed net procedures credited with reducing the dolphin kill from 133,000 in 1986 to 2,500 in 1996. (The latter figure represents 0.04 percent of the estimated 10 million dolphin population, realistically acceptable to any but the oversentimental.) Although observers represent supercargo as far as the boat's work is concerned, they put in long hours. Those in the fleets off Grand Banks are expected to monitor at least eighty percent of all hauls around the clock and to record the mesh size, species, and fish size among other data. They receive $183 Canadian a day—about $134 U.S.—plus food and lodging, no fortune, but sometimes more than made by the men around them on deck. (U.S. observers in Alaska make less, victims to competition among hiring agencies.)

Observing is a lonely job, dependent on the individual's own grace and resources, since he or she must avoid any compromising friendships. Most observers off Alaska are marine biology students and such, passing through. Some in Canada, like John Martin and Vikki Hammond, have made it a career and display a sense of profession. According to Martin, an observer since the earliest days in 1978, his job represents "a vanguard of conservation practices necessary to protect the world's marine resources." A Newfoundlander aged forty with three sons, he spends intermittent times at sea that have varied annually between three hundred days and fewer than fifty. At slack times he works other jobs ashore, but by law not as a fisherman, which would be a conflict of interest.

"Don't count on it," says Aubrey, "that observers always know what they're seeing." Just last month, half a year after everyone committed to observers and strict NAFO-negotiated quotas, he and a different partner became suspicious from spot checks in the hold of the Spanish trawler *Rio de Pontevedra*. The two officers knuckled down to inspect 540 boxes, moving the heavy containers themselves since "you don't get the crew to help if there's a problem." They found that unregulated witch flounder had been reported as eighteen percent of the catch when it was actually about three percent—most of the boxes labeled "witch" contained the more valuable turbot. In addition, high-ticket plaice, reported at two percent, was nearer twenty-three percent of the catch. The inspection lasted fifteen hours, from 7 A.M. to 10 P.M. The observer was new to the job, trained in England. "They put it over on him, seems."

What about the Portuguese? I ask. Fellow-Iberians with a long Grand Banks history, they also fish turbot on Sackville Spur. Not many infractions, Wilson and Aubrey agree. Neither recalls ever finding a sock, a liner, on a Portuguese. "But they're kind of smart," adds Aubrey. "Knows when you're comin', plays cat and mouse. Three boats fishing together, soon as they see us on radar—they're good at picking up a vessel not fishing—they take up gear and go off in different directions. You chase one, lose the others."

Next morning the weather has cleared enough to suit up and ride over to the *Yunaya Smena*. We approach the high hull. Rusty? Scabs of it. A framed square yard of this multibrowned metal could win a prize in abstract art. Our smallboat leaps at the ship's side in the surge against the hull. The crew has put over a Jacob's ladder, but placed it in the opening for a shoreside gangway too far down to grab an easy handhold of rope between rungs. We need to clutch a slippery rung and then at once the slick metal of the open rail. After making this one I'm a salt on the ladders.

A glum young seaman in grimy wool cap and stained coveralls acknowledges us and points toward rusty stairs. Kettle and Anderson know the way by heart since all the Russian trawlers of this generation have been built to the same design at fifty-four meters (177 feet). We pick our way to the wheelhouse through narrow passageways smelling of fish and machinery. The captain, a large man with shaved head, greets us cautiously. The mate, a younger man with carved cheekbones and a brown beard, shakes hands also.

The captain watches with gruff, anxious reserve as Officer Anderson copies the past month's log. The mate ignores the procedure. Officer Kettle, who alternates logbook duty with Anderson on other boats, chats in sign language to ask about their catches. The mate expresses little enthusiasm for their fishing luck or for anything else. There is a general air of poor upkeep. In one corner, tape barely holds together the stuffing of the captain's chair.

Trawlers at sea for long periods, given the repetitive work, do not necessarily have effusive crews, as I learned years ago experiencing boredom aboard trawlers out of Norway and Alaska. This ship seemed especially down, however. In Soviet days when I had boarded Soviet factory trawlers in the Bering Sea and on Georges Bank, even under the dampening eyes of a commissar in suit and tie, there were jokes, yapping mascots, offers to barter fish for girlie magazines, even small cameras aimed with a shout and wave. The status of Russian high-seas fishermen has changed. In the old days they expected to earn about three times the back-home wage. Now, according to reports, they earn very little. Observers on Russian ships confirm that depression is deep, and drinking heavy. On one that I visited someone showed me a locked room stacked to the ceiling with cases of vodka and jugs of shipboard brew. He noted that sometimes the crew staggered on deck and worked the heavy, dangerous gear at snail's pace, and that one of the mates stayed senseless drunk for days at a time. "Russian crewmen are treated like serfs," according to a Russian trade union representative quoted May 1997 in *Fishing News International*. "Trips can last two hundred days, violating a 165-day limit set in Soviet times. Nor by Russian law is a 12-hour day limit now included in contracts."

Later aboard the *Cowley*, Vikki Hammond, the observer, who has served aboard several Russian ships, noted that the Russians' depression deepens further when they deliver ashore at Argentia or Harbour Grace, the two designated Newfoundland trans-shipment ports. The men see a living standard among ordinary people (and Newfoundlanders live modestly) far higher than that their families can expect back home. "The Russians are superb mechanics," she added sympathetically. "But with no experience in the newest technologies they're losing out." When one Russian crew was stranded in Newfoundland for three months, many soon had fixed bicycles and other possessions from things discarded on the town dump. Despite their growing despair, even anger, Vikki noted that the crewmen she has encountered "have a great feeling for the Russian soil" and care deeply for their homeland.

She, and another observer of several I met, said they enjoyed serving aboard Russian ships despite the present shabbiness, because of the people themselves. "They laugh at the same jokes we do." (The worst? According to the other observer: "Germans.")

The *Yunaya Smena*'s evidence of lean times, an echo of the situation back home, reflects also the fact that it has been fishing at sea for more than a month. Below decks the smell of cooked cabbage—a Russian staple—permeates the corridors. I'm told it is the only green. The cook in the cramped galley is chopping a small, very fatty piece of meat. A shower can be taken only every ten days—Vikki takes her laundry in with her to do it. Facilities are cramped and basic, although there is a sauna. The observer sleeps in a cabin that also serves as the infirmary. Crewmen bunk four to a small cabin with a sink, and must drape their work clothes in the corridor to make room. Toilets are a hole with treads, not particularly clean. A later conversation reveals that the ship is down to fuel for one day's operation. If the tanker for the Russian ships doesn't come they will have to stop and wait, earning nothing, or use the remaining fuel to reach Harbour Grace, and wait.

On another Russian ship we boarded later, the *Udarnik,* things appeared less worn, and the observer said that food and water were plentiful. It had not been fishing as long. Yuri, the third mate, gladly practiced his English and invited me around the ship. His cabin, sleeping only two, contained a niche with a hot plate, souvenirs (an orange fuzzy grinning monkey), and family photos. He showed postcards of handsome official buildings in his hometown, Murmansk. In the engine room, hundreds of small fish were strung to dry, draped from the ducts like bunting. The engineer insisted on giving me a packet of them. Leathery and high-smelling, they were edible within a fish culture. We joked together about the odor and, buoyantly, posed for my camera.

One of the officers on the *Yunaya Smena* takes position at the trawl controls in back of the wheelhouse facing the stern, and begins to bring in the warps. The crewmen assemble on deck. Officers Kettle and Anderson pull back into their float suits (rubber boots glide best through the stiff legs when covered with a plastic bag) and head down. On deck, with the stimulus of working the gear, the men manage to grin when I point a camera. Their oilskins are the most worn and ripped of any I saw during the *Cowley* trip.

As for the catch of a five-hour tow: about half a ton. During the ship's thirty-four days of fishing, according to Kettle and Anderson's calculations from the fishing log, the average daily haul has been 1.9 tons, not much to sustain this size ship and crew.

Kettle measures the mesh and grill openings. All OK. We next go below decks to check the holds. En route we pass through a cramped but clean factory area. Someone shows us a broken and heavily taped casting on a chute, and shakes his head. The operation is basic and the men go about it with set faces. A machine shake-sorts the shrimp according to size, then passes them on for inspection. The by-catch is virtually zero. A belt takes the shrimp through a tunnel freezer, and then the frozen shrimp empty into a funnel. One man controls the funnel discharge while another fills forty-pound bags from the mouth. The shrimp are small, but bright and wholesome.

Back in the wheelhouse after finding the hold satisfactory, Kettle fills out the inspection report and explains it to the captain so he can sign. The two Canadians sign it themselves. Kettle tries to radio the *Cowley* for the smallboat, but the Russian's frequencies fail to reach the Canadian ship. It ends with the Russians blowing their whistle, and Kettle standing on the bow waving for attention. The boarding has taken approximately two hours. Later that day, after boarding other Russians in the area, we return observer Vikki to the *Yunaya Smena* with bags of clean laundry and supplies. She waves merrily as the smallboat splashes from its davit into the sea.

Shrimping on the Flemish Cap in 1996 could not be called regulated even though NAFO had voted to limit vessels to those already in the fishery, since member nations had the option to object and continue fishing under their self-assigned quotas. In this case Iceland, Russia, and some of the former Soviet states objected to the ruling, and thus had not bound themselves by it. The Russians, in fact, disputed sharing a quota with the former Soviet states of Estonia, Latvia, and Lithuania, and all those parties were shrimping as they pleased. "But nobody can find the quota anyhow," wryly observed a Canadian fisheries official. The captain of a Faeroese we boarded, whose ship was newly fitted to haul two nets at once, presumably for a larger catch, volunteered that his double effort was bringing up no more than had his single net the year before, about a fifty-ton weekly average. The dismal story may have played here yet again, of desperate overfishing of a high-seas stock among those who need to make a living. Yet the shrimp continue strong (2000 update).

And what of the Spanish with their wicked reputation? The *Cowley* finally reaches them one morning. The fleet is fishing turbot as expected in an area of deep fathom curve called Sackville Spur, located beyond Grand Bank, about ninety miles north of Flemish Cap where the trawlers of other nations target shrimp. Seas remain high following several days too rough to launch a smallboat, but have diminished. Officer Kettle identifies two ships through binoculars towing a net in the water between them, and radios politely his intention to board. Consent comes back with equal politeness. The bad old days seem history.

The two Spaniards are pair trawling: pulling the same net in tandem a few hundred feet apart. Each vessel in this case acts as one of the otter boards—the doors—to hold open the net mouth. The *"pareja"* method enables using a larger net to catch more fish than two separate ones, a practice denounced in some quarters as destructively efficient although not illegal. Kettle learns that the two ships alternate receiving eight-hour tows, and one tow has just come aboard the *Nuevo Virgin de Lodiaro*. We'll go there first, and later visit the sister ship *Nuevo Virgin de la Barca* in time to watch the haul-in.

In the *Lodiaro's* well-kept wheelhouse, electronic boxes crowd against polished wood. The captain and fishing master smile guardedly as we shake hands and show credentials. With European formality they offer their cards (which list also the names of their wives). The captain, short and broad, has a quarter-inch of hair that covers his round head like grass. Suddenly he grins. Kettle, a head higher, grins back and tousles the grassy head. How many years ago? Kettle had caught the captain fishing illegally in Canadian waters and the man had served a jail term in St. John's. No hard feelings. That was in the past, cause and effect between realists.

The fishing master, tall and more reserved than the captain, busies himself with running the ship. Kettle chats with the help of the observer, a young friendly Brit growing comfortable with Spanish. How's fishing? Not good, not as good as last year, but they've only just arrived from homeport in Vigo, only seven days' fishing so far. All of it turbot except for very small by-catches of grenadier, plaice, and cod within legal limits. Kettle nods. He'll see for himself shortly.

The catch is being processed below, so we go down at once. A smell of fresh fish and disinfectant heralds the factory spaces. Men in aprons and oilskins stand in front of machines preparing the fish of the last haul for freezing. We find the catch to be predominantly turbot, both on conveyor belts and in the holding bin. The only significant by-catch, acceptably small, is grenadier, a long fish with snowy meat. Kettle and Anderson stand at a trough watching turbot carcasses sluice past. Headed and bobtailed but with brown- green skin intact, they resemble flying saucers fat in the middle. None are close enough to illegal size to warrant measuring.

Down in the freezers the two inspectors stretch a tape to measure the hold's dimensions, count the number of boxes, then spot-open several to check contents. Turbot, as labeled. They have already examined the ship's specs in the warmth of the wheelhouse. All appears in order. Back up the ladder to room temperature, my glasses and camera lens stay fogged for minutes, no matter how often I wipe them.

As things progress well the mood steadily lightens. Kettle and Anderson complete their report and cosign it with the captain. He has remained edgy, smiling without cause, probably worried that however law-abiding he's kept his ship, something might be wrong. The fishing master on the other hand has relaxed. By now I feel free to call them José and Manuel, respectively, and the mate Fernando. While refusing alcohol, we have drunk their proffered coffee and Cokes. We pass photos of our families back home. Fernando, a lean, swarthy man, enjoys what Spanish I muster, and squires me from deck to deck. The ship is clean by fishing standards. We pass through passageways narrowed by clothing draped on rails along both sides. (One T-shirt hung to dry says: THAT'S ALL, GET LOST.) An open door to a crew cabin shows four bunks in double tiers. Just like the Russian ships, except that these walls have newer paint, and the clothing is in better shape. I note that the washroom has scrubbed Western toilets. Good smells come from the galley.

José and Manuel invite us to lunch in the small wardroom. Would we like steak or fish? We're all sea people. A kind of bean soup comes first with a side of cheese and salami cut into squares. Then a platter of redfish arrives, cooked in light olive oil with tomatoes, green peppers, and potatoes. A second redfish course follows, lightly fried with lemon. Both are delicious by any standard.

An explicit sex flick on the TV monitor accompanies the meal, not my dinner fare but clearly an expression of hospitality since Brian the observer said it had not been shown before. Talk becomes rough and relaxed, its tone set by the movie. Everybody roars when the chief engineer, a robust grizzle-beard of sixty, declares that he still has plenty of virility, but only with the aid of a *"capsula."* The crew eating at long tables in another area also watch the movie, and call jokes about it when I walk in. Some play cards and pay no attention. Prominent on the walls of both messdecks is a full-sculpted torso of the Virgin and Child, the Virgin with hand outstretched.

We leave the *Nuevo Virgin de Lodiaro* in time to inspect the *Nuevo Virgin de la Barca* before observing its haul-in. The 184-foot ships, each with a crew complement of twenty-seven, have close to identical designs, but today the *Barca*'s men are less relaxed. The net coming up has fastened on a snag. The fishing master moves tensely between the wheelhouse and outside controls overlooking the ramp, barking commands by shout and loudspeaker. At his instruction the captain backs the ship cautiously to free the trawl while keeping it from the propeller. At length the maneuver succeeds. The sister ship transfers its end of net. The trawlerbag rises astern and snakes up the ramp. Gasping fish heads protrude from the meshes. Fishing is no prettier than any other of man's kills for food. There come faint pops as bladders rupture from the sudden trip up from depth. These fish have been hunted where they live deeper than most, at five hundred fathoms compared to about fifty for cod. They had remained relatively unmolested until overfishing diminished stocks easier to catch.

The haul contains mainly turbot of legal size, plus an acceptably small by-catch of grenadier and redfish. But the total is less than two tons. Not much for the eight-hour tow of two expensive ships. The deep sea is only marginally abundant.

The net has no illegal liner. Officer Kettle inserts a calibrated gauge into twenty consecutive meshes and calls out the readings to Anderson. By NAFO agreement the minimum size for turbot must be 130mm (5.1 inches), large enough to permit undersized fish to escape. The net complies. The inspection passes. We shake hands, and return to the *Cowley*, our piece of home.

Homeport for the Spaniards is Vigo, in northern Spain. The city harbors one of the world's largest far-seas fishing flotillas. This is the area's major economy, but there are no longer enough grounds open to keep the ships occupied. Recent assertion of rights by Namibia and Morocco, for example, have closed entire regions to Spain. The drawdown off Grand Bank from forty vessels to seven in a single year speaks for itself. A report in late 1996 noted that some of these ships then tried the far northern Barents Sea for black halibut until Norway imposed a moratorium on the species. Others went on to try their luck off Argentina and Mauritania, while several were scrapped. The Vigo farseas fleet has dropped from 220 vessels in 1989 to a present 90. The men of *Nuevo Virgin de Lodiaro* and *Nuevo Virgin de la Barca* know they're lucky to be employed.

CHAPTER TEN

Outporters

Newfoundland, 1991–1992

The Spaniards who burned Canadian effigies in Vigo after the arrest of the *Estai* off Grand Bank took no account of the blatant cheating by their countrymen that precipitated the incident. They would not have cared who was right. When there is not enough to go around, fishermen who lose grounds or stocks they think they own can turn unreasonable. In 1997 Canadian fishermen blockaded an Alaska-bound American liner because they claimed Alaskans netted too many salmon homing to British Columbia. French fishermen have raised similar blockades for perceived cause. Things went further on Indonesia's Java Sea when fish bound for the tables of village net fishermen disappeared into trawlers manned by foreigners dragging the grounds clean. The villagers paddled out in the dark and murdered a few trawlermen to convey their concern. The Indonesian government got the message and banned further trawling in the area.

Things erupted not so dramatically, although shocking enough for Newfoundland, on a March morning in 1991 at the Port aux Basques office of Fisheries and Oceans. Two hundred angry fishermen broke open the doors, told the officials to leave, and then trashed the place. When it was over, computers poked from the snow, files lay scattered over upturned desks, and a chair stood embedded in the wall by its four legs. The men then took to their boats and blocked the harbor to hem in the Nova Scotia ferry.

On the morning of the action the men had arrived at Fisheries expecting to continue a grim but peaceful sit-in begun the day before. They found the door to their public representatives primly barred. "It wasn't no plan, no sir, I don't think," mused Murray Lavers of the dragger *Night Breaker,* a year later. "We was just mad."

The men were protesting a reduced redfish quota, imposed just after each boat had paid its annual $1,500 license fee for the privilege of fishing. Without redfish, the boats would lay idle as payments came due and expenses continued. Usually violence in Newfoundland is confined to the weather. Months later, many of the men who had participated in the trashing returned to the restored offices one by one and apologized. "The fishery officers is OK, themselves, they just doo's their job," Lavers explained. I asked him what the protesters had achieved. He rubbed a puffy fisherman's hand over a few days' stubble, and flashed a sheepish young man's grin. "Bad name for we."

Fisheries took no action against the men, and did restore some redfish quota, but this was a Band-Aid solution. The real Fish—in Newfoundland people speak the word as if capitalizing it, to mean only the cod—remained scarce, for some nonexistent. When cod was plentiful, neither fish plants nor fishermen bothered with redfish. By 1992 the cod shortage turned so desperate that Ottawa began to close fishing grounds around Newfoundland.

Ironically the protesters were not local, even though their livelihood was locally dependent. Most sailed their boats from only a few hundred miles north on the same Newfoundland coast, but they were foreigners in more than a different regional accent. Resident fishermen, who worked different gear from smaller boats, considered the rioting draggermen themselves to be the cause of the crisis they protested.

Port aux Basques, a town of three thousand on the far southwest coast of Newfoundland, is the center for a string of fishing communities, some so remote that only a boat can reach them. The villages, especially those to the east of Port aux Basques facing the Atlantic Ocean along what is called the South Coast, have for generations fished cod with hook and line from small open boats. Their greatest abundances occur during winter, between December and April. This might be a time of thick floating ice and frigid gales, but South Coast men learned to bend to the weather for their living.

"But no more," says Austin Fudge, a fisherman in Francois. Around him the houses of some sixty families dot a stunningly scenic harbor enclosed by a horseshoe of low mountains still white in March. He stands in the snow beside his boat locked in ice. In previous years enough boats came and went to keep the ice loose. "The Fish got scarce nine years ago in 1983, and then four years ago they disappeared altogether. And it don't look like they're coming back." A quiet family man in his thirties, Fudge now spends idled days puttering. He and fellow-fishermen throw darts in their work sheds and "wharf-talk" around small woodstoves, surrounded by lines and nets that need no further mending, away from kitchens and wives accustomed to having their men at sea.

"The young people now, they're leaving, lots of them. They sees no future in fishing." Clarence Durnford says it, and Fudge and Harvey Baggs agree ruefully. Yet this has happened before. Fudge was born in Francois (pronounced "Franswah," reflecting the early French presence on the coast that remains only fifty miles over the water at St. Pierre-Miquelon). He left the village to live in the city of St. John's for six years while attending high school followed by trade school. "But, wasn't for me, I didn't like it. All my people grew up in Francois." The village graveyard traces his family's residence for 156 years. "But my boy, now, be a fisherman like me?" He touches his close-cut beard with fingers that have engine grease ingrained, as they'd not if he were pulling lines with hands constantly in water. "Who can say, when it's gone, the Fish?"

In earlier years, with Fish in the water the men were "down to" the sheds—called "stages"—by three in the morning to bait their longlines. "Best bait is squid and mackerel, 'alf and 'alf, we calls it patch bait," Fudge explains. "Gives the Fish a choice." The longline boats carry two men. "We fish six to twelve tubs depending on wedder. There's eight lines in a tub, 60 'ooks on a line, 480 'ooks in a tub." That means 3,000 to 6,000 hooks to be baited. They would travel to the fishing grounds by first light, but also, as another idled dart-thrower put it with a grin: "Out h'early so one fellow gets ahead of anudder."

After setting the line between anchors and letting it soak for at least an hour, they would haul it in while removing both fish and unused baits from the hooks and coiling the lines back in tubs. Then, after returning from the grounds, they would gut and clean the catch. "If you gets finished nine o'clock at night then you're lucky." And except for Sundays, "weather providin'," it's up again at three.

Where have the Fish gone? "The draggers," they say as a man. It may not be all that simple, but trawlers certainly helped bring down the stocks. Overfishing, by whomever, weakened the cod's ability to hold its own in the great numbers nature requires for robust survival against predators. Scientists keep busy figuring it out. One piece of the puzzle may be a drop in local water temperatures produced, ironically, by global warming, since more glacier ice now breaks loose farther north to float down and clog southern harbors. Cod need cold but not ice, and they head to deeper water when inshore temperatures approach freezing.

And fishermen point to a growing population of seals—voracious fish-eaters that multiply now that a commercial hunt off another Newfoundland coast no longer keeps their numbers in check. Canada in 1984 yielded to animal activists' pressures and banned the hunt for young harp and hooded seals. "We sees seals now where we never saw them before," Fudge and his friends agree. Other South Coast outport fishermen confirm it. From Wallace Meade of Margaree-Fox Roost: "Now you sees seals all the time." And, "When you start seeing seals around," according to Bill Bowles of Burgio, "the Fish is gone."

Newfoundland's South Coast waters once held enough for all fishermen with the stamina to work hard in wet and cold. But here as elsewhere, fish-catching technologies, and the pressure to use them, had changed the scene. It started—as did so much for North American fishermen—with the 200-mile limit in 1976, which allowed Canada to build a strong domestic fleet.

As part of its plan, Canada in the mid-1970s began to encourage Newfoundland fishermen through grants and protected loans to build larger, higher-powered fishing boats than the dories driven by oar or outboard motor that were common in outports like Francois. The plan did indeed lead to sturdier cabin boats of the kind Fudge and his friends now own. (Although "God knows it wasn't no gift," he declares. He paid only fifteen percent down on a $35,000 boat, but paid ten percent on the remainder. When hard times came to the fisheries, however, the Loan Board placed a freeze on collections.)

But Canada's new-boat plan aimed higher than this. One of the most promising projects focused on a large stock of shrimp off Newfoundland's west coast. These shrimp were untapped for lack of boats powerful enough to pull nets along the bottom where they schooled. The government with its partial subsidy encouraged local fishermen to buy small trawlers, boats that would otherwise have been impossibly expensive for men in a depressed village economy.

The sixty-five-foot trawler-draggers began by fishing shrimp in season during the summer. Then, under pressure to meet payments (and flexing the muscles of new capability), skippers journeyed south in the winter to tap the traditional cod runs off Port aux Basques and along the South Coast in Austin Fudge's country. At the time it seemed no great threat, since the larger boats fished farther out in deeper water. Eventually the dragger fleet grew to be one hundred strong (the government limit). Whether by coincidence or not, following their appearance the average fish size, as well as the numbers of fish, diminished. By 1988 cod had stopped coming close inshore to Fudge's line. Fudge and his peers are certain that the draggers intercepted them.

Feeling runs high. "A lethal pack of fish killers," Cabot Marton terms trawlers, declaring further: "There was never a failure of coastwise fishery until the draggers came along." Marton heads the Newfoundland Inshore Fishery Association, an organization that represents those most affected by the roving trawlers. And, on a raw afternoon by a pier in Rose Blanche, a South Coast outport: "We won't have Fish back here, sir," a moustachioed, muscular, solemn young man shouts against the high wind, staring from his pickup truck where he and two fellow-fishermen sit idle when in other years they would be pulling lines, "until *them* is all burned." He gestures toward a modest-size trawler moored at the local fish plant.

From near shore the draggermen might appear to be villains, but they, too, are going broke. They claim the government assured them a minimum fish quota when it encouraged them to go for it with sixty-five-footers. This has since been diminished year by year—not surprising since bureaucrats had not foreseen the line beyond which overfishing and shortages began, and finally needed to act.

Trawler fishermen are as beleaguered in some societies throughout the world as chain-smokers in others. When I went shrimping in 1981 with a man I'll call James, his new trawler was the talk of Port au Choix, an outport 250 miles north of Port aux Basques. A man of twenty-nine and a hard driver, James had become one of Newfoundland's highliner fishermen. The Canadian media interviewed him routinely as an example of the enterprising new generation. He harvested shrimp around home when they schooled during the summer, and then in December, displaying the initiative much admired, took his prized boat south to target the abundant cod in Newfoundland's only winter fishery. In 1991 a mutual friend reported finding James riding out a storm in a secluded harbor near one of the South Coast outports, wondering dispiritedly how long it would be before local fishermen discovered his boat and hassled him for clearing the Fish from their waters.

The place termed "Newfoundland" is both a province of Canada that includes huge, bare Labrador to the north, and an island of forty-two thousand square miles that is the easternmost landfall of North

America. The island, called by locals "The Rock," is my subject here, although I have fished along the lonely Labrador coast as far north as Inuit country in Saglek Bay. The Rock is all coves and peninsulas, and a community seems to have taken root in any natural harbor close to fish and seals.

The outports, as the communities are called, function with the rural family-oriented stability of people who labor hard and ask little beyond what they can do for themselves. Money may be scarce, but people provide most of their own food, shelter, and fuel, live in small houses easy to heat, and settle for only modest luxuries. (The supreme luxury? A color TV and a dish to bring in the signals. Imagine the universe this opens in a place reached only by boat!)

Outports like Francois retain values and traditions forgotten in much of the world. The weekly menu still follows a practical routine, at least among older families: Sunday a big dinner, Monday leftovers, Tuesday soup (outport soup is not thin stuff), Wednesday fish, Thursday corned beef or salt beef, Friday fish, Saturday pea soup. Old folks' homes are for elsewhere. Nearly every fishing household I visited in Newfoundland included an aging father or mother, sometimes both, some senile and not easy to care for. In Francois, however, there is also a bright modern school complete with computers and a small gym courtesy of the Canadian government, and rosy-faced children, although at high school age they must leave for larger towns at government expense to continue their education.

September 1979

One day in another year—thirteen years in fact before I visited Francois in 1992—I started from St. John's, capital of Newfoundland on the other side of the Rock, traveling first to the island outport of Fogo in Hamilton Sound to dory handline for cod in a fishery that had changed in little but its propulsion over the centuries.

The sun shone as I returned from Fogo Island on the ferry from Seldom Come By to the mainland. I was headed for Catalina, 350 kilometers away by road on a different peninsula (about 120 by crow flight), which had become a major trawler port for Canadians on the Banks. The scenery was typical of Newfoundland a few miles from the coast. Rock remains the dominant material. Stands of aspen and small spruce reflected in the dark water of ponds trapped in rock hollows. A drizzle started about midday. By afternoon, rain blew nearly horizontal, graying out the wide reaches of Trinity Bay and any sight of the small icebergs that still lingered in early September. Wet business for me, since I was hitchhiking.

At dusk, around 5 P.M., two weary men who had the odor of the boats about them gave me a few miles' lift in their clanking truck. The brothers, each married with children, had been jigging in their open punt since 2 A.M., this being the season when squid crowded into the bays. Until the year before, all squid went for bait, they said, but now—this was in 1979—the Japanese paid a shocking price for them split and cured. "It's a Klondike, sir," declared one man, wondering at his sudden fortune.

The men harvested the little tentacled creatures day by day, and the women dried them like draped laundry over lines and fences, or on flakes—boards laid in horizontal rows. Of course, said the two, squids laid out in rainy weather would cure mealy, and the Japanese bought nothing that wasn't to their fancy. It meant that on a day like this the women would have gathered back hundreds of splits to await the next dry, breezy weather. (In Japanese markets, I had indeed seen housewives feel and sniff leathery dried squid before purchasing. They allowed no quarter for less than top quality.) The men were headed home for a rest, then out to their punt again at 2 A.M.

I myself had gone with fishermen to jig the little squids by the bucketful to use as bait to catch more important creatures. The resource was abundant, although few Newfoundlanders considered eating them. Squid jigging was as much a part of outport life, in season, as sealing. By the late 1980s Newfoundlanders had fished out their squid. The supply turned out not to be so inexhaustible that it could supply both the Japanese and the local boats. For years Newfoundland squid jigging grounds stayed empty, where once in season there would be a hundred boats. Eventually squid returned, but only in enough numbers for bait alone. Japanese markets still have piles of dried squid; they simply buy them elsewhere in the world. For Newfoundlanders, who had lost the seal hunt to the high moral purpose of protesters—half their income for many—gone was another resource that their fathers had assumed to be God's protective bounty. At this time the cod loss was yet to come.

The cod closures started in 1992 when the then-Minister of Fisheries, John Crosbie, placed a fishing moratorium on most of the Grand Banks and virtually the entire Atlantic coast of Newfoundland. The

South Coast was exempted at first, but included by 1994. Crosbie took the extreme measure, essentially a sacrifice for the future, to protect cod aged five to seven. This "very low spawning biomass," according to Willy Bruce, chief of Resource Allocation at the government's Northwest Fisheries Center in St. John's, had become the principal catch in fishermen's nets, so that continued fishing along with natural depredations might have wiped them out.

The moratorium affected thousands of fishermen and plant workers in Newfoundland. The government provided them a modest stipend as a partial replacement for lost income. Whatever the toughness of the times, outporters do have a safety net denied fishermen in most other parts of the world. Recognizing the seasonal nature of fish runs and the extremes of weather that govern the Newfoundland coastal economy, the Canadians pay unemployment compensation based on weeks worked, and money earned when possible. "Without it we wouldn't survive," fishermen admit.

An increase in crustaceans, which now survive better without cod gorging on their young, has provided an alternate fishery. Queen crab is the major species (also called snow crab, or, in Alaska, tanner crab). Since so many now catch these, the fishery is probably receiving too much pressure. Queen crab brought a grand price—up to $2.50 Canadian a pound (about $2 U.S.)—in 1995, but prices since have stayed around ninety cents.

May 1996

The moratorium has entered its fourth year when in 1996 I drive around the Fogo and Twillingate-Durrell area of Notre Dame Bay where I had visited and helped pull lines and nets in abundant times. Reduced circumstance have not changed people's positiveness as I'd feared. As says Jim Winter, St. John's fishery reporter and one-time sealing witness: "Of course, this present adversity brings out the greatest of all Newfoundlanders' traits—unbridled optimism in tomorrow. Between the jigs and the reels we're hangin' in and the belly has yet to hit the backbone.

On Fogo Island Don Best, in coveralls, readies his forty-five-foot *Nancy Lou Ann* and fifty-five-foot *Northern Quest* for the upcoming crab season whatever the price. At sixty-four, Best has fished forty-eight years. His sons now skipper the boats. "Even if the Fish come back," he says, "We'll never make a living again on cod alone. Old days, you'd fall down in your tracks with work, still never make it." He is a charter member of the Fogo Fisheries Co-Op, a bellweather project started when Newfoundland became a province in 1949 and the new government tried to shut down Fogo as too difficult to keep in schools and other services. Fogo Islanders refused to leave, and the co-op they formed proved boldly that remote outport communities could remain in the swim. As for access to the bureaucrats who juggle quotas and closures: "You'll see the Pope in Rome sooner than they!" Midday dinner, for which Mrs. Best lays me a place as a matter of course with no invitation necessary, is a full-bodied soup of meat and turnips, with home-baked bread.

I don't lack for food. The kitchen in Mrs. Emma Payne's guest house, where I usually stay, is never closed for long. And I sup on fresh-caught lobster at the house of Lloyd Payne (no relation) with whom I helped pull cod with handline and then from a trap in 1979 and 1982, respectively. Lloyd still fishes jointly with his brothers, including Everett who lives in the next house up the hill. Later I call on Frank Harnett. I helped pull web for cod aboard his forty-six-foot *Angela Chantel* back in 1982. Ivy Harnett remembers me as the man who slept on their living room floor because the couch was too short. Frank's crew of six includes two sons. After being stuffed with tea and a meal, we call on his boat. It is newly fiberglassed ("can't believe there's no water in the bilge any more!"), long-needed work justified by last year's crab price. This year's sales were to pay much of the bill. The plummeted price has Frank losing sleep.

In Twillingate, where icebergs still float offshore in mid-May, Jack Troake also prepares his pots for crab. Jack's face has matured like a Toby jug, with creases from chin to forehead both from squinting into cold wind and from good humor. I've never seen him laugh outright, but even when he's damning the bureaucrats his features brighten. Energy drives him. As someone observed: "Jack's not a man for the house. He's always got a job." This means that, except for meal times or evening news with an arm around Florence, his wife, on the couch, he's aboard his longliner *Lone Fisher* or down on the stage.

A Newfoundland fisherman's stage is his haven, the building by the boat and pier where he keeps gear, guts fish, repairs and devises things, and hangs out with other fishermen. No stage lacks a stove, but wind blows through the cracks of some. Not Jack's.

When first I met the Troakes in 1979 their house was smaller by a room or two, since built by himself as times permitted. In the harbor packed with long crackling flats of ice, Jack had just returned from sealing aboard his longliner. Messy stuff. The *Lone Fisher*'s scuppers ran with blood, and everyone's oilskins glistened with fat, as he and a crew with his sons boomed floppy pelts from the hold to a waiting truck. Jack's dad, Captain Peter, stood by to kibitz and lend a hand.

Peter Troake is a legend in his own time: fisherman, sealing skipper, captain for twenty years of the Grenfell Mission hospital ship *Christmas Seal*, recipient of his nation's highest civilian honor, the Order of Canada, as well as an honorary doctorate from Memorial University. He walks with a slight limp. In his midthirties a terrible boat accident almost cut him down, as it would have a lesser man, when his pants caught on a revolving shaft that mangled his leg. Bracing against shock as he stumbled for help, he snapped off a "stick" protruding from his foot that turned out to be the leg bone. Two English physicians in residence at the hospital automatically prepared to amputate, but Dr. John Olds (another legend) intervened. Olds decided, with Peter's consent, on a painful procedure to save the leg. He reinserted the snapped bone, bound the leg, and kept the young fisherman immobile in bed for nine months. After the bandages were peeled, ulcers that had formed needed another three months to heal. The leg came out short, "But 'e gave me a lifetime on me own feet, sir," says Captain Peter reverently. A half-century later, Dr. Olds remains his hero.

Later, seated in the kitchen over a bottle of dark rum which I had brought, Jack expounded on irresponsible Greenpeacers but quieted respectfully when Captain Peter took over the subject. Florence, like a good outport housewife of the time, stood apart even though she contributed to the conversation and accepted a small glass of the rum.

Several visits later in 1996, the warmth of the Troake kitchen remains. I wear thick wool boot socks knitted by Florence and given me on a previous visit. (Boots of course removed in the mudroom.) Florence now takes her place at the table. Captain Peter, in his late eighties, walks with cane slowly from his house down the road. He speaks less while Jack has become more articulate. (Captain Peter died a year later, in December 1997.) Rum is no longer the drink of choice, although the tea is nearly as strong. Jack's longliner, on the ways for painting, bears on her bow the rueful words: "She's Gone Boys, She's Gone." It means the cod. "We'll never see them back for twenty, thirty years," says Troake. In 1996 the government has allowed a cautious inshore quota in Troake's region, but the stocks prove so vulnerable that next year it will be closed again. (Austin Fudge's country on the South

Coast fares slightly better since the "subsistence" quota holds. The small monthly allowance—trawlers need not apply—comes aboard the boats within a few hours of a single day.)

Troake's judgment of bureaucrats and scientists echoes that of fishermen along the entire coast of eastern Canada, who say they saw the crisis coming and warned officials when the government continued to encourage new boats and men into the fisheries, then opened quotas for everyone. "There's a reason we got into the mess we got today, Uncle Bill." Jack leans forward earnestly to make sure I understand. "In Ottawa they just don't listen. Seems like to be 'eard you got to be a scientist comes from... *New Zealand* somewhere. For them, if 'e's a scientist 'e must know because 'e's a scientist! You know?" Admitted, now: "They're not going to be able to take all the advice that fishermen give 'em, they'd have bullshit runnin' out their ears. But anything a fisherman tells our Department of Fisheries in Ottawa, they go opposite. That's the way the system is, Uncle Bill. You can't run our fishery here from Ottawa. Too far away."

One chilly wet 5 A.M. I ride in open skiff with Jack's sons Gary and Hardy to work lobster pots. I wear long johns, boots, everything, but the wet chill creeps in everywhere. The problem is, an open skiff leaves no room for me to lend a hand and get the blood flowing. About midmorning, after only four or five hours on the water, I think, *Thank goodness, all the damn pots are in and we're going home.* Ha. Gary guns the motor in the opposite direction, straight out the harbor into choppy water that crashes against high rocks. The guys have nets anchored out there to gather herring and other fish for bait. We're close enough to the rocks and the surge around them to smell barnacles and moss on the glistening stone. I shiver, thinking of Florence's seal stew promised back at the warm house, surely soon. Ha again. When you have bait, you bait your pots. At length I persuade Hardy to change places in the skiff so I can work. After a few pulls I can feel my toes and fingers again. The men return me to the stage for lunch, but continue on themselves to work more pots. The harvest is no bonanza: seven keeper-size lobsters for the day.

That evening over a beer I relax on Gary's carpeted floor as we listen to recorded piano jazz and he shows me treasured volumes from his collection of books on Newfoundland history. Some are rare, bought at collector's prices. Gary's house, built with his dad, perches on a hill just above those of his parents and grandparents. The decor is relaxed and unconventional, focused on the living room rather than the kitchen—the pad of a divorced young man. At night, shed of oilskins and wool cap, Gary is barely recognizable with a headband around long hair tied back. His interests take him on the long road that now leads from Twillingate to the outside world, but his purpose remains focused at home. He went to Norway to talk about fishery markets. He's just bought an abandoned lighthouse which, when fixed up, should draw tourists. (Later note: It has.) The boats still draw back sons of Newfoundland.

Next morning at five the rain is heavy. Gary and Hardy, already dressed in oilskins, head for the open skiff to gillnet for lumpfish. I open my eyes, look out the window, wish them luck, and roll back under the covers.

CHAPTER ELEVEN

Plankton Soup
Chile

October 1990

Soon after talking my way aboard those first fishing boats in Alaska, I began to attend Fish Expo, a yearly meeting that was the place to keep up with news, to see fishing not only as a lifestyle aboard individual boats but as a profession and an industry. Sponsored by *National Fisherman,* a journal that has kept the North American fishing community informed since 1903, the Expo at the time met alternately in Boston and Seattle. (It now meets in both cities annually.) Exhibitors display the newest technologies—an amazing show in itself just to see the latest in wheelhouse navigation and fish-seeking electronics—while men from the boats wander the aisles along with the industry's leaders and decision makers. The Expos show that fishing is a worldwide affair, target of boat and equipment manufacturers (money in it), target of politicians with coastal turf, even target of statesmen, since marine resources are national wealth.

At the 1990 Boston Expo, where the Marco (Marine Construction & Design) booth featured a new longline self-baiter, the talk turned to founder Peter Schmidt's renewed interest in Chile. Peter, a Seattle-based engineer with enough imagination to enjoy ideas, opera, and other civilized activity, first made his mark in 1958, when he introduced the power block. A hydraulically powered net hauler able to handle ton-weights of fish, the power block changed seine fishing worldwide by relieving human back-power while increasing the capacity of hauls. Schmidt's company continued to set patterns in fishing vessel design and equipment. His experience in Chile has become a tale of American energy and talent at its best, applied to raising the economy of a host country.

Schmidt became interested in Chile's fishing potential when he visited in 1958. At the time Chile had no industrial fisheries base. Extreme currency control discouraged outside development. The scene consisted mainly of small-boat fishermen, *artisanals,* who supplied local needs, although Peru to the north harvested great schools of small fish common to both coasts. Chilean anchoveta remained untapped; their potential as in Peru lay in meal and oil, an operation profitable only if done on an industrial scale with high-volume boats. Four small Chilean fishmeal plants struggled to imitate the Peruvian success, but their fish supply came with no regularity from only the small boats.

A new Chilean fisheries law in 1959 opened opportunities for Schmidt to import equipment and machinery, backed by a government now willing to encourage fisheries development through tax exemptions and export subsidies. Bolstered by the capabilities of his new power block, Schmidt decided to start a shipyard in Chile for the seiners needed to develop the fisheries. To gain experience he built three small seiners in his Seattle yard, geared them with the latest equipment, and sent them to prospect Chilean waters. They delivered to the struggling small plants while he decided where best to locate. As Schmidt tells it: "We settled on Iquique in the north, relatively close to Peru, as it was an extension of the Peruvian fishery. From the day we arrived and for the first year, those three little boats came in fully loaded virtually every day. Some days they brought in two loads, some days even three. This excited the authorities as well as private investors. Within a year Chile had projects to build about ten plants."

The resource Schmidt tapped results from an unusual combination of natural forces off Peru and Chile that is duplicated only in southern Africa around Namibia, Angola, and the Republic of South Africa (where explosive new fisheries are also occurring). A very narrow continental shelf bands the Peru–Chile coast: no more than twenty miles wide compared with the hundred-plus-mile shelves off Alaska and Newfoundland. Beyond the shelf, the seafloor plunges without slope to depths of ten thousand to twenty thousand feet. Normally this would be barren sea, since blue tropical ocean water contains virtually no plankton to support schools of plankton-feeding fish. Trade winds blowing from land to the sea (the very wind the *Kon Tiki* sailors counted on to reach Easter Island), however, move the surface of the water out: water that must be replaced. The action starts a circular motion that causes upwelling, bringing up from the deep seafloor the cold water of the Humboldt Current that is rich in the nutrients that generate plankton when exposed to sunlight. Masses of pelagic (midwater) fish—anchovy, sardine, and mackerel—converge to feed and multiply on the resultant plankton soup.

In years of El Niño, the trade winds slow and the upwelling stops, leaving blue tropical water barren of nutrients, thus of plankton, thus of fish. Fish patterns change throughout the eastern Pacific as the plankton soup moves or disappears and the fish follow to the new places or vanish.

By the time Peter Schmidt's new shipyard in Iquique delivered its first boat—seventy-three feet long with 140-ton fish hold capacity—it had received orders for some one hundred more. "By 1963 we were delivering a boat a week." Several competitors opened shipyards, but their production was half that of the Marco Chilena yard with its logistics pipeline out of Seattle. "I could finance delivery to Chile, in advance of need, the machinery and components required to build the vessels. Being so far from the industrial world is a tremendous handicap. You must work nearly a year ahead to ensure having adequate materials so that lack of them doesn't slow production."

By the mid-1960s approximately two hundred purse seiners in Chile supplied newly built fishmeal plants that produced up to one million tons of product a year. Besides building seiners for other companies, Marco eventually operated a twenty-three-boat fleet of its own.

In the early 1970s the scene changed. Schmidt sold Marco and left just before the communist-leaning government of Salvador Allende nationalized Chilean industries. After Allende's overthrow and death in 1973, the government of Augusto Pinochet began a military rule that lasted until 1990. Despite human rights abuses, Pinochet's free enterprise policies reopened the Chilean economy to foreign investment and encouraged market-based growth. In 1984 Marco repurchased its former company and returned. The present Marco Chilena, while a wholly owned foreign affiliate of Marco in Seattle, operates under Chilean law. Marco Chilena includes the shipyard in Iquique, center of the northern sardine-anchovy fishery, and a repair yard at Talcahuano in the heart of a newer mackerel fishery. Chile's high-volume fishing industries now produce five to six million tons annually.

By the 1990 Boston Expo, Marco Chilena had completed some 190 boats, and the meal fishery had become a permanent force in the Chilean economy. Thus within easy memory an entire fishery had been created. Compare this with areas of the world fished in organized fashion since recorded time, from the Sea of Galilee to the stormy Lofotens off northern Norway to the coasts of Japan, or to the Grand Banks with at least centuries of history. The lore of Alaska's Bristol Bay extends back just over one century. Since 1973 Chile's fishing has increased enough to advance it in volume landed among the world's nations from twenty-second place to third or fourth, depending on the year.

Northern Chile, December 1990

Because I have never seen industrial-scale fishing, I take myself to Chile. The nation is all coast, 2,650 miles of it: a cigar-shaped north–south nation all in sight of the Andes, little of it farther than one hundred miles from the ocean. The nation spans latitudes 18° to 56°S, equivalent to such vast climatic stretches in the Northern Hemisphere as those between Guatemala and southeastern Alaska, or between Ethiopia and Denmark. Chileans feel isolated on the edge of their continent. The country is not a pass-through to anywhere except Pacific Ocean for thousands of miles.

The range of latitude makes Chile a country of no typical climate, and this tells in the fisheries. The Atacama Desert in the north, served by ports like Iquique, border upwelling seas that nourish the same anchovy and sardine biomasses schooling off Peru and Ecuador. The waters of central Chile near the capital of Santiago host a growing industry for swordfish. In dramatic contrast to the desert are green tree-filled towns three hundred miles south of Santiago. The principal of these, Concepción and adjacent Talcahuano and Coronel, have become the hub since 1982 of a new fishmeal industry centered on *jurel,* jack mackerel.

Puerto Montt lies a farther three hundred miles south of Concepción at the start of terrain protected from rough open sea by hundreds of islands. Inland lakes beneath snowcapped volcanoes contain salmon farms whose production matches that of Norway. Historically this region has sustained only artisanal fishermen who rely on sheltered water and close landfalls. It is journey's end for industrial fisheries, since water, rugged mountains, and glaciers prevent roads farther south that might supply processing plants and transport their products. All the way south, an occasional trawler-processor drags its nets off the tip of the continent in the howling ocean around Tierra del Fuego and Cape Horn. In this sea climate, akin in the Northern Hemisphere to that off Alaska, Labrador, or Norway, there may be marine wealth yet to be tapped by those brassy enough to seek it.

My destination is Iquique. The northern town (that is, close to the equator) fronts the arid, hilly Atacama Desert, which once provided fortunes from nitrate, a world monopoly ended in the mid-1920s with the development of artificial fertilizers. Iquique still ships some copper, but the town's importance now lies offshore. Barren brown-red mountains surround Iquique like a dust bowl. Buildings seem cast from traditional old frontier days except for an oasis where nitrate barons of the last century built a charming opera house, bell tower, and other elaborate structures facing a luxuriantly planted square. The town has character. The new character takes over when a breeze blows from the industrial part of the crescent harbor and the stench of steam-processed fish permeates the air.

Iquique harbor is lonesome on the summer Sunday evening in early December when I head aboard the 146-foot seiner *Hurican,* built three years before at the Marco Chilena shipyard. Other hulls loom high and dark as I approach in a harbor skiff. At dusk a chilly wind has replaced the daytime heat that baked the desert mountains. Regular crewmen will arrive later from their homes. Two watchmen catch my bag. The *Hurican* smells familiar at once. A fishing boat never loses the faint odors of its catch no matter how diligent the hosing, and no work-deck machinery ever sheds the smells of grease and metal. A huge skiff is lashed atop a mound of net ten feet high, seine gear of greatly larger proportions than those of Chignik, made possible only by the power block.

The watchmen, both in their thirties with young families, fish on smaller boats and work on engines when they can find jobs. From their wistful talk it appears that not just anyone can crew aboard a big clean prosperous seiner. At 2 A.M. the service launch pushes its bow alongside, and to the thump of brogans and gear bags the men of the *Hurican* jump aboard. The watchmen leave. The engineer descends to his workplace, kept spartanly clean, dons ear guards, and starts the big diesel. On deck the lights of fish plants ashore reflect in the water, and a waxing half-moon outlines the bare mountains. Lights flicker and engines rumble aboard other seiners around us. Ten minutes later the anchor rises and we're picking our way with searchlight among dark smaller boats, headed with the rest of the fleet toward open water.

In the messroom—two tables with side benches connected to the adjacent galley by an open counter—Christian, the cook, sets out cold biscuits and tinned meat. Few speak. Soon all but those on watch have closed the doors to their double-bunk cabins. Up on the dark, wide bridge the captain, Juan Ayella, talks to other skippers by radio and studies charts marked with the last sightings of fish late Friday. Then he sets course, turns the helm over to his *piloto,* mate, and curls beneath a blanket on a padded bench. An hour later, in the dark, spotter planes begin to drone overhead as pilots scout ahead for the phosphorescent glow that will betray a fish mass. When the *Hurican*'s pilot radios information from the air, the captain jumps from the bench to discuss it, then returns to his catnap.

By first light at 6 A.M. the captain is back at the helm and cruises with his eye on the color sonar. Juan Ayella, in his early thirties, is a square-cut man close to the ground, gruff, good-humored, and confident. (Later, during the heat of making a set, he barks orders as fiercely as any other fishing skipper.) His face, nearly as brown as the desert, has the rounded Indian features of those who have inhabited the Atacama for centuries before the first Europeans came seeking wealth, Indians who once fished along the coast in primitive boats. Juan himself first pulled nets aboard his father's wooden boat, one of five brothers who have all become seiner captains and thus substantive men in Iquique.

It is still barely light when Captain Juan gives the alert. The *panga,* the skiff, itself the size of a small fishing boat, is launched from atop the stack of net and soon bounces astern. The *panquero,* skiff man, stands alert by the controls. On deck two other men wait at the ready by the lines that will release the panga. In the wheelhouse the sounder shows the creatures swimming beneath the surface in color blots. Juan looks for masses in red, the hue of densest concentration. An hour later— everyone stays alert—a sizable patch of red appears.

A single siren blast, and off goes the panga with the net attached. Corks bump and big rings clatter. As the last of the rings (which hold the weighted part of the net) leave the horizontal shaft that holds them, a man calls the number of remaining rings: *"Ocho!" "Cuatro!" "Dos!"* When the final ring goes, Juan begins to close in a wide circle. Soon the rest of the crew, who have been hastily buttering biscuits in the galley, jump into oilskins and take stations.

The *Hurican* moves irregularly as Juan swings the ship to keep ahead of the dynamic red patch on the sonar. The circle of corks opens as wide as a playing field. This is a seine on another level from that of Chignik. It measures 460 fathoms in circumference (2,760 feet, over half a mile), and 80 fathoms (480 feet) deep. Everyone has his job. Several begin to bang cleats against the rails, making a metallic din that hurts the ears but presumably scares fish that might try to escape back into the net. In Chignik we did this with a plunger.

Within five minutes the panquero delivers his end of the net back aboard, then catches a line and guns his skiff to hold the boat off the circle of corks in routine seine procedure. The men on deck pull both ends of the purse lines back over the winch drums to close the net beneath the fish. With the pursing completed, the heavy net begins to be drawn aboard in a thick column through hydraulically powered blocks: first guided over the rail by the net hauler, a revolving drum in a Y-shaped crotch, then passed through rollers and lifted high above the afterdeck by another revolving drum called the net stacker—both of these developed from the basic power block that Peter Schmidt's Marco pioneered. From here the net falls into a pile to be stacked manually for a snag-free next set. The captain or mate controls the power blocks from a rail by the wheelhouse.

Stacking the web, corks, and rings of a big seine like this one is a different experience from that aboard a small Chignik seiner, despite the similarity of the gear. Six or seven men handle web instead of one, and it piles underfoot to a precarious height. Once, I forget to climb fast enough over the gathering folds, and must pull legs and then boots separately from a tight trap of web. Eventually the web stacks ten feet high, and half the stackers slide down its cliff to start a second layer. The water is cold, but everyone works with bare hands. We do wear hard hats, and the reason becomes clear when heavy wads of fish flop down from the block high overhead.

The corks are big but, made of foam plastic, they handle lightly. One man can lay them, although he needs to leap back and forth over a long, lumpy stretch of other corks. During the hour that it takes to stack, two cork men alternate. At the other side of the seine the rings and leads have real weight. Each lead, spaced on the bottom line about an inch apart, weighs one kilogram (2.2 pounds). The thick iron rings are as big as horseshoes. Even after their trip through the block they retain enough seawater to pop a salty splash into the eyes of the man who shoves them onto the vertical pole, and to send a cold trickle inside the arm of his oilskin jacket.

The set is only middling, about forty tons. All hands except the captain go below for breakfast, grabbed from platters of heavily salted tomatoes and eggs, onions and eggs, and fried thin steaks. With it comes *palta*—a mashed avocado paste—and a biscuitlike bread hard on the outside and doughy in the center, both standard fare on Chilean tables at all social levels. No one bothers with plates but scoops the food informally into sandwiches. Soon the siren sounds again.

Juan cruises, barely removing his gaze from the color sonar for the next hour, calm but utterly concentrated. He talks to his spotter plane, now in daylight looking for the silver glint of massed fish just below the surface. At 8 A.M. he radios his position and intentions to the Navy, as he will also daily by law at 8 P.M. I count more than thirty seiners like our own on the horizon. Lines of yellow and white corks bob in big irregular circles around those making a set. Despite the size of the ocean (we cannot see shore) the sardines are schooling in only a small part of it. Maneuvering space is tight. Juan skillfully avoids the hulls and nets that we practically brush.

I don't settle in automatically although everyone is cordial from the start, willing to listen as I struggle with textbook Spanish, always passing me the common platters at mealtimes before they're emptied. I become part of things only when, after taking notes and photographs during the first two sets, I don oilskins to help stack the net. A rite of passage follows. During a pause in the stacking as we wait on the stern beneath a hill of web about eight feet high, bearded Alejandro drops on all fours behind me, and Humberto, with a peasant's open grin, gives a shove that lands me into a pile of net clogged with pieces of old fish. I duly tackle Humberto to bring him down in the mess beside me. After that, everybody wants a turn talking and joking with me.

If Chilean fishermen love anything, they love horseplay. "Macho" might have been a word invented for the strutting attitude of some ashore, but at sea they bounce over each other like puppies, unbashful about pawholds that would worry a Norteamericano.

We keep making sets, some good, others not. One set comes up with three sea lions, which flap a storm, and gorge with abandon on the fish of their common entrapment. They become distressed only when the seine closes tight around them, and then they thrash in earnest while still gobbling fish. It takes twenty minutes to free the half-ton glistening creatures and send them off to pluck other nets (losing all our netted fish during the process), then another two hours to mend the web they have ripped in their attempts to fight free. The Chileans display none of the anger against marine mammals that American and Canadian fishermen feel at sight of their salmon consumed and nets shredded. (I once helped mend web for a full day in a Kodiak bay as other boats caught fish, after a seal followed the salmon into our seine.) But each salmon brings a price at the dock equal to about half a ton of sardines. And the fortunes of North American fishermen, working aboard skipper-owned rather than company-owned boats, are tied more directly to a crew share.

After mending the net we set on another promising red patch. Juan Ayella points to bubbles rising from the encircled water. "Fish down there." As the net comes in, a sea of silver begins to churn at the surface. Everyone stops a moment to admire it. Captain Juan draws a relaxed breath, and laughs for the first time. Soon, with obviously a major set on its way aboard, everyone has turned-to on deck, including the cook and all engineers. (One engineer always has duty, to operate the winches.) You can tell the *motoristas* by the engine-room earmuffs they keep around their necks, and by the fact that they work in coveralls rather than oilskins despite the wetness of the work. Most jobs done proudly have their symbols. The earguards did come off one day when web snagged in the screw, and one of the engineers slipped into scuba gear to enter the water and free it.

When the seine has been stacked two-thirds of the way, masses of fish begin to surge like the boiling in a cauldron. The hydraulic rollers by the rail strain as the net hardens, and the plastic corks squeak when the net passes through. We scoop bucketfuls of random fish on deck and dump them along the rollers to be mashed for lubrication. The seething moneybag of fish that eventually floats alongside measures several feet in any direction, and who knows how deep? Sea lions frolic alongside, pulling fish from the web by their protruding heads or tails. Every creature rejoices except the frenzied sardines, whose raw oily smell and collective drumroll splashes fill the air. We lower the suction pump. Highways of fish begin sucking through the thick hose and pouring into the hold. On the other side of the ship the pump discharge leaves a red pool of fish blood in the water.

The hatch covers are numbered, and the chute has a series of doors that can be opened or closed to direct the fish into different compartments. One compartment becomes unduly clogged. Young Romilio, the least senior of the men, climbs down a ladder deep into the hold to kick the mass free. I lean over to watch, and gag on the stench of mashed oily fish. It seems toxic. I look anxiously at the others, remembering a near-death in Alaska from a putrefied fish hold. I gesture to augment my clumsy Spanish. "He needs a mask. At least a rope around his waist." They shrug, amused and tolerant of gringo precautions. Romilio, shy and still boyish, grins when he climbs back, flattered by my concern.

One of the engineers in coveralls spots a *congrio* flapping in the pool of sardines. Others in oilskins hold him by the feet over the side as he pikes the fish and then displays it triumphantly, muffs still intact over his ears. Congrio, an ugly half-eel creature, is one of the region's finest table fish, rich and firm, world-class. This one weighed at least thirty pounds.

The catch keeps pouring in. One compartment fills and we top it off, then another. The haul exceeds 150 tons, and the gaiety of such an abundant catch affects everyone. The horseplay intensifies. Juan Ayella strides his bridge with a smile. The *Hurican* has a hold capacity of 580 cubic meters (20,465 cubic feet), so plenty of room remains. One more good set follows, in the dark.

So it goes. Days pass without routine, since we fish in both light and dark when significant red blotches appear on the sounder. Gringo Spanish alone limits my communication, since everybody talks to me and Chilean Spanish has a rhythm of its own that chops last syllables from some words and slurs others. The boisterous men on deck slur and chop with greater abandon than the captains and mates, who have taken advanced schooling to earn their papers, but I need to hold tight with bilingual dictionary when conversing with anyone. For respite from the effort of deciphering thick regional Spanish I creep off to nap.

As for entertainment: Anibal the *Hurican's contra maestre,* deck boss, teaches me a game like bridge, played with Spanish face cards that have a different iconography than conventional cards. (The four pictured suits are *espada,* sword; *copas,* cup; *medallión de oro*, gold medallion; and *bastos,* resembling a baseball bat.) A video screen placed above the two messtables continuously shows the same American movies with Spanish subtitles. All depict some form of violence in the United States, so the speaker blasts a steady stream of yells and gunshots over the engine throb. No one watches them more than idly.

The easy horseplay continues. One day it's time for the next set to come aboard and I begin to hustle into boots and oilskins along with everybody else. I discover that one of the socks laid over my boots is tied into an iron-tight knot. Nobody seems to watch the unsuccessful tugs to open the sock. On deck the lead end of the seine is already snaking through the roller, so with no time to spare I run to grab other socks from my rucksack. About two hours later, after chuting tons of fish into the hold and hosing down for the next set, everyone has settled around the messdeck tables with coffee. I saunter in with a mock scowl, waving the knotted sock. (It eventually requires a fid to pry open its ruptured threads.) "OK, you guys, *who?. . .* " I growl in Spanish. The delighted roars and laughs bounce off the bulkheads.

On the *Hurican*'s bridge, crewmen lounge freely when not at work. Once, the sweeps of the sonar shows a patch of dark red. Everyone cranes over the captain's shoulder. But the patch is small. It comes and goes. Juan Ayella turns back into the patch to test its strength, then moves on. The atmosphere aboard is informal and democratic, but no one questions the *jefe*'s decision. These Chileans have different expectations than American fishermen. They don't aspire as they might in the opportunistic helter-skelter of North American fishing where crewmen save to buy their own boats—even large ones—and take charge. Crewmen expect to stay crewmen.

It is not impossible for a crewman to study and become a captain—Juan Ayella and his brothers all rose from the oars to the wheelhouse, and Peter Schmidt's son, Hans, with his own boats, often helps his crewmen to do it—but it does not happen routinely. Chilean fishing captains, as with merchant marine officers in most countries, must attend a university or vocational academy to study pertinent subjects like navigation, meteorology, and safety, and then must pass difficult exams. The *motorista,* engineer, has also trained and become qualified. The thirty-two-year-old captain of another seiner I rode, unlike Juan Ayella, was a university graduate who took to the water without seafaring background. Trim, polite, preoccupied, soft-spoken but firm, he had learned his fishing skills at the national fisheries college. After passing his exams he worked on deck for a few months to learn the gear, then shipped for his *practica,* apprenticeship, as mate aboard a seiner.

Not even a deck hand in Chile can work on a fishing boat—except small village-level craft—without first being trained in his duties and receiving his papers, unlike a would-be American fisherman who can be hired green by any skipper willing to take him aboard, to learn the ropes hands-on. (Further, according to one captain: "It's controlled by the Navy, so that if you have a criminal record, or a history of your family being Communist, it's not too easy to get a crew's license.")

"Men on deck don't take initiative," my captain-informant said. "They don't feel the incentive to learn new things. But they consider their work their career, they're very responsible, very professional. They're in for the long haul and they behave. If you work year-round in an economy where your pay makes you an elite, you don't risk arriving drunk and getting fired." A young Englishman, Michael Combes, who had managed to crew aboard a Chilean fishing boat, told me: "I found them all nice guys, upstandingly honest, not wishy-washy. All solid. For them, experience is a thousand screw-ups. That's how you learn. You never get sympathy for an injury. It's assumed you've screwed up. One guy cut off his finger. Looked at it, said the equivalent of 'Oh shit,' and soon was back at work."

A modern company fisherman in Chile expects Sundays off like any other worker. On Saturday the *Hurican's* owners decide to deliver in Tocopilla, close to the fish, rather than use ship's fuel to return home. A bus will return everyone to Iquique, then late on Sunday night will reverse the five-hour trip with all hands so that by early Monday the nets can be back in the water.

We head in and scraps of fish swirl everywhere as the hosedown begins. We moor to a barge, from which our catch will be pumped ashore through submarine pipes. A dozen waiting men walk aboard, throw off the hatch covers, and take over the unloading at once. Within minutes a service launch has pushed alongside and the *Hurican's* crewmen, in shore clothes, jump aboard. The launch passes among the seiner fleet picking up other crewmen. These vessels are trim by any fisherman's standard, painted and maintained. The black steel hull and white superstructure of our own *Hurican* glisten as fresh as if it were a cruise ship.

A collection of local fishing smacks bobs at anchor close by. Some are painted brave yellows and reds while others show bare wood, but all betray a different level of the fishing life than that on hosed metal decks. As with small-boat fishermen the world over, the fortunes of the men on these boats hang daily on the chances of web and hook. The volume and quality they land close to shore will likely never make them prosperous. In contrast the crewmen aboard the modern Chilean seiners receive a guaranteed 44,000 pesos a month (about U.S. $140) plus an 80-peso bonus for each ton delivered beyond a fixed amount.

Their paychecks could be triple those of other local skilled workmen, higher yet than others.

Even though the faces of the *Hurican*'s crewmen run the Chilean ancestral range from Indian to Spanish-English-German, the faces on the wooden boats are darker, leaner, less shaven. Their deck clothes appear less washed than ours hanging back aboard in lockers. Few elements of life, after abundance of food and quality of shelter, draw a line among workmen more firmly than the availability to them of fresh water for cleaning (which on a boat is a product of afforded equipment). The two classes of fishermen stare at each other. Both groups nod with friendly impersonality, but exchange no waves.

The launch discharges us at the end of a pier. Everyone lines automatically outside the covered window of a building guarded by soldiers, and withdraw papers from their pockets. Augusto Pinochet's military dictatorship might have been voted from power but the old suspicious authority remains strong. We have traveled no more than 125 miles down the coast from one Chilean town to another but a Navy official checks each man's papers and compares them with the *Hurican*'s manifest. Another officer, polite and friendly but firm, motions me into a separate office to examine my own passport and to search my bag. Indeed, the Peruvian border lies only 250 miles to the north, so smuggling might have occurred. Back at the boat the captain had notified the Navy and an officer waited to check our cargo and fuel level. (Unaccounted fuel might have betrayed travels beyond authorized waters.) Ashore, the captain delivers his manifest and catch report immediately.

We board the waiting bus. I glance around Tocopilla with wistful interest. I've been here before, four decades ago in 1949, as a kid tanker seaman. The town is still dusty, frontier-like, backed by bare, coppery mountains. My shipmates have fun looking for evidence of my features in people we pass. The bus travels straight through town, then enters a wilds of loose rock and climbs a sinuous grade. Soon Tocopilla is a mere band of roofs against the water, a smudge in the desert that enlarges around us. Not a piece of greenery grows on the stones or hills that now glow orange under the late sun. Someone hands me a paper cup filled with *pisco,* the region's clear drink akin to tequila or vodka, laced with a sweet softdrink. I toast and down it goes. Everybody toasts. Some then lie back to sleep, but a holiday buzz begins to fill the bus.

It has been a sweaty December summer's day. When the bus reaches a plateau between foothills and mountains the air blowing through open windows turns chilly, then cold. Jackets emerge from overnight bags, along with more bottles of pisco and rum. The sun has disappeared, but dusk lingers. The dry land whizzing past—more crusted than sandy—turns pastel russets and lavenders against a deepening blue sky. A perfect yellow moon rises.

A young crewman from one of the other boats begins to sing. The agreeably dirty lyrics soon have shipmates from all the boats laughing as they join in. By the time the moon has turned pure white to shine across a blackening umber desert, the singer has drained several cups and turned so foolishly wild that the rest try to ignore him. He staggers down the aisle challenging others to sing, often losing his balance to flop across their laps. Nobody takes offense. Some rough him playfully, others right him and push him on. These are all men of the same community, neighbors both aboard boats and back home who know each other's weaknesses and strengths.

The inclinations of Chilean fishermen, like seafarers everywhere, vary with the length of time they spend at sea. The *Hurican* seinermen on the bus are headed straight home, although some unsteadily. Fishermen I meet later from smaller boats in rougher waters farther south, who stay out for weeks and may work harder (no Sundays off when onto the fish), are more likely to declare: *"Hola!"* and head for female company at a favorite *casa* before turning to home. At a *casa,* not to be confused with a blatant brothel, men can survey things without committing further as the ladies sell them drinks, while the casa ladies themselves had the option to say *si* or *no.* ("You want to know a good body for a woman?" declares one fisherman to me thoughtfully, without bravado. "Big thick legs. Something to bury yourself in.")

All that we do riding five hours between Tocopilla and Iquique is to become a bit drunk. Close to midnight the bus rolls into a residential section of town. Wives and collective taxis wait to take everybody home. "Please visit my family for tea tomorrow afternoon," says Jorge Hennings the motorista as we part. "I will come for you, whenever you say." I promise.

Back in my hotel room I shower. But a fish odor persists, stronger it seems than on the boat or the bus. I scrub my fishing clothes. The odor remains, strong and pervasive. Question answered when I go on the balcony to hang the garments. A true stench engulfs me. It blows from the fishmeal plants, miles upwind across the crescent of harbor. The process of heating fish to render them into meal produces a gagging, acrid odor much stronger than any other seafood smell except that of rotting fish. The stench dramatizes the tradeoffs for those prospering in northern Chile.

Jorge picks me up on Sunday afternoon as promised. First we watch strollers and vendors promenade along the Playa Brava, a beach with such murderous waves that nobody swims. Farther down the road, a collection of shacks stands on a rock inlet. Nets hang to dry and small wooden boats, weathered to the grain but brightly painted, lay at anchor. This is Sunday, so no one fishes although some men, barefoot in the sand, mend nets. The shacks, their bare boards and tarpaper exposed, have small windows or none at all. Here is the lowest end of the fisherman's scale, men with whom we'd exchange nods on the water but pass on land without recognition.

Next we drive around the residential part of Iquique where Jorge lives. New houses on land claimed from the desert cling to hillsides pleasantly facing the ocean. Modern, low buildings like these bear no resemblance to the mahogany-paneled mansions of the old nitrate rich, but they come from another world than that of nitrate laborers and artisanal fishermen. Juan Ayella's home has a terrace above a garage, and curtains frame a wide picture window. The same prosperity shows in the home of the *Hurican*'s spotter pilot. Ayella's four skipper brothers also live in the same neighborhood. If they had followed their fisherman father without the opportunities of the fishmeal industry begun only in their time, their homes would more nearly resemble the shacks on the rock.

Jorge lives a few blocks away in a less affluent development, but in a terraced house of substance. His wife, Daisy Marguerite, greets us at the door, and we settle over tea and snacks in a small living room with stuffed chairs and sofa. A painting of the *Hurican* hangs on the wall. Daisy Marguerite is round and friendly but, speaking no English, stays reserved as we work with my rudimentary Spanish. Everything has the feel of comfort and permanence. When I ask Jorge and Daisy to pose for a photograph he leads her to the doorway. "To take the three of us," he says. The third is a small ceramic figure of Christ on the lintel.

The occasional stench from the fishmeal factories is, after all, not an impossible price to pay.

CHAPTER TWELVE

Siwashers

Chiloé Island, Chile

December, 1990

Puerto Montt sits at the top of Chile's southern third, at the same approximate latitude as Boston and Marseilles in the Northern Hemisphere. It is there that Hans Schmidt, the Marco founder's son, receives me in the office of his company, Pesqueria Omega, wearing jeans and sneakers. When Hans speaks, his quiet voice pauses with seeming uncertainty at key words, but this trait masks a clear-eyed drive as he studies weather reports and then radios instructions in Spanish to one of his boats far at sea. In deep water with waves at least twenty feet high, the boat's gear has snagged on the bottom. Hans explains step by step how to free it. He himself has fished in the waters under discussion, aboard the same vessel, and knows the way his boat handles.

The compound of Pesqueria Omega has the fresh-painted look of new construction. Two high warehouse roofs loom behind the office. Inside, workers of both sexes stand by tubs of coiled fishing line, patiently attaching whole sardines to thousands of hooks. The oily smell of salted baitfish fills the enclosure. In a shed standing apart, a blacksmith and helper construct fish traps; they forge steel rods into hoops, then weld struts between pairs of hoops to form cylindrical frames. Another group, out in the rain wearing oilskins, stretches and sews stiff mesh over the frames to form the tunnels and walls. "We have to build the traps ourselves—nobody makes them," says Schmidt. "We're going at this by trial and error, but possibly all our boats'll be converted to traps, instead of hauling baited longlines. In the deep water we fish, you can imagine how you lose fish by the ton, drawing 'em up a mile on nothing but a hook. So we've experimented with traps, and we think they're more efficient."

"Tough luck for whoever supplies your salt bait," I observed.

"Well . . . Plenty of small boats use longline. Fishermen don't change around here too fast."

A low building away from the work area houses a galley and messhall. Now, in the afternoon, it is scrubbed and deserted. "Everybody gets a free hot lunch," says Schmidt. "People are so poor, a lot of them, it's their big meal of the day."

Hans came to Chile in 1987 after college, already a veteran fisherman of Alaskan Bristol Bay waters who knew the craft he wanted. He spent eight months at the Iquique shipyard supervising construction of his first boat, with which he planned to begin exploring south Chilean waters. The design itself was based on a Marco seiner built for rough Alaskan waters, with raised fo'c'sle and a wide afterdeck. Working under the desert sun, amid the clangs of steel plate and the sputter of welding torches, Hans dealt with Chileans and relearned Spanish. Recalling the experience, he declares: "There's not one weld there that I didn't see, I think."

Schmidt hired a Chilean captain and crew for the completed fifty-eight-foot *Elva S,* and they navigated south to the Puerto Montt region he had targeted. Government regulations prevented him from captaining his own boat without being Chilean, but he remained aboard for more than a year, *jefe* in all but name. His goal was to find untapped species farther from the coast and in deeper water (rough that far south toward Antarctica) than artisanal fishermen were equipped to catch. He started tentatively, first venturing beyond the protection of islands for the same species, mostly *congrio,* that local fishermen caught in waters close to land. In southern Chile, weather dominates all fishing. The *Elva S* easily landed its money's worth of congrio in water beyond the weather endurance of small boats without compromising local inshore stocks.

The farther-out waters yielded also *bacalao,* Chilean sea bass. (This grouperlike fish is not to be confused with cod, also called bacalao in Mediterranean countries.) As the *Elva S* fished deeper it began to average forty-five tons of bacalao a month. Bacalao brought a better price than congrio. "So we went for it, went deeper and concentrated on sea bass." On the strength of his catches Hans ordered two *Elva* sister boats, and built a shore facility.

Puerto Montt, with weathered frame houses on steep hills facing the water, has the look of a southeastern Alaska town like Ketchikan. Small islands buffer the harbor from open sea. A *corderilla* of snow-coned volcanoes rises in a near distance, and the white peaks of the Andes gleam beyond. On the quay, women in aprons call with laughing urgency from beside their iced displays of crabs, sea urchins, huge barnacles, mussels, and fish like the fleshy congrio. The creatures can be purchased fresh, or eaten cooked at long tables amid metallic and mellow fishy smells. Across the road a coastal steamer heading south loads clanging flatbeds of penned cattle, regular cargo, and passengers. On a nearby beach, brightly painted wooden fishing smacks of a size and condition not intended to go far to sea rest on their sides in the mud of a receding tide.

The *Elva S* has just arrived from the grounds. Baskets of coiled longline with hooks attached along the sides lie stacked several-high on the covered stern. Leathery young men in wool caps and oilskins, many with a week's growth of beard, nod to Hans as they shout and continue working. From within the open hold others call instructions. The boom cable raises a box out of the hold as ice spills from a thick fish tail that flops over the edge. A single huge, gray, slimy, ugly-snouted fish lies inside. "About thirty kilos, an over-sixty-pounder," Hans declares appreciatively. "We get many like that?" he asks in Spanish.

"A couple, boss. But most average ten kilos. Two were maybe fifty kilos, another one seventy."

"That's the *bacalao*, Chilean sea bass," Hans explains. I have eaten sea bass in a Santiago restaurant. Its firm texture and agreeable flavor place it among the region's best-eating fish. "When we first started bringing in these guys. . . ." he continues, his eyes coming to life, "people wouldn't believe they came from around here. Nobody had ever fished this deep and far out before."

The fishermen of the *Elva,* like those in Iquique, have the drive and good fortune to be hired onto modern boats. What of the artisanals in wooden boats who pull nets for smaller trophy? Men closer, really, to the fishing that first attracted me. Bait for the *Elva*'s hooks comes from Chiloé, a large remote island south of Puerto Montt that lives by farming and fishing. Hans sends me on.

The village of Dalcahue lies on the Chiloé coast about twenty miles from the island's capital, Castro (population 26,000), but accessible only by boat or through high rolling hills over an extremely potholed gravel road. Its frame two-story houses seem maintained more to keep out the wind than for appearance. The village consists of a main drag along the waterfront, and two other parallel paved roads encompassing altogether no more than a sixth-of-a-mile grid. The few fruits and vegetables displayed in front of a grocery shop appear to have come a long way since being picked. Yet Dalcahue is not remote by Chilote standards, since trucks can bump their way in. Two miles across the water a boxy steeple rising above trees marks a village beyond such easy reach. Many such Chiloé communities depend solely on boats.

Hans has referred me to his bait supplier, Pepe Montt Letelier. I expect a muscular peasant chap of the wide good humor seen on other Chilean boats. Instead I find a brisk, educated young man from Santiago, who has set up a business attuned to local standards and settled here with his American wife and five children. Beneath a shock of fine black hair, Pepe wears large wire frame glasses from which his eyes peer with seriousness and curiosity. His voice has cheerful authority. He turns out to be the kind of man more likely to tap his child's rear end fondly than in anger, able to shrug when something breaks, and then to start at once fixing it.

But Pepe is a bold entrepreneur. At thirty-three he owns two well-maintained wooden seiners, the *Elefantes* and the *Fomalhaut,* and shows them off proudly. The former is larger, at nearly fourteen-and-a-half meters (forty-seven feet), than any other in the Dalcahue harbor. Both have sound engines. Both have a deck winch of sorts for the heaviest pulling. The bait *sardinas* that Pepe's boats and others in the fleet deliver to the village pier are salted in his own warehouse with local labor. Pepe runs his company, Los Elefantes SA, with the help of a Chilote, José Arroyo. Pepe handles the boats and the customers, José the paperwork. From their rented office, in a big old wooden house once grand for the island, under the shuddering stomps of a family on the second floor, they employ more than two dozen villagers.

After drinking coffee twice as strong as Norteamericanos like it, I follow Pepe along the waterfront. Beyond a pier and shops stands a roofed pavilion open on the sides, a shelter for boatmen traveling the islands. Inside, a platform of benches surrounds a blackened pit. The platform leads around to an attached outhouse. The planks smell of old sweat and burnt wood. In late afternoon sails appear over the water. The first boat to arrive off the pavilion is a scuffed wooden sloop rigged with gaff-hung mainsail and jib, carrying a deckload of crates. The people aboard—two lean men and one large woman—wear clothing as brown and smudged as the canvas around them. After dropping anchor the men wade ashore through tidal shallows. One of them carries the woman on his back, her skirts tucked around fat legs. She snaps something, sounding both tired and fierce, and the other man hurries back to the boat to fetch a box of provisions.

The woman soon has a fire going in the pit. The pavilion's ingrained odors are replaced by new ones of smoke, sour woolens, and coffee. I ask if I may take a photo. The men face the camera, grinning. But the woman waves her arms and rasps a string of invective that translates roughly to "Hell no, beat it, mind your own business!" Pepe leads me away at once. "Chilote women are very strong-minded," he mutters. "They boss the men. What they say is done."

At 6 P.M. it's time to go fishing. A few hundred feet from the boatmen's shelter—all places in Dalcahue are close to each other—the floating pier rises with the tide. At midday fishing boats bobbed at the pier unattended, but now men are converging. Nobody is boisterous, but they smile as they shake out nets or lean with cigarettes against the cabins, chatting of gear and families (in that order) like fishermen the world over. The boats, all wooden, have comfortable, predictable Latino names: *San Pablo, Kitania, Don Diego, Roxana, Pisces, Don Victor.* They show enough care to have been painted within recent memory. The prows of Pepe's *Elefantes* and *Fomalhaut* jut higher than the others, and their planking looks sturdier.

The boats start their engines—some of them ancient, to judge by their thumps—and leave the pier one by one. As we clear the harbor, we can see at the boatmen's pavilion that several other weathered boats have assembled. One of the sail crews is wading out in water up to their waists. "They must go now or wait ashore," says Pepe. "Seven-meter [twenty-three-foot] tides. Currents up to four and a half knots."

The *Elefantes,* with Pepe and me aboard, travels together with the *Fomalhaut,* each with a crew of six including the captain. It is a clean boat, with no engine smells filtering into the small wheelhouse or the tight berth-and-galley space below. I comment on the roominess: similar boats often crowd steering and living spaces together. Pepe brightens. "You notice this?" he says in English. "I have designed *Elefantes* myself after converting it from an old boat I bought that, yes, had everything together." My interest encourages him. "The engine is 145 horsepower. Reduction one-two-three, an economic velocity. Speed average eight knots." His hands accompany the explanation. His fingers have patches of grease from tinkering with the winch. Chileans of family and education more typically follow the Spanish tradition that expects a gentleman to keep hands clean and leave manual work to peasants.

The wheelhouse holds barely the two passengers, along with the captain Sergio "Pirincho" Mayorga, and the *motorista* Francisco "Pancho" Arroyo (brother of Pepe's assistant José). From below come the other crewmen's easy laughs. They are all young Dalcahue men (skipper Sergio is the oldest at thirty-five), all with families. Soon all hands stand on deck at points from bow to stern, chewing a dinner of hard biscuit and thick-rind ham while peering for signs of fish. We cruise between hilly islands of rolling green. Any ground the least bit level bears rows of crops, while sheep graze on steeper grades. The volcanoes and snowy Andes rise from the far haze. It is a beautiful place at a softening time of day. Nobody seems hurried despite the intentness of the fish watch.

"Seagulls, there," murmur Sergio, Pancho, and Pepe simultaneously. The skipper snaps on the sounder and changes course toward a patch of birds on the water. Other boats head for the same patch, but ours, the fastest, reaches it first. The needle swishing across the echosounder paper records a few smudges identifiable as fish, but not enough to warrant dropping a net. We cruise on. Besides the sounder, a modest one by current fishing standards (no color), we carry a high-frequency radio over which Pepe and the others chat with the skipper of the *Fomalhaut.* These are the only pieces of fishing electronics aboard.

We cruise four hours to reach a bay surrounded by small islands where sardines have schooled in nights past. This is December, late spring with long days, considered a good fishing month throughout Chiloé. At other times fish migrate and boats sometimes need to cruise more than a day to Quellon on the southern part of the island.

Pepe's two boats anchor together. The crews visit as the sky darkens, facing each other with backs against the cabins and boots braced against the rails. The land is close enough that odors of greenery and manure mingle with those of briny water and boat's oils, but our feet have left the land and talk becomes merrier than ashore. It is still boat and family talk, among brothers and cousins who see each other daily and expect to do so (*Dios* willing) for the rest of their lives. Their hair is black and fine, their faces dark-skinned by Pepe's city standards, men from an Indian heritage.

"They're extraordinarily sweet people," Pepe's wife, Rodney, said later. "The lieutenant of *carabineros* in Dalcahue once told me that, even though in Chile military service is seen as good for poorer people since it gives them clothes, food, training, and a chance at a career, military service for Chilotes was a bad thing because it corrupted them, took away that good-natured sweetness."

The rocks and trees along the nearest shore have become a dark mass.

Splash! A silhouetted fish jumps from the water. One more jumper
follows in another direction, but then the water remains still. It doesn't
look promising. By now other boats have arrived to the pock-pock of
engines quickly silenced as anchors drop quietly. By twilight nineteen
sets of lights reflect on the water. The bay is wide enough that the
assemblage seems more companionable than crowded.

Inside the cabin narrow bunks along the sides double as benches
beside a table that can be raised and snapped to the overhead. Everyone
bunches shoulder to shoulder to watch a television screen the size of a
snapshot. The old Beatles movie, *Yellow Submarine,* with Spanish
voiceover (except for the songs) comes in faintly from Castro beyond
the hills. The single low-watt bulb blinks, then goes out. With a flashlight Francisco, the motorista, checks wiring, then replaces the bulb. A
collective "Ahhh," as low brown light fills the cabin again.

Outside it turns black. The time has come for sardines to rise to the
surface in search of feed, and for men to stalk them. Each takes his
station on deck. They start a kerosene lantern but shutter it tightly. So
not to spook the fish, no light shines on any boat except for port and
starboard running lights. Fish betray themselves by stirring phosphorus
in the dark water. Searches are so ineffective in the brightness of a full
moon that seining stops for about ten days each month.

With the sight of land obliterated by night, the small red and green
lights of the fleet move disembodied. It's a time to believe in the folk
creatures of Chiloé Island: *El Caleuche,* a mesmerizingly beautiful ghost
boat manned by fishermen lost at sea, or *La Sirena,* a mermaid who
dances on the beach to lure them to their grief, or even *El Trauco,* the
ugly bent-over fellow who makes girls pregnant while their husbands
are off fishing. Only *La Pincoya,* the lovely seaweed-garbed fertility
goddess of the sea, offers fishermen any benevolence: She has powers to
control the abundance of fish if approached properly, for example with
a smooth rock placed close to shore on which to dance. Does anyone
aboard believe in Pincoya or Sirena? I ask quietly. Uneasy chuckles in
the dark. "Only our grandmothers," says someone.

We cruise, sometimes passing close to other boats but never
touching. Skipper Sergio studies the water temperature, which fluctu-
ates between 11.8° and 12.1° Celsius (52° to 54° Fahrenheit), and
frowns. Sardinas should be around, although a temperature later in
the summer between 14° and 15° would be better. The warmer the
water, the more feed grows to attract fish. Sergio gives his greatest attention to the echosounder. Once the needle makes a significant smudge,

but he shakes his head. Then a larger smudge grows on the paper stroke by stroke, and the sounder begins to beep.

"*Larguen!*" Sergio cries: "Let 'er go!" Dark figures spring into motion. Carlos in the skiff draws one end of the seine away from the boat, then drops it in the water attached to a lighted buoy. Others by the rail pay out the net layer by layer. The boat drives in a wide circle that closes back at the buoy. Pepe the educated owner grabs a plunger and pops it furiously into the water to scare escaping fish back into the seine. Shadows bark quick commands and faces flicker as they pass the shuttered lantern. An exhaust pipe rising from the engine at center deck creates a scorching-hot obstacle in the dark. After the circle has been closed, a small cranky winch helps purse the bottom of the seine, trapping the fish. Now the fish can spook all they please. Someone opens the lantern and its raw light covers the deck.

Time to haul. Purse seining can be done with all sizes of nets, depending on the capacity of the boat and the weight of the catch. The *Elefantes'* seine makes a 650-foot circle 115 feet deep—compared with the *Hurican's* industrial-size, half-mile enclosure worked by two big power blocks. Aboard the *Elefantes,* as still on many village boats the world over, they "siwash"—pull by hand, general practice before the hydraulic power block of the 1950s. The word is probably a corruption of the French *sauvage,* for primitive. Primitive it is, interacting with the water as we lock bare fingers in the web. The half-inch mesh for fish this small accommodates thick fishermen's fingers as neatly as slots. The skipper jumps from his wheelhouse to haul web with the rest. All hands heave in unison with musical grunts. The first handfuls of net over the rail are simply slack, easy stuff. Everybody mutters, without heat. Probably not going to be much of a night, *verdad?* Maybe the fish have already started south? Then the net begins to harden.

Not bad. The set produces ten brailer loads of flapping silver sardines. The *chinguillo*—the brailer—holds about 440 pounds (two hundred kilograms), so this is two tons of fish. They flop into the hold with a satisfying tattoo. The little winch raises them slowly from the water on a rope wrapped around the drumhead and passed through a block on the boat's small boom. At load nine the winch wheezes and the drum begins to slip. Francisco is there even before Pepe. They putter over it. The drum regains its power, but only at half speed. Slowly the next dripping brailerful rises, just barely over the rail, and everyone grabs to swing it across deck to the open hatch. The final chinguillo rises even more slowly.

The set has taken about an hour, and it's now half an hour before midnight. Sometimes the men make as many as seven sets a night trying to fill their eighteen-ton hold. Often two tons must satisfy them. Shutters go back on the lantern and Sergio resumes the search. Pepe and Francisco put their faces into the workings of the winch while one of the others holds a flashlight. Everyone else peers over the water. The lights of other boats slip by, close enough for men to call over the water comparing notes. "Zero for us," reports the *Fomalhaut.* "Your gringo's not such bad luck so far, eh?"

From another: "*Three* tons in our hold. You'd have that much yourself without your gringo aboard."

The size of the nightly catch is definitely of interest, since boat-owners split fifty-fifty with their crews after deducting expenses off the top. Only captains and motoristas receive a guaranteed minimum whatever the boat's luck. During the previous month Pepe's crewmen have each made 400,000 pesos (about $1,200 U.S.: phenomenal pay for a Chilean villager), but sometimes they're lucky to pull 150,000 pesos (or $450 U.S., still better than most nonfishermen in Dalcahue could earn).

Suddenly a large mass appears on the chart, so large that the sounder beeps steadily and the smudge covers the paper down to the twenty-meter depth line. Sergio sucks his breath as he slows the engine and turns. *"Madre Dios,"* he mutters. The boat's abrupt motion is all the signal needed to those on deck. Except for Pepe and Francisco still bent over the winch, everyone takes station. The sounder stops beeping, then begins again as we reenter the mass. An outsider might think that if sophisticated equipment discovers fish, scooping them up follows automatically. What else would be the advantage of modern electronics? But boats and nets must be coordinated in three dimensions, and not everyone is made to be a skipper able to keep track of relative positions between fish and nets.

At Sergio's signal off goes the skiff to set the lighted buoy. As he moves the boat in a circle, the big smudge on the sonar chart slips away. He groans. "Too soon, I set too soon, they're gone!" Suddenly he springs to life. Maybe he can find the patch and set again before they disappear or find their way to other nets. The slightly tense but mild-mannered young captain becomes a madman. He races around the cramped wheelhouse, from the sounder on the starboard wall to the wheel on the port side, maneuvering the boat, barking commands to the bow out the window by the wheel, leaning his whole body out a rear window to scream around the superstructure to the men astern. "Hold the net, don't let it all out. Haul in." He leaps to deck to pull lines himself.

In come the purse lines. All hands at the rail start quick hand-over-hand pulls. After a few laps the net begins to have weight. "*Ole,* something here." The weight increases with each heave. We begin to use our backs, in unison. It feels like tug-of-war with a wall. The net may only have snagged the bottom, except for its springy feel as the mass inside shifts to give up inches. Then the web begins to vibrate against our bare fingers. "*Ole, ole.*" That vibration is the collective thrashing of trapped fish. We heave with grunts in unison, soon sweating. The net tangles in folds around our feet, each fold another small gain from the sea. Talk becomes staccato, only the few words that can ride a shortened breath. Then talk stops altogether.

The vibrations from our prey increase. Then, out on the dark water, the opened lantern catches the silver of fish tails breaking the surface. Suddenly the water explodes into spray. A field of thrashing fish covers the surface. Fish spray and slime leap over the low rail into our eyes. This is no remote machine-harvest. The briny fresh smell of fish enters our nostrils. Their struggle shakes our arms. We're part of their lives and they are part of ours.

Other boats pull near to watch. Faces under bright-colored wool caps stare. "Hey, give us your gringo!"

"Keep your gringo too long and you'll see La Pincoya dance in the wrong direction. Bad luck not to share!"

Off come the hatch covers. We lower the brailer by hand and the skiff man, his boat now tied to the corks, pushes its rusty steel rim into the mass of sardines. Pepe and Francisco, their sweating faces as streaked with grease as their arms, step aside from the old windlass and switch it on. The repaired drumhead turns with a grudging rumble, but it holds the brailer line and steadily raises the first load. The creatures continue thrashing inside as the last of their sea home drips through the meshes. "Ahhh." A crowd watching fireworks light up the sky could not have been happier.

This windlass is not one on which to make great demands. As soon as the brailer bottom reaches the rail, sagging with more than four hundred pounds of fish, we take over by hand and swing it only inches above deck to the open hold. Silver sardines cascade out. They disappear into the depths of the hold, swishing against the fish already there. The brailer rises five times more at the windlass's normal deliberate speed—all the hauling needed for a usual Dalcahue set, but it makes no dent in our present catch. The drumhead begins to jerk and buck, and during the next five brailer loads its speed gradually diminishes. Then a load stops between the water and the rail, and that's it. Everyone jumps to grab the line between the drumhead and the boom, and heaves up the load, while Pepe and Francisco huddle back over the machinery. The sea of fish still in the water remains barely touched. There's nothing for it but to raise each bursting chinguillo hand over hand.

Other boats have stopped watching. Their lights cruise past as they search for equal good fortune, now long past midnight. Overhead the stars shine in a moonless sky, and a chilly breeze blows. By now the fish in the brailer barely twitch, and slime drips from them as much as water. The winch never works again for more than half a pull. The rest of twenty tons come aboard slowly, siwashed all the way. Who minds? The fish in the hold become a peaked mountain. Crewmen take turns easing into the mass to slosh with their boots and distribute the pile. Eventually no corners of the hold remain unfilled. The pile rises above hatch level, then spills on deck. Still we grip the rope and haul up fish, our oilskins and faces slimed and shining with scales.

Pepe and Francisco continue to cluck-cluck over the windlass, holding the flashlight for themselves. "I think that I shall fix this machine for tomorrow night, but shall also buy a new one," Pepe pants with the boldness of prosperity. "Yes, and also I am thinking to buy the first power block in Dalcahue for my *Elefantes*."

By 2:30 A.M. fish slide all over the deck. The *Elefantes* can carry no more without capsizing despite the dead fish remaining in the diminished circle of corks. The *Fomalhaut*, Pepe's second boat, comes over to brail the rest into its own hold. Such is the luck of the chase that they have caught nothing all night.

It ends at last around 3 A.M. By now, winds cold enough to match the distant snow peaks sweep across deck. Everyone prances and some pose waist-deep in fish (the way they've been working) while I take photographs to record the event. It is the biggest haul in memory. On the way home I wrap in a damp blanket and climb into one of the narrow bunks, shivering with chilled sweat. Everyone else, joking quietly, crowds by the little table to cut slabs of cheese and canned meat with their knives. Someone spreads an extra blanket on me solicitously and offers a piece of cheese. Anyone who can bring them such a catch rates looking after.

I remember nothing more until the *Elefantes* bumps gently against the pier back in Dalcahue. A dawn mist hangs over the village. Some of the other seiners are already moored. No other has had our luck. The boatmen's pavilion stands empty, its occupants, including the grumpy fat woman, long departed in their sailing boats. I follow Pepe home. He talks with unabated energy. An old drumhead in the back of his warehouse might fit the windlass better. He's already told Francisco to meet him there in a couple of hours. But soon, why not?, he continues, a power block for the *Elefantes,* the first hydraulic machine on a Dalcahue boat! But, I ask, won't a power block on your *Elefantes* make cousins and brothers on your *Fomalhaut* jealous? "No. Healthy competition."

Pepe has already left the house when I wake at ten and stroll back to the quay. The sun shines brightly and people, none of them crewmen, move everywhere. In the *Elefantes'* hold one man stands waist-deep in fish. He scoops them into buckets and lifts to a man on the pier who empties them into plastic boxes. Others carry the thirty-five-kilo (seventy-five-pound) boxes of fish between them, up the ramp into waiting trucks. Everybody at work grins over the *Elefantes'* luck. Pepe pays them each two and a half pesos a kilo for what they carry. Farther down the road other of Pepe's employees, white with salt dust, carry the baskets of fish up a swaying board from a truck to the raised floor of the warehouse. The chilly interior smells of fish-leather and brine. The men empty the basketfuls onto an open canvas sheet, shovel salt on top, blanket-toss the load until the salt clings to the fish, then stack the fish in rows like bricks. The cured sardines will go to customers like Gringo Schmidt for longline bait.

The sound of heavy objects being moved bounces from a back storage room of the warehouse. Pepe hurries out, wiping rusty hands on his coveralls when a buyer, hunched in a fur-collared coat that declares his managerial status, arrives in his truck to negotiate for a load of bait. José joins them from the office. Pepe talks with friendly attention, but his gaze keeps returning to the recesses of the warehouse. As soon as politeness permits he steps gingerly around the men salting and disappears back into the storeroom. Francisco arrives. They carry out a heavy, rusty winch drum larger than the one on the *Elefantes.* Maybe it will hold where the other failed. They carry it across the road to the beach, discussing how the job should be done. Later that day Francisco changes the drums. The new one works.

That night neither the *Elefantes* nor any other boat catches many fish. Nor the night following, nor the next. What kind of witchcraft did this gringo bring with him, then take back? A year later: "If Chilote men are anything it's adaptable," writes Rodney Montt, Pepe's wife. "They are famous throughout Chile for their seamanship, but they're equally at home as small farmers, etc., ready to turn a hand at anything practical." That is good, since for a long time after our bonanza night the sardines stopped returning in quantity. Pepe postponed any thought of buying his *Elefantes* a power block.

In 1991 the Chilean Congress passed a comprehensive new fisheries law imposing limited licences and quotas, based on the assumption that many of its fisheries were fully exploited. Especially reduced were efforts in mackerel off central Chile, anchovy in the north, and *merluza*, Spanish hake. The mackerel fishery in particular has suffered, although according to Peter Schmidt: "Many think it is much larger than anyone realizes and that a continuous large exploitation will not harm the resource." A new government in 2000 may change the picture.

The story for both Pepe Montt and Hans Schmidt remains ongoing since both remain flexible. In Schmidt's operation, *bacalao*, Chilean sea bass or toothfish, grow slowly and are believed not to reproduce until about age ten. It proved a fragile resource. He diverted his boats to test the waters for *centolla*, a king crab that had appeared on the lines as by-catch, found new stocks, and became the leading Chilean producer. He has now changed venue farther north to Coquimbo where his vessels longline for swordfish, another new-found resource.

After sardines disappeared around Dalcahue, Pepe, intent on surviving with his workforce as intact as possible, sent his boats south to see what they could catch around Quellon at the far tip of Chiloé, and even farther south around the multitudinous small islands of the Chonos Archipelago. They caught enough sardines to supply the needs of local fishermen and pay expenses, but not enough to support the saltery in Dalcahue. Pepe took to processing any fish the boats could bring back. The business has grown. The saltery ("That nasty warehouse," Rodney called it) has become a little processing plant with sixteen employees. Pepe continues to be good for the economy.

Captain Peter Troake, Twillingate, Newfoundland, 1996, age 88. In the background, his grandsons head to their lobster traps in an open skiff. Captain Troake died in late 1997.

Chile, 1990: Crewmembers mend web aboard the seiner *Albimer*, a vessel targeting jack mackerel. Stacked net and corks of seine appear in back. A berth aboard a large ship fishing industrial volume means success and prosperity for local fishermen. Their good humor here reflects it.

Chiloé Island, Chile, 1990: Crewmen of the *Elefantes* gleefully harden the net of a huge sardine catch landed by hand, while, after helping to pull, boatowner Pepe Montt watches.

Chiloé Island, Chile, 1990: Men of the small seiners *Elefantes* and *Fomalhaut* visit while waiting for dark to set their nets.

CHAPTER THIRTEEN

Barefoot on the Java Sea

Indonesia: November 1991 and September 1983

The Chilean fishermen I met had the advantage of young, ambitious bosses willing not only to pitch in at the nets but also to generate action and income. Thousands of other small fishermen in Chile remained as far from the mainstream as ever, putting to sea in mostly wooden boats more colorful than efficient. This in a developed nation with stability at the top. One monsoon season in south India near Madras, I watched an entire fishing village wash away in a debris of mud and corrugated metal—a cycle played out in severe monsoon years that went unnoticed, even nearby. What of such *artisanals* in the third world?

To find out, I crossed the Pacific to Indonesia and talked my way aboard little boats on the Java Sea, an area vastly different from lightly populated Chile. Indonesian fleets must feed millions rather than thousands. The Java Sea, nine hundred miles long, is encircled by several great islands and island complexes of the huge Indonesian archipelago including Java, Sulawesi (formerly called the Celebes), Kalimantan (formerly Borneo), and the Moluccas (formerly the Spice Islands), and by smaller islands such as Bali. Java itself is one of the most overpopulated islands on earth, supporting 1,500 people per square mile, compared with 844 in Japan, 666 in India, 306 in China, 68 in the U.S., 44 in Chile, and 32 in New Zealand.

Around the Java Sea, villages must depend on what they produce themselves. Fishermen-farmers put out daily in basic wooden boats or plant in season. (The monsoon that roughens the sea and makes fishing dangerous fills paddy fields with the necessary water.) Rice, grown on flatlands and mountain terraces, is the staple. Fish provides the major protein, in hauls that range from several-pound dark-meated silvery skipjacks to oily small sardines sun dried by the thousands. The Indonesian government has become wise enough, although it contracts rights in hard currency with foreign fishing interests on more open seas surrounding its numerous islands, to protect the enclosed Java Sea against big efficient trawlers with foreign interests. Only local boats may fish the area. Wisdom was helped by midnight boardings in the 1980s, when villagers murdered fishermen on foreign boats to make their point that not enough existed to go around.

In Sulawesi I ride aboard the twenty-five-foot (eight-meter) wooden *Indahsari*. Bare toes curl into the grain of the planks. The sun dropping near the horizon still radiates steamy heat as the skipper starts a sputtery engine. Up comes the anchor. We bob out slowly over the low waves. Zul Sukiman, one of the younger crewmen, starts singing in a thin, Asian whine that rises at the end of each phrase. *"Sorongi biseanta, sorong sai,"* he begins in Makassarese, one of the two main languages of the Celebes. Push our boat, push together. It has the quick-step cadence of a college cheer: *"So-rong'-gi bee-see-en'-ta"*—full stop and change of rhythm— *"So'-rong sah-ee'."* A crewmate standing opposite sings the next phrase.

A few minutes earlier, back in Borombong village whose tin roofs now receded from sight, the men were playing cards to kill time until the moment to go fishing for the night, seated cross-legged on reed mats and laughing as they shared a single large bottle of local beer. As with all the village houses, built on stilts, the roof beams at the gables extend in a carved X. According to Zul, this denotes the harmony between earth and sky, between temporal and spiritual. Beneath us in the shaded sand under the house, children played and chickens squawked while two women of the house, in faded turbans, shelled beans and joked on their own.

When the shoreline swells have been safely negotiated we hoist sail, a breeze begins to propel the boat from amidships, and the skipper shuts off the engine. Someone starts another song at once. It translates from the Makassarese: "Waves come together, big waves be little. Oh Allah (*Eaule: eh-ah'-uh-leh'*) our boat is small, but give us fish this evening." Bare feet stomp on the deck in unison, to help Allah flatten any rough seas. Zul's voice and the others' caress the wiry grace notes of the melody, which might have sounded tuneless to ears unaccustomed to mullah chants.

These are Makassars. Along with the Burgis, also of south Sulawesi, the Makassars are renowned seafarers. Both peoples have the same features, but they speak languages as distinctly different as Spanish and French. Their regions lie less than fifty miles apart, separated by Ujung Pandang, the Sulawesi capital city formerly known as Makassar. Tell me the differences between the two, I challenge Zul, who speaks both their languages, as well as Bahasa Indonesian and English. "Makassar men are fishermen," he says brightly. "Burgis men are sailors, taking cargo across the Java Sea in big *prahus* with great sails. Oh, beautiful." His look becomes pleased and dreamy as it does also whenever he throws back his head to sing. "But I am Makassar. Makassar men love to sing. Not Burgis to sing."

We fish all night, barefoot, pulling in the net hand over hand. Two of the men in an outrigger skiff light a lantern to attract the fish, and then the main boat lays the seine around the skiff. The singing continues sporadically, especially from the young men. Most songs have minor-key grace notes and trills, and all deal with bereavement for loved ones far away or not yet encountered. Such misery seems to be the general pleasure to judge by wistful smiles. "Makassars are a romantic people, very sad," confides Zul, not unhappily. His uncle and one other aging man in his forties sing less and smile only at the sight of fish thrashing in the net. Their married sons, also in the crew, can play at yearning.

Zul, a man of twenty-five, is not yet married, as other village men would have been for the past five years, because everyone recognized that he has ambitions. He pulls nets with his father and uncle but also attends university in Ujung Pandang whenever he can save 500,000 rupiah ($250 U.S.: 1991 figures) for a semester's tuition.

At dawn, several of the eight men say the first of their five daily prayers, bowing to Allah on the cramped deck. By now we've caught a reasonable number of fish, enough to celebrate with a less-sad song as a bottle of palm wine passes the rounds. Among more than a hundred other boats we head to the *lelang,* the fish auction.

At the roofed auction shed in Ujung Pandang the hulls of other boats have already crowded too tightly around the slippery steps of the quay to permit maneuvering close. We transfer our fish in baskets to a ferry-canoe and wade behind it. Depending on how the breeze blows, the odor inside the pavilion is fresh from the sea or, from the crowded dusty courtyard, stenched with decaying offal. The men arrange their catch artistically by species on the concrete floor, as does everyone else, and the younger crewmen take turns throwing water over it since the heat is already intense. The displays range from big grouper to near-minnows of cobalt blue and yellow. Buyers walk around checking the piles, sometimes making individual deals before the auction begins.

The courtyard leads to the road, part of an esplanade lined by palm trees where pushcart vendors sell hot curries and seafood every night. Drivers of bicycle rickshaws compete noisily with air-conditioned taxis for anyone needing a ride. Zul walks off for a few hours' sleep in a friend's room before classes. The others return by sea to the village. It is only a few miles over water, compared with a two-hour drive on bumpy roads among backed-up vehicles puffing black exhaust. The state of the roads keeps villages isolated. Each man takes home 6,000 rupiahs, about three U.S. dollars. The night's pay is much better than the national average but for perspective, a meal at one of the best seafood restaurants in town (not above two-star) costs 25,000 rupiahs, while the better hotels charge upward of 150,000 rupiahs ($75 U.S.) a night.

I see no starving Indonesians during travels that take me across 1,500 miles of that country's 3,200-mile archipelago, but also no fat ones. The villages are the nation's backbone, housing seventy-five percent of the population. Away from the slums of overcrowded Java they remain low-key places with space between huts for children and chickens to run. From those villages dotting the coastline, boats averaging fifteen to thirty feet long, carrying crews from one man to two dozen, venture from local piers under sail and rudimentary engine power.

In another village, in Bali, 350 miles southwest of Sulawesi across the Java Sea, men fish the same type of hand-pulled gear as the Makassars in craft more gaily painted, but the security of their lifestyle is more tenuous. When I first go fishing with Embli Astara in 1983, his village on Jimboran beach shares the sand with a single small collection of tourist huts. Eight years later the village remains, but now, separated by only a cinderblock wall, stands a hotel that accurately calls itself *Kraton,* Balinese for palace. A tiled path leads under palm trees from a lobby of fairy-tale grandeur to air-conditioned cottages of carved red sandstone. Packloads of tour groups occupy the grounds, connected to the sea only from shaded deck chairs within the compound. An artificial waterfall splashes into a sumptuously curving pool. The rocks of the waterfall rise over the shed where the villagers keep their boats.

Worse, the noise of hammers heralds the construction of yet another kraton, this one hemming in the village from the opposite end.

"Hotels, hotels," Embli grumbles, shaking his head. He is a man who walks erect through the single dirt path of Jimboran village. Born there in 1952, he now raises his children on the same sands. A young son plays with a model of his dad's boat while we talk. Embli's own parents, still young-looking, live a few huts away, as do four brothers and their families. All the men fish. They live modestly in homes built of wood covered with blackening plaster, standing in a single row facing the beach. The two to three rooms contain a minimum of furniture. Tin roofs keep out the rain at monsoon time, while palm trees shade from the driving sun at other seasons. It is not a place to start a tourist's camera shutters clicking except for a little carved Hindu stone pillar where incense curls among bright red flower petals. Flies are everywhere, as well as constant smoke from burning trash that includes debris from the great tourist kraton.

A store the size of a closet sells oil, milk powder, and other basics. Embli urges me inside despite the heat. We crowd onto two chairs in front of a board to share a large bottle of local beer. Faces darken the doorway to look me over. Photos I've brought from my previous visit pass hand to hand as people exclaim over their younger selves. They do not appear to possess other likenesses, despite the proximity to tourist sophistications.

Jimboran follows an easy pattern. The men fish all night and sleep most of the morning. People live outdoors. The women prepare food and talk with bright chatter, while the men mend nets in a section apart. It is a mellow and cheerful place. On the hundred yards of beach between houses and low surf, the women place coconut shells in little sand-pockets to hold arrangements of palm leaves, blossoms, and rice. This keeps the sea spirits happy, but it also expresses the Balinese delight in bright colors and patterns. Beside the nets, the hulls of the catamarans, which serve as skiffs, are painted purple, orange, or blue, embellished with such specifics as a friendly animal eye. The larger boats at anchor have red or brown stripes that sweep along the hull to the prow painted a different color. Little bells top some masts and hang with woven tassels from the rigging.

At dusk an orange sky silhouettes masts as the red sun sinks in the water. Within minutes the sky turns black. Later Embli and his nine crewmen paddle to their boat by lantern light. The light flickers on the bright curlicues of the prow as we draw near and climb aboard the open deck. Embli pulls the whipcord on a cumbersome twenty-two-horsepower engine, and a small propeller at the end of a long shaft churns the water like an eggbeater. With an exhaust-pumping rattle the boat slowly moves. We cruise far enough to sea that the lanterns of Jimboran village disappear, although the illuminations of tourist hotels never leave the horizon.

One of the men climbs the mast as lookout. The mast, cut from a medium-size tree not entirely straight and painted glistening red, white, and blue, has a cross-stick nailed near the top to anchor his leg. "Ah-ah!" someone cries. Phosphorescent gleams betray a school of fish. Embli stops the engine, and in silence, so not to spook the prey, we pass part of the net to a smaller purse boat that has followed us. Embli barks commands in classic skipper fashion until the net is positioned, then joins the rest at the rail to pull. Our bare feet press into the slippery deck as we harden the net hand over hand, then hand-brail the catch.

We seine all night, taking turns on the mast to scout fish. Eventually the air chills under a profusion of stars. The sarongs that the men wind around their heads like turbans while hauling become covers to wrap in for a doze on the open deck between sets. I myself, having anticipated no chill as I sweated ashore in steamy heat, cover as best I can in the little I wear.

At first light we head in. We pass other Jimboran men, in smaller boats that work gillnets closer to shore, returning to unload directly at the village where wives meet them to help. We ourselves go up-beach (on the other side of the newest tourist hotel) where some twenty-five boats our own size assemble daily from several villages. The early sun has already turned hot and it throbs on the brightly painted hulls. Just outside the break point of the mild surf we anchor, nearly scraping the rails of other boats. The catch goes off in baskets suspended on poles. A swell covers one man in the water and nearly swamps his load. Everybody laughs in high spirits, including the man himself.

The baskets of fish continue on shoulder poles to a high point on the sand where a thatched roof shelters a scale. Despite the early hour people have gathered in numbers. The basket men run a gauntlet of women and old men who pick out fish for themselves without challenge. Embli stands by the scale with pencil and a scrap of paper. He now wears his sarong wrapped around his waist, no mere net puller who shouted and sweated but a dignified captain. The fish go from the scales to the back of a truck where a man with a shovel ices them for the jog over rural roads to a co-op fish plant.

Back at the village, the men nap on cots or mats in their huts while outside the women and children lead their own noisy life among the flies and chickens. By afternoon the men have returned to their shaded spot around the nets. But one youth, who pulled nets all night long with his father, instead strolls past the wall to work for wages at the newest hotel. How long will he, or the rest of Jimboran's youth including Embli's son, bother with the uncertainties of fishing?

It is a question that fishing fathers ask all over the world.

CHAPTER FOURTEEN

Unseen Forces

It was reassuring to join others stamping bare feet on the deck of the little wooden Indahsari to help Allah calm the Java Sea. And the dark night in Dalcahue with gliding red-green lights and phosphorescent water had seemed right for the wickedly dancing La Sirena to lure us to the rocks.

Those who live to be old fishermen never take the sea for granted as they work on deck. Most also have a respect, admitted or not, that goes beyond the practical. The great dark pile-driving waves that rise above the wheelhouse still call the shots. Coolly used training, experience, knowledge, and equipment keep the killer at bay. Yet if ever an unseen Force has a medium through which to manifest Itself to puny man, to prove superior powers now and then, it is the ocean.

Fishermen have a literature of prayers, cabals, and jinxes that vary from place to place but serve a common purpose to cope with that they cannot control. Who is to disprove it, that the Unseen can be offended or urged by wrong words to do harm, or that an unguided action can disarray the order of things.

Spanish fishermen may cross themselves in a dangerous situation, but—according to William Warner in his 1983 book about the big-trawler era, *Distant Water*—they consider "priest" their most taboo word (to do with last rites?). "Snake" and "fox" follow. Spilling olive oil can harbinge enough ill fortune to make a captain return to port, while predicting the weather is an act of arrogance that might bring down the worst of storms.

Cajoling the gods for fair seas goes back at least to the ancient Greeks. Agamemnon sacrificed his daughter Iphigenia at divine behest so his ships could sail to Troy (a bad domestic decision, it turned out). Italian fishermen in Bristol Bay, Alaska, in the old sailing days before

1953 always added their penny under the mast before stepping it up for the first time each season, careful not to remove the pennies of others before them. The Gloucester *Fishermen's Own Book* of 1883 notes that a horseshoe nailed to the mast wards off witches, while sticking a knife in the after side of the mainmast brings a fair wind. Among acts that invited bad luck a century ago: a partly filled bucket of water on deck, driving nails on Sunday, and leaving port on Friday. Friday midnight, the start of Saturday, still sees dockside activity from Kodiak to New Bedford.

"I've got no superstitions," declares Jack Troake, lifetime Newfoundland fisherman. "You make your own luck." But he adds that his dad taught him, as a boy first on the boats, "Never turn around against the sun." No examining the why of this. Unless emergency dictates otherwise, Jack turns his boat always to the right. "That's the way the sun travels around the world, right-handed. It's as much me 'abit as saying grace. Like me gran'fadder said: 'When you set to the table, always honor your grub, boy.' Those two things I never forget to do."

Among the bastions of older fishermen with Norwegian names and accents, a green-painted hull awakens a boat's desire to head toward grassy shore. And a boat with a hatch cover replaced upside down might decide to roll over to point its cover back in the right direction. An umbrella invites bad weather, and a black bag aboard brings with it the need for a doctor. This is only the beginning among the oldest Norwegians. Don't even think of letting a female cross the gangway. (Picture a grim-faced Norwegian purging the deck of an unavoidable female visitor, just as she leaves, by pacing a grid on deck with a roll of burning newspaper. I've noted this manly precaution also in Taiwan, where female dock workers, who work as hard as the men, automatically stop short of the ship's rail.) Best not to wash windows on the boat just before going to sea: that can invite a storm. And don't say "horse"—nobody likes to explain a taboo, which might in itself upset the balance, but as near as I can gather, horses bespeak land. (The dean of Kodiak king crabbers, the late Oscar Dyson, carried this to the point of allowing no cowboy boots aboard his *Peggy Jo.*) Young Olsens and Nilssens pooh-pooh all this but they still, some whistling pointedly, watch how they replace a hatch cover.

Alaskan Indians fishing wild Lituya Bay, according to fisherman-author Joe Upton, have a care for the monster Kah Lituya who lurks "forever wrathful over the advances of man." Village boats from Vietnam to Indonesia, and even in parts of the Mediterranean, have eyes painted on the bow to guide them in the dark.

Once I rode a Japanese fishing ship and we did so well that the wheelhouse radio crackled with urgent invitations from other boats to host the "famous American fisherman." When I left, the vessel's catch returned to normal, and I learned years later that my presence had become a kind of legend. And, of course, what of that spectacular Chilean Dalcahue haul with Gringo McCloskey aboard? But this credit stuff can backfire in case of misfortune, and I want no part of it. A Bering Sea crabber I once rode later capsized, as did a tuna boat in New Zealand. I came closest to being an immediate Jonah on a Bristol Bay gillnetter when, on the run, I committed the ultimate error. Knowing better a thousand times, I replaced a hatch cover upside down. It challenged the most observed superstition of them all, since in practice an ill-covered hatch might indeed leak in heavy seas. Fortunately I was with young Americans who shrugged it off (though gravely), while the boat never stopped catching its share and never came to harm. Maybe the gods shrugged it off also, watching how much the mistake troubled me.

Young fishermen these days take their relationship with the hidden world more lightly than earlier generations. I've even heard some of them whistle in the wheelhouse, known to be a surefire way to bring on a storm. I myself, a compulsive whistler on land, find it a severe discipline at sea to keep lips unpuckered. I learned this one the old-school way. When first I went to sea in 1948, still a teenager, I started to whistle during my maiden trick on deck, happy in my good fortune to have begun seafaring. Within seconds a big hand gripped my shirt around the neck and raised me a few inches. "What the hell you doin', kid? *You don't whistle.*"

"Why not?" I gasped.

"Because you fuckin' don't!" My deck boss, an American, would not voluntarily admit what even the stupidest sonofabitch knew about the correlation between whistling and typhoons. He did invite me to be slammed across the deck, and maybe into the water, if he ever heard me whistling aboard again. It was quick education. (I learned something else that trip when a twelve-foot maverick wave swept across deck during work: Flatten fast and grab something, as did the others. I braced into it like meeting a jolly wave at the beach, and but for an intercepting stanchion that merely fractured a cheekbone, my name would now grace a forgotten cenotaph.)

Unseen forces may be beyond human control, but not necessarily beyond reach through faith. At Sunday service in the tiny Pentecostal church on Square Islands, Labrador, fishermen able to endure cold and cruel waters grovel like mice and sob out their sins to the Great Fisherman. A fisherman's family in India can maintain altars side by side to the Virgin Mary and to Ganesha the Hindu elephant god in their hut, and feel no conflict of interest. Shoreside grotto Virgins await South American fishermen just off the boats from Pucusana, Peru, to Zapallar, Chile, and on down the coast. Blessing the fleet remains a profound part of boat-related festivals especially in communities with fishermen of deep Catholic ancestry. Coastal churches with maritime motives fill on Sundays. Even Protestant hymnals have a smudged page at:

> *Eternal Father, strong to save*
> *Whose arm has bound the restless wave*
> *Who bids the mighty ocean deep*
> *Its own appointed limits keep*
> *Oh hear us when we cry to Thee.*
> *For those in peril on the sea.*

In late 1997 three Mexican fishermen were lost at sea for fifteen days, surviving on raw fish and a bottle of water. Then an El Niño–induced hurricane blew their dinghy to shore and rescue. Don't think they detachedly credited nature for their salvation.

A Japanese boat I rode to the North Pacific squidding grounds carried its temple-blessed *omomori* in a special shrine, while for extra measure a Shinto priest blessed the ship in homeport just before sailing. Hindu fishing villages in India and on Bali, constructed of nothing more solid than mud or scraps of plywood and sheet metal, are centered around an altar to Shiva or Vishnu. In Muslim Java, the mullah's midday chants from little tin-domed mosques stop men briefly from delivering their fish, while at sea with the chant unheard the work stops when the sun's position indicates prayer time. The sultan of Jogjakarta, on Java, once annually presented a ceremonial coconut to the sea goddess *Njai Loro Kidul.* A few years ago during an El Niño episode, *anchoveta* vanished off the coast of Peru, leaving a huge industry and its dependent communities destitute. Then suddenly, in place of *anchoveta,* appeared equal masses of *sardinas* able to be caught and processed with the same fleet and plants. "God is Peruvian," declared those affected, happy in their grotto Virgins.

In Taiwan the goddess of fishermen, *Ma-Tsu,* presides over some four hundred temples. I've seen her presence also in Chinese communities from China to Singapore and Vietnam, but nowhere with the intensity of Taiwan. Ma-Tsu has interceded for fishermen braving winds and typhoons since long before engines replaced sail and oar. According to the history of the faith, her mortal birth occurred to fishing parents in A.D. 960. A devout Buddhist, she revealed saintly qualities from the start. Her childhood abounded in those tales of miracles deemed necessary to establish divinity, and when she died at twenty-eight the miracles, especially sea-related ones, were said to continue. Fishermen soon began to pray for her protection. In 1684 the emperor of China declared Ma-Tsu officially Empress of Heaven, a title she retains. Modern Taiwanese fishermen still enjoin and consult her, even as they stock their wheelhouses with the latest in color fishfinders.

Ma-Tsu's temple in the fishing town of Tsinda, an hour's drive from Kaohshiung on the southwest coast of Taiwan, stands high enough to be seen from the water. At a distance, a lacework of carvings races in silhouette around its curved roofs. Up close the temple dominates every other structure, rising at the end of a square, set back from the bustle of bicycles and trucks. High white steps lead up to the interior. Five-story pagodas flank carvings and gold designs. Rampant gaily painted dragons dart from the roof like flames. Nothing else in the town of tile roofs has remotely the same presence.

I mounted the steps with my host, Quo Ming Tsong, a fisherman and head of the local fisheries association. We passed through big carved doors into a smoky interior pulsating with golds and reds. At a side altar a man in flip-flops knelt before a gleaming gilded figure and patiently tossed two curved pieces of wood onto a mat. The pieces landed repeatedly both up or both down. "He wishes advice," Mr. Quo explained through an interpreter. But Ma-Tsu would only be prepared to give it if the two pieces landed one up, one down. It was remarkable given the averages, for one inclined to doubt, how consistently the pieces refused to land other than in tandem.

The image of the sea goddess watched impersonally from an altar of urns and gilded ormolu. Her face, as in other Ma-Tsu temples, was an auspicious black. The gold in her robes gleamed under bright lights. After centuries of divinity she had evolved beyond the humble fisher lass, hardly ready any more to scale a fish (any more than the Divine Carpenter appears ready to saw a board in most Christian statuary).

In a bare upstairs room away from the glitter, two young men in sport shirts, whom Mr. Quo identified as fishermen, stood before a table. They held the legs of a wooden stool. An old woman and a boy stood to one side backed by three men, while a serious man who appeared to have a priest's authority stood opposite. The stool began to wriggle in the fishermen's hands. Their arms, veined with the muscles of net-pulling, seemed incapable of holding it steady. Suddenly the stool reared above their heads as if grabbed by invisible forces. The men held firm and a supernatural tug-of-war commenced. Sometimes the stool careened down to slam on the table. Whenever it hit, the authoritative man recorded the position with brushed Chinese characters on a square of paper printed with a red border. The stool would bounce out several taps before flying off again. The priest's notes accumulated. After twenty minutes the two fishermen, now sweating and breathing heavily, gave over the rampant stool to two equally strong-looking comrades. The spirits on the other end showed no sign of tiring as quickly as humans.

Had the old woman asked about the boy's career? Or did they inquire the fate of some fisherman dear to them all, lost to the sea as are many Formosa Strait fishermen each year? We moved on as the spirits continued to chatter, to the temple's rooftop incinerator. Looking out above tiled roofs to the sea, Mr. Quo burned a packet of spirit money. The money, on thin paper crudely printed, curled and blackened quickly in the flames, and the smoke conveyed up the money's spirit essence for the use of gods who lived in a practical heaven of trade and barter.

Downstairs, the man with the curved blocks had finally gained Ma-Tsu's attention. With the blocks having landed on opposite sides, he was free to pick an "advice stick" from a tall urn with the goddess guiding his choice. The stick had a number. The questioner presented it to an old man with authority among several quietly playing a board game. The old man matched the number to one in compartments along a wall and handed over a thin printed paper. The goddess had directed answer X. The man donated a sum and left, apparently satisfied.

Next day I went fishing aboard one of the Tsinda boats, and later we delivered ashore into a busy, noisy auction shed. Some thirty other boats lined the quay in various stages of offloading. Most, like ours, had a tree branch attached to the mast for good fortune (a dramatic reversal of the Norwegian proscription against land-based objects on board). There on an adjacent deck, washing down after delivery, stood one of the young stool trancers. He glanced from under the straw coolie hat he wore against the sun, and nodded shyly.

There's reassurance in sharing the blame with higher powers, but accidents are tangible, and the foolkiller waits. It makes great sense to keep the hatch cover right-side up, and there begins the crossover into practicality. A responsible skipper and crew anticipate harm: They maintain engine and machinery against failure under pressure; they invest in gear for survival and fire-fighting, then conduct drills to know how to use it on the run. They stay alert, take only calculated chances.

"An old skipper told me this one time, back on the old schooners," recalls Newfoundlander Jack Troake. "He said, 'You know, son,' he said, 'safety is good seamanship and common sense, mostly the latter.' I remember, and that was a lot of years ago." On the other side of the continent: "It just amazes me how a lot of people don't have common sense," says Al Burch, trawlerman-owner of the pioneer Kodiak draggers *Dawn* and *Dusk*. For both men, each a healthy survivor with decades of fishing experience, unseen forces have nothing to do with the cause and effect of, say, footing a net or chain in the zip of paying out, or stepping into the bight of a line in motion, or wearing floppy clothes near a turning winch, or leaving slick oil spilled on deck, or standing in the snapback path of a cable under tension, or straddling a cable that might whip. Or, while the boat eases into berth, putting a leg or hand over the rail to invite its being crushed if the rail scrapes the pier.

Like alert skippers everywhere, Al Burch adds his own boat rules gathered empirically. He outlawed earphones in his wheelhouse after losing a $30,000 net when a crewman on watch during a dull tow failed to hear a chain snap. "And there could be a Mayday on the radio that you'd miss." In fact he deplores loud music—on some decks pounding rock eases the long cold and wet labors—because it blocks all sounds of warning. Among other routine precautions, Burch guards against storing cardboard where water might mush it against a drain. And he cautions crewmembers coming to the galley for a quick snack to take care starting a cold stove, since the heat can build to incendiary levels.

Fire is dreaded at sea above all other disasters. There is nowhere to go. Fire extinguishers, smoke alarms, care when welding around fuel, drills so each man knows his immediate duty—it all matters.

"One thing I tell my guys," says Burch, "and I'm dead serious: you don't pee over the side of the boat in the dark. If you fall in, nobody hears or sees, and that's it. More kids have been lost that way. If the bathroom's in use and you've gotta go, then pee on deck."

Jack Troake's rules for safety start with checking everything large and small before leaving the pier, and again before the return. "Even if it's calm as a clock, everything best kind and sun shinin', might not be for long. You break a shackle or turnbuckle in forty-knot winds, now you got a problem. Batten down and secure everything that's open to the ocean: 'atches, gear, cargo. And keep listening to the weather forecast. Know the limitation of your vessel, what you can do wid' it. Seas breakin' on deck, I don't mind that, long as everything's secure. You make a policy on board, then you don't have to speak about it no more. When everybody knows the policy, they go do it."

Thor Olsen of the Kodiak-based *Viking Star* equates checking everything from fuel filters to rusty cables, as "being professional." The first safety rule that came to his mind when asked: "Never give the wheel to someone you don't trust."

Joey Testaverde, of the seventy-seven-foot dragger *Gloucesterman* out of Gloucester, has crews so ingrained with fishing culture that they take safe work conduct for granted, from "no drugs or booze" to survival suits and tested life rafts. As for superstitions. "Ohh, . . . " he laughs, not sure where the question will lead. "I don't believe in bad luck. You make what happens happen: destiny. Any superstitions I do, me and my brothers, we don't really believe in them, stuff we just carry on from our father, that he learned from his father. Bunker plate upside down and they say the youngest person on the boat might get hurt, maybe die. A thing if you turn bread upside down on the table it's bad luck. Bad if birds get trapped in the boat. They had a million of 'em, stuff they grew up on." Joey, a big man, throws out his arms. "Not that I believe it. But—I don't do it anyway."

And, best remember to say grace, and always turn the boat with the sun.

Some Positive Precautions

Monitor weather reports
Keep knives sharp for emergencies
Secure equipment not in use
Trail a permanent rope or ladder over the side for man overboard
Install alarms and keep them activated
Hold regular drills
Check all gear from rigging to engines before putting to sea
Clear debris that might block scuppers or pump filters

How Not to See Land Again

Invitations to Harm
Maintain engine and machinery poorly
Leave spilled oil on deck
Work in rough seas and high winds
Work in poor or no light
Stand watch with distractions
Load deck unevenly
Install low rails
Leave ladders loose or wobbly
Leave hatch open
Fail to contain a fire
Ignore emergency drills
Fatigue, fatigue, fatigue

Easy Accidents on Deck
Place foot in bight of line
Lift a load carelessly
Step into path of out-of-control object
Catch loose clothing, hair, or jewelry in machinery
Fall through open hatch

Ways for the Sea to Grab You
Tangle a limb in a line or net zipping out
Stand in path of rogue wave
Draw a bucket of water from the sea while underway
Urinate over the side
Run on a slippery deck
Step in front of a free-swinging block
Work near shifting or poorly battened gear
Roughhouse or fight
Work alone on deck
Use drugs or alcohol

Most Efficient Way to Die Overboard
Work without a float vest or jacket

CHAPTER FIFTEEN

The Unforgiving Bar

Greymouth, New Zealand

July 1984

The work might be dangerous—hovered over by unseen forces—but fishermen, most of them, do seem to have as many lives as a cat. Their wildest barroom yarns of escapes are only part fantasy. The safety devices of the 1980s and 1990s have helped save enough lives—several in fact of my own shipmates—to make modern fishermen more cocky than those of other generations. But it doesn't always work.

The night in New Zealand I board the *Golden Star* with Ian and Mike, to fish by handline for four-hundred-pound bluefin tunas, we were all too involved in the businesses of life—radio banter, Ian's prospective new boat, the horses at Westport—to worry about the twists of Nature.

After oystering far south in New Zealand's South Island, I have traveled north from Invercargill through rainy mountainscapes for twenty hours on four separate buses to reach Greymouth. It was an informal trip. Now and then the drivers stopped to shove newspapers into an isolated mailbox, or to deliver a package into the hands of someone waiting by a sheep fence, bundled against the July winter rain. The towns we passed through were distinguished more by misty mountain backdrops than by architecture, except for monuments of British colonial pretensions.

In Greymouth the rain slacks but a chilly breeze blows across the piers. The outlines and lights of fishing boats move in the dark. It happens that this is high tide, when boats can return to port or depart safely across the bar. The Greymouth harbor entrance has a reputation. Open sea lies just beyond the rocks at the Grey River's mouth, and the water seems never still. Later, when I watch from the breakwater, a southerly breeze blows hardly at all yet lifts spray off swells two feet high. "It's when a westerly blows, and the waves it makes hit the river's current, that's when," says an old man, a retired fisherman, who happens to be watching also. "Then, mate, it's a tempest at harbor's mouth, and you don't want to be there." Sometimes the rolls are heavy enough to keep fifty-foot boats locked in harbor for a month at a time. But few large sheltered harbors exist along the northwestern part of South Island's coast, so fishermen deal with what they have at Greymouth.

Greymouth, population eight thousand, is a utilitarian fishing town with scenic overviews. Houses along the hills face level waterfront. Mountains and a rocky coastline isolate it except for a northern coastal road to the ports of Westport and Nelson. A highway and railroad connect it through a pass to the major city of Christchurch, miles away. On the busy wharf at the Westfleet Fishermen's Co-Op, you have to dodge forklift trucks moving fish from boat holds to pierside bins to the filleting and freeze plant. A slate outside a fresh-seafood market shows the variety of the area's winter catch: sole, turbot, grouper, and tarakihi (the four most expensive, in that order); skate and squid (the two cheapest); as well as hoki, snapper, star gazer (a nicer name for monk-fish), lemon fish, red cod, blue cod, ling, wharahou, silver kingfish, and flounder. Not listed, whether from absence this day or because it has all gone for export, is tuna, the target of my trip.

Fishing for the quality-obsessed Japanese bluefin tuna market requires special equipment. Prior to leaving, the *Golden Star*'s crewmen spend the day in a work shed adjacent to the piers, building long aluminum "coffins" reinforced by wooden frames, in which to quick-chill the big tunas when they come aboard. The boxes need to be strong enough to hold a fish of several hundred pounds along with a slurry of ice. Everyone pitches in with shears and hammers, including Ian Colville the skipper, and owner Tom Fishburn.

Fishburn, a thickset, weather-burned, cheerfully gruff man in his forties who wears a ribbed blue watch cap wherever he goes, is cred-ited with pioneering the local fishery for bluefins. He has fished all his life, like his father and grandfather. In the early 1980s, testing rumors of the price the Japanese would pay for fresh quality, he went with an advisor from the Fishery Board to land a bluefin and explore the market. "Then," according to Phil Prendergast, in his sixties the patri-arch of active local fishermen, "Tom helped fellows get started who wanted to join him." It became a major area fishery. Fishburn now manages three boats and a supply base that keep him generally ashore.

We load the newly built coffins aboard the seventy-five-foot *Golden Star* as the late afternoon sky darkens. While waiting for high slack I find a warm and noisy pub. Mugs line a shelf, and photographs of fishing boats hang on the walls. Most of those inside wear the boots and woolens of men from the piers and boats. I order a mahogany-colored draft. Before I have finished, New Zealand hospitality being what it is, two other mugfuls stand alongside it. The men themselves, however, are too preoccupied with talk of fish business to do more than throw a friendly question to a stranger before reimmersing themselves in the main topic.

Ian Colville's pregnant wife, Trish, and small son wave us off in the dark despite rain. The *Golden Star* crosses the harbor bar at high slack, and takes a dip as the bow pushes into conflicting currents. Open water is mildly rough, and lights from other boats leaving on high water sometimes disappear in troughs. Ian chats in rough good humor by radio with several fellow-skippers. Only twenty-six, he is considered one of the most promising young skippers of the Greymouth fleet, according to Prendergast. He captains the *Golden Star* for Fishburn but by next season expects to have his own boat.

The boat carries two crewmen. Mike Tinnelly, Ian's age, grew up next door. They know each other's jokes almost before hearing them, and banter rapid-fire. Brian Topliss, at seventeen, has fished less than a year. While not subdued, he listens more than talks when the two shipmates nine years his senior get going. Ian owns half shares in a pacer that races at Westport, and he loves to bet nearly as much as to fish. As for yarns, they have in me a fresh audience. A while back during albacore season, begins Ian, a sudden storm caught them. All the other boats had gone in earlier. "The Greymouth bar, the gate was closed, eh? Hell of a big roll. So we sat there and rode it out." He has youthful confidence, gruff rather than cocky, with head tilted back in a characteristic pose. "But, next day, we got straight on to fishing. Had one of our better trips, and no one else could get out for the next twenty-six hours; lucky to get out then."

Mike speaks of the time in 1978 when he and Ian fished together aboard a boat named the *Kowhai*. "Remember, mate?" he says brightly, then turns to me. "A narrow escape we had when she sank off Barrytown." Ian busies himself with his radar and makes no reply.

Once the boat reaches open water, Mike and Brian alternate tricks at the wheel and a nap in the bunks below, while skipper Ian settles into a cubicle with blankets just behind the wheel. I wake at 4 A.M. to a chopping sound as the boat rolls easily. The engine noise has diminished to a hum. On deck, in the dark, Brian stands with a cleaver cutting fish on the rail for chum. Chunks of tails, bodies, and heads sink, their scales momentarily glinting from the deck light before black water closes around them. Farther forward, Mike sorts fishing lines and readies one of the coffins, while Ian in the wheelhouse studies the markings of his echo sounder.

Down to business. We bait hooks surprisingly small for the size they are meant to catch. Each hook is attached to the line by a leader or "trace" several meters long that has a one-hundred-kilogram (220-pound) test. Each line is wound around a big spool. Over go the hooks, cast in a high arc, and the spools bounce on deck as the line pays out. With the boat adrift, the water pulls the lines until they disappear in the dark. The depthsounder reads 340 fathoms, but the fish will be feeding only in the first few fathoms of the water column.

"Don't wrap that line around your hand now, mate," Mike cautions me. "Let it rest in the open palm."

We stand passive with the lines on top of our palms, and wait. The deck rocks gently. Now and then someone secures his line and chops more hoki for chum. Mike's bait-chopping has more style than Brian's. He holds the fish out over the water and slices through the air, leaving no mess on the rail to be cleaned.

"Got to keep the chum to 'em," Ian tells me.

It might be midwinter in July, in a latitude that in the Northern Hemisphere would have required heavy woolens, but light hooded jackets suffice. The talk flows in New Zealander accents with a Cockney cast that jumps some syllables. Mike, lean and bearded, is the bright presence, ready always with a quip. When a fishhook snaps from the water to lodge in a stay, he shinnies up monkey-style to release it. Brian defers to his senior crewmates. He is sweet-natured, ready to laugh at anything, still boyish. His pleasure ashore, he tells me after friendly prodding, is his motorbike: two of them in fact.

Ian is less voluble. He already has the worried quietness of the man on whom rests the responsibility. His moustache has the bushy presence of authority, and his eyes penetrate under a cool frown. Although he holds a line and works on deck with the rest (one suspender of his yellow rainpants always hangs loose over a woolly gray sweater), he also slips into the wheelhouse often to check his sounder for the blips that might betray big fish. Sometimes he barks with a half smile at Brian, who takes it in good cheer. Mike says Ian is the season's top fisherman in the co-op. Ian takes fishing seriously; it has been his occupation and preoccupation for a decade, since leaving school at sixteen to go to sea. He passed his coastal skippers' ticket after only three years, so that since age nineteen, except for a year on deck in Australia to enter its prawn fishery, he has commanded his own fishing boat. Ian notes it with quiet pride—twenty-six and seven years a skipper—as he stands with head thrown back and eyes half closed.

During a run between grounds, after Ian snaps a bit at Brian: "The skipper's always more on it than the others," he tells me apologetically. "You've got the responsibility. Never leaves you. When everything gets down at night, crew can sleep. But you yourself, you get up, you know, up and down all night, checkin' things. Then if the fishing's bad, that's the worst. Your crew, they can want to go home, even leave. You've got to keep their morale up, make 'em keep at it, even though you want to say 'bugger this' and go home yourself."

After Ian's year on deck in Australia, the shrimping company put him in charge of a seventy-three-foot trawler and he became their top catcher. His wife, Patricia, sometimes rode aboard and cooked. They remained in Australia for five years, flying home between seasons. "Then Trish returned to Greymouth at seven months pregnant to be with our folks." Shortly, with the aid of a low-interest New Zealand Rural Bank Loan, Ian would take possession of his own forty-five-foot *Galaxy*. He produces a photo. Buying a $90,000 NZ (about $50,000 U.S.) boat will bring a new set of problems, of course. "Pull your socks up and watch what you spend, I s'pose, and put in plenty of days at sea. Can't afford to get sick. If you can get a good year under your belt, not so bad. If the engine doesn't break down, that sort of thing that eats up your money while it uses up fishing time." A new alternator aboard the *Golden Star*, for example, has cost Tom Fishburn $1,200. "But, I don't think I could do anything else but fish. When the weather cracks up and I end up with two weeks at home, I get fidgety and niggly. Don't think I could handle a shore job."

Bluefin handlining is a waiting game. Unlike fisheries where the crew can break while the gear does the work, we hold the lines constantly. It makes for lots of conversation on deck. Mike too found his way across the Tasman Sea to Australia. He fished for prawns off the desolate far north coast of Northern Territory. It was different than fishing out of Greymouth, where a man can have a life ashore. The Aussie boats went out for three months at a time. "Not really bad, you got used to it. No booze on board, probably good, you put it out of your mind." They cruised off places with nothing more ashore than aboriginal missionary stations. Then they'd come to Darwin. "A pretty little town. Plenty to drink. We'd have a rowdy. Girls mud-wrestling at the bars, all that sort of thing. And the fellows, for bets you know, we'd go into a live-tank of crabs, those with big nippers like a lobster? Wearing nothing but shorts. You'd try to tie down their bloody nippers before they clamped on you. Drunk of course, wouldn't do it otherwise. A good rowdy. Aussies know how. Different life than here in Greymouth."

Young Brian listens with the attentiveness of a fellow ready for adventure across the water himself. (He's told me privately that he "might have a go" at enlisting in the Navy.) All at once his line gives a pull. "Got one," he announces simply, and focuses full attention on the thick cord zipping overboard across his gloved open palms. The spool clatters on deck as the line unwinds. A big fish is off and running.

The fish must be played. Brian allows him to run as long as the force is strong enough to snap the line, while keeping a steady drag to tire him. The tuna's underwater dash shows on deck as a line taut enough to be plucked like a banjo string. The instant the fish pauses, Brian pulls in. The fish gathers spirit for a second run, and the line pays out again. Unlike a sportsman, who can work his catch *mano-a-mano* for hours if he chooses, Brian has no more than eleven minutes to bring the catch to deck. Fighting, the big fish would generate enough body heat to start cooking its own meat, making a B- or C-grade product for the Japanese. After all the waiting, the intensity of the work has to be explosive.

The others shovel ice from the hold into one of the coffins. With gaffs, we line the rail as the shining, blue-glinting body of the fish surfaces. He still emits spasms of energy, swimming slowly in a half-circle, but the fight has ended. Our gaff hooks drive into his head as the line pulls him alongside, and with the shouts that men need to heave a heavy load, up over the rail he comes.

"Three hundred fifty pounds, I'd judge," declares Ian.

The next push: reach the backbone and stop the heat. Mike's knife slices into the fish to bleed it along each fin (the Japanese also reject tuna meat with blood), as Ian spikes its head for a quick kill to prevent thrashing. Mike cuts the gill plates, then opens the stomach and rips loose the intestines. Brian inserts a hose that gushes cold seawater into the opened belly. Mike tears out the gills and stomach as a unit and tosses it on deck. The heart within the mess is still beating.

"Not over the side!" cautions Ian as I step in to help. "Gills in the water spook other fish."

It all happens with the intense concentration of a blood rite. Each step is precise and defined, and within minutes of the tuna's arrival on deck we have dropped its gutted and gilled carcass into the ice slurry and Mike is packing ice into the stomach cavity against the backbone. Japanese prices give great incentive for action.

The sun rises. We have left the sight of shore, but the snowy mountains some fifty miles away catch pink gleams of light. Mike cooks a breakfast of pancakes and sausage—served on deck along with Ovaltine and animal crackers to keep us going—as the rest give the lines renewed attention. But chum as we might, no other fish strikes. We hold lines for another six hours. Then a fishing buddy announces on the radio that a Japanese trawler a few miles away is preparing to haul in. Ian tells us to reel in as he starts the engine. Why chum when a multiton cod end of bottomfish will scatter scraps of fish everywhere? "Tuna get used to trawlers," says Ian, "just like a pack of dogs gets used to good food."

Big Japanese trawlers need to search farther for catch following the 200-mile declarations. New Zealand in 1984 suffers them to fish as part of a joint venture, since the Kiwi nation has not yet developed a fleet large enough to exploit its own deepwater stocks. The foreigner is useful for our present purpose. Ian and Mike remember, though, that only a half-dozen years before, a small inshore fisherman could drag up eighteen cases of sole where now he'd be lucky to get three. And, when longlining for grouper and ling, the 150 to 180 hooks that were all they once needed have become a thousand and more hooks for fewer fish. "It's these big draggers that did it."

Near the high black steel hull of the *Koyo Maru No. 2* are other boats of our own size, wooden-hulled like ourselves, bobbing expectantly like pups waiting to be fed. The warps aboard the Japanese ship vibrate under the tension of haulback. Crewmen in hard hats watch us from the high bow, fishermen of a different life, but we all wave. Eventually a huge trawlerbag floats up astern in the gray chop, and seabirds pounce over it wildly. Tons of fish bulge against the meshes. We throw over our baited hooks as do all the other boats. The effort brings nobody a tuna. "Too many boats," Ian declares. "All our noise splits up any group of bluefins under us. Intelligent fish? Oh very. If things don't suit 'em, if anything's not in their favor to bite, you'll see 'em swimming around with four or five hunks of bait in the water, they just won't take it. Where a normal fish—a shark or anything—they're so easy to catch with chum."

Ian cruises, slowly in order to pick up signals on his sounder. He interprets some large smudgy blips to be tuna following the churn of our propeller, and slows further to make sure they keep up. "They associate screw noise with bags of fish coming up, you see," he explains, and sends Brian on deck to chum. "Just keep a steady dribble of bait, keep 'em interested." But we lose them (if we ever had them). Ian shuts down and waits, hoping they'll find us. When the sounder continues to show empty water, Ian heads to another area he knows. He chats with other boats, and occasionally one comes alongside for a friendly exchange of shouts, but he tries to fish at least three miles from anyone else.

We fish throughout the day and into the night, catching a big fish now and then, although the periods between amount to hours. One gets away. I help chum, gaff, and ice, but my own line remains slack. On the second day, suddenly, as all such strikes happen, the line zips over my hand. When I grip to make friction as the force on the other end of the line charges ahead, I could be trying to lasso a locomotive for all the good it does. I apply more and more tension. All at once the line is weightless. I haul back with speed, hoping that I'm taking up slack. But it's empty line, deceptively heavy. I've held too tight and lost him. The others are not upset. We all cast with fresh bait to lure the fish for another strike. After two hours: "Well, he learned a lesson and told his friends," says Brian.

We trail a small New Zealand dragger for a while, since even a modest-size cod end releases scraps. The dragger's skipper, with a wave to Ian, motions us close and tosses aboard a bag of fresh-caught hoki for bait. Local fishermen look out for each other.

It has turned dark when the line starts to zip over my hands once more with that sudden force. Only eleven minutes to tame the locomotive. I keep tension, but not with the same heavy hand as before. The others watch with more casual concern than I feel, although Mike keeps reminding me quietly not to wrap my hand around the line. Out the line continues to pay until I yell, "What the hell do I do when there's no more line?"

"Then you wrap it around your waist, mate, and jump in. Don't worry, we'll follow in the boat." Quickly as the fish charged, it slows. "Now you haul, Bill. *Pull,* man!" About four minutes have passed. I grab in line by the hundred-foot. Like dragging a rock over gravel. By minute five I sweat and pant. The line accumulates around my feet. "Don't get your leg wrapped in any loops, Bill." I'm too concentrated to declare that I knew to step clear of bights. Nobody offers to help. I'm grateful. "Don't play him too hard. Don't count on he's given up."

I have him practically to the boat when off he goes again. The padded rubber glove on my right hand starts smoking from the friction, and suddenly the line burns over bare skin. I shift the hand to another position as my recaptured line zips away. Around minute six I start pulling rocks again. By now I'm drenched and my arms feel ready to lock. The fish makes one more charge, taking back half the line. I groan and cuss and laugh, but the minutes are passing fast. "Hey guys, this is your living, you'd better take over."

"Doin' fine, mate. *Pull* now!" They're enjoying it too.

No stopwatch counts the minutes. If I've brought the tuna alongside on schedule, it's with barely enough arm left to help gaff him aboard. I watch, dizzy with fatigue but spirits hopping, while Mike and Brian pounce with their knives over my fighting, noble adversary. Minutes later the sleek, blue, beautiful tuna lies coffined in slurry. This has been no sportfishing idyll that would have allowed me to return the fish to the sea as now I wish I could.

Fishing continues. Our smaller tunas stay in slurry for eight hours and the largest ones for ten. Then we loop a line around their tails, lower them into the hold, and pack them in ice. Ian's mood hinges on our landings. When a new fish enters the coffins every three or four hours, he and Mike banter and even horseplay on deck. When longer periods pass without a strike he frets. A little bird flies into the rigging and, hurt, hops crookedly around deck. Brian at once scoops it under his arm and carries it about, even as he handles lines. "You'll be cleanin' up after that thing, it'll die anyway," says Ian roughly. He mumbles it standing, legs apart, with typical head thrown back. Brian smiles, knowing the skipper, and pets his new charge.

When we return from three days' fishing, Ian steers over the tricky bar without a hitch. He has timed it for high slack at 3 A.M. Sure enough, a flashing buoy reflects in calm water. The bar is always a subject for talk. "Sometimes you get a big roll that builds up here," says

Ian, pointing. "And even though the weather here's good, something farther south'll just keep the roll building up and the bar stays unworkable. Just closes the gate. But now, some bigger boats like ours, we can push the bar harder than what we used to."

A canal flanked by silhouetted masts leads toward the darkened town, where lights at the co-op pier glow like a beacon. At the wharf someone comes out yawning, starts a loading crane, and sends down the hook. Each of our three- to four-hundred-pound bluefins rises by the tail from the ice below decks, lovely fish as round in the middle as wine goblets. They glisten pink under the first streak of dawn as a forklift truck moves them into a holding room.

A Japanese in short white boots appears. He stands a head shorter than the New Zealanders. Perhaps his size, cultural isolation, and delicate job contribute to his frequent smiles and chuckles. One by one the big fish go onto a scale. We watch tensely as the Japanese bends down, all business. He saws off the cardboard-like fins, then cuts into the tail and studies the circular slice of meat. Finally he thrusts a tubular tool into the fish's back section to take a core sample. The color of all the meat has to be red—everyone knows it. Signs of marbled fat would be good. The slightest whitening or splotching is bad news. He scribbles his verdicts. "A" grade will fly iced to Japan in hours for the lucrative sashimi market. "B" grade might also fly, or be frozen, but it brings fishermen a fraction of the price. "C" can do no better than the local market. We have mostly A's.

The Japanese passion for seafood has changed the face of fishing in more places than Greymouth, because no one else in the world pays such a high price for quality held to exacting standards. It has raised the level of seafood care throughout North America, from Newfoundland to Texas, as well as in other ports around the world where the yen can stimulate or subdue an economy. The spin-off is fresher seafood in every market. And more careful fishermen.

All this happens in July 1984, but as far as method is concerned it could have been 1997. In the interim, however, the stocks of New Zealand bluefin tuna plunged, and the Greymouth fleet searched longer for each one it caught. Biologists and fishermen time the fall with the appearance of Japanese driftnetters in the Tasman Sea. The miles-long floating nets were intended to catch a single target species, but they managed to take also any other creature they encountered that swam near the surface. Thus the Japanese, who had been instrumental in creating the bluefin fishery, became its nemesis. The southern bluefin stocks became so endangered that in 1989 the three nations fishing them, Japan, Australia, and New Zealand, agreed to reduce quotas. Under international pressure the Japanese stopped driftnetting the Tasman Sea in 1991, while by the end of 1992 all boats in the world stopped using long driftnets. More on this later.

Ian bought his boat in September 1984, the forty-five-foot *Galaxy*, smaller than Tom Fishburn's *Golden Star* by more than thirty feet but the accepted local size, and his own, for fishing albacore. Next summer a few days after Christmas he and Mike set out, over the Greymouth bar (which in late November had built higher after a flood and needed to be negotiated with new care), for the *Galaxy's* maiden trip.

After fishing, Ian pondered whether to deliver to Westport farther up the coast or come home. He had "a little wad" in his pocket for the Westport races. But with three-month-old Adam back in Greymouth along with Trish and young Matthew, he decided on January 4 to head home.

"It was not meant to be," Patricia Colville wrote me later. "After sitting off the Greymouth bar for some time and in contact with another boat by radio they decided the *Galaxy* would go in for a closer look to see if an attempt should be made to cross the bar. A combination of rough seas and a broken partition in the freezer led to disastrous consequences. They were sideswiped by a huge wave, causing the boat to roll; the catch moved to one side, and the boat rolled completely over. Mike was washed ashore, and Ian has never been found. . . . We all miss him so much."

Commercial Fishing magazine of New Zealand, in reporting the tragedy, quoted tributes from both Mike Tinnelly "who made his way to shore through half a mile of breaking sea," and from fellow-fisherman Bill Brennan, skipper of the *Helga* and president of the West Coast Fishermen's Association. A year later, the *Helga* went down in a similar accident, taking with it both Brennan and his crewman. The good fishing off Greymouth comes at a price.

CHAPTER SIXTEEN

The Fish Habits of Japan

Around midnight fresh tunas flown on ice from New Zealand, and from other parts of the world including the Atlantic harvest from New York and Boston, begin to be laid out on the auction floor inside Tokyo's Tsukiji Market. Sweating stevedores in towel headbands race their handcarts—each bouncing with one or two silver carcasses—through a gauntlet of other vehicles. Nobody relaxes. The men thrust meat hooks into the gills of the glinting heads and the tunas, bluefins weighing upward of four hundred pounds each, thud to the concrete. The big fish have bright identifying numbers painted on their skins, and enough pasted tags in scrawled Japanese characters to make them look like international luggage.

Graders in official caps slice a disc of meat from the tail section of each tuna and lay it alongside. The exposed meat glistens a dark red. Buyers shine flashlights on the tail discs and into the gutted bellies, then scribble notes. This is the place where the exacting Japanese demand for quality reaches its payoff. Only the best can justify the prices charged in restaurants that serve *sashimi,* raw fish.

The first work of the day at Tsukiji, arranging fish for display, soon enters into full swing, an activity that lasts from midnight until 5:30 A.M. when the auctions begin. After the auctions end around 8 A.M. the focus shifts to the market for wholesalers, or "middlemen" as the Japanese call them, and Tsukiji becomes a 2.7-million-square-foot fish store. By noon everything has cleared but the janitors hosing the concrete.

At 3 A.M. I check in with management on an upper floor of the complex. Windows along the corridor of the circular main building look down on docks and ramps where men hustle cargo from boats and trucks. In the wide, dingy office, clerks peck away on pads and computers. They sit at long tables, each presided over by a section head who watches them with suitable gravity. My escort issues me boots, then leads upstairs to a long chilled room. Boxes of produce by the hundreds lie on tables under the bright lights of a low ceiling. The odors have the delicate tints of small sea things dried, salted, or iced, in contrast to the big fishy smells below. Like bean sprouts, glistening unborn eels fill tubs profusely, each eye a nearly invisible black pinpoint. All manner of roes fill other containers—pollock roe of an electric red, brined orange salmon roe sacs arranged in rosettes, white herring roe clustered like crystals on thick kelp. There are tubs of squid paste, boxes of small dried fish and squid, slabs of salted salmon. This only suggests the variety.

Tsukiji (pronounced Skee´-jee) lies a mile from Tokyo's Ginza shopping district. The largest clearinghouse in the world for seafood, it employs over fifteen thousand directly but involves seventy thousand counting buyers. Deliveries of a daily 2,500 tons occupy twenty thousand trucks. (Boats can also reach Tsukiji through a canal.) Auctions and market generate two hundred truckloads of garbage each day. The four hundred office employees tabulate sales on 330 species. Products come from around the world. Sixty-four nations alone ship in prawns and shrimps. Octopus come from the Indian Ocean, Mediterranean, and Australia; cuttlefish from the South China Sea and Africa; cod and crab from Alaska.

All this organization and effort distributes seafood to a nation smaller than California. The Japanese eat fish—a word used here for convenience to mean all edible sea things from whale to seaweed—on a scale equaled only by Icelanders and small Pacific islands like Palau and Tokelau. For perspective, according to latest Food and Agriculture Organization figures (July 1997), Japan's 147-pound annual per capita fish consumption compares with a mere 101 pounds in Norway, 48 in the United States, 65 in Chile, and 30 pounds in New Zealand. Japanese eat fish routinely fresh, dried, or salted; as paste called *surimi,* shaped into forms to be fried or boiled; and as *sushi,* bits of raw fish on rice rolled in seaweed. They also eat it expensively as *sashimi,* raw fish by itself, and as delicately placed single items: glowing pink tiger prawns, ochre sea-urchin gonads, or chilled orange-purple mollusks, each accompanied on the dish by a lovely flower.

At 5:30 A.M. the tuna auctioneer strides to a platform trailed by assistants. He glares at the buyers beneath him identified by uniform caps with yellow licenses. An assistant hurries to a grouping of tunas and calls out their numbers. Japanese auctions have a different psychology from American ones. The auctioneer starts high and works down. First bidder takes. (Or the bids then rise from there.) It saves time, but increases tension. The auctioneer barks into a microphone, his exclamations as fierce as challenges. Buyers bark in return and shoot hands in the air. It has the unforgiving heat of a Fascist rally. As soon as the assistant walks to another area, stevedores heave the purchased fish onto handcarts and move them away. By now traffic has increased in the crowded, dark aisles. Men with handcarts of lesser sea creatures dodge for space. Nobody smiles or laughs.

In a quieter area by piers, stevedores lay out albacore. These smaller tunas, frozen hard, clunk as they hit the concrete. Their frosty white surfaces make vapor in the warm air. The buying goes calmly. The money at stake is less than half that of fresh bluefins, no matter what the level of care. In an adjacent shed, men at a bandsaw cut the frozen tunas in halves and quarters. They are unpressured enough to grin when I take photos. One unsmiling young man in boots and apron, looking wan and tired, leaves his cart to sit and smoke on a pile of boxes. Other auctions proceed throughout the huge main building. One centers around live fish in containers of water, another around crabs kept live in wet sawdust. In most, the men (I saw no women) stand on bleachers. The auctioneer, who faces them, shouts in a steady rhythm. At the end of each round he rings a bell to signal the final transaction and an assistant slaps the number of the successful bidder onto the containers.

The wholesale market opens around eight in a building adjacent to the auction. The aisles among closely jammed stalls seem impassable, yet carts push through, and buyers linger critically. Men with crosscut saws cut big tunas into salable chunks. Merchants (women now included) call and chatter as they arrange wares with aesthetic precision: little fish nose-to-tail, maroon octopus in rows with suction-cup tentacles curved like umbrella-bursts of fireworks. Here stretches the range of sea creatures that the Japanese eat. There are finfish of all sizes, in colors from silver to bright yellow-and-blue; crabs, from little spidery fellows with hairy carapaces to heavy purple kings; snails in shells resembling black marbles; clams as big as dinner plates; leathery dried squid in stacks. Before whaling bans there was ruby whale meat (very expensive) in cubes. Some items would never sell in the West. I try one for the record, a gelatinous purple blob. It's indeed food for a specialized palate: the flavor to me wavers between nauseating and disgusting.

Outside, food stalls serve all manner of seafood out of steaming pots and sputtering pans. Customers sit at long tables, or eat as they walk. Nearby stands a small Shinto compound, its trodden ground enclosed by a low wall. A balding man hurries over, his money pouch flapping against his side. At the altar his pace changes. He bows reverently several times, and repeats the bows before a high carved stone. Then he sits on the wall, removes one rubber boot, scratches his instep, adjusts the sock that had pulled down off his heel, and hurries back to market. The Japanese practice two religions comfortably together. Buddhism addresses the soul. Shinto balances duty and nature which, on a practical level, translates into worship for good business. Every office and ship I visit has its Shinto shrine.

The Japanese bring as realistic a gusto to their seafood consumption as to their religion. During fishing sojourns it has sometimes tested my sensibilities. Even modest village boats tuck soy sauce and chopsticks in their bows. After nets or lines have been worked and fish fill the bottom of the boat, someone will select an attractive specimen. Within minutes the creature, still flapping, will be filleted into bite-size strips and we, seated cross-legged among the fish (in boots and waterproof trousers) will be dipping the strips into the sauce. The flavors are fresh and delicate. One morning during breakfast at a *minshuku* (boardinghouse) in Ayukawa, the proprietor comes from a dawn pull at his nets with a big salmon. As everyone exclaims appreciatively, his wife places it on a platter in the center of the table to be admired. The fish, still twitching, slowly loses its sheen. None of the Japanese seem remotely troubled to watch the handsome fish die under our noses.

Most Japanese meals are wrapped around seafood. Here's a fishing family's breakfast near Nagasaki, after we have fished all night: raw bream sashimi and a beer; raw mackerel with soy and green horseradish sauce; pickled radish and fresh cucumber; dried small fish we chew like corn crisps; rich fish broth with chunks of fresh bream; *nori* seaweed strips (like crackly pieces of green paper, flavored like iodine) and cold rice; *wakame* seaweed soup with floating raw eggs (the wakame bland and slimy and the eggs slimier, textures quite acceptable in Japan); more fish soup, more beer, finally Japanese Scotch whiskey. A less leisurely daily breakfast aboard a fishing ship I rode at sea for several weeks: fish-and-tofu soup, pickled octopus, rice, and a raw egg.

As for Japanese dinners: Modest meals include fish paste products. At one boarding house the plates contain brown balls shaped like potatoes, and slightly slimy. These surimi balls, fried but often served cold, are rubbery, tasteless, basic protein, the end-product of Japanese factory trawlers that roam northern seas for months at a time. Banquets and dinners at expensive restaurants are something else, combining flavor and aesthetics.

Here is the menu of a two-hour dinner in Kanazawa on the northwest coast, along with my notes scribbled at table between courses. We start with the subtle flavors of sashimi: strips of raw tuna, octopus, urchin, yellowfin, and shrimp, nested on plates decorated with picturesque rosettes of raw vegetable. Beer accompanies this course. Warm sake follows. Regional delicacies start with a platter of exquisitely arranged squid in murky ink, pickled seaweed garnish, a dark-grained salty roe that has been marinated for four years (*"strong taste with depth, but not really worth the effort"* according to my notes), local river "sweetfish" pickled in sake (*"tastes like stale candy"*), and fresh sweetfish accompanied by a stalk of red ginger (*"small, fat, delicious"*). Next the waiter brings us each a rounded gray stone in a bed of salt, warning us not to touch. (*"We put little 'firefly' squid on the hot stones. They sizzle, eyes pop. After my initial shock, what the hell, do as the Romans. Juicy, many subtle flavors."*) Next a local fish called *gori* served whole uncooked (*"small, black, ugly little fellows, still twitching, delicate flavor"*), followed by gori fried to a skeleton (*"crunchy and good"*). The banquet ends with *"fungi etc. in slimy good sauce"* and a clear broth with vegetables.

Some of the banquet courses, and the twitching snacks aboard village boats, imply a cultural assumption different than in the West: It is OK to eat creatures so fresh that they die in your mouth. Squeamishness is relative. The Japanese are simply honest about the fact that they kill to eat. Americans who feast on steamed hard crabs, still deliciously warm with juices intact, conveniently forget that a few minutes earlier a cook pushed the creatures alive and protesting into a pot of scalding steam. Diners on veal *au chef* allow delicate wine-and-butter sauces to erase the fact that stockyards raise the calves barbarically without the light, exercise, or mother-contact that we consider necessary when we turn sentimental over the rights of all creatures.

Japan has a natural orientation to the sea. The nation is an archipelago of four large islands that stretch 1,500 miles northeast–southwest off the coasts of Siberia, the Koreas, and China. Climates vary from cold to subtropical in latitudes akin to those between Toronto and New Orleans. The "mainland" and largest island, Honshu, is home to Tokyo, Osaka, Kyoto, Hiroshima, and most other large and famous Japanese cities. The exception is Nagasaki, on Kyushu in the south. The northernmost large island, Hokkaido, bears some parallel to Alaska for its icy winters, its inhabitants more outgoing than most Japanese, and for the amount of seafood off its coasts. The Hokkaido chum salmon runs are as famous as the Bristol Bay sockeye runs in Alaska.

Despite trade, conquest, the American occupation after World War II, cultural interchanges, and a resultant obsessive delight in things Western that has altered the face of the cities, the Japanese remain homogeneously Japanese to their core. They outproduce many larger nations through an ethic that allots more time to work than to play, and that expects fewer privileges on the job. It remains a basically feudal society, good for assembly line effectiveness, but not necessarily for creative fiscal management. People obey the rules and bear down on those who don't (and enter shock if someone in authority doesn't).

Fish plant workers in Alaska learned this when salmon eggs for Japan became a prime enough money product that American companies hired Japanese supervisors to ensure Tokyo-level quality control (as they still do). Deborah Buchanan Adams of Cordova, who eventually fished aboard her own boat, remembers in her teens working a roe line. "You work faster?" the Japanese supervisor, a small nervous man, urged his female charges repeatedly. Once Deb paused from bending over the table to yawn and raise her arms. The supervisor ran up and snapped: "Stretch on break, not while work!" She barked back, "Stick it, buster!" in good Alaskan style. He retired in confusion. The Japanese whom I have seen riding aboard Alaskan processor boats during salmon season, usually alone and shorter than even the women aboard, are linguistically isolated, insecure except in the knowledge of their duty for which they will answer back home, and very lonesome.

Japanese mask sternness toward convention by a graciousness beyond belief, at least to those considered equals or above. They have treated me with embarrassing kindness as a visitor with credentials. It woos an outsider mightily if he can forget their World War II barbarism, but their graciousness does not necessarily extend to subordinates. I learned this during my maiden stint at the Kodiak shrimp plant, which was owned and partially supervised by Japanese. During hosedown after an eleven-hour shift on the peelers I accidentally splashed shrimp offal across a gutter into an area already cleaned for the night. Rectifying it was the work of two minutes. A Japanese foreman rushed over shouting vituperations in my face. I reacted physically. The American foreman, who though darting everywhere quickly appeared, pulled me off (and intervened for my lowly job, which I later ungratefully left to go fishing). The violent insubordination dazed the Japanese, who wilted the moment I touched him. Mere workers in Japan are expected to bow heads and listen. "Japanese don't like to deal with something they can't control," an American businessman in Japan told me later.

I have tested Japanese graciousness to the limit at times. While riding with whalers in Japan (before general whaling stopped) I asked to work a day at a tryworks. This desire for hands-on puzzled my hosts, but after polite negotiation they agreed. I duly reported at five thirty and spent the morning cutting blubber into chunks for rendering. Several workers found it hilarious, a few ignored me disapprovingly, and some gravely or smiling took me under their wing. The work was slippery, stinking, and sweaty, no picnic despite the laughs. After several hours we ate in a long cook shed. Fellow-workers showed me where to fill my bowl with rice and fish-seaweed soup, then how to chopstick choice pieces from platters of raw and cooked fish, whale meat, blubber, and whale intestine. Back at work, the foreman declared it time for me to cut into the whale carcass itself: an expression of hospitality, not judgment. As my mentors watched, I incised with my long-handled flensing knife and then sawed along the length of the whale, as I had observed the others do it. A polite sucking of breath halted me. Instead of slicing just through the blubber I had continued into the meat. With Japanese graciousness nobody told me what I learned later: My random jag had downgraded the value of the meat. Moral: If in Japan you make a stupid work error, be protected by hospitality.

The Japanese commitment to foods from the sea, their consequent intolerance for poor quality, and their ability to pay top money for shipments up to their standards, have revolutionized the way fishermen around the world treat their product. Fellows who once gaffed a hooked fish aboard in the belly when convenient, now aim carefully for the gills, leaving no broken flesh to mar the aesthetics of a fillet. And the catch they once pronged from boat to shore now goes by hand despite extra slime on the fisherman himself. The power of the yen also directs that catches once left to slosh for hours in the bottom of a boat be bled and iced within minutes. (Some, including Norwegians, have done this routinely, by law, but the practice was not universal in North America and elsewhere.) And fish once iced layer on layer in a boat's hold, left to turn mushy on the bottom layers while the weight increased during a several-day trip, now go neatly into boxes that, stacked, absorb the pressure and keep the fish firm.

Japan's ability to pay has created new fisheries and consequent dependencies. In Alaska's Bristol Bay, salmon was canned until the Japanese started a huge market for the product frozen. Now, in years when enough salmon storm into Japan's own nets to glut the domestic market, the price in Alaska plunges. New Zealanders like Tom Fishburn and the unlucky Ian Colville ignored bluefin tuna until Japan declared its interest in buying them. Fisherman from Maine to the Maritimes found that the prickly sea urchins they called "whores' eggs," which spiked through rubber gloves, were transformed from a nuisance into a lucrative commodity. In Chesapeake Bay country, eels previously considered fit only for bait became a product for Japan that watermen harvested during the gap between winter oystering and summer crabbing. Japan's interest in dried squid changed the small creatures from mere bait to a hard currency product in Newfoundland waters in the 1980s. The siren call has a dark side. By the 1990s squid were overfished, and for years Newfoundlanders needed to find other bait. (Squid *have* returned.) The same overfishing for quick yen leveled bluefin stocks off New Zealand and for a while virtually wiped out Chesapeake Bay eels.

The dependency runs deep. Responding to the Japanese market, the prawn farms of Indonesia, China, Thailand, Taiwan, Philippines, and other Asian nations multiplied severalfold during the 1980s. Because the United States also bought tons of the large Asian shrimp, few realized the extent of Japan's hold. Then in August 1989 Emperor Hirohito lapsed into what became his final illness. The Japanese canceled everything from festivals to business meetings. Prawns are banquet food in Japan, and wholesalers keep inventories frozen to supply ongoing occasions. Abruptly they stopped buying more. After the emperor died in October there followed a three-month mourning that overlapped the traditional December wedding month. Thousands of engaged couples postponed their ceremonies for a year. The Japanese market disappeared temporarily, and the world shrimp price crashed. It moved, for example, from $12 U.S. to $7.50 per pound for shrimp of a sixteen- to twenty-count size, a category in which the industry considered $11 to be the break-even price. Bankruptcies followed on the new shrimp farms throughout Asia. (Disease has since then, incidentally, decimated most Asian shrimp farms.)

In Japan, the government does not own and run fishing companies, but the ties are so close that government–business decisions often appear unanimous. This is probably not graft—as might be suspected in the United States, where bureaucrats and fishermen routinely square off as adversaries—but such comfortable mutual interest does resemble a cartel. The solidarity presents a monolithic front to outsiders trying to deal in Japan. Jay Hastings, a Seattle lawyer who works with the Japanese, puts it in the best possible light: "Japanese say very little and their language is vague. But their understanding and sense of trust among themselves is tremendous. They don't have to discuss every little thing—unlike Americans who must clearly spell out everything."

Since seafood commands an accepted priority, the Japanese government invests more in the fishing occupation than does, say, the United States. Every coastal village of any size has a modern concrete quay and auction shelter built with civic money. (All in the same design.) The Japanese are generous also with fishery advice and funding overseas, given both to help underdeveloped nations, and pragmatically to raise the level of product to standards that can supply the Japanese market. A new quay facility in Puerto Montt, Chile, that served the young American entrepreneur Hans Schmidt's initial new fisheries, has a design recognizable at once even to the offices above the long concrete auction floor. The *lelongs* of Indonesia also show a familiar hand—Japanese money built entirely the major one outside Jakarta—although the Indonesian level of village fish delivery still lacks the scrubbed Japanese cleanliness.

Except in the high mountains, virtually every inch of soil in Japan supports either a building or a crop. Inshore waters receive the same close cultivation that utilizes everything available. A drive along one of the scenic Japanese coasts passes bays and inlets filled with the buoy markers and beadlike floats of fish traps, pens, and sunken pots.

Cooperatives serve Japanese fishermen in jurisdictions from village to city, whether they be crewmen, mom-and-pop loners in little weathered wooden boats, or owners of small fleets. All know the security of being part of a group. In Taiji, a southern fishing town once also a center for whalers, everyone in the co-op owns a share of the trap. Members go out to empty it twice a day in long wooden boats that carry eight or nine men each. I have visited co-op villages committed to cultivating only a single sea crop, among them such fish as *buri,* or "yellowtail"; nori seaweed; wakame seaweed; oysters (raised on strings suspended from floats).

Miles off a deserted coastal road connecting the hectic old city of Kanazawa to the scenic Noto Peninsula, the co-op village of Saiki supports an impressively large fishery with the self-sufficiency required of a remote area. Saiki's black-tiled roofs and red-decorated cemetery figures all face the sea, and its few steep roads lead downhill to the harbor. The Japan Sea provides the co-op enough sardines and mackerel inshore to fill the nets of forty seiners, while farther offshore rockfish, bream, and cod school around seamounts and the two-hundred-meter curve to support a gillnet fleet. Besides dockage, the co-op maintains plants to freeze, dry, and salt the fish. It stores fuel in bulk and runs plants for purifying water, making ice blocks, and farming fish. And it runs its own marketing association. Local initiative has not generated all this without a helping hand. The remarkable thing, for free-enterprise people like Americans, is the amount of investment the Japanese government provides to strengthen such rural fishing industries.

While Japanese conglomerates like Marubini and Nichiro (and formerly Taiyo) own hundreds of ships that hustle for fish wherever in the world they can negotiate their nets, small family-owned companies are the bedrock of the domestic fishing economy. In Shiogama, a deep-sea fishing port on a central coast facing the open Pacific, in 1980, seven owners of small companies have assembled to meet with me in the office of their co-op above the unloading pier. As the first business we exchange cards. My single card remains on the table before each, to remind them of the difficult name. (I was "Mr. McCroskey," since no *L* exists in Japanese). For my part, their cards arranged in seating order—at least those not printed in Japanese alone—help me address each by name.

It surprises them that I ask their personal histories, but they answer with amused good grace. Four of the seven started on deck as fishermen. This background overlays their natural Japanese formality to erupt often in robust cheerfulness. All have sons and daughters, and the older men grandchildren as well. Their memories hark back wistfully to the golden days before 1977, the year when the United States and other coastal nations took control of their own 200-mile fishing waters and began to exclude foreigners. That was when the troubles began for Japanese fishermen, they said.

Mr. Nitta, sixty-four, a man with high cheekbones and a shaved head, directs a company he founded that includes a trawler, a longliner, and a salmon catcher. Mr. Endo, wiry, straight-backed, and far younger-looking than seventy-three, founded his company in 1952. It consists of one trawler and one gillnetter. Round-faced Mr. Suzuki, forty-nine, heads a company founded by his father in 1956 that operates one middle-size trawler and a smaller one plus a tuna longliner.

Mr. Maruama, a lined but robust seventy-four, started at age fifteen as cook on a fishing boat, and now heads a family fishing company that he founded. Over the years he rose from cook to captain, bought a boat of his own, and sailed it to fish for herring off the Soviet Union and for salmon and groundfish off Alaska. "Those were good days," he declares through an interpreter. He speaks with such warmth that without translation it would seem a recital of present prosperity. His company includes one medium-size trawler and three smaller ones. The latter three are trade-offs for one large trawler that once traveled to Alaskan waters but has become impractical with the loss of American fisheries. The local co-op bore some costs for scrapping the large surplus trawler and acquiring the three smaller boats, but the company itself needed to absorb most of the bill while coping with suddenly reduced profits as it scouted new, less abundant fishing grounds.

The meeting continues, low-keyed and informal, as a secretary brings in a sushi lunch in plastic pans covered with cellophane. The small-company men want to tell me that they all feel squeezed. The limited stocks of seafood in Japanese waters cannot support all the boats unable to fish longer in foreign waters. Their companies have been forced into layoffs to survive. It greatly disturbs the men around me. In a society where an employee expects to remain with a company until retirement many of their fishermen have found themselves, in middle age with only fishing skills, required to drift into a job market locked tight by other traditional employees.

Many times in Japan I have sat with sympathetic people while wondering, especially among older men like these, what part they played during the Second World War. A friend, knowing I was headed to Japan, wrote without further comment at the bottom of a letter: "Remember Pearl Harbor." He didn't need to remind me. I grew up intensely during the early 1940s. Yet whatever the urge toward savagery begot by the Japanese samurai tradition, it remains hidden beneath suits and oilskins during my present experiences.

The founding dates of the companies run by Messrs. Endo, Suzuki, Nitta, and Maruama, all in the early or mid-1950s, is significant. Fishing might be a traditional Japanese occupation, but Japan's massive presence in the waters of the world began with the technologies and opportunities opened by World War II. During the 1930s Japanese boats pursued lesser, unchallenged fisheries in Alaskan waters for king crab (at that time ignored by Americans) and salmon. Pearl Harbor halted this. For several years after the war the conquered Japanese were not permitted to return. And then. . . .

In 1952 I was serving aboard the 180-foot Coast Guard cutter *Sweetbrier* in Alaskan waters. Junior officers inherit the dreariest jobs, and one of mine involved deciphering encoded classified messages. This unromantic labor required hours of running cardboard strips of scrambled letters through the slots of a manual decoding board. The messages that emerged were invariably trivial, sent from headquarters to keep us alert. Suddenly, scrambled messages began to arrive by radio rather than by mail, at 3:30 A.M. local (start of 8:30 A.M. office hours back in D.C.), with SECRET. TRANSLATE AT ONCE. The messages instructed us to pick up a man with a Japanese name who would fly from Seattle to Adak Naval Station halfway along the thousand-mile Aleutian chain, and to escort him to a rendezvous with two Japanese fishing ships fifty miles at sea. The messages directed that all personal cameras aboard be impounded and no photographs taken. They further required censorship of letters to ensure that no wives back in Ketchikan gossiped about the happenings. The sleep-robbing communiqués had at least become interesting.

The Allies had signed the peace treaty with Japan in September 1951, ending the Occupation and opening the Japanese economy, and the Truman Administration decided without fanfare to allow a Japanese return to their prewar fishing grounds. Yet, as elections approached in 1952, incumbent Democrats facing Republican Dwight Eisenhower wanted no political hot potato to develop over the decision. The best way to avoid a possible surge of popular feeling, led by thousands of Americans who had suffered at Japanese hands within vivid memory, was to say nothing, to keep the Japanese return a secret until it could no longer affect the election. I played my part. The ship's safe was opened only behind a bolted door.

As the rendezvous approached we headed across the great stretch of Alaskan waters to Adak. Less than a decade before, the Japanese army had occupied islands not far from here and bombed Dutch Harbor during the only part of World War II to reach American soil. Rusting American Quonset huts and bunkers still lined Adak's barren hills. Our secret passenger, a Japanese American who said virtually nothing, moved quickly aboard and, despite our hopes in the wardroom for insights, stayed seasick in his cabin during the rough trip.

Next afternoon the *Sweetbrier* rolled in sight of two streaked black ships with Japanese lettering. Not only had cameras been impounded, but all hands stood at quarters to assure no sneaked photos on undeclared cameras. (Pictures of those dreary rustbuckets under a leaden sky would have needed remarkable captions to have caught anyone's interest.) We lowered the motor surfboat and watched it buck away with the huddled gentleman and our captain and executive officer. Seas were high enough to kick a spray over their heads—seas of no consequence compared with others we worked in routinely. In the Japanese wardroom our two officers accepted a hospitable snack and joined in a toast before heading back, while the fisheries representative hastened to the stateroom provided him. Soon we were headed back to duty in Dutch Harbor, having participated in a snatch of history.

When we returned to homeport in Ketchikan four weeks later, one of the wives held up a small clipping from a Seattle newspaper reporting that the Coast Guard cutter *Sweetbrier* had made rendezvous to open Alaskan waters to the Japanese. The news made no flurry, after all. Alaska was a distant place, not even at that time a state, known to few Americans. None of us guessed that within the following decade hundreds of Japanese fishing ships would have gathered off the Alaskan coasts, and eventually thousands of them, to harvest seafood by the million-ton of species that did not then interest Americans. Japan had begun the formidable far-seas fishing that opened an entire industry at home for the Mr. Nittas and Mr. Endos and for the giants like Taiyo and Marubini.

Pekalongan, Java, Indonesia, 1991: Just in from two weeks of fishing red snapper, a longliner crew clowns for my camera in their cramped berthing space.

Konbumori, Hokkaido, Japan, 1988: During a fishermen's festival, young fishermen carry a shrine down the single main street. The structure weaves wildly as those on each of the four sides exuberantly contest strengths.

Ian Colville, lost at sea, January, 1985.

New Zealand, 1984: Crewmembers aboard the *Golden Star* prepare to gaff in a 350-pound bluefin tuna caught by handline. From left: Brian Topliss, Mike Tinnelly, and foreground, skipper Ian Colville.

CHAPTER SEVENTEEN

Fencing the Ocean Commons

The Winners and the Anxious Dispossessed

The Mr. Nittas and Mr. Endos had reason to worry. In their youth, getting started, creatures of the sea were assumed to be common property, especially by those best equipped to catch them—certainly by Japan, but also by other nations seeking to expand food resources beyond their ocean borders without military conquest.

Before hydraulics, marine engines, and freeze refrigeration had been developed to a level practical for use aboard fishing vessels, the world's largest far-seas fishing fleets consisted of boats with limited capacity to catch and store. Iberians and Yankees converged annually on the Grand Banks off Newfoundland to catch cod. They worked lines by hand from bobbing dories, and salted the catch until their holds were full enough to return home. Such an inefficient method lacked the capacity to deplete stocks. People could assume that the abundance of the sea had no limit.

World War II stimulated technologies and applications that, a decade later, changed all this. Ships could be made into fishing factories able to camp on distant fishing grounds and harvest continuously with vacuum-cleaner efficiency, then freeze or can the fish and send the product home in cargo ships. Several nations built such ships, especially the Soviet Union and Japan, but also West Germany, Poland, South Korea, Spain, and Bulgaria among a dozen others. They began to rake fish excessively from the waters off North America, where a huge portion of the world's edible seafood resources are concentrated. As the number of efficient ships increased to catch more and more fish, the volume of catches began to diminish, as well as the average size of the fish caught. There turned out to be no infinity of fish at all.

Before the 1950s, the recognized right of a nation to the resources off its coasts extended only a simple three miles from shore, an old concept said to be based on the enforceable range of cannon. By the mid-1960s many nations, including the United States, had added another nine miles for twelve-mile exclusive fishery zones. Living resources beyond this remained part of the world commons, owned by everyone until possessed by the catcher.

During this time Iceland forced national rights by claiming control of the fish within fifty miles of its shores in waters British fishermen thought they owned. At stake for the Brits was the livelihood of entire fishing communities, and they fought it. In the "cod war" showdowns Icelandic gunboats held firm despite the worried deploring of Western nations, and the once-defiant British trawlers went home for good. A concept of extended fishery jurisdiction had taken hold. Then, the governments of Peru·and Ecuador announced rights within two hundred miles of their coasts and impounded American fishing boats that pursued highly migratory tuna into the area, in the process roughing up crewmen, which added to the American outrage.

To provide internationally accepted rules for such disputes, the United Nations in 1958 and again in 1960 convened conferences to write a Law of the Sea. Both sessions failed, because they called for the powerful nations (the ones who paid the bills) to relinquish too many rights.

Into the 1970s foreign trawlers fished casually off Kodiak town in Alaska and Long Island in New York. Residents could see bright deck-lights as the ships fished through the night. In 1975, according to U.S. Department of Commerce figures, there were 2,339 foreign fishery vessels working off the Atlantic coast (over half of them Soviet), 476 off California, 382 off Oregon–Washington, and 3,477 off Alaska (over two-thirds of them Japanese).

It might have infuriated local fishermen to be bullied off their own grounds by boats that came from a thousand and more miles away but, as experts in the Department of State and elsewhere argued, a nation declaring rights over more than twelve miles of its contiguous waters would undermine the very roots of high-seas freedom, including unchallenged passage of cargo and military vessels.

In U.S. waters, the State Department managed to negotiate some control over the foreign fishing effort through quotas and closings. But those around the bargaining table who represented the United States knew painfully the limits of their clout. Laws passed cautiously had extended U.S. jurisdiction to twelve miles in 1964 and in 1974 declared possession of bottom-dwelling crustaceans as "creatures of the continental shelf." Using the latter, National Marine Fisheries Service inspectors riding with the Coast Guard could board foreign ships, and make arrests if they found lobster in the freezers. (Coast Guard crews pursued this duty imaginatively. One technique included quickly sending a smallboat astern of the ship about to be boarded to pick up any hastily jettisoned crustacean parts.)

In the Bering Sea off Alaska the Japanese ran factory operations. A dozen or more trawlers fished grids, efficiently scraping everything in their path from the seafloor, delivered the catch to a mothership for processing, and returned their nets to the water at once. They termed their highly organized effort "order in the fishery." The Soviets and others ran big trawler-processors that prepared the fish on board. All offloaded to freighters bound for home, generating income that never touched ashore in the United States, and continued fishing around the clock for months at a time. This same exploitation occurred off Canada, and other world coasts in the world where the catch proved worth the effort.

Americans, fishing for king crab in the shadow of foreign trawlers many times their size, felt the foreign presence in their very gut. The foreign ships overran and destroyed American crab gear with the casualness of any unchallenged bully. We watched through the sweat and spray dripping from our caps as fish bags thick as a house snaked up the foreign stern ramps. Birds screamed over broken fish and crab squeezing through the outer mesh. Our crab! And our fish whether we were prepared to catch it ourselves or not. What would be left? Raping the resource is what we called it, for good reason.

During the mid-1970s I rode aboard a U.S. Coast Guard ship patrolling the Bering Sea to monitor foreign fleets, and received permission to accompany boarding parties. A 1976 visit that seared itself on my mind occurred aboard the 566-foot Japanese factory mothership *Soyo Maru*. As the boarding party approached in a small boat, the *Soyo* rose on the horizon like a warehouse on a plain while the ships delivering to it appeared no more than outbuildings. Most boarding parties climb a Jacob's ladder bouncing against the hull. On the *Soyo* this would have meant a two-story climb (of which we were all capable). Instead, from deck high above they lowered a rope and canvas basket. We grasped the edges as the basket rose. It hovered several feet above the deck before depositing us safely, and we viewed a stunning panorama of superfishing.

Below stretched two field-size bins thick with pollock. Each bin extended more than a hundred feet along the length of the ship and, except for a walkway, filled out the sixty-eight-foot beam width. Men waded through the fish with wooden pushers, distributing the load and easing portions of it onto a continuous feeder belt.

The ship's end-product was *surimi,* the protein-rich fish paste that the Japanese eat in various processed forms (and which a decade later Americans accepted as simulated crab legs). Our guide, with polite cordiality, issued us white gloves. He took us over wooden trestles with water gushing beneath, past the high bins, into the factory area. Batteries of men hand-fed fish at two per second into machines that dressed, skinned, and eventually converted the creatures into mush. The quantities were overwhelming. So were the numbers: a crew of 437 serviced nine trawlers that delivered around the clock. Yet the *Soyo* group was one of the smallest among seventeen Japanese factory fleets fishing off Alaska. Some motherships exceeded 650 feet and processed the haul of two dozen catchers.

The tour ended two hours later, close to dark. On the vast decks loading and sorting continued under floodlights. Beyond the factory ship an orange twilight glinted on the swells, and work lights twinkled on nearby Japanese catcher ships. From the *Soyo Maru's* lofty bridge any American boats scraping for crab were too small and insignificant to notice.

In the United States a popular groundswell was building (not necessarily from the wheat farmers of Kansas) for greater control of the nation's waters to save the fish stocks from extinction. Moderates had first suggested a fifty-mile extension, radicals one hundred miles. Opponents of such territorial expansion could point to the reprehensible behavior of Peru and Ecuador toward American tuna fishermen. Did we want to legitimatize such actions? By the early 1970s, with technology steadily changing the realities of seafaring, the United Nations tried Law of the Sea again with a third conference. By 1976, after five extended sessions, the concept of a 200-mile exclusive economic zone had become accepted (though excluding, at the insistence of the United States, highly migratory tunas to keep Peruvian impoundments illegal). Two hundred miles, in fact, was virtually the only tenet of the conference to gain international consensus on the rights and obligations of maritime nations. Several Central and South American nations had indeed already followed

Peru's 200-mile example including Chile, Argentina, Brazil, Uruguay, and Panama.

Unfortunately, the Law of the Sea negotiations moved too slowly to address immediate overfishing off North America. In the United States the constituents of coastal states pushed for action before the fish disappeared and local fishermen permanently lost their livelihoods. After five years of hearings congressmen, principally from the West Coast, Alaska, and New England, finally crafted a bill that in 1976 passed. President Gerald Ford signed it reluctantly, listening to a State Department that still feared the erosion of all other rights on the high seas.

The Magnuson Fishery Conservation and Management Act—named after its senior sponsor, the late Democrat Senator Warren Magnuson of Washington—declared U.S. possession of and responsibility for the marine resources within two hundred miles of the U.S. coasts. Many other coastal nations, including Canada, followed suit at once. (Japan, an exception, declared for 200-mile rights only in 1996; its heavily fished near-shores had little left to protect from big foreign fleets compared to grounds it lost.) The action altered forever—or at least for the present generation—the rules of a coastal nation's rights to the resources within its contiguous waters. New ownership had been established in the fishing commons.

Any winner presupposes a loser. The losers of the world's new 200-mile jurisdictions were the far-seas fishing nations. Within a few years most of their great trawler-processors and motherships had been dismantled or lay rusting in ship graveyards. Those nations with economic and diplomatic clout, like Japan and the Soviet Union, had done all they could to forestall the U.S. law. With it accomplished, they maneuvered within the new order to negotiate for resources they once had grabbed. They managed not to be swept off U.S. grounds at once, as many Americans expected. (Nor, incidentally, did free passage of the high seas evaporate.) The Magnuson Act, during its long passage, had evolved from a simple law to possess coastal resources to one that also set up a management structure for conservation. One realistic provision allowed the foreign fleets to phase out and avoid ruin. Quotas would be determined scientifically, and American fishermen would receive all they proved able to catch, while foreign nations could negotiate for the remainder as long as it existed.

Given the modest sizes and numbers of American fishing boats—they could not be called fleets—it appeared that while the foreign ships needed to cut back their effort they could still fish indefinitely if they followed the rules. The story changed quicker than anyone had envisioned. The United States (and Canada) made credit and tax concessions to encourage domestic investment in more capable boats, and it worked.

By the early 1980s, four and five years after the Magnuson Act, Americans had vastly increased their capacity to catch fish, if not their facilities to process them, and they had absorbed far more quota than projected. Catching ability had increased enough that a new fishing arrangement evolved called Joint Ventures. JVs provided that American boats caught the fish, then delivered them to foreign processor ships allowed into domestic waters to buy (but not to fish). Canadians permitted a similar arrangement. JVs provided work for a relative few large foreign ships—predominantly Japanese, Soviet, and South Korean for Americans; Portuguese, Soviet, and Bulgarian for the Canadians. Americans were certainly now catching fish and making money from it. But like the workers of a colonized country, they delivered raw material for someone else's greater profit as manufactured goods. JVs became merely an interim step. It allowed Americans to acquire larger boats while they learned to handle factory-volume catches.

In a Japanese fishing town, Kushiro, officials squired me to a modest home in a crowded workmen's neighborhood where two wives and a mother of men fishing far at sea offered cakes and tea while delivering a message. The men's ships depended on fish in United States waters soon to be closed to them, as Americans proved able to harvest everything within U.S. 200-mile waters. My notes record a translator's version of one wife's speech as her children hugged around her: "American people eat little much fish, Japanese people eat very much fish. It makes us very sad to understand why Americans wish to make quotas to Japanese so much smaller and smaller, of fish they do not need, so that soon my husband will have no work to feed our family." Another question: "Are you in so much hate against Japanese fishermen?" I replied gently that Americans ate much more fish than my hostesses realized, and that they were eating more all the time. The news upset them. It negated their hope that the problem had a simple solution.

By the late 1980s the United States had drawn down to virtually zero the quotas for foreigners, since Americans proved able to do all the catching and processing themselves. An earlier assumption, voiced and counted on by the Japanese and others, had it that U.S. factory ships could never make a go because no Americans in any number would consent to work at sea for months at a time sliming and gutting fish on a factory line. Everybody was wrong. In a saga covering only a handful of years, Americans (albeit with much foreign capital) built a fleet of factory trawlers, and manned them with Americans (these days, many are first-generation citizens from other countries). The trawlers fished the very pollock and other groundfish stocks that I, only a decade before on the Bering Sea crabber, had watched the Japanese and Russians take when no competing American boat existed.

The tale of the American fleets continues. There are success stories, but with the pitfalls of success: turf battles, shortages, overcapitalization, waste, politics.

For fishermen of loser nations like Japan the new 200-mile declarations meant for many a return to home grounds and older ways, even to other livelihoods. The bulk of the huge motherships like the *Soyo Maru* soon rusted at anchor and long ago became scrap. As for the governments and owners of such fleets, it meant more subtle negotiation, and a more imaginative pursuit of the world's ocean resources in new areas for different targets. One thing was certain: Most traditional fishing grounds of the world were no longer open for outside grabs. The nations whose exclusive economic zones contained continental shelves on which the sea creatures of the world reproduced had claimed their heritage.

CHAPTER EIGHTEEN

Mr. Bigfoot on the Raw-Bacon Circuit

Japan, 1980 and 1988

While Japanese entrepreneurs sought their way around the new 200-mile fences erected by other nations, traditional fisheries on home grounds continued as before. Whenever I have found my way to Japan I have seen new aspects of Japan's domestic fishing culture, from little boats to collective community enterprises to the small-company fleets. The variety befits a great fishing nation, but it does have the cultural collective sameness of Japan itself. On none but the smallest, most rickety boats, does it appear that individuals work for themselves rather than in some co-op or company. And even individuals belong to some organization. The geography of my visits has ranged from chilly Hokkaido in the far northeast to the semitropical Goto Islands in the southwest. I stayed in one isolated village where the main business was seaweed culture, and another where whaling was the traditional occupation. I turned-to on the decks of seiners and trawlers, helped pull village setnets, and sociably drank gallons of *ocha,* green tea, (plus some sake) as I met with company officials and bureaucrats.

The Japanese Pacific, May 1980

Kushiro, population about one hundred thousand, is a busy utilitarian port in Hokkaido, northernmost of the four major Japanese islands. For Japan, Hokkaido is the cold frontier: their Alaska. With open space and less crowding the people seem heartier, even taller. Kushiro faces directly into the Pacific Ocean and a rich continental shelf. In pre–200-mile days it was a major staging port for the factory fleets heading to Alaskan and Siberian waters. Its trawlers, jiggers, and gillnetters continue to sail to wherever they find permission to fish.

Tied alongside a river that bisects Kushiro are the small boats of the inshore fisheries that go out in season for salmon, big clams *(hokki-gai)*, crabs, kelp, scallops, and a variety of other fish including sole, flounder, and sardines. Farther upriver are moored the deep-sea vessels, including trawlers such as that I will ride. On the bridge connecting the city's two segments, statues help relieve the town's general bareness, but loudspeakers drone relentless music and advertisements above the traffic's din. The quays are always busy. From my hotel by the river I can watch a steady line of boats return from overnight fishing. Every morning around six a bald old man with a towel around his head, and his wife in a nunlike bonnet that hides her face, sit in their scuffed wooden boat picking and mending a torn gillnet. A short walk across the bridge takes me to a quay where fishermen unload salmon, weigh them in wooden buckets carried by two-man poles, and empty them into waiting trucks.

In the office of the Kushiro Middle-Sized Trawlers Association I wait over cups of ocha, while owners of companies with one to three vessels each debate my request to ride on one of their ninety-foot trawlers. The association manager gladly offers all the statistics I want, and more. But to wish to do more than walk aboard one of the fishing ships in port, to go out for several days and to "handle the equipment" besides? A puzzling request, since, as he points out several times, all information is available right in the office.

More members arrive, their faces masks of polite concern as they button suit jackets over waists wider than those of fishermen. One phlegmatic gentleman, the owner of a company with several fishing ships, including ones that once had traveled all the way to Alaska for its catches, regards me severely. I ask through an interpreter supplied by the Japan Fisheries Association how the 200-mile limits of all coastal nations have affected his business. "Very deeply," he growls, eyeing me as personally responsible.

The discussion swirls over my head in Japanese for an hour, and then they retire to another office to discuss the matter in private. Whenever I empty the cup of ocha a lady from one of the desks in the office bullpen beyond the visitor's nook hurries over to refill it, smiling. I feel all eyes follow me politely as I rise, killing time, to inspect the office Shinto shrine mounted high on the wall. It contains a neat arrangement of rope and foiled paper shaped into a boat. All offices have such a shrine with objects symbolizing the company business.

A long time later, over more ocha, I draft a paper absolving the trawler association, the trawler company whose boat I will ride, and the government (both local and national), from any injuries I might sustain aboard the *Mito Maru No. 55*. Yes, permission is granted. The atmosphere changes at once. Even the scowling gentleman—owner of the ship to host me—turns cordial. The association director hosts a multi-course dinner with many sake toasts. Then as the sky darkens we drive along piers of steel hulls, into a world that smells of metal and old fish, to the *Mito Maru* preparing for sea.

Around eleven, the eighteen crewmen come aboard and disappear into bunks below decks. A storm at sea the day before has allowed them time at home. In the large wheelhouse the fishing master, a lean and preoccupied man, nods curtly, climbs into one of four bunks flanking the chart table, and snaps shut the curtain. The round-faced, affable captain offers basic courtesies to a stranger, and arranges his own bunk for my sleeping since he himself will be on watch all night to reach the grounds by dawn.

Next morning, in rough weather, the thumps of bobbins and cables wake me. It is only 4:30 A.M., but in summer this far north the sun already gleams on the choppy waves. O-san, my interpreter, more bureaucrat than fisherman, emerges from his bunk unsteadily. He has, in fact, never ridden on a fishing vessel during two decades' employment in the fishery business. Conscientious and sincere though he is, he's come aboard in a suit, carrying a briefcase. To the bundle of oilskins and boots under my arm he had said worriedly, "Oh, Mr. McCloskey, you will not need those. The vessel is very dry, you understand."

It seems that aboard the *Mito Maru*, whatever the negotiations in the co-op office, it is assumed that I will keep to the wheelhouse. (Indeed a stranger to any fishing gear should always stay clear when it is being run. I have no intention of doing otherwise.) It seems also assumed that I will eat in the wheelhouse. As the ship pitches agreeably for those with sea legs, the cook appears from below to present me an "American" breakfast. With exquisite Japanese taste he has arranged strips of uncooked bacon like spokes of a wheel atop lettuce and sliced tomatoes. A graying nervous man older than the rest aboard, he awaits my approval. I can only nod brightly as I stall for time.

Fortunately the first haulback of the day begins, and the cook leaves to join the others on deck. The beautiful bacon breakfast goes discreetly into a corner as far from sight as I can push it. By now Akio Yoshida, the fishing master, holds the controls and has become cordial. The early sun glares through the windows, etching shadows on his cheekbones. He is a calm but perpetually moving one-man show as he steers, maneuvers, consults his echosounders and other electronics, and calls orders to the decks fore and aft.

The crewmen shoot the trawl, then cable it back aboard. I assume that the captain has reclaimed his bunk after working all night, until I recognize him working on deck with the rest. Captain? It takes a while to get it straight, coming from fisheries in the United States, Canada, and Norway where the captain of the dirtiest scow is skipper next-to-God. In Japan only the fishing master occupies a position that competes with the Almighty. The Japanese "captain" is responsible for the ship only between harbor and the grounds, although his position is considered a route to becoming a fishing master.

Each drag lasts between thirty and forty minutes. The fish of the catches are relatively small but of six target varieties. The men lift the mass by the tubful to a long table, sort and ice them into low wooden boxes, then stack the boxes in the hold. Fish other than the six species go en masse into another part of the hold between layers of support boards and ice.

After a few sets, the catch begins accumulating faster than the men can sort it and I become restless to help. I start to ease toward the wheelhouse door with my roll of fishing clothes. O-san turns anxiously from where he holds on, greenfaced, his tie askew. "Oh, Mr. McCloskey, you must stay dry in here," he exclaims. "The equipment is very dangerous." As if in answer, the cook bursts in with a steaming pot of fresh-boiled "hairy" crabs from the incidental catch. (Hair covers their carapaces.) Delicious odors fill the cabin. O-san holds even tighter to the rail he clutches. While I crack and eat with gusto, his eyes glaze. Half in generosity but half with other intent I hold out a shellful of crabmeat swimming in its dark yellow fat. "Try this, O-san, it'll make you feel better." Poor O-san disappears into his bunk.

Sure, I feel guilty.

Within minutes I walk on deck dressed for work, to start at the bottom shoveling fish into tubs and lifting them to the table. There are uncertain chuckles, then grins and laughs as I keep at it. From the wheelhouse window the fishing master, grinning also, points his camera. Soon I'm sorting fish into boxes with the rest, invited into the circle and shown the different varieties.

After the set I follow to the crew's galley, a damp and smoky space centered around a stove that burns open charcoal. They include me immediately, passing tea and chopsticks from the common jar. As we all dip into a pan of curried squid on the stove the cook brings my American breakfast from the wheelhouse and offers it reproachfully. (He probably rushed all over town the night before to buy it.) I graciously pass the uncooked bacon around, but no one else wants it either. They cringe: Westerners are obviously barbarians to eat such stuff.

The sea remains rough all day. I become a regular on deck and then around the stove between sets, grilling chunks of fresh fish with the rest—and eventually the pieces of bacon. We exchange appreciative looks at photos of our wives and children, and perform other friendly sign-language communications. One of the bachelors invites me below to see his lusty Japanese pinups. In the berthing area low boards partition off spaces for sleeping.

Eventually O-san acquires sea legs of a sort and gamely follows where his duty lies, down to crew country from which he had tried to shield me. With his translation I learn that the crewmen have all fished together for the five years since the company bought the ship, and that most transferred as a group from a previous company ship. How are fishermen making out? I ask, expecting the same long faces as those from boatowners. A young man with thick fisherman's fingers answers proudly that he makes better money than an office worker. When he states figures, O-san quietly confirms the truth of this compared with his own salary with its years of tenure.

The final set comes aboard at 4:30 P.M.: a twelve-hour fishing day. We eat a meal of raw and baked fish, then head to sleep as the cook cleans the galley. After working as hard on deck all day as the others, he still dips plates and chopsticks into soapy water. This is the fate of old-timers on the world's fishing boats, their way to remain aboard in competition with younger men. I offer to help. He politely waves me aside, either from pride or in memory of his scorned bacon.

Back in the wheelhouse the captain has appeared at the helm again for the trip home. His job gives him no more quarter than that of the cook. Yoshida-san, the fishing master, now haggard-tired, is just climbing into his bunk. He has been too busy all day to talk privately. Now he agrees to postpone sleep long enough for a quick interview. He is forty-nine, and has four children. His fishing career began on deck, where he advanced to boatswain. Then, five years ago, the fishing master of a large trawler aboard which he worked for ten years recommended him for promotion.

"You learned well," I comment. "Your hold is full."

He smiles to show teeth laced with silver bridgework. "Much of what I know comes from my father. He also was a fishing master."

We arrive back in Kushiro around 9 P.M. with a haul of approximately fifteen tons. Buyers wait on the dark pier, both men and women. The crew unloads. The cargo net brings up the boxed species trailing ice, and then the loose fish of other species that have been placed between boards and layered with ice. They lay out the quality stuff in a shed adjoining the quay, and negotiations begin between buyers and a company representative. The bulk fish go at once into trucks, iced again. Some of the crewmen's families wait for a visit after the fish have been unloaded and the hold scrubbed. They have an hour together before the ship sails again: Fishing for a Japanese company can be as driven as, in the United States, fishing for oneself with payments to meet.

1988: Fish Pens and Sing-Along

"My hatchery salmon all swim to Alaska to get fat. Then one hundred percent they swim back to Shibetsu because they are *contented* in Shibetsu!" Mr. Minami laughs and laughs at his joke, which would have elicited no merriment in Alaska. The health of chum salmon off little towns like Shibetsu along the coast of Hokkaido dictates much of the price Alaskan fishermen get for salmon—even different types, including sockeyes. A bad Hokkaido season leaves a Japanese market willing to buy more imports at a higher price, while conversely the price to Alaskans plummets when Hokkaido chums storm the weirs. This Hokkaido season is a good one.

I am ending a long day with officials and fishermen of the Shibetsu Cooperative in the company of my interpreter and of Hiroshi Minami, general manager of the co-op. After a dinner of sashimi washed with beer and then warm sake, we drink and sing songs to each other in a warm little karaoke bar where shelves of bottles line the walls. Minami-san, a graying athletic man of fifty, has been abruptly businesslike during the day. Now, as our host, he grows progressively expansive. He studied German and Spanish at university to prepare for a career in international trade, but gave it up and returned home to Shibetsu when his father became ill. Starting at a laborer's salary in the co-op, he worked hard and soon had doubled his pay. "Now—" his eyes open wide and his brows arch triumphantly: "*Twenty-one* times double salary. Doing very well!" At nine we wave *sayonara*, since the boats will leave at four the next morning and I plan to be aboard.

In Shibetsu, a place of utilitarian low buildings a several-hour bus ride from Kushiro, seven salmon rivers empty into the Pacific Ocean. During the major runs from late August through November, these rivers collectively supply the largest salmon pack in Hokkaido, averaging between eight thousand and ten thousand metric tons a year. The Shibetsu Cooperative, organized by local fishermen, is comprised of thirty-two small fishing companies, some of which own only a single fish trap. It has existed for over sixty years. The co-op has its own processing plant for fresh-frozen salmon as well as for frozen and salted salmon eggs. It runs the local fish auction—but by its charter must buy fish for the plant competitively with other buyers.

The co-op also operates a salmon hatchery, Mr. Minami's pride. It has been very successful in increasing local runs. "These are my *aki-aji* come home from Alaska," Minami reiterates with perhaps not all bravado, since salmon swim far enough at sea for these to have touched in Alaskan waters. At the hatchery I watch the unfortunate aki-aji that have struggled upriver, now trapped and penned before they can pursue their destined spawning. Workmen cull females and send them down a sluice to tanks where others de-egg them without the comfort of an attentive male. The males, too worn from their journey to provide first-grade meat, go without ceremony into bins to be butchered for the cheapest product.

At 4 A.M. in the chilly dark Mr. Minami, now too businesslike ever to be pictured singing expansively, drives onto the pier to introduce me to the skipper of the open, wooden forty-five-foot *Kyo-ei Maru No. 7* and see me off. I climb aboard with the half dozen regular crewmen. By the time we reach the farthest of three fish traps two miles to sea, orange streaks lighten the sky.

A fish trap on the surface seems nothing but confusing lines of floats. It is in fact an elaborate series of submerged nets constructed into diminishing cones fed by a mesh wall that intercepts fish and leads them in. The cones terminate in an enclosure. Few fish swim free again through the small mouth of the cone. Fishermen harvest from the trap by pulling up the meshes of the enclosure.

The skipper, whose leathery earth-colored skin stretches over taut cheekbones, tosses away his cigarette and turns the bill of his cap backward, then steps to the rail with the rest. Everyone pulls in unison. When the net hardens and the weight becomes like rocks, the men slip into a chanting grunt: *"Yat-see, yat-see."* It helps. Soon thrashing seven-pound chums of silvery green fill the brailer and flap around our legs. Working the three traps takes hours. We deliver the catch back to the auction floor of the co-op. Fishermen from each boat sort their own aki-aji by sex and size. Roe-bearing females fetch more than double the price of males.

One man in our crew wears glasses and has a complexion less swarthy than the rest. He has pulled web as vigorously as anyone but now, rather than bending ankle deep in fish to sling them into categories, he removes oilskins and enters the glassed-in office adjacent to the auction shed. He takes a clipboard from a slot with his name on it, scribbles notes, and consults with the grave and efficient Mr. Minami. Later he follows the auctioneer, noting further. The man, age forty-four, is the heir to the fishing company that owns the boat and the fish traps we worked. A law school graduate and father of three, he still participates in the business at all levels until such time as his father turns it over to him.

Following the auction, the six-man crew of the *Kyo-ei Maru No. 7* hoses the hold of their boat and themselves, then go to their quarters for an 11 A.M. dinner before the next pull of the traps. They live in a dormitory, within a compound for its transient fishermen run by the co-op. Each year they come to Shibetsu as a crew from three hundred miles away in Aomori Prefecture, arriving in early June to prepare the nets and staying through the end of November. (In mid-August they go home briefly to celebrate the national holiday *Bon.*) The dormitory consists of a large central room, a basic but chrome-lined kitchen, and a large back room with separate four- by six-foot cubicles for each man. Futons are neatly rolled. The main room has a long table near the kitchen and a wood-burning stove by a wide window near the door. Clothes and rubber work gloves hang on drying racks near the stove. As we wait for dinner the men, changed into clean clothes, sprawl on the floor to watch a television program. Above the color TV hangs a little shrine.

Skipper Kenichi Nihon-yanagi has been a Shibetsu man for thirty years. His wife accompanies him to cook for the crew. "I'm fifty-eight," he declares through my interpreter, "And in another three years I'll be too old to come here any more." He doesn't appear old, nor, in the softened light of a room, as creased and leathery as he had under the sun. His younger brother, Ryuzo, whose missing teeth do nothing to inhibit a frequent grin, has been a Shibetsu man for seventeen years. Ryuzo shows me photos of his wife, three children, and stooped old mother who lives with them back home. My interpreter notes in English that Aomori Prefecture is very poor, and the men earn far more during their annual Shibetsu stay than they could ever make back there. This year, Ryuzo declares happily, they've had *"tai-ryo,"* fantastic catches.

Mrs. Nihon-yanagi, a trim and efficient woman in slacks, wearing an apron embroidered with a cluster of roses, shuttles from kitchen to table. When she calls, the men go at once to the low table and sit cross-legged. Dinner includes salmon steaks, pots of curried chicken and of rice, briny roe, and assorted pickled vegetables. I have barely begun to fill my plate and grasp chopsticks when, six or seven minutes later, everyone else has finished eating. They smoke, then leave the table. One of the men helps clear the dishes and another stacks them. Within fifteen minutes the table has been washed clean. The men lie on the floor watching TV again, then stroll outside yawning to mend a large net. By early afternoon they have reassembled at the boat for the next haul and auction.

1980: Midnight Shoals in Village Waters

The tiny Goto Islands lie about 1,200 air miles from Hokkaido, nearly as far south and west as it is possible to go in Japan. Goto temperatures are nearly tropical compared with Hokkaido's Alaskan cold. Katsutoshi village is no more than a single lane of houses along a bay. A quay and pier lie at the far end of the lane. Low forested mountains rise behind. It is 1980, and I've been invited here, a three-hour ferry ride from Nagasaki and only 110 miles across the East China Sea from Korea, by the Kotobuki ("very happy") Suisan ("fishing") Company, Ltd.

The company president, Mr. Torao Natsui, a dignified but relaxed gentleman of middle age, escorts us to his office in the home of the fleet fishing master. We park shoes at the family entrance among neat boxes and boots, and settle cross-legged on a tatami to be served ocha and snacks. Six feet away in the same room, Mr. Natsui and a clerk conduct late business by phone from swivel chairs, their knees swinging at the level of our noses.

Fishing master Katsutoshi Tanaka joins us yawning, having fished all night and just awakened. He is a compact, tired-eyed, unshaven young man of thirty-five. When the three Tanaka kids come in from school, they creep with several friends as far as the doorway to sneak a look at me. Whenever I wink their way they scurry from sight amid general giggles, but they pass in notebooks and souvenir scrolls for my distinguished autograph.

Fourteen small fishing companies including Kotobuki form the fishery co-op of nearby Narushima town. Each company, consisting of one six-boat purse seine fleet, provides the chief subsistence for a village in the area. The fleets fish every night including Sundays, except in February, the month of roughest weather, when crews repair boats and gear. The boats target *saba* (mackerel) and *iwashi* (sardines). The mackerels go to Tokyo on ice within two days while the less grand iwashi provide local bait and fish-culture feed.

Tanaka-san, relaxed but bashful, speaks through an interpreter as his wife continues to fill the teacups. He's been fishing master since age twenty-two, thirteen years ago, inheriting the post from his father, who had trained him. The company finances go like this: Expenses include fuel and ice, plus three percent of gross to the co-op. The fleet uses six tons of ice and about 2,700 liters (712 gallons) of fuel a night. The company takes forty percent after expenses and the fishermen divide sixty percent. The company guarantees each crewman a minimum salary in the event of poor catches. ("Never necessary," declares Mr. Natsui from his swivel chair just above our heads.) Crew also receive a percentage bonus for unusually large catches.

As time draws near to put to sea, we walk along the harbor to the boats. A misty rain hazes the mountains like a Japanese watercolor. Our fleet of wooden boats moored to the pier consists of one sixty-five-foot seiner that holds a twenty-man crew, three forty-two-foot collector boats each crewed by three men, and two sixty-five-foot fish carriers with six men each. On a wide open space by the boats the forty-plus crewmen stand, many barefoot, surrounded by a bright maroon net that they are sewing into a new seine. Behind them on a low hill stand the stones and bright cloth decorations of a Buddhist cemetery. Everyone continues to work, but at the sight of me subdued laughter ripples among them. I smile back, not sure why I'm so amusing. Japanese individuals may display the quintessence of civility, but collectively workmen are unabashedly direct. Finally one of the men, a head shorter than me, places his small boot next to the big rubber clompers on my feet. Everybody laughs, now freely.

Before casting off we straddle mounds of net to dine on raw fish and squid washed down with fish soup. Sitting cross-legged in boots is clumsy and I remove mine. To the sound of suppressed chuckles I glance up to see the boots passing from foot to foot as the men try them on and wiggle their toes inside.

At dusk, in blowing spray, our six-boat fleet puts to sea. I ride aboard *Kotobuki Maru No. 1,* the seiner and operations center. We pass low mountains and bluffs with a small house or two huddled beneath and nets strung along the rocks. As soon as Tanaka the fishing master steps aboard, his reticence vanishes. The others jump to his every muttered command. Soon he's settled cross-legged in a wide three-foot-high alcove behind the wheel, his bedroom and command post, with bedding on one side and a range of electronic sounders and gauges (as well as a color TV) on the other. For me, standing in the wheelhouse becomes subtle torture because the overhead drops three inches below my height. Tanaka-san clears back an assortment of blankets and quilts from his alcove and insists I join him.

An hour later we reach clusters of boats from the other thirteen fleets of the co-op. Tanaka stations his three collector boats. Each turns on powerful lights that form a turquoise ring in the water. In the dark, a dozen other blue-green glows spot parts of the black water where other village fleets have set. The fish need time to collect under the floodlights. Tanaka rolls himself in the blankets for a nap, and I wander aft to eat strips of raw fish with the friendly crew. When I yawn, they insist on leading me into a waist-high crawl space under the main deck. The space contains two facing rows of open boxes separated by low boards. Someone produces extra bedding to pad my compartment (or gives up his own), and I wriggle in. It measures less than three feet wide by five-and-a-half feet long, but I fit by propping my big feet atop the board facing the narrow aisle between the rows. Snores soon surround me.

Three hours later, near midnight, someone shakes my foot, and I join in the general scramble to dress in tight quarters. The foul-weather

gear—pants and hooded jackets of rubber as thick as inner tubes—
sways on hooks under an awning by the galley suds bucket. It's a
struggle to get into it elbow to elbow on a rolling deck slippery with
seawater. Rain dumps outside on choppy waves. Nearby one of the
collector boats swoops up and down in its turquoise pool of light. Our
boat stays dark so not to counteract the effect.

In the pilothouse Tanaka stands by the wheel with two microphones
in hand, crisply shouting orders to his fleet. At his command the net on
our deck pays out, carried off by one of the carrier boats. The net forms
a necklace of floats around the bright-light boat, circling the fish that
have come to cavort in the great illumination.

We purse at once. Two crews of six stack the center of the web, alter-
nating heats. It seems excessive manpower until I join one crew. We
pull column after column of dripping net across deck from the overhead block, many times a minute, and each man's armful of each
column weighs about forty pounds. I last the heat, but only with
panting effort. Fishermen sometimes become as much a part of the
sea as the creatures they pursue. Water and jellyfish from the net
cascade on us from above, rain pelts our faces, and the ocean washes
around our feet.

By daylight we've returned to the village, most having slept a bit on
the way. Tanaka, his work done and no longer the driving boss, walks
home, while some of the crew take the boat around the bend to a central
unloading facility. Mrs. Tanaka greets us with low bows and soon places
ocha before us. We take turns in the family bath, a deep three-foot-
square tub in its own small room. I follow the Japanese procedure,
soaping and rinsing first, then entering the tub clean. The water is
painfully hot, but once I'm immersed, the heat's dizzying comfort nearly
puts me to sleep. Without question my muscles ache and it feels good.
A long breakfast follows, of fish—fresh, dried, and pickled.

On the second night we corner an immense school of iwashi. The
netful runs the sixty-five-foot length of the boat, and the thousands of
gleaming fish thrash a stew. At one point masses of *hagi,* a lesser fish,
emerge in a clot. From the wheelhouse Tanaka cries orders in a high
voice, and with sub-shouts the crew poles down one side of the floats.
A huge wash of hagi swims free along with masses of the target fish. The
loss can hardly be noticed. The first carrier boat brails until its holds
fill and fish pile on deck. The second carrier takes over. Some of the
men from our seiner swing over Tarzan-style to help with the icing,

which becomes feverish to keep pace. This school is so immense that if it sounds collectively it could carry the boats with it, so hatchets lay ready by the rails to chop the net. The weight is too heavy for the power block, so we tug the net aboard inch by inch with arms and backs. The spray from the massed fish salts the eyes and leaves a metallic taste on our lips.

When it is over we sit in the rain atop the net. With blood still pumping no one cares to sleep yet, even though we're headed home with all holds plugged. The men have pulled choice stray fish from the mass—mostly black-and-white-striped *ishidai*: bream. These they deftly slice into bite-size strips. Out come bowls, chopsticks, and a big bottle of soy sauce. Bream sashimi, a favorite on all the boats I have ridden in Japan, has firm red meat and the delicate flavor of the best raw fish. I eat a good fill, along with rice carried out in a big pot from the galley. Then the cook appears on deck with a tureen of fish-and-seaweed soup made from more of the fresh bream, too rich and creamy to resist. We finish with green tea, mixing it with leftover rice and a touch of horseradish in a concoction called *ocha-zuke,* common among frugal working Japanese.

By now I'm as warmly a part of the crew as a foreign-speaking stranger can be. My big boots remain a curiosity, although it is too wet now to pass them around (as indeed I have done once again). It has become our running joke whenever everybody relaxes, my entry ticket.

I've barely curled into my box under the deck, satiated and more, when the cook (by whose side I sweated at the net) tugs my leg to present a bream he has baked especially. I'm dizzy with eating, but I finish it and smack my lips to reassure him of my pleasure.

CHAPTER NINETEEN

Harpooners

Ayukawa, Central Japan

As soon as she recognizes me Hanako Chida prostrates herself on the tatami of her doorstep. I have returned. A small woman in her midsixties, she mumbles over and over in Japanese, "Cannot believe the honor." I bow repeatedly, playing my part and making no effort to dissuade her from playing her own. In 1980 she was shaped like a dumpling, but now, in 1990, more like a pear. Nothing else seems different, even to her apron and brown kerchief. Minoru Chida, Hanako's fisherman-husband and a former Antarctic whaler, comes from behind, smiling. He is less robust than a decade ago, but this diminishes none of his surprised pleasure. The husband and wife operate a *minshuku,* boardinghouse, and, ten years ago, I was their only Western visitor ever. I have returned to Ayukawa to acknowledge old friendship and to see what has become of the former whaling town. During my first visit in 1980 I rode a whale boat and formed my judgments on the ethics of whaling compared with its necessities.

Ayukawa lies two hundred miles north of Tokyo on a hilly, scenic stretch of the eastern Honshu coast. The harbor centers around a workaday esplanade backed by food stalls and shops. During my first visit, the low sheds of the Sanyo Hogei whaling station dominated the harbor. Now in place of this a scaffolding surrounds what is to be a giant whale monument built to satisfy camera-snapping tour groups that once came to watch an industry in action. Whaling no longer exists, only its souvenirs. Relentlessly cute cartoon whales decorate shops that sell whale trinkets. Tourists wait in line outside one shop in the picturesque hills to have their photos taken by a lacquered, nine-foot-high whale penis.

Much of the town's economy was built around a fleet of seventy-five-foot wooden boats with sweeping bows and crow's nests high on the mast, designed to catch the relatively small minke whale during its migration off the coast. A single minke—pronounced "ming-key"— yields 800 to 1,000 kilograms of meat (1,760 to 2,200 pounds) plus 150 to 200 kg of blubber (330 to 440 pounds)—all of it edible and considered a delicacy by the Japanese. The local industry employed hundreds in work ranging from crewmen and harpooners to butchers and whalebone craftsmen.

In an identification with the slaughtered prey similar to that of Eskimos, Ayukawa had a special Buddhist temple, surrounded by pines and reached by a high flight of steps, where whalers went to bless and thank the creatures they killed. One tall polished stone cenotaph, its inscription clearly legible, commemorated the deaths of one thousand whales during a period of years.

June 1980

At the minshuku, Hanako-san's smiles fill the small dining/living room as she hurries from the adjacent kitchen to load the table with food. Guests for the occasion include Yasuji Iwasaki, harpooner or gunner of the boat I will ride, and Teruo Miida, the captain. Both men, although very polite, regard me cautiously, unsure of my game in a time of frenzied antiwhaling activists. We sit cross-legged, flanked by windows overlooking the harbor. A samurai movie roars its course on a color TV set in the corner, ignored by everyone.

We start drinking beer from large bottles, and about halfway through the meal switch to warm sake in the usual order of beverages for a large Japanese meal. In polite Japanese fashion, no one refills his own glass, but only his neighbor's. A toast with the exclamation *"kampai!"* follows each round of fish served baked, raw, and fried—fish all caught by the master of the house himself, Minoru-san, who acknowledges modestly.

The harpooner is fifty-one, father of a family that includes both young and teenage children. His whaling career spans thirty-five years, twenty-five of these as a gunner. Life in the sun has left his face brown and shiny, especially the cheeks, and under the bulbs of the Chida living room his high forehead glistens. "I wished to be a whaling man from the start," he declares through an interpreter. He attended a vocational high school that specialized in fisheries, then went to sea. "Twenty-five years ago, when whaling was good, the company selected several crewmen for gunner training. I was selected." He pauses, then adds modestly: "Only very good men were selected."

Did young men still have such an opportunity? I ask. The veteran harpooner gives no real answer. "Only the company can decide," was the closest he comes. But, he adds, "There are more whale gunners now than ships to hire them. Back then there were fourteen whaling ships in Ayukawa. Now only five. The time is different now." The International Whaling Commission (IWC) has succeeded in reducing worldwide whaling quotas drastically year by year. The reductions are not academic for those around the table. Our host, Minoru Chida, was a former whaler whose ship stopped going to the Antarctic for lack of quota. He and his wife used savings to convert their small home into a boarding house to make ends meet, and he fishes now as he can.

The world outcry against whaling left Japanese whalemen puzzled and resentful. For harpooner Iwasaki, a whalingman's job is to take food from the sea rather than to moralize about it. Looking at me firmly, he declares it arbitrary and unfair of other nations, meeting generally in England on the other side of the world, to set limits on the livelihood of Ayukawa. I explain that many whales have been hunted to near-extinction and that it is important to protect the surviving herds. "Yes, but please we wish to say, no danger of extinction to minke and sperm whales off Ayukawa!"

I do not tackle the more complicated explanation. The West finds whaling repugnant. Particularly vocal are the British, who were once enthusiastic whalers, and the Americans, who deplore present whaling but grow wistful over the bold Yankee whalermen of a century ago who cleaned out the greatest herds of whales, even from the Japan coast. As Richard Frank, then-U.S. commissioner to the IWC, told the House Foreign Affairs Committee circa 1980: "Our goal [is] to halt all commercial whaling. . . . The United States will continue to support [a moratorium] as the cornerstone of our whaling policy." In 1998 the policy remains the same, although the U.S. continues to insist on a small annual quota of endangered bowhead whales for Alaska Eskimos.

With strong American and British support the IWC packed its voting membership with nonwhaling nations, even landlocked Switzerland. The ten nations that in the early 1980s still kept a stake in the industry were out-voted within a membership of thirty-six. The organization, formed by whaling nations in 1946 to self-police the industry, has, since the 1980s, appeared to work more toward eliminating whaling. The substantive reason is the fear of depleting stocks. The unofficial but intense bottom line, however, is the "immorality" of killing creatures as special as whales, a cause espoused by pressure groups with that most dangerously intolerant of all motivations: high moral purpose. Since morality is shaky ground at best, given its varying interpretations throughout the world, the newly focused IWC relied on computer models to show that even the most robust whale stocks were endangered along with the *truly* endangered stocks. When the Japanese proved a computer model on sperm whale stocks faulty in 1981 (making the difference between endangerment and abundance) the antiwhalers verbally shrugged. That attitude continues.

Alan Macnow, a spokesman for the Japanese, reversed the morality issue during 1980s testimony before House Foreign Affairs: "The Japanese see this very much as a moral issue. When science says this is a resource that can be utilized, and when science points out that it can be utilized to a certain extent [with] quotas. . . why should the Japanese then say, 'Well, we're going to respect the Americans' opinion about the whale, that it is an intelligent, semi-Godlike creature, and we are going to give up eating it because the Americans and the British don't like the idea of us eating whale meat.'"

I had attended a conference of the whale protection people in Washington, D.C. Their complacence and self-reinforcement left me aghast and wry. They listened avidly to long jargon-laden talks proving high cetacean intelligence (since questioned by responsible scientists with no connection to whalers), then chatted or leaned back glassy-eyed during Japanese attempts to explain their own view. Whatever their method, the goal of the antiwhalers to halt all whaling was possibly valid. This was why I had come to Ayukawa.

The boat I'm to ride, *Taisho Maru,* has a minke whale quota of fifty-five. According to the harpooner, they need closer to seventy whales a season to assure each man a living wage. The *Taisho* thus far has landed only twenty-seven whales. Unseasonably frequent fogs have kept boats in port for many days of the high season, and now in late June the main minke herd is already migrating farther north. Every day at sea now counts. On the first morning we assemble on the dark quay at 3 A.M. The six crewmen nod cautiously as the harpooner and captain introduce me, while those aboard other whalers tied nearby strain to watch. We leave harbor with four other boats like ours.

Aboard the *Taisho* a long open afterdeck allows little room for quarters. One of the men shows me a place to lie comfortably on the cramped, clean cabin deck. Everyone except the captain at the helm naps until we reach the grounds. By daybreak three hours later, fog lies over the ocean and visibility extends no farther than a quarter mile. No land can be seen. A single man climbs the mast and settles in the bucket to scan the water. As the fog lifts, more join him. By ten the sun has burned the air clear and all hands watch. Iwasaki, the harpooner, takes his place alone in the bucket, while others climb higher to a small crow's nest or hook a leg around the rigging.

Most of a whaling ship's duties turn out to be lookout. The rigging and crow's nest fifty feet above the sea increase the scope of the horizon but also place us in the path of a chilly breeze. We peer all morning. The sun grows hotter, but the breeze still cuts across the water. Everyone seems tense. With fog, no boat has caught a whale for four days. As the sun sparkles on the choppy water, black wave-shadows begin to look like whale backs. No one but the harpooner speaks. Occasionally he mutters a course change into a microphone, and a loudspeaker near the wheel in the cabin echoes it back. The captain at the wheel obediently repeats the command like any disciplined helmsman.

By the time the cook calls lunch, my face smarts from wind and sun. One man, the boatswain, remains in the bucket. We settle on the scrubbed wooden afterdeck. The crewman who serves as cook, Hayao Abe, is a happy man in his fifties who later tells me pointedly several times how glad he is to be whaling when so many other whalemen are out of work. Abe-san serves an impressive meal for a man who has also been standing lookout all morning. He brings out a big pot of steaming rice, along with a whole grilled fish apiece, a tureen of thick fish-and-seaweed soup, and assorted common platters of raw fish and squid. We select red lacquered chopsticks at random from a vaselike jar. A bucket of hot suds nearby shows that everyone takes dish washing and sanitation for granted.

Suddenly the boatswain shouts from the bucket. Off run the gunner, engineer, and captain at once. Soon everyone crowds back on lookout with legs and arms wrapped around the rigging, scanning the choppy water with binoculars lashed to sticks for stability. The boatswain has seen, in the sun's path, what he thinks was a curving black hump and splash about a mile to starboard. If the sighting results in a captured whale, the man who first sighted it will receive a small bonus. Twenty years before this in more prosperous whaling times, they tell me, the bonus was many times higher.

"*Hakken!*" ("Sighted!") barks someone. A smooth black shape slices gracefully through the water before disappearing. Harpooner-gunner

Iwasaki snaps a course change in the direction he last saw the whale swimming. He uses the English "port" and "starboard," but in a heavy enough accent that only after many calls do I recognize it. Soon: *"Iro!"* The word, literally "color," means in this usage "whale over there close enough to see its color"—the signal for action. Everyone turns tense. The whale, after sounding off the starboard bow to leave the horizon blank for five minutes, reappears astern. He had reversed course underwater. The *iro*s become hoarse barks. This is to be no straight-line chase. Either the whale enjoys swimming zigzag, or he already senses pursuit.

The whale, an air-breathing mammal, initially has simple mathematics on his side. He can disappear underwater for five minutes and more without surfacing for air. And he can race at sixteen knots, while the *Taisho*'s engine delivers no more than twelve knots at full throttle. The ship must creep close before alarming him. A whale, however, tires quickly under pressure while a diesel engine churns indefinitely. And as a fatigued whale becomes winded, he needs to surface more often, which lessens his chance of escape.

The ship carries a low, wide speedskiff equipped with an engine good for thirty-five knots. It rides in tow after reaching the grounds. Seiichiro Ito, a full-chested young man with flying black hair, has pulled into a wetsuit at the first confirmed sighting, and now he stands ready in the skiff. When we've closed to a quarter-mile of the whale, the gunner signals and off Ito goes with a roar. The water is choppy. As he speeds toward the whale his little boat thuds and bounces. "Young man's work," observes the captain glumly. "No good after thirty." He himself was a speedboat man before rupturing his spleen on the thud of a high bounce.

The speedboat circles behind the whale, then zooms closer and closer to harass him toward the ship. When the whale sounds, the gunner guesses his direction and calls a course by microphone to both ship and skiff. No one expects the whale to remain still. Sometimes, in the long chase, the whale surfaces at a point unpredicted. We gain ground, then lose it. The speedboat turns precipitously, bucking waves head on that toss it several feet in the air. This is wild duty. An hour into the hunt, the speedboat breaks down. The ship chases alone. Ito bends feverishly over the propeller shaft until he fixes it and re-enters pursuit.

The whale outfoxes us, and we search anxiously. Then one of the lookouts sights him again and cries *"Iro!"* That "iro!" becomes a cry almost frightening. To add to the frenzy, seabirds fly wildly before us.

Swarming birds sometimes betray the whales. In these waters both gorge on the sardine-size *shirasu*.

I become gripped enough by the heat of the chase to contribute excited "iros" myself. The more the whale fights and maneuvers, however, the more I root for him even though the crew's payday hangs in the balance. At length I try silently to will our prey into the sun path that half-blinds us, while only nodding in his direction without calling out if I spot him before the rest.

The whale begins to move more slowly and sound less often. The ship homes in. Iwasaki moves down to his harpoon gun on the fore-peak. The boatswain takes the chief lookout position in the bucket to shout helm commands to the captain at the wheel. The whale surfaces about twenty-five meters away. Iwasaki fires but misses. Two crewmen hurry forward to haul back the thirty-meter line and barb. Iwasaki rearms and waits, legs apart and body bent, his eye in the sight.

Suddenly, the whale surfaces ten meters to port. *"IRO!"* Bang. Blood seeps into the blue water, but the whale remains submerged as they quickly winch him alongside. He is thrashing, and it would be deception to pretend it is not from pain. The harpooner and the two others stand ready with long pikes that they thrust repeatedly into the shiny black body. From the bucket we lose sight of both victim and hunters in the welter of water. Then one of the pikes reaches the heart, the whale dies, and the water suddenly calms.

The chase has lasted an hour and a half. It takes between seven and eight minutes to complete the kill following the strike. Everyone grins his satisfaction. As in the case of game hunted by thousands of Americans, the hunter becomes hardened after a while, or at least philosophical, over the fact that suffering can occur between the hit and the kill. I am not trying to negate the ugliness of this part of whaling, but to place it in the perspective of other cruelties that our society accepts for convenience.

At this time (1980) an exploding harpoon that detonates immediately after penetration, developed for quickly killing large whales, cannot work on twenty-foot minkes without destroying half the meat. Thus unless a minke takes the conventional harpoon direct to the heart, he dies neither instantly nor painlessly. The Japanese will later develop a harpoon with quick-kill, high-shock, low destructive capability that they claim works on minkes. A conventional exploding harpoon, in the hands of a skilled gunner, does work on larger cetaceans. During a hunt for forty-five-foot Brydes whales that I observed off another Japanese coast, such weapons killed two animals within a few seconds and one other instantly. (The proud gunner declared the latter to be a "*pan-koro*": a bang-dead.)

Everyone aboard the *Taisho* pulls on a line to maneuver the big floating carcass astern, then winches it up the stern ramp and onto the deck boards where we sat eating a while before. With deft incisions from long-poled flensing knives they bleed, gut, and clean the carcass. The cook and radioman do it with the greatest skill. The opened whale emits a raw, gassy stench. Organs tumble onto deck, at least a ton of little *shirasu* fish fall out, blood gushes everywhere, as it does on any slaughterhouse floor, and none of it is agreeable. Nor is it in a conventional abattoir, where hoses quickly send the blood down drains so that the gore is less apparent, but where I have seen kills neither as instantaneous nor anxiety-free for the animal as generally supposed.

Japanese whalers traditionally eat a piece of their catch soon after the kill. It appears to be for them equally a reward and a symbiosis. The cook cuts meat and blubber into thin two-inch slices. My crewmates combine a piece each in their chopsticks, since they like the taste of fat while minke meat is lean. They exclaim over the quality of the blubber, and urge me to eat more than I want. The taste and appearance of minke whale meat is not far removed from rare beef except for a mild nonfishy sea flavor. I prefer it chilled to body temperature, perhaps from squeamishness. Raw blubber is white and firm, with a rind crunchy like weak cartilage, and though I can get it down, its subdued oily flavor gives me no pleasure. Cooked blubber on the other hand takes on a nauseating flavor exactly like the acrid and oily-sweet stench of a blubber tryworks in full swing. Abe-san also prepares fried whale meat, which has a stronger sea flavor, and slices of whale intestines boiled in salt water that taste like conventional organ meats.

As I write this in 1997, Ayukawa whaling is in the past and the once-prosperous town is economically depressed. The Chida minshuku appeared shabby when I revisited in 1990. Few people within their customer range came to town on business any more. Only tourism jogged along, since the town is a way-stop to a famous shrine. Was it really necessary to kill a fishing food industry?

Lack of management and greed of men to grab all they could had led to a terrible endangerment of whale stocks. The numbers of such great cetaceans as the blue, humpback, and right whales—the largest and therefore most profitable—had diminished to possibly mere hundreds.

Only with the formation of the IWC, comprised of whaling nations willing to self-police, was the slaughter controlled. This fight had been won by the 1970s.

The new IWC majority voted an indefinite moratorium that started in 1986. By then only Japan, Norway, Iceland, and two small Caribbean islands still protected whaling investments. While these nations fought the moratorium, arguing that minke, fin, and sperm whales in particular were abundant enough to sustain a limited hunt, and while they chafed under the IWC charter that weighed their votes equally with nations that had nothing at stake, they acceded. To appease them the IWC declared itself willing to reconsider the moratorium following the accumulation of more accurate data on whale populations.

By 1993 Iceland had left the IWC in order not to be bound, and in 2000, began whaling again. Japan and Norway began to take a limited number of minke whales for research, an act they claimed necessary to collect data for the studies. Though this limited take was part of the agreement, thunderous denunciations followed from animal rights groups, and continue with pressure for sanctions. This is not playing by the rules. During its 1992 annual meeting in Glasgow, the IWC received a report from its scientific committee that dismayed the anti-whaling members. It said that certain whales could indeed be hunted in limited quantity without harming the stocks. The report suggested a management procedure to allocate one percent or fewer of counted numbers to the whaling nations. The United States has helped lead attempts to block any allocation and continues to support the effort against all whaling. Other nations, however, began to support a limited resumption of whaling at the 1997 IWC meeting in Monaco. They recognize a greater danger to whales in the possible breakup of the IWC if whaling nations leave and make their own rules.

International agreement now protects all endangered whales, except for the native "subsistence" exemptions, and this is challenged by no one. But if certain edible whale stocks off fishing communities are not threatened with extinction, and the creatures can be killed within the bounds of cruelty that society accepts for the slaughter of other food creatures, then a case can be made for a limited continuation of monitored local whaling, no matter how unattractive to some with nothing to lose.

The strongest voices for extreme animal rights come from city people, who need never to bloody their hands or participate in a death agony to obtain a package of steak or chicken. They find it easy to demand, for sentimental reasons, the sacrifice of other peoples' livelihoods in which they have no stake. Many of these urbanites also march frenziedly against any practical means of controlling human births. Yet the overpopulated planet packs in more people by the day and they must be fed. Thousands starve as it is. Humans need protein, all that the planet can provide from every available source. We cannot indefinitely save all potential humans while protecting every attractive individual creature that is a source of human food.

CHAPTER TWENTY

Hanging Genki with the Squidders

Ishinomaki, Japan, June 1990

The Japanese regard outsiders and their motives warily when it comes to controversial matters of the ocean, as well they might. Visitors treated openly in the past have been known to respond on returning home with thundering denunciations of dolphins "sensibly" slaughtered in the Iki Islands to protect the local fishing industry, or of whales harpooned for food, or of miles-long squid driftnets set efficiently. Thus, when I challenged and cajoled Japanese authorities to let me sail with one of those driftnet fleets that had earned contumely throughout the world, negotiations took nearly a year. The Japanese deal with such matters step by step through introductions, allowing time for all parties to establish a gradual trust.

Do these floating nets ensnare devastating numbers of birds, marine mammals, and other fish as they were accused of doing? Or, as the Japanese claimed, do their meshes capture only the targeted squid or other species? I could only promise to report truthfully what I saw, while cautioning that, whatever the persuasion of Japanese hospitality, I wouldn't gloss my observations. I also made it clear that I expected to ride aboard a vessel in the main fleet, not some special boat that might be designated to fish "clean" for the eyes of a foreigner.

Eventually my trip aboard a Japanese driftnetter was arranged for June of 1990. It began in Ishinomaki, a fishing town on the central Pacific coast of Japan, where the two-hundred-foot (sixty-three-meter) *Sumiho Maru No. 75* lay at dock ready to sail. On deck brave marching music crackled through the overloaded speaker. Families lined the quay, awaiting our departure for the North Pacific, a trip scheduled to last from mid-June to mid-September. The men had been home only four days since returning from a fishing journey to the Falkland Islands off Argentina that lasted from December to June.

On deck Mr. Shikahiro Sumida, the gravely cheerful young president of the three-ship family company that owns the *Sumiho,* assembles the crew of seventeen to introduce me. He reads a reassuring statement I penned on the advice of an American friend versed in Japanese custom, stating that I have ridden aboard other Japanese fishing boats, look forward to this trip with equal pleasure, and will report with fairness and objectivity. Then Sumida pours sake into plastic cups from a large bottle and we toast the voyage.

The sake of our toast comes not by casual purchase but from one of two bottles placed inside a small Shinto shrine in the ship's wheelhouse. Just half an hour before, a Shinto priest came aboard, changed from street clothes into vestments, and blessed the ship and its voyage. He faced the shrine, which is enclosed in a cabinet placed between the radios and the sea-temperature gauge. Behind him, backed against electronic fishfinders in the cramped space, stood owner Sumida with the fishing master, captain, chief engineer, and office manager. "Let there be a safe trip for all aboard, and let there be a large catch," was the essence of the priest's chanted words. He took a small-leafed branch from the shrine and waved it ceremonially over the men. They in turn bowed, and clapped to draw divine attention.

The blessing centered on a foot-long wooden panel that bears the ship's name and other identifications. Three days earlier, Sumida-san and Yoshiteru Abe, the fishing master, carried this *omamori,* or *ofuda,* by boat to the island shrine of Kinkazan to have it consecrated in a special ceremony. We traveled by fishing boat among beautiful hilly islands. The sun shone although a haze softened the low, forested mountains along the coast. From the shrine's pier we climbed a mile uphill past blue-water vistas framed by the gracefully twisted trunks of tall pine trees. Deer roamed free everywhere, as befits the Shinto emphasis on living in harmony with nature. The Japanese consider deer to be sacred, and regard the Western taste for venison with the same horror that some in the West regard the Japanese taste for whale meat.

The shrine complex covered three levels separated by stairs and a courtyard. Tourists on the lower level chattered and laughed in holiday spirits as they bought nibbles for the deer and charbroiled squid-on-a-stick for themselves. In the buildings above, bells sounded in deep, gonglike tones, and voices chanted. We passed a large pavilion where people sat on straw mats, praying individually. Others bowed and clapped before an altar with a chubby figure that held a fish in one hand and a fishing pole in the other. This was *Ebisu,* the deity of fishermen, one of seven Shinto gods of wealth, who is enshrined at Kinkazan along with another deity representing good fortune.

Two priests conducted our own ceremony in a separate, open pavilion. As we knelt back on our feet and the priest chanted for our ship's safety and good catches, visitors gaily passed down a stair just outside. Shinto, a practical religion concerned with the present life, can intertwine ceremonies and outings without losing spiritual effectiveness. Buddhism, the coexisting religion of Japan, takes care of the afterlife and individual salvation. On the way out, we received a sip of sake from a common dish, much in the manner of communion.

Back on board the *Sumiho Maru,* our temple-blessed omamori replaces in the shrine last year's omamori, which will eventually be returned to Kinkazan for burning. Such objects in this transitory life cannot be expected to retain potency forever.

On the quay, men whom I will soon know better visit their families for a last time. They hold or walk hand in hand with children they see barely enough to be remembered. My snapshots identify them for me later. There is Kishio Satoh, in red workout pants, his muscles bulging from his undershirt. He holds a thumb-sucking little boy who snuggles close against his chest. His wife alongside holds an older girl. The photo catches Kishio watching his son wistfully as sisters crowd close and parents stand discreetly apart with disciplined smiles. Soon he'll be checking gauges in the engine room as first assistant, with a wrench in his white-gloved hand and a sweatband around his head. Morio Abe, in his thirties, ten years Kishio's senior and chief engineer, holds a squirming little girl with a flower tied in her hair. His shaven chin will soon have a black stubble and, with calm cheer, he'll be one of the steadiest men for any work on deck or below. Hiroshi Itoh, the cook, a grave, self-conscious man in his forties, stands with middle-age relatives and a high-school-age son, smiling more than he ever will on ship. An hour later he'll be setting his galley in order, wearing apron and boots, unsmilingly concentrated.

Kazue Oono, a round-faced man of about thirty with full black hair, stoops to talk eye-to-eye with his six-year-old son. His expression is a serious version of the friendly one, just on the verge of a grin or chuckle, that will characterize him daily on ship. Nearby stands Yoshishero Abe, the moustachioed radioman, his hands around a gift as two women holding children talk. Within a day he and I will be hunched over a big Japanese-English dictionary in his cramped quarters, interrupted only by his duties to transmit and receive lengthy reports.

During the farewells, people unroll ribbons of colored paper. The ship's whistle blows and the men, some without looking back, troop aboard with the streamers. The gangway rises. The men attach their strands of paper to a block suspended from the ship's boom. The relatives ashore hold the other ends. Off go the mooring lines. Water separates us by inches and then by a widening gap. The volume of the music rises. The streamers—yellow, red, white, green, and purple—stretch farther and farther until those ashore can hold them no longer and must let them drop in the water to follow their men.

Those who decided to permit me aboard *Sumiho Maru No. 75* might have placed me within the action as agreed, but they made sure I will experience one of the newer vessels within a fleet that has seen hard service in other fisheries before being converted. I'm relieved despite my bravado insistence during the negotiations that any boat fit for Japanese fishermen would be good enough for me. Some vessels of the squid driftnet fleet are reported to be rustbuckets, poorly maintained by companies half-broke, even dangerous if hit by a violent North Pacific storm.

The *Sumiho* crewmen live two to a small cabin furnished with bunks and cabinets, a refrigerator, and a video TV. Private cabins go to the fishing master (three times the size of any other), captain, chief engineer, and to the radioman, who shares space with all his equipment. The men have converted a storage space for me, installing a bunk and a new carpet but, Japanese-fashion, no chair. I soon learn Japanese proportions as I slam my head into the doorposts and even small vents protruding just an inch from the overhead. My own six feet equals exactly that of the ceiling, a comfortable height for crewmen a few inches shorter. I feel like Gulliver in Lilliput. After a half-dozen scrapes during the first day aboard, when my head begins to hurt, I take to wearing a cap at all times for padding, and I learn to walk stooped.

Then there are the footwear-changing ceremonies. To keep the mess-deck cleaner than the workdeck, and rooms cleaner than corridors, everyone slips from boots to different sandals in each part of the ship, intensifying a common Japanese practice. It makes sense to keep quick-rotting fish matter out of the living quarters. Sometimes to move from one place to another, even on the run, requires multiple changes. Once while working below decks, when I discover a sudden photo opportunity but have left the flash attachment on my bunk, I switch footwear six times on the run to retrieve the equipment.

I must make other adjustments. Everyone chain-smokes, having never heard of the American Surgeon General, although I, the nonsmoker, develop the only cough. As for food, I've traveled enough to try in good cheer anything my host eats first. Raw squid that was spouting ink on deck a few minutes earlier is just fine (although slippery), as is a ton-weight mambo fish caught in the net and shortly after served raw with its liver. I don't question the origin of some dried, slimy, or pickled sea things as I eat them along with everyone else. But, a raw egg for breakfast with my pickled octopus and seaweed-fish-and-tofu soup? After the first morning I skip the egg.

I am on my own with the language, bolstered in basic sentence structure by a five-session evening class at Johns Hopkins University back home in Baltimore. Bushy-haired Yoshishero Abe, the radioman, knows a smattering of English and has the energy to search out idea-words in a thick Japanese-English dictionary. The tissue-page dictionary has such fine print that we need a magnifying glass to read it. *"Mo'ment!"* he'll declare, and rush for the book. We teach each other, laboriously comparing families and cultures. Sometimes the dictionary gives multiple definitions. When Abe-san's meaning could be a choice between "decoration," "disarmament," or "fumigation," I nod sagely and pass to a new topic.

Whatever the effort, struggles with words break the ice. While working on deck one day in the early part of the trip I receive a minor bump and everyone turns solicitous. I shrug and declare with elaborate enough unconcern to be clearly joking, "Oh, *itai itai*"—it hurts—and mean to follow with a call for a doctor. Instead of *"isha"* I say *"ika,"* which means squid. Everyone looks puzzled. Then I correct myself and we enjoy the joke loudly.

The Japanese—these fishermen at any rate—are by no means inscrutable. Among themselves they joke and banter all the time. During the leisure portions of the trip to the grounds they play mah-jongg with slam-bang glee. At work their horseplay ranges from taking long slides into each other on a deck slippery with squid ink to snapping the jaws of a dead shark at each other's bottoms. They follow events back home and most take time to read a long daily news sheet in Japanese that arrives on the telex each morning. The portions of the sheet that people read me, however, deal with the world outside Japan only if it pertains to Japan.

To know the men I approach each individually with a crew manifest in hand, and venture in Japanese rehearsed beforehand: "Hello. I am named McCloskey." Handshake. "Now please show me *your* name." With his name duly pronounced (some, like Shizukuishi, require amused coaching before I get it right) I draw from my breast pocket—never from a back pocket and never with the left hand, both indications of disdain or uncleanness—a big white pen printed with a Baltimore Orioles logo. "My home is Baltimore in the USA. Do you know Baltimore Orioles, famous baseball team?" Since the Japanese love baseball, most have indeed heard of the Orioles and nod with evident relief that they can pull some sense from the speech. "Please, accept this little souvenir from my home." The first man to receive a pen brightens with obvious pleasure. Since my self-introduction process takes several days to assimilate each name and face, the final men on the list know what to expect. I'm unprepared for the avalanche of reciprocal presents, from prized ceremonial cups to cases of drinks brought to ease a long trip, that begin to pile in my cramped room. I feel guilty accepting them, but to refuse would be insulting. Soon I can no longer stretch on the carpeted deck, the only alternative sans chairs to lying in the bunk, without propping either my back or legs against boxes.

The ship rides as a little enclave from Japan. Head-bump ceilings keep me reminded, as well as Asian squat toilets, and a tiled tub filled with blistering hot seawater for traditional Japanese relaxation following a soapdown and rinse, but more: We maintain a Japan-oriented clock even though we eventually travel five time zones west, in addition to losing a day by crossing the international date line. Thursday 9:30 P.M. by the sun at our actual position south of Alaska remains "Friday 4:30 P.M." in our artificial time sequence. Thus despite the northern location in late June, our sky turns dark by 4:30 P.M. and light again before midnight.

The man in charge dictates the personality of any ship. In Western countries, the captain holds this place, but to Japanese fishermen it is the *sendo,* the fishing master. (There is of course also a captain, who dutifully works on deck when he isn't steering the ship.) Our sendo, Yoshiteru Abe, is a man for the part. "It's the dream of any fisherman to become sendo," he declares flatly at our first meeting (as translated), regarding me with hooded, direct, confident eyes. His back is straight and his head erect as a fighting cock's, a self-contained man of fifty-two whose entire manner exudes the robustness of mind and body that the Japanese call *genki.*

This sendo marches so confidently to his own drum that his title could be capitalized. On the first day out Sendo draws a stool in the messroom and shaves his head (leaving mats of hair for the cook to sweep) and this completes his resemblance to Yul Brynner's King of Siam. At table if he holds out a teapot, anyone at hand, captain included, will refill it at once. Emperors, though, can lavish personal hospitality more grandly than commoners. If I fail to make it first to the big rice urn at the end of the table, he dishes out my food along with his own, and even tries to empty my leftovers himself in the galley slops bucket. Sendo rules because he delivers. Everyone knows that finding the catch depends on his talents alone. Back home in Ishinomaki stands the proof. In his spare, elegant sitting room we sat on mats as Mrs. Abe served ocha and cakes on a low table and their teenage daughter (who was studying to be a concert pianist) helped quietly. With a deprecating nod, he indicated a shelf with half a dozen gold-plated trophies. Each, presented by local seafood processors, named him highline sendo of the fleet for a given year.

On the foredeck I help bring nets from the hold and sew them together. As we complete joining a section, a pair of rollers sucks it aft through a long tube where the entire stern of the ship serves as the net bay. The nets come in thirty-meter (roughly one-hundred-foot) bundles called *tans.* One hundred sixty tans lashed together form one *nagashi-ami,* a driftnet roughly three miles long. We put together eight driftnets: twenty-four miles.

Each species of sea creature follows a pattern. Those that travel en masse can be caught with compact nets—seines on the surface, trawls or short gillnets below. The big North Pacific squids of our quest travel on the surface in scattered groups. A net to catch them in any commercial quality must drift on the surface and be long enough to snare them at random. Drifting nets suspended like a wall have been used for decades, but not in the lengths employed after advanced technologies made them possible in the late 1970s by fishermen from Japan, Taiwan, and South Korea. Back when a fisherman used arms and back to pull, when nets were made of natural fibers heavy in themselves and heavier after absorbing water, no one considered stretching nets for miles. This came only with the development of tough, light synthetic fibers, and the hydraulic machinery to pull them.

We travel seven days due east at thirteen knots to reach the area where the Asian fleets have agreed with the United States and Canada to confine their squidding. We pass groups of other ships from South Korea and Taiwan—the oblong corks of their driftnets bob like endless tapeworms—but continue in a straight line since Sendo has no intention of fishing among foreigners. Sitting cross-legged in the wheelhouse with a yellow towel around his head samurai-fashion, he talks with fellow-sendos already fishing among the Japanese fleet. They often break into the laughs and chuckles of longtime friends. He consults also the radioman, who spends hours each morning receiving and plotting the positions of other Japanese boats and the catches they report. When we reach the Japanese fleet Sendo still cruises as he checks temperatures and studies the sounder for evidence of the small-fish masses that attract hungry squid.

The squids pursue feed in a northerly pattern as they seek a colder temperature when summer waters warm, while the ships follow as close as their agreements permit. In July the Japanese fleet may fish as far north as 43° north latitude (within a specific longitude roughly due south of Anchorage but outside the U.S. 200-mile zone), and in August still farther north, but now, in June, 40° marks the limit, even though the main schools of squid have crossed. Most of the fishing boats crowd as close to the northern boundary line as possible without going over. Respecting the line is no casual matter. Two years ago, to Sendo's humiliation and the Sumida company's loss, a patrol vessel of the Japanese government's fishery agency found the *Sumiho Maru No. 75* to have strayed over the line and ordered it home, and *Sumiho Maru* lost two months' fishing time. The Japanese were trying hard to make their maligned driftnet fleet acceptable to the world.

At 2 P.M. on June 26, after more than a week at sea traveling some 2,500 miles, Sendo sounds two sets of blasts on the ship's alert system. Within minutes several crewmen stand at the stern in wetgear, and jets of water shoot horizontally over the ocean from deck level just below the great stack of nets. Sixteen radio flashing buoys stand in a row at the rail. They will mark the beginning and end of each three-mile segment. A shout from the bridge, and over goes Number One buoy. The attached net zips out at a terrific speed, guided by a large roller and then by the jets that spread it apart before hitting the water. The men use bamboo poles to keep the net from snagging, careful to stay clear of flying meshes that could sweep them overboard.

With brisk ceremony, Sendo strides aft holding the second large bottle of sake from the Shinto shrine in the wheelhouse. He sprinkles some of it on the pile of nets, then hurries back to the bridge to fill a ceremonial cup. The objects inside the boxed shrine were crammed helter-skelter even while the priest blessed them, and have remained so during the sea voyage, but now they are straightened. A miniature temple stands in the center, a purple curtain frames the top, a large gilded bell hangs from a thick red cord, lighted filigreed lamps flank the sake cup, a vase holds the leafed branch of the priest's blessing, and the omamori stands in back.

Sendo moves everywhere, watching, directing, laughing, scowling, never shouting except in good humor. The net, as it flashes over the stern, seems part of him.

It takes four hours to lay the net. Fitted with corks on the top and weighted line on the bottom, it unfolds from the surface into a floating twenty-four mile barrier thirty-five feet deep. The ship moves a steady ten knots, paying the net in a straight line among the nets of other ships. The Japanese vessels stay at least a mile apart, although when not crowding the latitude line they keep a three-mile distance. We have set in daylight. Hours later, in the dark, we start to haul back. When light fades, the squids rise from depths to feed on masses of small creatures that also rise to the surface. The long net drifts, waiting.

The net comes aboard amidships on the main deck, its corks and line drawn through separate rollers that spread them apart so the mesh can be pulled hand over hand across a wide stretch of rail. The first squid arrives. *"Ika, ika!"* (ee-kah) shouts everyone. Sendo looks down with fierce pleasure from his perch in the wheelhouse, and blasts the whistle.

The only ika I've known have been little quarter-pounders jigged in Newfoundland dozens to a bucketful. Four of this five-pound North Pacific creature would crowd a bucket. It resembles a big party cracker. A purple-orange tube about two inches in diameter and a foot long, called the mantle, encases its body. One end of the mantle holds two muscular tail fins. From the other end emerges a cylindrical head with round eyes larger than human ones. Eight stubby "arms" and two foot-long tentacles protrude from the head. Little suction cups cover the arms like barnacles. One arm slaps my hand and I jump from the sudden pain as the cups attach themselves. The squid scouts prey with the tentacles, then suctions them tight against its arms to be fed into its mouth. Now, the efficient predator-machine lies helpless on deck. Ripples flicker across the dying creature's translucent mantle, caused by camouflage pigments that flash within its body. A jet of black ink spouts against my foot, the squid's ultimate defense against all but his biggest predator.

Ommastrephes bartrami, called neon flying squids, live only a year but reproduce heavily from a single female's five hundred thousand eggs. They inhabit both tropical and temperate waters, but fishermen find commercial quantities only in the North Pacific. The creatures are tigers when on the offensive. One night at anchor I watch them feeding and see the origin of their colloquial name. They pinion little fish and plunge after others, darting above the surface in slashing arcs. Beneath the surface their bulletlike bodies flash lights like a Las Vegas marquee.

Japanese eat the big squids in several ways. No fish market of any size lacks piles of them dried and stacked like cordwood, ready to be chewed like jerky or soaked and cooked. Carts sell them braised over a charcoal fire and served on a stick. Chewy, almost rubbery, with a mild flavor, they take a long time to eat but sell briskly at parks and temple sites where people come unhurried in a holiday mood. At expensive sashimi restaurants, milky white slivers of squid mantle lie in ice along-side tuna and sea urchin. My clumsy Western palate finds raw squid too bland to compete with the rich subtleties of the other sashimis. It improves when dipped in a mixture of soy sauce and hot green horse-radish. Slippery? Try picking up a slice with lacquered chopsticks!

It takes ten and a half hours to bring in all eight nets, starting in the dark at "9 P.M."—more realistically 2 A.M. local time—and ending next morning at "7:30" under a bright afternoon sun. The sky begins to lighten at "midnight." There are a few hundred squids, although some entire one-mile stretches of net come up completely empty. "Aghhh," growls Sendo under his breath, and points to the water-temperature gauge, which shows 19° Celsius (66° Fahrenheit). The ika must already have moved north, across the 40° latitude line to colder water. To add discouragement the bright new green of the mesh begins to turn a sickly yellow. Slime flies off in globs to coat our faces and oilskins. It's the warm-water algal growth of a single night. Slime doubles the weight of the net, which constantly has to be hustled back from the rail quickly to make room for more. Soon the decks stream with muck so thick that we slide in it.

While some pick nets, others below decks in the factory "dissect" (direct translation) the squids. They slit open the mantle and remove innards with one sweep using a concave tool designed for the purpose. The mantle, cut and hand-cleaned, emerges as a thick, flexible butterfly-shaped sheet of food about a foot wide and longer across. Fifteen or sixteen fill a tray. We also cut arms and tentacles as a chunk, as well as a meaty piece of the head, before discarding the rest through scuppers. Water gushes from hoses and sloshes underfoot, carrying squid offal and squid eyes as big as mashed ping-pong balls. It's wet and messy work, not for the squeamish.

After all the nets have come aboard and been restacked astern, everyone turns-to below to finish the cleaning and packing. The workday ends to the clatter of metal trays as the mantles and parts go into flash-freeze lockers like books on a library shelf. Later the frozen contents of the trays, now hard blocks, glide down a chute to the freeze hold. The cold down there is claustrophobic despite padded thermals. No one else seems to mind, even though the breath of their talk freezes on the fur around their hoods.

Catches remain sparse, and slime drips everywhere in increasingly bigger globs while jellyfish sting our hands and faces. Better things surely lie over the 40° North line that we hug as close as we dare. At last, in late June, we move over the line and speed some eighty miles north. The sea temperature over just this short distance drops from 19° to 15° Celsius (66° to 59° Fahrenheit), a good sign. Sendo studies his notes from previous years, and cruises as he watches the echosounder. Finally he lays the nets and waits. At exactly one second after midnight, Tokyo time, legal under the international agreement, we enter the month of July and start hauling.

More squid indeed! A bright rising sun gleams on their dark shapes in the net. But several sections still come in sparse. Sendo growls and mutters to himself as he studies his notes. Then, twelve hours later and still hauling (but having moved and drifted at least twenty miles from where the set began); "Ha *ha,* ika!" Big squids hang like melons in the net, taut between water and rail. At once the loudspeaker blares

Japanese pop music. Soon squids carpet the deck, and tangled heaps trapped in ink-blackened nets begin to pile up no matter how vigorously everyone picks. When a hundred or more of the floppy creatures accumulate on either side of the net, too deep to step through, someone takes the time to push them into chutes that lead to bins below decks.

Before this I've been a supernumerary on deck, allowed to help out of courtesy. Now I step to the rail and become part of the operation. The rollers bring corks and line aboard inexorably, but the web between sags so with squid that it needs to be hefted over the rail. Sometimes alone I grunt aboard a dozen five-pound squids at once, always on the run, trying to pick out those lightly entangled as we haul. After an hour I'm sweating enough that my cap slides over my eyes, and my knees shake— and this hour has serviced only a fraction of one net in a string of eight.

On deck, amid the abundance, everyone shouts and jokes. Short, husky Shizukuishi-san, who during the leisure trip out learned a card game from me and then, with glee, how to flip-shuffle the cards, grabs my waist and shakes me. Sendo himself arrives on deck to pitch in, wearing a Baltimore Orioles baseball cap I've given him.

The final flag comes aboard fourteen hours after the hauling began. Without a break all hands converge below to complete the cutting and stowing. Before they have finished, Sendo is laying the nets again. Finally at sea anchor, after seventeen hours' steady work, they sleep for five hours while the net soaks. Then the buzzer sounds, and within minutes the next set starts aboard.

A few nets still come in virtually empty. Squids are clearly concentrated in a patch, so the sendo races the ship back and forth gathering barren nets and placing them in more fertile waters. Eventually he sets only four nets because they take three to four hours each to bring aboard. At their fullest, one three-mile *nagashi-ami* yields between 2,000 and 3,800 squids.

As the days pass with set after set, many of them marathons, it becomes impossible except by keeping notes to remember when one set begins or another ends. Days turn to nights and nights back to days. A patch of sleep—never more than five hours within twenty-four and usually less—might be granted in the fullness of sunlight or in the dark. The world becomes a nightmare of squids spouting ink on deck or being chopped apart below. (For me it does at any rate, even though I freely disappear for naps.)

The men never stop their joking and horseplay as they plug along.

Most have grown up together, their families know each other, they've worked for years as a crew, and they roll with the conditions of fishing as their life. Their *career.* The crew's share comes from thirty percent of the gross. (The company's seventy percent absorbs all expenses for the costly voyage.) In 1989, a poor fishing year, ordinary crewmen earned roughly U.S. $2,000 a month, the fishing master double that, with the captain, radioman, and chief engineer getting about $3,000. Such earnings raise Japanese fishermen from peasant to middle class, but in inflated Japan these are still modest amounts. "Once," observes the sendo, "a fisherman could buy a house in two or three years. Now it takes him a lifetime."

Sitting around the hatch for a bite or a smoke, still dripping from the deck or the factory, everyone is as ink-black from face to boots as coal miners. No fixed mealtimes exist anymore, although food remains always available. On the messdeck, for anyone with the time to remove wet gear, the big electrically heated rice urn stays full and steaming twenty-four hours a day. A similar pot alongside it always contains some kind of soup, most often one based on seaweeds and tofu that sometimes also includes fish and sliced root vegetables.

Once a day Hiroshi Itoh, the cook, leaves the factory to prepare a dinner. (Printed on his pink apron is a teddy bear, and the words: "Every day the see [sic] to come up with something new." His teenage son, whom he tells me must "struggle, struggle" with schoolwork to qualify for university, gave it to him.) The meal is a big one. It usually centers around fish or pork cutlets, accompanied by a thick-battered tempura of green peppers as well as fish paste and fried eggplant. There might be also thin fried Chinese dumplings with meat inside, and always—while it lasts during the three-month trip—shredded lettuce with a chunk of tomato. Itoh leaves it all on individual dishes in a cabinet with sliding glass doors, since flies ride with us from Ishinomaki. Sometimes the plates stay there for hours before anyone finds the time to eat.

All of this is heartwarming, to know that Japanese far-seas fishermen work hard but remain conscientious and cheerful, and that they have a precious family life like everyone else. But that was not my purpose in joining the crew of the *Sumiho Maru No. 75*. What did their nets bring up besides the squid they had come so far to harvest? Like the blind man feeling part of an elephant, I can report only what I saw. During the time I rode aboard we hauled more than 150 miles of driftnets. I observed about half of this directly, either on deck while helping to pull and pick the nets or from the wheelhouse, and remained in proximity for another quarter of it while helping below decks to cut and wash the squid parts.

There appeared to be no attempt to hide anything. Someone called me from below to photograph the single porpoise (dead) that I saw in all the nets. And no one seemed to be sneaking drowned birds over the side, since I disposed of a few myself that had been lying around for hours. My notes record eleven dead seabirds altogether. We tangled the leg of one large seabird of the hundreds that collected around the ship to feed on offal disgorged from the factory below. He flapped angrily, very much alive, and flew off at once when freed. The only creature besides squid that the driftnets caught in significant quantity—sometimes dozens—were "*echiopia*," or pomfret, a gray fish the size and shape of a dinner plate. The crew dressed and froze the pomfret until a space allotted in the freezer hold had filled, then kicked them overboard, except ones saved for table. There were one to six gray "salmon" sharks a day weighing five to about thirty pounds each, a single round half-ton fish called a mambo whose meat and liver were all saved, two swordfish, a tunalike fish called a louvar, and a one-time school of two dozen yellowtail.

Squid alone constituted the rest of the sea creatures that came aboard. The *Sumiho*'s driftnets proved able, for this time and place under these fishermen, to target relatively clean on the species it sought under one self-propelled Japanese fishing master aggressively seeking to fill his hold. It may have been different with other driftnet operations. But I have seen more by-catch of harvested or wasted sea creatures in some trawl nets.

Two years after I rode aboard the *Sumiho Maru*, world pressure closed in enough that Japan agreed to discontinue fishing with miles-long driftnets and called back its fleet of 457 ships. Taiwan and South Korea with some 150 ships each did the same, as did China and some European countries with fewer vessels. The Japanese and Taiwanese governments offered to buy the newer boats and assisted in converting any of them to alternate gear. On the final day of 1992, high-seas driftnetting ended.

What now? I asked Mr. Sumida, owner of the *Sumiho Maru*. He replied to my letter of mid-1992, as he prepared for the closure, in his own careful English tempered with stoic Japanese cheer: "*Sumiho* has last fishing of Net now. I will finding other ways and or Jigging only, but not yet fixed. In a worst case is scrap by Government. Anyway, let me go other ways. S. Sumida." In fact, Sumida and others found that jigging with banks of machine-jerked hooks could catch enough of the big neon flying squid to pay. Such ships required less crew, however.

Back aboard the *Sumiho*, the squid driftnetters are to stay out for three months. After seventeen days, having other agendas, I transfer to the fifty-meter Japanese patrol ship *Koyo No. 1*, which is headed to Vancouver for supplies. I leave the *Sumiho*, shaking hands removed temporarily from inky waterproof gloves, feeling myself unnaturally clean after a bath taken while everyone else is working. We shout *sayonaras*. Quickly the work on the squid deck resumes. I bounce away in a rubber raft manned by two blandly pleasant, scrubbed young sailors from the patrol ship who have no fishermen's juice in their blood.

A few hundred yards of choppy blue Pacific takes me from noon Thursday to 5 P.M. the previous Wednesday, since the patrol ship uses local time. Really I transfer from one world to another, though both represent the same culture. Part of me yearns to be back pulling nets in noisy company. As I near the spanking white *Koyo*, still watching the *Sumiho* streaked with scupper waste, Sendo-san appears on the flying bridge. He waves and waves in full-armed genki sweeps. I wave back with all the genki I dare generate from a swooping raft.

North Pacific Ocean, 1990: *Sumiho Maru* crewmember Kazue Oono, free to eat after sixteen hours on deck, his face still covered with squid ink, digs into a meal of squid sashimi.

Goto Islands, Japan, 1980: The crew of a Narashima seiner eats aboard before all-night fishing. When I'm not looking, they merrily pass around my big boots and try them on.

Japan, 1990: Joined by ship's officers and the owner, a Shinto priest blesses the wheelhouse shrine aboard *Sumiho Maru #75* before the ship embarks on a three-month trip to the North Pacific. The fishing master, or sendo, Yoshiteru Abe, whose personality will soon dominate the ship, claps his hands reverently to draw divine attention.

CHAPTER TWENTY-ONE

Floating Cities

Bristol Bay, Alaska

July 1980

Back in Shibetsu, the salmon co-op's Mr. Minami could crow with impunity about the Alaskan travels of his *aki-aji* because the fish themselves chose to do it. The migratory pattern of salmon remains their own secret, but the fish in question clearly traveled off the Aleutian Islands, because fishermen there encountered quantities of both Hokkaido chum salmon *(aki-aji)* and the red/sockeye salmon of Alaska's Bristol Bay. Shibetsu's ranched chums probably did fatten on American plankton. The story was quite different for Mr. Nitta and Mr. Endo in Shiogama, whose trawlers had been legislated from U.S. waters, and later for Mr. Sumida's driftnetter, prevented from freely following the squids' northern migration. In these cases the vessels might intercept sockeyes definitely spawned in Alaskan rivers and headed home. The United States, after taking control of its 200 miles, was having none of it.

With new bargaining clout the United States immediately nego tiated Japanese and other foreign vessels away from most of the Aleutians, even beyond 200 miles from shore. Salmon in U.S. rivers near the start of the Aleutian chain increased at once. The greatest beneficiary—the place where salmon had always come but where suddenly they stormed as in the old days before far-seas fishing—was Bristol Bay. The sockeye runs of Bristol Bay are known to be cyclical, with two or three large catches every five years and the others smaller. But in 1973 the run fell so low—2.4 million—that President Richard Nixon declared Bristol Bay a disaster area. The foreign fleets, sensing inevitable U.S. controls, were taking all they could before it was too late. In 1978, just a year after 200-mile controls, the run rose to 19.6 million.

The Japanese rebounded quickly after losing intercepted fish from their own boats. Scarcely a year passed before they started buying the same fish out of Bristol Bay and freezing them for the home market. The Bay had been traditional cannery country. The new freeze market absorbed the vast new quantities pouring in, and inevitably changed the scene for both fishermen and processors.

Bristol Bay is north of the Aleutians, off the eastern edge of the Bering Sea. Its system of lakes feeds eight main short rivers and numerous smaller ones to sustain the largest sockeye run in the world. It is hospitable country for this salmon species, whose cycle requires a first two years in fresh water, then easy passage to and from the salt ocean for the two to three years needed to mature before returning to reproduce. In the frenzy of its abundance the Bay resembles only Norway's Lofoten Islands in my experience. At both remote northern locations fish (cod, in the Lofotens) come spawning from afar in gargantuan numbers and for the brief time of the runs fishermen converge also from afar to transform the waters into a city of boats. To cannerymen Bristol Bay is a place with a century-old history of enterprise and risk, of fortunes gained, lost, or never realized. To fishermen Bristol Bay is one of the grounds of legend, the Alaskan equivalent of the Grand Banks or the Lofotens for its concentration. But it is also, like these others, a graveyard of capsized boats and drowned men.

When I first arrive in late June 1980, the activity at the little King Salmon airport resembles a circus come to town. No one seems bothered by rain or the mud that clings underfoot. As boxes and crates emerge from the cargo hold, men swarm to load them into pickup trucks of all variety. These are supplies for a month of fishing and canning, stuff from apples to crankshafts, no more available locally than tickets to the opera.

In downtown Naknek, permanent population 350, about five times that many hustle to be ready when the fish arrive. Trucks splash muddy gravel over the rare pedestrian along the single main road, and create a traffic jam outside the marine supply store. Welding torches crackle and blue-flash. At the municipal pier, men in glistening oilskins share a crane to lower cargo to their boats from a pile that grows as trucks back in to be unloaded. Others pass down hoses to take on water and fuel. They have to shout to their mates, since at low tide boats rest on black mud twenty-some feet below.

All seems productively busy, except that suddenly the roads and docks clear. From a nearby meeting hall come angry shouts. All's ready for fishing, but fishermen are voting whether to strike. The Japanese, having created a new market for the great new Bristol Bay runs they had lost for themselves, already control the price. Last year, in 1979, fishermen received up to $1.25 a pound but this year are offered only forty cents. The plummet may reflect the reality of buyers in Japan who find Alaskan salmon more viable in years when Hokkaido salmon turn scarce from nets like those of Mr. Minami's Shibetsu co-op. But the general angry opinion in Naknek: "The Japs are jerkin' us around." (I've never felt this opinion to be entirely wrong.)

At Red Salmon Cannery, a community unto itself about a mile from town at the end of a primitive road—a bear lumbers boldly through the scrub and watches the truck bump past—people dodge forklifts along boardwalks and ramps that lead in all directions. Barn-red buildings range over an upper level. Roofs of long, high sheds hide the water below. Signs point the way to the office and messhall. Other signs identify the laundry, showers, and dormitories: for men, "Waldorf Hysteria," and for women, "The Hen House."

I know of Red Salmon by reputation. It is Brindle turf, one of the names of Bristol Bay cannery lore that also includes Daubenspeck, Bez, Gage, Calvert, Tarrant, Murray, Daly, Hanover, and Barthold. The brothers A.W. Brindle (Winn Sr.) and H.A. Brindle (Harold Sr.) entered the Alaska salmon business together in 1928. Winn was the hands-on force while Harold managed the business, which grew to include several canneries throughout Alaska. In Naknek Winn became his own legend, a power in the days when the Bristol Bay canneries owned and controlled everything a fisherman had except his boots and oilskins (which they'd probably sold him at a price). "Winn was a hard-nosed businessman and a tough old bastard," recalls one former fisherman. "But honorable and honest: more than you could say for many of the others. And the kind of guy who'd personally drive the cannery water truck to Naknek if there was a fire, and pitch in doing both the directing and the dirty work himself."

Harold Jr., the man I want to meet, has been Red Salmon's cannery boss since his uncle Winn Sr.'s death, part of a second generation that has begun extending to a third, now apprenticed on the cannery lines. I corner someone long enough to be pointed to a man operating a crane on the pier. Brindle, an engineer by education, is doing a precise enough job dropping cargo gently onto pallets that it might have been his life's work. After storing the crane, down he steps: a square-rigged man in his midforties, all business, whose coveralls need a scrub with Lava soap. He strides in such a fast line to his red electric cart that I have to run to catch him. He regards me directly from under the yellow tractor cap that shades his eyes. "Look around, help yourself." The voice, though curt, has an agreeable ring. "Stay to dinner, we'll water the soup for one more." The red cart moves away. "Hey," I call. "Can I trail you on your rounds?" Faint smile. "Nope." And he's off.

The big, clean messhall has long tables, and people line up cafeteria style. Supervisors eat in a smaller room with shorter tables. The menu for all includes large tender steaks, heaps of potatoes and vegetables, and fresh-baked pie. People eat elbow-to-elbow, but even a quick glance shows their division into groups. There are tired-eyed mechanics with grease on their faces and clothing, and noisy kids in college sweat-shirts. About two dozen men, some middle-aged and others resembling them enough to be sons and nephews, speak combined Italian and English, waving their hands for emphasis. A group of set-faced Filipino men eat in silence. Within twenty minutes trays are cleared and everyone has gone. Brindle, with whom I hoped to chat, has come in like the rest, eaten with no small talk, and disappeared again.

I finally corner Brindle back at the wharf. It is close to midnight, although no one appears to be sleeping. Lights blaze halos against the wet black sky, and the crane and forklift motors gun louder than ever. The river is on flood, and a container barge lies alongside the dock. By 2 A.M. the tide will have peaked, requiring the container ship to leave, cargo discharged or not, for safe passage out the river and through the Bay before the next low tide grounds it. Brindle sits for a moment. I ask him what the vans contain. "Supplies," he mutters. "Cans enough for two hundred thousand cases. A case is forty-eight one-pound talls," and up he springs again to check the numbers on a crate against the manifest he holds.

Brindle has reason to be preoccupied. The cannery needs to accom-modate five hundred workers for the one-month season, including 110 canning line workers, eighteen machinists, a fifteen-man dock gang, three carpenters, ten cooks and kitchen help, payroll clerk, accountant—and the crews of one-hundred-odd fishing boats when they come ashore between openings. When he returns he notes that everything from butter to the smallest machine replacement part must be ordered months in advance for shipment from Below—everything.

"Fuel enough for generators and boats, food, towels, dishrags, all this delivered and working before you even get a smell of fish." This is near the end of June and the fish will arrive any day. Biologists predict possibly the biggest run of sockeyes in the century-old fishery—sixty million fish, of which they require only a seventeen million escapement to provide the healthy next generation. The entire apparatus from gillnet to filled can will suddenly have to begin clicking.

Back in Naknek I head to join the *Gail T,* a new aluminum thirty-two-footer crewed by Dick Nes and Otto Holgersen of Norway. It's a steep downward climb to deck gripping a slippery thin ladder. We're tied at the base of a pier with other boats of the same size—legal limit in Bristol Bay—beached on the mud. The tides of the Naknek and the other rivers reach twenty-five feet. Nothing moves at low tide, and all plans take this into account.

All is ready, but tensely. By the time the strikers and buyers reach a grudging agreement the first fish have begun to thrash upstream. Frustrated anger turns to action. "Let's fuckin' fish!"

By the first flood tide the pilings under the piers empty. Boats gun to be free of each other, tossing off lines as wet cold wind lashes hands and faces. The river turns as crowded as a freeway at rush hour. Nobody has time to lose since the first Naknek run usually peaks by July Fourth and this is already the morning of the third. In the *Gail T*'s warm cabin, Dick Nes at the wheel mutters to himself in Norwegian. We peer through splats of water on the windshield to maneuver among rain-grayed boats, ships, and barges. Some loom up only seconds before we might brush or collide.

We head straight across Kvichak Bay (it and Nushagak Bay are the major subsystems of Bristol Bay) for a place on the west side that Dick remembers well in past years. The water has become a floating city, a battlefield swaying to wind-driven waves. We pass a wall of anchored processor ships, deck lights ablaze under dark clouds. The hum of their engines and machinery surrounds us. Figures on deck in bright yellow oilskins bend over tables gutting fish. Strike breakers, or fish wouldn't already be aboard! Cause for new anger to be settled later. A crane hoists brailerloads of fish from a boat tied alongside. The sight makes Dick throttle even harder.

None of the thirty-mile-wide Kvichak is deeper than twenty-five fathoms, but the salmon returning through it to the rivers of their natal lakes mill in greatest numbers along the shoreline. We reach our position along the shallows of Copenhagen Creek. Dick maneuvers for a place among the other boats while Otto and I stand at the ready astern beside the nets in a green fluffy heap on deck. Our net by law consists of only three "shackles," each fifty fathoms long—nine hundred feet of gillnet altogether—a miniature version of miles-long driftnets. Bleak, marshy land lies a few hundred yards away, with only a single scraggly tree high enough to provide a reference point. "Banana Tree," explains Otto. The old-timers call it that.

"Ja, OK," shouts Dick. Otto tosses the first plastic buoy over the stern roller, and the attached gillnet zips quietly after. The light wiry strands need little guidance. The white corks pay out like beads, snaking around individual waves as they make an irregular line astern. If the fish are here in any quantity they will bob the corks. Nothing happens. "Shit, ve missed 'em." Then some of the corks begin to dip, and water splashes around them. *"Ha!"* After a soak we haul back the net over the hydraulic roller, one of us guiding the corks and one the leaded bottom line. It is not heavy work, even though a fish flops aboard with every few feet of net, since the treads of the roller do most of the pulling. (Later, when the fish start coming, I learn a different story.)

Only a few of fish fall free as they come aboard. Each of us has a toggle hook that fits in the hand comfortably. With an expert twist Otto or Dick can hook web and quickly pull the trapped creature through a mesh that seems half the width of its belly. The denser tangles take me three times as long to handle. A thrashing fish can enmesh itself tail-to-head like Br'er Rabbit in the Tarbaby, and it seems impossible for some ever to be freed, but for the experienced it takes merely a moment longer. The fish emerge whole but streaked with blood. We toss them forward into a hold where they land with a thump, some still beating their tails.

As we pick, two other boats ease alongside. The men aboard study our catch and converse in combined English and Norwegian. The *Gail T* is part of an informal Norwegian fleet in Bristol Bay. I've been hired aboard only to help with the peak of the run. Dick and Otto live in Norway but come over every summer to work shares for a relative in Seattle: a fellow-Norwegian, now an American citizen who has fished all his life, has saved and prospered, and owns two Bristol Bay gillnetters with accompanying permits. They are all Karmøy men, an identifying fact to those who work among Norwegians. An island off the south Norway coast, Karmøy is a rocky and windswept place famous for its hard-driving fishermen. (My Bering Sea king crab skipper Leiv also comes from there.) In Ballard, the Seattle suburb where most Norwegian Americans who fish in Alaska live, the Karmøy subcommunity is sometimes called wryly the "Karmøy Mafia" for tenacious fishing, cautious investment, and consequent prosperity.

This is to say that Dick and Otto are considerate but taciturn crewmates, who speak little in English (or at all) except for words necessary to do the job. They are kind enough to seem undisturbed by my initial slowness picking gillnets even though I draw an equal crew share. Dick, the skipper, moves and talks quickly. A beard, bushy but neat, helps his look of authority. He never shouts, but sometimes his eyes flash and the bearded chin tightens. Otto is more deliberate, his voice deeper, his hair already gray.

The first set brings in only a few hundred fish, not much for the peak of a heavy run. Dick speeds to Half Moon Bay and we set next on a falling tide to try for fish that have entered the bay system on the flood and now should be milling. The nets come aboard heavier than before. It's no longer a snap to guide them over the roller. Now we must pull. Sometimes the five-and-six-pound sockeyes come up bunched in knots, with the weight of other fish dragging from the opposite side of the roller, so the pull involves sixty or seventy pounds. Nets full of fish pile around our legs, since we can no longer pick them clean as we haul. But Dick shakes his head. There should be more somewhere. He guns next to a point off King Salmon Creek, racing the tide, while Otto and I pick furiously. By now the tide is so low that when we try to lay the net again it grounds.

With a light bump, then a stronger one, the boat stops rolling and itself grounds. Around us points of sandy mud appear, then wide stretches separated by narrowing rivulets. Within an hour only a pool of water remains here and there. A salmon trapped in one flaps helplessly. A gull swoops down and pecks out its eyes. "Candy for dose noisy bastards," growls Otto. I remember pulling some eyeless fish from the net. Now, over the emerging land, gulls scream around other puddles. I jump ashore hoping to rescue a few of the noble reds for a less mean death. The bared land holds firm in places, but when I touch a boot-sucking gumbo I venture no farther.

After two hours the water returns slowly to reclaim the land, and the net floats. Suddenly the corks begin to bob under in a frenzy of splashes. We give what passes for a whoop in Karmøy terms. Silver-glinting salmon are riding the incoming tide straight into our nets!

Whole sections of cork disappear, and tails thrash all the way down the nine hundred feet of shackles. We start hauling even before the boat floats free again.

Now we have work. The net comes in clogged with fish and mud. What men the old-timers must have been, pulling such weighted nets aboard without a hydraulic roller. We grunt and grit teeth as we heave in unison, grabbing a tangle of fish at a time. No question of picking, only of getting it all aboard. We plank the bins to extend the deck, and drag armloads of net and muddy fish all the way back to the wheelhouse. Fish pile around us so thick and heavy that we must pull from the knee to free our legs. My foot sucks straight out of its boot. Mud and fish slime sweat into our eyes. Now and then we exchange taciturn Karmøy grins. But: "Oh boy oh boy," Otto mutters, his bad back hurting. The pain does not slow him.

Out over the water the remaining few hundred feet of net seems to stretch for a mile, all of it weighted so only a white cork shows here and there. Imagine pulling nine hundred feet of rocks on a string. At last the net is all aboard. Our railings ride so low that waves splash in. Dick heads the boat for open water as Otto collapses on top the fish, kneading his back.

We lunched on peanut butter and pickles while beached five hours earlier. After we anchor: "Guess we'll eat before we start picking?" I say, and volunteer to fix something. Otto and Dick regard me strangely as they take their hooks and begin extracting fish from web. The junior member joins them.

The short summer darkness falls around eleven. We pick nets under deck lights. Bursts of rain alternate with chilly drizzle. At around 3 A.M. the sky streaks brief orange as the rising sun sends rays through a narrow gap on the horizon. Then it all dims again under the overcast. Occasionally we tear off a piece of fish jerky from strips hanging to cure outside the cabin, but no one wastes the minutes to hose oilskins, peel down, and go to the stove. The fish, so silver in the water and firm to the touch, have turned the color of gunmetal and now ooze white slime. They even smell of gunmetal, an acrid odor that seems always to grow around fish heaped in numbers, but especially from salmon. Dark net marks crisscross their backs along with blood marks. They have lost their beauty. However, men do not fish for aesthetic reasons, certainly not Karmøy men.

The chill creeps into my buttocks as we sit on the hatch disentangling nightmare wads of dead salmon. My fingers ache from tugging at wiry web, and smart from cuts the web makes through soaked cotton gloves. It's miserable, but I wouldn't change places with anyone, would not even want to ship with easier fishermen. Just as the battles of history stir some men to daydream over, say, the grit of Antietam, tales of fishermen who pulled nets in Bristol Bay for the past century stir my own circulation.

Bristol Bay has a lore based on hardship, like that of the Lofoten cod fishery. Anyone fishing either place these days must accept at least the minor discomfort of working gear throughout a cold raining night to claim part of the heritage but this, comparatively, is nothing. Until 1952, the men who fished the ferocious tides of Bristol Bay each summer did so from wooden "double-enders" powered only by sail. Photographs taken in our time, already historic, show grimy, exhausted, rough-looking fellows hunched in oilskins against the cold, sometimes grinning self-consciously at the authority represented by a pointed camera, often with a cigarette or pipe in their mouths. They stand knee-deep in fish, in boats open like large bathtubs, men who take hardship for granted.

"Well, damn it," I say finally, some time in the morning after about ten straight hours of picking. The atavistic hardship business has limits. I rise, stretch, hose down, remove wet gear, and pad with thick wool socks into the galley. While coffee perks I chop a salmon into chunks and drop it in boiling water. A half hour later I'm back on deck with some of the chill eased from my bones. My crewmates gladly accept the steaming mugs, and take refills. But they glance reproachfully at the platter with fish. It would spoil his appetite for dinner after the work was done, says Otto, and Dick adds his polite refusal. For my own needs, the boiled salmon is indescribably, dizzyingly delicious.

Eventually, in the dark, we haul anchor and go back through the city of bouncing lights to our contracted processor–freezer ship. We tie astern of her and continue to pick nets without the bother of adjusting to tides and currents. Other boats have done the same, and a line of them stretches in the direction of current. No one speaks between boats. Each remains its own island of work. The noise of winch motors blows back occasionally when crews less fortunate come alongside the ship to unload smaller catches, perhaps to climb aboard for a hot meal, then to drowse by a warm galley stove as they wait the next tide. Poor fellows. Rain-hazed clusters of lights from other vessels on all sides reflect against the low clouds, brightly in the dark, then dimly in the gray daylight. There are dozens of hundred-foot Bering Sea crabbers here to tender with their circulating seawater tanks, plus all manner of scows and barges in support. The processor ships, some three hundred feet long, like the one from which we drift, form a wall of big hulls and masts illuminated day and night.

It is past noon of the next day when at last we take our turn to unload. Indeed then, stiffly, we do shuck our oilskins and climb aboard to settle at a warm galley table. The cook, a middle-aged woman both tough and motherly, dishes out pot roast, then seconds, without question. There's plenty to eat. Fishermen from other boats enter and slump, as do men and women from the ship, all of them subdued with fatigue.

Dave, the owner of the floater–processor, draws coffee and sits beside us. His bushlike sandy beard and red-rimmed eyes in fierce fatigue give him the look of a Biblical prophet. Before he has taken two sips someone summons him to the freezer deck. Soon he stands glaring at a Japanese half his size across a metal table piled with salmon. "What do you mean, number two's?" he demands.

"Bad net mark," says the Japanese firmly.

The difference in grading represents thousands of dollars, and both men know it. "Net marks? That's how you fuckin' *tell* a Bristol red, it's accepted in my contract, written in English and Japanese both. You want to come to my office and read it? Feel this fish, feel him!" Dave tosses the fish. The Japanese anxiously replaces it on the table. "Don't try to dick me out of number one goddamn price for high graders like these!"

The Japanese glances uneasily at the large Americans around him. Someone explains later that he probably feels as much overpowered by their noise as their size. "Half number one, maybe," he says in a quiet, firm voice. "Some of them OK. But still half number two."

"Eighty percent are number one," growls Dave. "Net marks are in the contract."

The Japanese turns over one of the fish. "This fish not number one. Very bad marks. Belly burn here, broken tail here." He picks others. They all have light purple crisscross marks across their backs. "This fish... number one, OK. This fish OK. This fish, seal bite or knife cut, number two." He studies the last of the fish on the table, finally concludes: "Sixty percent OK."

"No. Seventy-five."

Long pause. "Seventy."

"Yeah, OK," says Dave, relieved. Back on the messdeck he concedes that of course there are some twos. "But you got to fight 'em all the way." He understands the fishermen's gripe about fallen price, but from his perspective of four years in the Bristol Bay processing business: "Last three years the market's gotten stronger and stronger, more demand for frozen fish. The Japanese companies had a lot of money, and they came in with open-end contracts. I'd negotiate a fixed fee for every pound I processed. They'd pay so much, then any more it cost me to buy from the boats. They'd even *advance* money. Essentially they drove up the price by outbidding each other. Then this year came the big crunch. Frankly, some product they bought last year had quality problems, and I hear it's still in their freezers. So, no advance money this year. They'll pay fixed cost, no adjustment for what I'll have to pay fishermen, just so much for frozen salmon dressed in the box and delivered to the freighter."

Somebody comes to report a dispute on the gutting line. Dave waves it aside, says wearily he'll be there in a minute, continues. "A buck twenty-five for grade A's, ninety five cents for grade B's. Might sound good, but listen. Right now I'm paying fishermen forty cents. I figure my ceiling is fifty cents. After that I've got no profit, or not enough to bother. Say I buy thirty thousand pounds of fish in the round. After dressing that's only twenty-one to twenty-two thousand pounds of product in the freezer. Then there's another two percent weight loss in the freezer before it gets delivered to the Japanese ship. Figure in fish tax to the state, then insurance for my employees, then for hauling, for cargo, for boxing materials, plastic liners, metal bands. I pay my labor regular time and then overtime. I maintain a tender to collect fish. It comes to this. Before labor costs, which eat up everything, if I pay fishermen forty cents, it'll cost me fifty-five to produce a fish in the round. But if I pay fishermen fifty, my cost goes up to sixty-eight-and-a-half cents a pound. That's before figuring in the rest. Doesn't leave much margin when you're paying overtime to a labor force and shipping up high-grade meat and other food to keep everybody happy and producing. I run close to the edge."

But the drop in price to fishermen is no academic matter. "Caught between the dog and the fireplug," says one skipper-owner, not laughing. A lifetime fisherman in other waters, no amateur, last winter he decided to go in hock to have a part of the Bristol Bay bonanza. For about $200,000 he bought his gillnetter and an accompanying limited entry permit—both good only for the short Bristol

Bay seasons (most store their boats at this distant site between seasons)—the debts secured on the strength of high salmon prices. Then he paid out another few thousand just to outfit the boat with grub and other supplies.

The 1980 strike turned out to be seminal. It had been called by AIFMA, the Alaska Independent Fishermen's Marketing Association, following a successful strike the year before when, with small runs predicted in both Hokkaido and Bristol Bay, Japanese buyers decided that any investment would hold for salmon-hungry Tokyo consumers. In 1980, however, both sides of the Pacific expected heavy salmon runs. The union failed to note that they no longer bargained from a seller's market. AIFMA had performed a pioneering and necessary function in gaining rights for fishermen from the monolithic old canneries, but with the coming of freezer-oriented Japanese the times had changed more than they realized. The union never entirely recovered its near-mystical clout. Nowadays this and other fishermen's organizations no longer bargain collectively. Some settlements are consummated with an old-fashioned handshake, with the final price not settled until after the fish have gone. Much depends on the health of Hokkaido salmon, and the health of the yen itself.

Observed Harold Brindle, a man capable of viewing both sides: "The Japanese are almost totally dependent on the sea for their protein, they pay high prices for it, and last year [1979] the Japanese buyers had a lot of money. Unfortunately they didn't recognize the pitfalls that come with indiscriminate buying, and they bid themselves right out of their domestic market. Quite frankly, these people are now very frightened."

In an ironic reversal, canneries ended after the 1980 strike paying fifty-seven cents compared with eighty-five cents in 1979, while the floating freezers paid only forty cents compared with $1.25 the previous year. Only those who delivered to the canneries made up their losses. Those committed to the freezer ships held the bag, having sacrificed a large portion of their catch with no rise in income to cover it.

Back aboard the *Gail T,* with the tide ebbing, we anchor and catch three hours' sleep. Then we lay our nets in time for the slack before flood and fish throughout another night and day. Any sense of time disappears. There is dim daylight, even once a few hours of sunshine. Then next time I glance it has turned dark and the processor ships again form the familiar wall of hazy lights. We're having a typical Bristol Bay nightmare of good fortune.

CHAPTER TWENTY-TWO

Generations

Past Meets Present

Bristol Bay, Alaska, 1980, 1986, 1995

One 1980 Bristol Bay night in bad weather I stand anchor watch for several hours as others grab sleep. Mists and squalls pass alternately, playing hide-and-seek with the lights of the river traffic. When the tide changes direction, every craft at anchor shifts on its chain in a simultaneous circle so that the relationship between land and water creates a new landscape. The wheelhouse radio crackles with the talk of men waiting as their nets soak.

"I don't know if I'll stay out here any longer. I don' see nothin' at all."

"Yeah, OK. Well, haul up and try someplace else, I don' know." I recognize the voices, from the Italian American community out of Monterey that fishes for Red Salmon Cannery. "*Aw* right, see what happens."

On other channels, men talk in Norwegian, Aleut, Yupic (Eskimo), Japanese, Filipino Spanish, and a Slavic language probably from the Russians aboard a joint venture ship off the coast but possibly from a Yugoslav community out of Anacortes, Washington. Asian languages fill half the radio space. The Japanese are busy, to judge by the frequency and length of their conversations. Some of what I think is Japanese might be Korean to my unpracticed ear, since Koreans also operate a nearby joint venture.

At 8 A.M. and 6 P.M. conversations in English cease. This is "Peggy" time. Peggy Dyson's voice comes across in a thin squeal, the signal distorted by the mountains between Bristol Bay and the radio room in her Kodiak home. I have heard her more clearly a thousand miles farther away with less obstruction. "Cape Constantine to Port Hayden. Winds southeast twenty-five knots diminishing to fifteen knots or less, small craft advisory. Six-foot seas diminishing to three, periods of light rain. Outlook southwest winds to fifteen knots. . . ."

The Alaska-wide marine broadcasts conducted by Peggy Dyson since 1975 are an institution within the Alaskan fishing community. They usually start with a greeting between Peggy and her fisherman-husband Oscar aboard his *Peggy Jo* wherever the fish or crab have led him, with Oscar's direct observation of his local weather. Peggy then follows with an area-by-area Alaskan marine forecast, from southeast to the far western Aleutians to the far northern Bering Sea. Fishermen within the thousands of miles covered then ask for repeats, offer local observations, and relay messages to families they might not have seen for weeks. "Sometimes Peggy has to break bad news like a death or good news like a birth," observes one Kodiak fisherman. "And she's saved a few marriages by seeing that flowers get delivered when guys forget anniversaries."

Six seasons later in 1986 I return to Bristol Bay. Peggy is still broadcasting (as indeed she continues to do in 1998 despite Oscar's death in 1995). Bristol Bay remains the site of the world's largest sockeye run, providing eight to sixty-plus million fish each year in cycles of relative poverty and abundance. I check in with Harold Brindle at the Red Salmon Cannery. Same isolation through bear and mosquito-infested scrub. Harold now drives a green electric cart rather than the old red one, and the color of his tractor cap has changed. Most of the same production heads and staff still self-gun through the plant. Only younger faces are new. On the main canning belts, the same scowling middle-aged Filipinos gut and clean in sou'westers and long oilskin coats. They come annually as a crew hired in Seattle, from a dependable cadre relied on for decades by many Alaskan canneries.

But across the runway stands a large new freeze facility from which a heavy rock beat blares. Something *has* changed. Inside, rosy-faced kids in waterproof aprons and college sweatshirts also gut and wash salmon. The fish flop from chutes overhead accompanied by clattering ice saturated with fish blood. Everyone works steadily, but in contrast to the classic business-like Filipino line the kids laugh and call freely across the noise.

On Brindle's desk papers are stacked in bunches. He leans back restlessly in a swivel chair and props thick workshoes on the desk edge as he listens to men in coveralls who enter to give routine morning reports. Elroy Kowalski the plant manager says he's short twelve to fourteen people. "OK," snaps Brindle, and calls Bill Ady his office manager. "Fly me in fourteen bodies." That was 8 A.M. By 10 A.M. fourteen young people with knapsacks stand at the reception rail waiting to be logged in. Up from the Lower Forty-Eight for a summer adventure, some have waited weeks to find work, camping in rain by the road-accessible canneries in the Kenai near Anchorage.

This year I ride aboard the *Manhattan Kid* with John Crivello out of Monterey, California, part of the dedicated Sicilian American enclave that also includes Vince Aiello's *Sea Prince,* Jack Aiello's *Katherine A,* and Ed Genovese's *Lady Phyllis.* Crivello, a good-humored, heavy, deliberate man in his sixties who runs a restaurant during the rest of the year, has fished the Bay since 1948 when sail was the only propulsion allowed. So have the other older men, and now their sons and nephews crew with them. Like the Filipinos on the sliming line, the "Monterey Mafia" is part of the traditional scene even while changes swirl around them. Their wooden boats, well maintained, stand in contrast to the latest in aluminum. And, with no costly new boats or new licenses to pay off (permits having become a negotiable commodity sometimes sold for as high as $300,000) they have less hustle.

We return to the Red Salmon Cannery before dawn after three days' fishing and a 2 A.M. delivery to the scow. (My notebook records "Midnight haul of three fish in blow and cold. John says hell with it for a while.") Crews that store their boats and gear and deliver here have rooms, a benefit not enjoyed by crews who sell to the floating processors. The padlocked Aiello quarters up the creaking stairs of the "Monterey Beach Hotel" have chairs, bunks, and an old sofa: bare and chilly by *Town and Country* standards, but we settle in like home with whiskey and ginger ale. "You'll never pry those old California Sicilianos from their cannery privileges," observed one longtime cannery hand. He admired them, he assured me, because they fish hard, stay loyal, and bring their own younger generation along. "But when the fish go slack in one place and other boats go prospecting a hundred miles away, which means living on baked beans for a week, these guys stay close to home."

Maybe they've earned a snatch of leisure. Commercial fishing in Bristol Bay began in 1883, and from the first an early pool of fishermen came from first-generation Sicilians (and Sardinians), the great-grandfathers of present Aiellos and Crivellos, who had immigrated to the sardine waters of Monterey from sailboat fisheries back home. By the turn of the century cannery buildings stretched along all of Bristol Bay's major river systems. And since skiffs, nets, food, everything needed to be shipped at a cost impractical for individuals, the canneries operated as fiefdoms. Fishermen were hirelings, caps off in presence of the boss, shipped up and sent back home under company control. Working-class men expected little in those days, particularly immigrant fishermen on the poverty end of the social scale. Until 1952 they were allowed to fish only under sail despite the treachery and force of the tides. Crivello's father fished the Bay from 1913 to 1938, and little had changed by Crivello's first season in 1948 with his father-in-law.

That first year: "He says, 'go on up in the loft and select a pair of oars that fits your hands.' That's what he tells me, a green kid, you know, my own father-in-law. Didn't say fit your hands because it's *you* gonna do all the rowin'. I found that out the hard way!"

Two-man sailboats had been the Bristol Bay method since the early 1900s. Pointed at both ends like whalers, the "double enders" could take punishment. Typically they had ironbark keel, bowstem, and sternpost, ribs of Vermont white oak, and planks of Port Orford cedar, secured with galvanized cut nails, solid craft still respected by boatmen. Everything was heavy, from the boat itself to the linen nets that absorbed water (as modern nylon nets do not). "Yeah," said Crivello, "when you went to assemble your gear from the stacks in the warehouse, you'd sort through for the lightest—oars, mast, booms, sprits. You'd even sometimes shave the sides of a twenty-five-foot mast to lighten it. You think there wasn't hernias back then? Then, of course, before you first stepped the mast you'd put a lucky penny in the mast step. Older boats had a lot of 'em, but you always made sure to add your own."

The engineless boats were towed in long lines from cannery piers to open water and then left to fend for themselves. A lot of your well-being depended on the fish boss and the scow skipper. You needed to stay on the good side of both. The fish boss assigned the boats, and some leaked more than others. And he lined up the boats each Monday morning for the scow to tow into open water. You wanted to avoid being one of the first boats in the tow. It meant you couldn't cut loose when you wanted, you were at the mercy and whim of the scow captain. He could cut you adrift a mile or two from the grounds or take you to the center of it as he chose. "You pulled those fourteen-foot oars two miles to get on station you knew the difference!" Or maybe you needed a tow as a sudden wind shift blew you toward the beach, or just a tow against the wind and current to a better fishing area. "A little money behind the back to the fish boss and the scow skipper didn't hurt!"

Crivello tells of his first day out with his father-in-law. "He says, 'OK we'll make sail now.' Riptide a while later, got in such a swell you kissed the water every time the boat rolled. He says: 'This is nothing yet, you'll get used to it.' *Used* to it? I was so scared I was dead."

The double-enders were seaworthy, sure, Crivello continues. "But of course all open, no place on 'em to warm up. Bow had maybe a two-foot cover that's all, a piece of canvas. Two men to a boat, we'd sleep with our heads under that little bow cover, feet sticking out with boots—you never took 'em off, hip boots—and a blanket over your oilskins. That long oil coat, you put it over your head like a nightgown. You couldn't even walk it was so tight around the knees." He turns to one of the bearded Aiello sons. "You looked like a priest."

The young Aiello nods politely as if the information is new.

"Cold?" Crivello continues. "We'd wee in our hands to keep 'em warm. Mornings you'd get up, hands all stiff you couldn't open 'em, no feel till you pissed 'em open. Breakfasts, it was raw eggs, a little sugar, a shot of whiskey, and you drank it. You wanted to shit, you hung over the side, not even a bucket, no room for one. Boats did each have those little coal stoves, remember? A chimney, a little vent in the bottom? Just enough heat to make coffee if you bent over to hold in the fire. Coal smoke got your face so black, you'd come to deliver to the scow, nobody recognized you only by the number on your boat, you came to deliver."

Fishermen drowned routinely back then: at least a dozen each season. When a storm held those double-enders helpless under nothing but sail power, and they swamped or capsized, men in hip boots, woolens, and long oilskin coats sank easily. Even if they swam, the cold water did not sustain life long—any more than it does today except that another powerboat might now rescue in time.

Why, in some of the meanest waters imaginable, where men drowned each year for lack of engine power, were Bristol Bay fishermen required to fish only under sail until 1952—decades after the technology of small-boat engines was taken for granted in any other developed fishery of the world? The influential "packers" had the 1922 law passed in the name of conservation when newly developed small marine engines threatened to free fishermen from cannery ownership of all the boats. (A man with a powerboat could have brought himself to Bristol Bay—gear, grub, and all—to deliver where he chose.) Even men returning from duty in World War II, who might have rebelled, put up with the self-serving danger for another half-dozen years. Maybe it was pride. The law certainly kept the amateurs at bay and weeded out incompetents.

"Those old men," Crivello reminisces, "we said old, they were thirty, thirty-five . . . they were tough, they had stamina. You'd pull those nets, like pulling rocks, then row back after you'd tacked across by sail, all soaking wet, sweaty, tired, no sleep." He laughs. "So I say, after that first year, this is too hard, next year I'm not comin' no more. Then I go home, spend the money, forget about how hard." He throws out his arms with open palms. "Next year I was there again, and next year, and next year. Look at me."

Al Andree, reminiscing for *Alaska Magazine* about his own Bristol Bay days in the 1940s, detailed hardships enough but also conceded: "In some ways sailing for salmon was a joy. It was relaxing. There was no engine noise, no exhaust stink, no vibration. You could yell across the water to someone 150 yards away and be heard. When under way, if you wanted you could lash the sail and rudder and play cards as long as the wind didn't change."

At the start of the season when everybody arrived, the fish boss made lists and divided men into gangs to launch the boats, ready the gear, stack supplies. "You had your ship gang, warehouse gang, net gang, . . . " said Jack Aiello, who had eventually become a fish boss. Working ashore was part of the deal. Whatever the fortune of the season, a fisherman could count on that $150 or so "run money" for the work of about a week setting things up. Then you made equal run money at the end of the season stowing gear and loading the season's pack of canned salmon onto the ships that would take it south. "Best part of the season, that final" says Crivello. "Paid-for work that didn't keep you wet and cold on the water? We'd party." In a good season, hundreds of dollars might change hands over the cards each night. After such hard work to make the money? "I don' know. . . . You had to be there."

The tide is rising and we return to the boats. Water already surrounds the hulls, and fingers of it edge into the beach fast enough to see them move. We climb down a slippery ladder from the pier. The

Monterey boats have the solid sea affinity that seasoned wood provides. Wood also retains the odors of fish, sweat, and engine oil more than steel. The stuffy cabin of John Crivello's *Manhattan Kid* has the air of many seasons' accumulation, home-smells to a fisherman but potentially the sort to unsettle a landlubber without leaving the pier.

One boat from the Monterey group has stayed on the water to keep an eye on things. We head to his nets even though he reports only a so-so haul. We set on the rising tide, and settle back to let the nets soak while radio-chatting from boat to boat within the group. Crewman Chris Rivera, an electrician and diver ashore and Crivello's partner aboard, keeps an eye on the net. A splash explodes against one of the corks. "Got a hit!" Crivello relays the information in code. Chris makes spaghetti and we sit on bunk edges. He puts ours on plates and eats his own from the pot without comment, delicate hospitality aboard a two-plate boat.

A radio voice calls. John picks up the VHF microphone attached by string to the overhead. "Riptide here," says the voice. "Pickin' up fish, but the riptide . . . " Tide rips mean waves and turbulence, but fish seem to seek them out. "I'm watching them come aboard. Another big bunch, another thirty or forty. But the tide's takin' us, and this loran of mine, I dunno, it gave a reading the other day I thought it was busted, I dunno. . . ."

His worry is the boundary designated by Fish and Game. The line for this opening cuts across the bay from a point just below the Naknek River on the east shore to Deadman Sands on the west shore. Essentially it closes fishing on salmon returning to the Kvichak River farther south and allows boats to target only those returning to the Naknek, as biologists fine-tune escapements into individual river systems.

The radio voice sounds worried. "What the hell, all the other guys are on the outer line, looks like we're close in." Muffled shouts in the background and the voice declares "Oh my God I don' know what I'm goin' to do, I'm over the line, my crew's screamin' back there."

Chris has been studying the chart. He holds it to the light and takes the mike. "How deep are you, amigo?"

"Twenty-eight feet, twenty-eight."

"Wait then, outside the line's shallower, wait a minute, you'll be all right there."

"He's OK," John confirms. "Let's haul."

Loran coordinates had appeared to define the line. By the time I return again in 1995, Global Positioning Satellites have placed the line absolutely. Before this, lines were less exact, delineated by markers on land that darkness and foul weather obscured, and enforcement was less stringent. Nowadays boats and even planes patrol, and violators can be fined enough to bust their season. It is tricky since a man might set close on the legal side—a great temptation, to get as near as possible to the forbidden fish—and then while hauling gear be pulled across by wind or tide.

We've been too busy on the radio to monitor the white corks of our net that snake behind the boat. Now we see that stretches disappear under lapping waves. "Yo, it's a piano man," purrs Chris, pointing to corks that bob and reappear like white piano keys. After only a few feet of net has come aboard we know we have fish from the strain on the hydraulic roller. We need to pull, holding the web tight against the revolving drum. Fish begin to flop over the roller in bunches. They pile against our legs, six-pound sockeyes, the weight of their mass shifting as the boat rolls, their sea-chill penetrating through oilskins and thermals.

Crivello wipes his hands and leaves for a minute. His voice comes from the wheelhouse, talking in code to his buddies. Later a spotter plane from somebody else's group begins scouting overhead. We bunch a tarpaulin over the tangled mound of fish astern, and sit on deck looking indifferently in any direction but that of the bobbing corks until the plane passes. By then a couple of our own boats have appeared close by, scouting for themselves in answer to John's message.

It's a dream of a haul, fish unencumbered by mud or seaweed, lots of them. They take hours to pick as the bins fill. These fish are going to be paid for by the pound. "When I started," says Crivello, "we got twenty-four cents a fish—not for a pound, for a fish. Cigarettes those days cost twenty-five cents, so we'd say each fish we picked: OK we got a pack of cigarettes. Earlier, fellows in my dad's time, they got three cents a fish. So, you get paid by the fish, what do you do? When we picked the net we'd throw the big fish overboard, keep the little ones, get more in the bins that way. It made sense."

We've anchored to pick. The *Manhattan Kid* rolls steeply, its housing sheltering us from a chilly wind. The sunset glows around us in wide bands of scarlet and gold. Then lights pop on all over the horizon like those on a Christmas tree. Braced against the motion, and warm except for hands inside cotton gloves needed for gripping, we pull sockeye bellies through the wiry meshes by the hundreds as we compare the relative merits of baseball teams. When the gloves become slicked with slime we wring them out in the sea. It begins to drizzle, forming halos around the twinkling lights and blanking some altogether.

The wind increases and drizzle becomes pellets. "We'll make market," John announces after we've cleared the nets. After delivering to one of the cannery scows, we anchor and leave the nets aboard. A bucket's icy rim serves as a toilet seat. You cut the wind by putting the bucket in an empty fish bin and hunching down. We brush teeth, crawl into sleeping bags slightly damp and long unaired, and sleep at once as the radio near our heads crackles with "Well, I dunno . . ." and "How's it goin'?"

At five I wake to the grind of the engine underway. Rain drips down the open doorway against a slate sky. By the time I've pulled pants and wool shirt over the long johns I slept in, we're bobbing rail to rail by the *Sea Prince*. "I came over," John explains affably, "so Chris can eat pancakes and eggs at a table." Chris, in fact, can be seen through the porthole forking in chunks of pancake. He appears on deck a few minutes later wiping his mouth and smiling, refreshed.

The rain ends and clouds begin to open. The *Lady Phyllis* and the *Sunshine Lady* join us and tie alongside. (The skipper of the latter named the boat after his wife, who loves to lie in the sun.) Aboard the *Lady Phyllis,* Ed Genovese and his sons sit on deck in their oilpants, eating from plates on their laps. Ed Senior's hands have black ridges of grease, remnants of engine work not washed off by endless water. "Shows I don't have to pull nets no more," he declares, drawing on a curved-stem pipe. He cooks. And he frets because he's forgotten to pack enough tomato sauce in the supplies brought from California. We visit like back-fence neighbors. Chris and young Eddie Genovese in hip boots (Eddie a Little League coach back home) talk with quiet laughs from adjacent bows. Amidships the older men hold family conversations in both English and Italian.

When next I return to Bristol Bay, nine years later in 1995, John Crivello and Chris still fish the *Manhattan Kid* and Harold Brindle still holds reins at the Red Salmon Cannery (as indeed they still do as of the 1997 season with John now a rugged seventy-four). Changes there are, but not at first sight. The eternal tides flush the Naknek River, and all traffic stays geared to this. The sockeyes remain among the world's great fish. The Japanese market still controls so firmly that whenever prices fall—as they do now regularly with the influx of farmed salmon—angry rumbles and even strikes continue among fishermen convinced they are being jerked around. Five old cannery complexes still hug the Naknek River as they have since the 1920s, enclaves of self-sufficiency devoted to a month of heavy food production, but they are now as realistically called freezer plants despite continued canning.

I myself am inevitably older. It has been nineteen years since I picked candlefish on the Kodiak shrimp line in my late forties and first talked my way into a crew share aboard fishing boats. My trips with fishermen continue, but now I'm likely to be no more than a passenger ready to pitch in (as indeed I am this year in Kodiak, gleefully stacking web again on the seiner of my former skipper Thorvold Olsen, alongside crewmen unborn when I'd first come aboard).

In 1995 I arrive in Bristol Bay on the crabber *Trailblazer* at the invitation of its skipper, Yogi Briggs, storm-tossing through the Bering Sea from Dutch Harbor, where I've attended a meeting of the North Pacific Fishery Management Council. Yogi has been hired to tender salmon for Trident Seafoods, which now owns two of the cannery complexes (as not when I first came in 1980). In Dutch Harbor I've seen again my friend Tom Casey, who in early Kodiak days had bigbrothered my son and me. He now represents the beleaguered crabbers in a fight to reopen former grounds. Old times abound. When I reach Bristol Bay I radio Bart Eaton, who once skippered his crabber *Amatuli* within sight of my own stint with crab pots in the Bering Sea: We met again in Indonesia, where since his young Peace Corps days he has helped to foster new fisheries. Bart now manages the Trident South Shore plant in season as Trident's executive vice president. He diverts the company helicopter to bring me ashore and meets me. Usually groomed, he's now a few days whiskered, given Bristol Bay pressure and informality. Soon my knapsack lies on an actual bed with sheets in the frame hillside house of the old cannery bosses. (Bart has his own trailer with sophisticated communications gear.)

The twenty-five-foot tides quickly become a concern because Trident has plants on both sides of the Naknek River. Save for the priority helicopters, only skiffs connect the isolated South Shore to the active North Shore with its plants, village, and airport—and this for only the few hours of high tide. Across the river's expanse at low tide, boats lie beached against pilings, the sun gleams on roofs, and gulls swoop over midwater-exposed mud flats, attacking any trapped edible creature.

The offices of both Trident plants look over the water. Within the camp out atmosphere of weathered frame buildings and chow lines below, they buzz like combat centers. Locator maps on the walls, covering an area expanded beyond the Kvichak and Nushagak systems to include new hot spots farther down the coast at Egegik and Ugashik, show the positions of tenders and the tender-processor *Bountiful.* Radio voices direct aircraft and tenders, relay messages, alert a net scow to replace a boat's torn net on the run. One voice asks if a kid hired for the cannery, who couldn't cope, has tried. When the answer returns affirmative the voice directs that the kid's airfare home be paid. (The usual cannery contract in Bristol Bay pays airfare only if a worker remains the whole season.)

On the North Side pepper-bearded Chuck Bundrant, Trident's founder, seems to be everywhere if only by the force of his presence. Trim, enthusiastic, wired but coolly in charge, he personifies the new Bristol Bay of international markets and opportunity. He delivers his favorite mantra, "We're humble but we're hungry," with a positive cheer that makes it sound like a call to arms. Part of Trident's pride is one hundred percent U.S. ownership, an arrangement not shared by most companies with plants in Alaska, where Japanese and Scandinavians own as heavily as U.S. law allows.

Bundrant has, in common with Harold Brindle at Red Salmon down the road, a respect for his product as food. He expects boats to deliver every twelve hours to keep the fish fresh. "Quality is the key to surviving. If the market's strong you want your fish to be worth a premium, if weak you want 'em to sell before your competition." A dynamo with eyes still bright after sixteen-hour days when everyone else droops, motion is part of him. Immediately at the close of the Bristol Bay runs, Bundrant and Eaton will head for Japan to meet the fish there. If you can't sell before *Bon* (an important mid-August Japanese festival when people consume lots of seafood) you might have fish warehoused until spring. As for the vicissitudes of the fish business: "Change is a way of life. We should look forward to it. Should create and force change, not react to change created by others."

An example of change shows in the boats tied rail to rail along the pier, a village in itself. The law still limits the length of a gillnetter in

Bristol Bay to thirty-two feet. But no law governs width. Some boats, resembling aluminum wading pools, now have beams nearly as wide as their lengths, which virtually doubles their hold space.

Trident, as does Red Salmon, looks out for fishermen committed to delivering to its tenders exclusively. They have their own mug-up room in one of the buildings. One of the tender skippers tells me that uncommitted boats might be stopped in mid-delivery to make way for one of the family. Such priority in the heat of a run could mean the time to catch extra hundreds of fish.

This year I ride aboard the *Katherine B*, owned and skippered by Guy Piercey. The season has taken a break to allow escapement. Then at falling tide comes radio advice from Fish and Game to those at the piers: "Do not go dry." The air fills with revving engines. Soon the Naknek River turns mobbed as boats race for anchorage in open water. Suddenly I'm bunked with different fishermen than the dogged Norwegians or the familial third-generation Monterey Sicilianos. Piercey and his crewmen Dave and Scott are young hunters ready for the chase. Guy fishes in touch with his brother and friends on other boats, but his *Katherine B* stays intensely a community of one.

He calculates and observes. Overhead his pilot flies the area scouting shadowy concentrations of fish, to report options at Dogleg, Gravel Pit, Deadman Sands, Honey Hole, Banana Tree, South Line, other locations both traditional and privately discovered. "Fish going upstream into the wind," notes the pilot. Fish and Game announces the opening for thirty minutes after midnight at the start of flood. By then Guy has chosen his site, raced to it, and is waiting, keyed up and positioned. The sky, still orange, darkens rapidly.

We set. In the old sail days the men would have then secured the net astern and drifted with the tide—"flagged"—as did my own earlier crewmates in 1980 and 1986. This skipper, lean, unshaven, perpetually alert with a forward thrust, buoys both ends of his net and cruises it back and forth, inspecting, tuning, never relaxed. While he runs the net he surges prop wash to shoo fish into the meshes. If a concentration appears at one point but not another we "grab and pull" to tow the net to a new position. Scott and Dave also watch closely. If Guy sounds a signal from the cabin they respond on deck at once. There seems no correlation between number of rings in the signal and intent, so I ask. Guy grins. "Means what I'm thinkin' at the time. They know." They do, having fished together for years.

Days follow days on the water. A cool hand wherever he senses fish, Guy once maneuvers into a squeezed parallel with other aggressive boats off an abandoned cannery site called Libbyville as do no others in his group. ("It takes a certain kind of nerve," he observes modestly.) He risks falling tide for a fine netful off a notoriously tricky shore of Half-moon Bay, as a hill of a dark sand rises before us and wind drives the receding water against it like surf. A miscalculation could mean a battering such as has claimed lives in sail days and still gives no quarter to a propeller full of earth. Once the tide leaves us dry in a less threat-ened location, and we wait to go back afloat while clouds of mosquitoes descend to torment us off deck into the battened cabin. We deliver to *Trailblazer,* the tender I had ridden up from Dutch Harbor, some-times in fog or rain at three in the morning. Yogi Briggs's wife, Vicki, passes over fresh-baked brownies whatever the hour.

When the nets come aboard, there is no question of stacking them loaded on deck to pick for hours. With a new rigging used now by many boats, the net is winched straight across deck and the men flank it, freeing the fish as they came over the roller. A simple snap of the wrist sends many salmon thumping to deck, but the three men extri-cate even the tangled ones on the run. Dave, on the side where I help, attacks the work with such consuming focus that his hands bounce in my face if I don't watch out. The flapping fish around our legs are far fresher than those that die and soften in meshes for hours.

We head regularly to the South Line for predicted strong flood tides. This is the boundary that Fish and Game sets and enforces, the entry line for sockeyes incoming. I have fished the line before. In 1980 it was a town of boats that jockeyed to intercept the fish. By 1986 it was a city, and I even saw an angry pistol fired overhead to settle the matter of a boat edging too close to another. Now the line is a metropolis. Flanks of masts across the horizon move like rush hour in Rome or Tel Aviv. Following traffic rules is only for the timid.

Boats maneuver, churn the water, and leave zigzags of foam. Black smoke puffs from gunned engines. Hulls pass within literal touch. Aluminum bows bump. It's like being a microbe squirming among thousands in a petri dish. Fish and Game patrols, its location of the line exact with onboard satellite receivers. As the tide pushes them back, boats preempt each other's place at the line's invisible edge, trying to be first to intercept incoming fish when the signal allows boats to set. Planes buzz overhead, risking collision to radio fish movement. (Spotter planes have since been outlawed during openings.) Guy drives through it to the manor born, tensed but cool. Once he strays a fraction over the line. A Fish and Game boat speeds by and an officer in an orange float suit holds up a single finger. One microsecond over: friendly warning with too much noise for shouting. Guy nods back and adjusts. Farther over the line we see one boat arrested, put out of business. It's not a game.

The tide changes. Suddenly corks snaking everywhere begin to disappear in froth. Millions of sockeyes are running the gauntlet. They hit the nets thrashing. The water smokes but the boats are now passive because committed. We haul and pick as fast as we can, panting and laughing. Sweat pours into my eyes from under a wool cap while flecked slime mingles with the sweat. Boats all around become a blurred jumble. Big sockeyes beat our hands and thump our legs. This is why we've come.

CHAPTER TWENTY-THREE

Dividing and Protecting the Loot

Outside an Anchorage hotel one January in the middle of this tale, cars slipped on streets that had remained icy for weeks, while pedestrians hunched against a blowing snow. Inside the hotel, besuited men and women with briefcases headed toward two conference rooms. The sight was unremarkable except that this was a fish-business meeting in Alaska. A few years before, these participants and witnesses would have come to a session of the North Pacific Fishery Management Council in work-faded (not boutique-faded) jeans and plaid shirts. Now they came in business costume, with lawyers and hired guns to represent them.

The councils are a creation of the Magnuson Act, which established eight such regional bodies to prepare management plans for each fishery in its area, and to advise the Commerce Department while remaining independent of its jurisdiction. The councils lack the ultimate power to pass regulations, but strong language in the act directs that the commerce secretary heed their decisions. The rules for appointing council members were written to ensure that their interests (and inevitably self-interests, since they are individuals involved in some aspect of fishing) remain regional.

The North Pacific council meets five times a year. During this session its scientific committee and the advisory panel met first to receive testimony on twenty-seven proposed changes to fishery management plans that the full council expected to consider. On the third day the two panels reported to the eleven voting members and four nonvoting members of the full council. The agenda ranged from such routine items as clarifying the term "prohibited species" and redefining the concept of acceptable biological catch to matters that demanded a triage between legitimate but conflicting domestic interests.

There were two proposals in which a win for one side meant a clear loss for the other. One sought to limit the number of boats that could longline for newly profitable sablefish in the Gulf of Alaska. The proposal was submitted by fishermen already established there, pioneers in the fishery who ironically lived and kept their boats in Washington and Oregon. It was opposed by Alaskan fishermen planning to enter the fishery located in their own state—who, if they came in great numbers, might overfish the stock and spoil it for everybody. The council by its makeup represented both interests. Voting members just short of a majority came from Washington and Oregon. Keeping an Alaskan voting majority on the council was a running fight in Washington, D.C., for Senator Ted Stevens of Alaska, an original force behind the Magnuson Act that in 1976 established an American 200-mile fishing zone and required fishing councils. (Stevens' name was later added to the title.)

For those who understood the language, the other proposed change held a bomb in practically every word of its title: "Establish priority access for domestic processors around Dutch Harbor." In conflict were two American interests, both valid, neither of which could have developed to the point of hiring well-rewarded lawyers and consultants without the opportunities created by the Magnuson Act. The circumstance symbolized all the progress achieved by Americans during the heady first years of 200-mile jurisdiction.

The proposal would create a protectionist zone in the waters around remote and booming Dutch Harbor, requiring that any fish caught there be harvested by and sold to Americans. Advocates wanted Bering Sea fish manufactured into food at the local shoreside plants to create a stable local economy. The new American trawler fleet, they charged, used Dutch Harbor for only limited logistical support (they bought most supplies in Seattle before leaving), processed their catches on board, and either sold it at sea to foreign buyers or took it back to plants in Washington or Oregon. In contrast, shore plants in Alaska paid Alaskan taxes, and hired local people or at least transients who paid state tax on what they earned.

The trawler-processor spokesmen from the Lower Forty-Eight argued that their capital and initiative had created the American groundfish industry once monopolized by the Japanese. Now that the risk was over and the market flourishing, they balked at sharing allotments equally with shoreside plants.

Don Collinsworth, at the time a council member as head of the Alaska Department of Fish and Game, expressed the concern of many when he said: "We're dealing with common property fisheries. I've watched people come to this podium to testify, people whom I've known for years and have enormous respect for—creative, hardworking entrepreneurs. However I vote, I'm going to be disadvantaging one of those people's economic interests."

Ironically the very success of the American trawler-processor fleet in the Bering Sea had led to some of the worst of its problems. The now notorious roe-stripping incident off Kodiak was bad enough, but the pressures the big boats felt to generate income on their investment led to worse. Pollock is a low-price, high-volume fishery, and fierce competition in the world market allowed only a small profit margin. The trawler-processors carried as many as forty crewmen for the deck and factory, Americans who expected to be fed and housed agreeably enough to keep them content for several months spent in rough seas doing long shifts of uncomfortable work. It was an expensive proposition, and the ships needed to fish hard to pay for it. Lawyers representing the trawler groups frequently pressed the council for larger quotas (never granted), and also for more lenient restrictions on protected species such as crab and halibut that would be allowed as by-catch.

The shoreside people charged further that the Seattle trawler-processors caught vastly more than their quotas, and got away with it because nobody was there to watch them. (In truth this is often the case for more than big trawlers, no matter how often fishermen call themselves conservationists.) Another claim, supported by a volunteer witness: The ships worked grounds where their nets took greater quantities of undersized fish and unauthorized by-catch than they reported. The witness, who had worked on one of the ships, said he saw more fish wasted, thrown back dead, than he saw processed. He became progressively more articulate, terming it "rape and piracy," a haunting reminder of the accusations leveled fifteen years before against the foreign fleets.

Since that 1989 meeting, the council has created what amounts to a new occupation in the fisheries: observer. Every Bering Sea and Gulf of Alaska fishing vessel over 130 feet must now carry a full-time trained observer, vessels 60 to 129 feet a rotating part-time observer, whose job it is to oversee the contents of the nets and collect data. Observers are recruited and assigned by agencies that train them. While many are students in one of the marine sciences, passing through, there already appears to be a professional cadre, male and female. What does a crew of sweating fishermen make of a supernumerary who produces nothing and in addition is a sort of spy? Answers I receive vary from support by the Bering Sea trawler companies who welcome proof that their by-catch is not as vast as charged, to individual boatowners hostile to the considerable extra expense of guaranteed pay and transportation. Courts have dealt strongly with occasional sexual harassment and attempts at bribery. By 1997 observers had become accepted in Alaska, as well as in Atlantic Canada (but not necessarily other regions of North America or the world) as an inevitable part of the scene.

The hot inshore-offshore issue was resolved in 1992 after passionate lobbying by both sides. Bering Sea boats delivering to shoreside plants receive thirty-five percent of the quota and trawler-processors the remainder, except for seven and a half percent reserved to develop remote native communities. The original allotment, made for three years, left the option to thrash out revised divisions after seeing how it worked. While some expected a fresh battle at renewal time, the council in 1995 passed on another three years without contest. By then, other issues promising reward or disaster were drawing the heat. By mid-1997, however, the inshore-offshore struggle resumed in light of lowered overall quotas.

Thus the pressures and opportunities among fishermen of the same nationality. Fish, however, are careless of national boundaries as they pursue their feed. Since continental shelves alone produce most sea creatures in commercial numbers, the world's great fishing areas are known and numbered. In parts of the world where 200-mile jurisdictions overlap on continental shelves, or where such lines leave open gaps of fish-productive international zones, there is bound to be a scramble. The area around the Grand Banks is one of the most dramatic examples, where Canada's zone does not extend far enough to control the whole ecosystem, and foreign ships gather outside the 200 miles to take what they can. Among most other major hot spots, affected nations have organizations or agreements to exert some control. Their effectiveness varies since they rely on consent rather than force. Besides off Grand Banks, such international waters include:

- The Pacific "Donut Hole" in the Bering Sea, a space between the U.S. (Alaska) and Russian zones; mainly pollock; competing nations are Japan, South Korea, China, and Poland. Presently closed to all fishing.
- The "Peanut Hole," thirty-five miles by three hundred miles, Sea of Okhotsk; enclosed by Russia (mainland and Kamchatka Peninsula); mainly pollock; competing nations are Japan, Korea, China, Poland, and Panama. Presently closed.
- "The Loop Hole" in the Barents Sea between zones of Norway and Russia; mainly cod, capelin, and redfish; competing nations are the European Economic Community, Greenland, and the Faeroe Islands. Norway, Russia, and Iceland signed a trilateral agreement to manage it in mid-1999.
- The Atlantic "Donut Hole" in the Norwegian Sea bounded by Norway, Iceland, Greenland, and the Faeroes; mainly herring.
- East central Atlantic, off West Africa; horse mackerel and squid; competing nations of the European Union.
- Off Namibia, southwest Africa; hake and horse mackerel; competing nations are the European Economic Community and the Republic of South Africa. (A formerly uncontrolled area heavily overfished by former Soviets, Spain, and Portugal with international conservation attempts ignored. Namibia became independent in 1990 and claimed 200-mile jurisdiction, starting its own fishing industry.)
- Patagonian Shelf off Argentina; squid, hake, and whiting; competing nations Poland, Spain, Taiwan, Japan, South Korea, and China. (Cooperative agreement in 1989 between the United Kingdom and Argentina regarding zone around the Falkland Islands.)
- Southeast Pacific, off Chile–Peru 200-mile coasts; mainly jack mackerel; competing nations are the Soviet Union (before its collapse), Bulgaria, Poland, Cuba, South Korea, Japan, and Spain.
- Challenger Plateau off New Zealand; orange roughy; competing nations are Australia, Norway, Japan, Korea, and Russia.

In mid-1995 the United Nations completed a six-session Conference on Straddling Stocks and Migratory Species that followed the 1992 Earth Summit in Rio. The goal was to write a set of rules to govern high-seas fishing that all nations would agree to follow for the survival of the world's living marine resources. The rules would also govern informally an individual nation's approaches to managing its own seafood stocks. The conference agreement, cautiously endorsed by some one hundred nations (many with stated reservations) but subsequently signed by only fifty-nine, will become international law only after thirty nations actually ratify it. In mid-1996 the United States under President Bill Clinton ratified and took the lead in urging other nations to join. By early 2000 only twenty-four other nations had ratified, a majority of them small players except for the U.S., Russia, Norway, Canada, Uruguay, and Iceland. World players whose signatures await ratification include Argentina, Australia, Brazil, China, Denmark, France, Germany, Indonesia, Japan, New Zealand, Pakistan, the Philippines, South Korea, Spain, and the United Kingdom. Some of these, including Japan—which has stated it officially—have begun to abide by the agreement in good faith. Among major fishing nations that never signed are Chile, India, Peru, Taiwan (not a UN member for political reasons), and Thailand.

In essence the U.N. agreement focuses on three main tenets: conservation/management, enforcement, and settlement of disputes. The agreement would apply in all waters "outside national jurisdiction" (that is, outside 200-mile and other exclusive economic zones) but signatory nations would also comply with the precautionary measures within its boundaries.

Conservation and better management are based on "a precautionary approach and the best scientific information." Nations would agree to act conservatively when the viability of stocks is in doubt. This would be a colossal change in the way many nations regulate their seafood resources. In the short run it could make fishing a survival of the fittest by distributing quotas so thinly that many fishermen give up. In the long view such personal misfortune might save the resources from the pressures of need and overcapitalization, and allow them to regenerate or remain healthy.

Cooperative enforcement would ensure that no nation undermines conservation measures. Flag states must allow a coastal state suspecting a violation to board a suspected offender of the flag state. Serious violations include fishing for prohibited stocks, fishing without a license, using illegal fishing gear, and concealing, tampering with, or disposing of evidence needed for an investigation. This tenet for several nations appears the stumbling block of the agreement. China flatly opposes it, and nations like Japan with the greatest stake in far-seas fishing have expressed concern.

Peaceful settlement of disputes would be achieved through "compulsory and binding" third-party decision. No more cut nets or guns across the bow, as occurred in March 1995 off Grand Bank when Canadians forced the issue by arresting one Spanish trawler and cutting the nets of another suspected (correctly) of fishing illegally.

The issues that govern a fisherman's livelihood have grown beyond his immediate control, unless he stops fishing and becomes a lobbyist, or helps hire one. It isn't my purpose here to present all the issues or debate them but, only in this chapter, to hint at their complexity and importance. They are as fluid as the ocean itself, so that one problem met can beget another; the hot issues at this writing may not be the same tomorrow.

Informed regional and national management must stay above greed and narrow interest to pick its way through. On the international level the threat of overfishing the world's productive waters beyond national jurisdictions is acute enough that only a consensus to conserve can reverse the tide. The U.N. agreement offers new hope and our best chance to date. But only if all agree, and get tough together.

CHAPTER TWENTY-FOUR

No Promises

One night I stood lone watch on a shrimper traveling the Shelikof Strait from Mitrofania to Kodiak. Before stowing our nets we had pushed to the limit the cannery-imposed ceiling on the time shrimp could stay iced. Now we needed to deliver by early morning. I hurt from three long days' fishing, aboard a boat whose design quirks necessitated brute labor with shovel and crowbar. Whatever I had taken for pain, while nothing more than an over-the-counter drug, did not help my alertness.

My two crewmates slept. They too were exhausted. I had drawn this watch fairly, and would in three hours wake one of them to relieve me, so asking for help was out of the question. My eyes kept creeping shut against my will. I craved the comfort and oblivion of the warm sleeping bag waiting in the bunk below. Lights swam and it was difficult to focus. To sit would have meant falling asleep at once. I grasped a rail, unbalanced myself, and took few-second naps that I could trust to end when I stumbled. I held my breath and did pushups to make the blood flow. I drank black coffee until my stomach rebelled. The boat chugged steadily into rain and choppy water. Through sleepy vision I saw the lights of other boats in time to avoid collision, and I checked the radar often enough to ensure against groundings, but the line between safety and danger that night stretched very thin.

Fishermen hope they've learned to balance fatigue against the desire for income, which can be called either greed or expedience in an uncertain business. According to the late Norman Holm, an ex-fisherman and marine surveyor out of Kodiak who in a long career assessed hundreds of fishing boat accidents and disasters, fatigue causes more marine wrecks than any other circumstance.

Fishing remains statistically the most dangerous occupation in the United States. According to the Bureau of Labor Statistics, a fisherman has twenty times more likelihood of getting killed than does a miner, who plies the next most dangerous occupation. The names of the drowned peel off each year during observances in fishing towns from Gloucester to Pascagoula to Newport to Kodiak. Between 1990 and 1994, 118 fishermen died at sea in Alaska alone, seventy-three due to vessels sunk or capsized, while injuries were seven times the state average for other industries. (Logging came next.) Between 25 and 40 fishing vessels still sink annually in Alaska, according to the U.S. Coast Guard. No area or country has found the secret to absolute safety. Norway averages twenty to twenty-five fishing dead a year, with as many others made invalids in fishing accidents. The count on Asian boats runs higher. In 1993 an official in Taipei clocked off for me Taiwan's previous year's toll: 143 dead in fishing accidents, 70 more missing, and 94 severely injured.

Kodiak, during my first years there, was a chancy apprenticing ground for fishermen, swim or sink, in some of the world's most dangerous waters. In practice, the only skippers willing to hire a green hand were those with the least local reputation: those who for reasons of low catches, poor boat maintenance, frequent accidents, a tendency to scream and berate, or some combination, could not keep an experienced crew. Once a marginal skipper hired me. The boat was ill-kept, but we fished in a bay not far from Kodiak, thus seemingly removed from the dangers of open seas. I came aboard with my own survival suit—a loose foam rubber garment completely sealed from foot to chin (impossible to work in) that when donned in emergency floats and keeps out the terrible cold of northern water—assuming the other crew had them also. After we had made it through a nasty storm, one crewman, larger and stronger than I, said with a friendly grin: "Dale and me was drawing lots to see who'd get your survival suit if we went down."

At that time in the late 1970s, U.S. law required life jackets aboard a fishing boat, but nothing forced a skipper to conduct periodic maintenance nor to carry survival suits (relatively new gear back then) and emergency communications equipment. The best skippers took such provision for granted, but not necessarily the worst. Nor, unlike Japan, Taiwan, Norway, and several other countries, did the United States require a fishing captain to pass any qualifying test.

My son, Wynn, after he had followed me to Alaska in the 1970s, eventually found boats to hire him. By luck, or under the eye of a benevolent Force, he survived. Once he might have been caught praying to that Force. Fortunately his mother, sister, and I didn't know of it until he called us from the raining safety of a phone booth on the Kodiak pier. The engine died on the boat he had joined, leaving them powerless more than a hundred miles from any land during a Gulf of Alaska storm. For two days waves crashed over the wheelhouse and plunged the boat helter-skelter. Diesel oil from a ruptured line slicked the cabin deck, making it impossible to walk and trapping the crew in its stench. The radio malfunctioned, so they could not have called for help. Since they were alone in transit, no other boat would have spotted them if they had capsized. The skipper, a fatalistic older man, took to his bunk and left his three teenage crewmen to cope as best they could. Wynn reached port at last, well sobered but, being young and strong, still quite ready to go fishing. A few years later this same boat hit rocks and sank as it traveled Shelikof Strait (where I had struggled with sleep and pain) from one fishing ground to another. The weather was not bad and all hands survived. The man on watch had fallen asleep from exhaustion after having worked on deck all day.

In 1985 Peter Barry, a twenty-year-old Yale junior who had gone to Alaska to seek adventure and make summer money, drowned off Kodiak with his five crewmates. The boat of the skipper who hired him (the only one who would) was the seventy-year-old wooden *Western Sea*. According to later investigation, the vessel had rotten planking, a loose hatch cover, and a heavy skiff lashed too high above deck for stability. It carried neither life raft nor survival suits, only pleasure-boat-style life preservers for water that would freeze a man to death in minutes. Nor did it have emergency signaling equipment or a standard engine-powered bilge pump. The vessel sank without word or trace. The corpse of the skipper-owner, when found, betrayed traces of cocaine. The man whom Barry replaced had quit in fear for his own safety.

The tragedy galvanized the youth's parents. Robert and Peggy Barry, he an American ambassador, made it their mission to lobby for compulsory safety standards on fishing boats. It was more of a fight with the establishment than might be imagined. Fishermen detest bureaucracy—they must already cope with enough of it. Many Alaskan fishermen, macho and fatalistic, hardened to taking their chances yet also professional enough to ensure their safety without laws to force them, resented the fact that it was the death of a landlubber "preppie" not committed to the fishing life that caused the stir. A whole group of fishermen's *wives,* however, turned out in support.

Representative Gerry Studds of Massachusetts, then a senior Democrat in the now-defunct House Merchant Marine and Fisheries Committee, had already begun work on a legislative package to increase fishing boat safety and lower the cost of insurance. Liability premiums had become ruinously high for fishing boats in the wake of multimillion dollar judgments. Studds sought incentives to reduce insurance through boat licensing and mandatory inspections. Studds sought also to require an EPIRB (emergency position-indicating radiobeacon) on board each boat—a signaling device that would activate automatically in case of a disaster. He indeed convinced the insurance companies, but the powerful Association of Trial Lawyers of America opposed the bill because it limited the amount of a judgment for injuries (although only those not due to vessel negligence).

Peggy Barry, clear-eyed, informed, articulate, and calmly passionate, became the catalyst for stronger safety measures. Her speeches and testimony drew enough public awareness to rouse wider congressional interest. Studds, with other congressmen, notably Mike Lowry of Washington, gradually modified the insurance provisions and finally dropped them. By September 1988 both houses had passed the bill, and President Ronald Reagan signed it into the Commercial Fishing Vessel Safety Act. The Act, enforceable by the Coast Guard, requires that vessels operating more than three miles from land (that is, in federal rather than state waters) must carry enough life rafts and immersion suits for everyone aboard, radio equipment sufficient to call the Coast Guard, specified navigation gear, fire extinguishers, life preservers, flares, first-aid supplies, and an EPIRB. The organized trial lawyers had successfully killed the section on capping liabilities and thus preserved for themselves a formidable source of income, usually one-third of the settlement plus expenses. While not all that the Barrys and Studds envisioned, the Act removed some of the needless fatalism from fishing.

Approximately a decade later *National Fisherman,* principal U.S. organ for commercial fishermen (there are also several regional publications) surveyed safety in the U.S. fisheries and reported that there is now a decrease in "the risks, the long hours, drugs. . . . " The May 1997 issue ran an editorial by then-Pacific Editor Brad Matson entitled "Peg

Barry Was Right." Matson noted that in 1985 when Peter Barry went down: "News of a fisherman lost at sea was as common as sunrise to most of us"—102 fishermen died nationwide that year. Matson continued: "Weather, of course, was and is the big killer. For hundreds of years before 1985, though, safety was more of an instinctive after-thought than the energetic preoccupation it is now. . . . In 1994, only 75 sons and daughters died on the fishing grounds; in 1995, only 68. Thanks Peggy." Note that word "only," though. Fishing remains the most dangerous occupation in America.

As the editorial noted, no promise of safety can guard a fisherman entirely. One day I received a call from Terry Mason, the bright pres-ence in the king crabbing crew of the *American Beauty* in 1976 who had joshingly dubbed me "the Baltimore warbler." We had not seen each other since that November on the Bering Sea. Now, five years later, in 1981, Terry fished closer to his home in Oregon. "Bill, I've just survived a really crazy accident."

Terry and his brother Todd were crewing for groundfish on the forty-eight-foot trawler *Odyssey* off the Oregon coast. When a strong south-wester started blowing, skipper Gary Cutting decided to weather it out. The boat, a new one and well tested, slammed and rolled, but fish-ermen in northern waters have always accepted this as part of the work. Suddenly a big wave hit the boat broadside. Todd, on watch, had just made himself a snack. The skipper was dozing in a bunk near the wheel, and Terry lay asleep against the bow in the cramped fo'c'sle. A later investigation determined that the wave knocked off one of the six-hundred-pound steel trawl doors chained to either side of the boat, and the sudden weight loss on a single side tipped the balance.

No one had time to put on his survival suit. According to Terry: "It felt like the boat was immediately on the verge of tipping over. I jumped out of bed. By the time I got to the top and reached the radio my brother had shut off the engine. Then another wave hit, just imme-diate-like, and we rolled over. Didn't have time at the radio for a Mayday. It was like, for me, like being from a dead sleep to being upside down." Terry, thirty-five, was a short man with a kid's bright-ness. He discussed his ordeal a week later with such a quiet, steady voice that he might merely have watched it on TV.

"Then we kind of panicked, all three of us there. Tried to get the door open, the door leading from the galley to the deck, get out fast as we could. The door wouldn't budge. Water pressure, I guess. Then we tried to bust the window open, but it's got that bulletproof Plexiglas stuff. Beat at it with a frying pan." Remember, these men were now in a boat with everything tumbled into reverse. They stood on the former ceiling, with the deck they had walked upon seconds before now bumping their heads and every familiar object that had not broken loose hanging over them the wrong way. "Then Todd opened a drawer that had in it our really big frying pan—everything inside tumbled upside out—and beat at the window. Todd's a big guy. He broke off the frying pan handle but the window didn't budge."

It had to be the two-part Dutch door or nothing, even though it would flood them immediately and require a frenzied swim to the surface. "We tried to figure out which way to turn the handle from upside down. Just got it cracked enough to let water in. A wave slammed and crushed our fingers—a couple of mine still won't hold anything—but we held on 'cause it was the only way out. We finally got the door partway open. But by that time water was up to about our waist, and we'd got disorientated."

Soon, the water was up to their chins. "We were kind of floating. Sometimes we had to hold our breath when the water washed over our heads." The hatch to the engine room was a little trapdoor less than two feet square. A short ladder inside, built to lead down to the engine and bilge, now led up at least to a space above them that still had air. "Gary was still obsessed with getting out the door. But we had to go up. I said 'Let's go.' I'm not sure but I've been dreaming this, but I think Gary just shrugged me off. So Todd and I went up to the engine room, popped right up, and just stood there and waited, on like a little mantelpiece. Waited for the skipper to come up. We figured he was right behind us."

The Mason brothers made it up to the engine space none too soon. "We didn't have time to even look around when there was this big *whoosh*. The door had come loose evidently, 'cause the cabin below us got completely full of water. We figured Gary had got out. But then, in the cold water, we wondered what happened to him. Anyhow, I thought we were dead. Plenty of guys I've known, fishermen, they've been drownded. So, I figured, now it's my turn. Will I see God? Then we stayed floating, like gettin' a reprieve. If somebody found us."

They had capsized around 3 P.M. It was mid-June, so the days were long. Daylight, seen as a glow through the engine-room hatch, slowly faded. For a rescue to start, somebody first had to find them. But the

Odyssey had been fishing alone. How long before somebody missed them, even their wives? (Both men were separated but, with children, were still in touch; fishing and an easy home life do not always go together.) There was no comfort except for being still alive. Terry had burned his arm against a hot engine pipe as they climbed to safety, and they could barely move their fingers after crushing them in the door. And, Terry added, "We were completely saturated with oil, black oil." At first the engine radiated heat, but the metal soon cooled. The sea temperature was fifty-six degrees. "We could crawl up out of the water on a ledge but it was still cold. We was only wearing sneakers, jeans, and T-shirts—you know, the cabin had been warm inside when it happened, we weren't on deck hauling nets. So we kept moving our hands and arms to stay warm." A broken vent pipe let in a trickle of fresh but frigid air, and also water. Alternately they plugged it with a sock or opened it for ventilation.

The brothers muttered contingencies to each other. If the boat hit rocks and ripped apart . . . if the waves rolled the boat to a new angle and flooded their prison. . . . if nobody came to rescue them. . . . "The only answer to any of it was, to swim for it, under the water," Terry said. They practiced holding their breaths. "I had to go under once to find something to stick in the door. *Scary.*" His voice tightened for the first time. "I don't like to swim, don't like the water that much."

By a fluke, some people on a sailboat lost in the same storm had radioed the Newport, Oregon, Coast Guard for help. The Coasties had their hands full escorting boats out of the weather, so they asked for an exact position to help them reach the boaters. The boaters thought they saw an orange vessel tossing in the waves and approached it hoping to get a radio fix. It was the overturned *Odyssey,* discovered against all odds before darkness would have made a search impossible until morning. The message, according to newspaper accounts, reached the Coast Guard at 6:27 P.M., three and a half hours after the accident.

The Coast Guard dispatched a helicopter, the first of many heroic acts during the night, because this was no weather for safe flying close to the surface. The chopper reached the scene at 7:16 P.M., radioed the exact position, and began to shine a powerful light around the water, looking for survivors. A special Coast Guard self-righting lifeboat arrived from Newport at 8:10 P.M. In the furiously raining twilight, with whitecaps snapping over the water, Petty Officer Second Class

Richard White volunteered to have the helicopter raise him in a harness from his boat so that he could crawl onto the *Odyssey's* rolling, pitching, slippery hull and tap on it for survivors. Terry and Todd tapped back strongly with a piece of pipe they had nursed for hours in hopes that someone might come. Except for the taps, the only sound that had filtered through the overturned hull had been the throb of the helicopter rotors.

In Newport, a close-knit fishing community, people began rushing supplies and equipment to the waterfront and the airstrip, much of it helter-skelter since nobody knew what the rescuers would need specifically. Some fishermen set out in their boats to see if they could help, while others prepared to go if the Coast Guard failed. The wives and ex-wives of the three men gathered in the Coast Guard operations office. Other family members waited by their marine radios. (Terry and Todd came from a family of thirteen.) Eventually word of two survivors reached the community, but no one knew which of the three they were. In town one of the churches opened its doors, and throughout the night people came to pray. And, of course, the media arrived in force with lights and cameras.

The Coast Guard reviewed the options, all of them dangerous in the storm and darkness. They could try to cut a hole in the hull, but the bubble holding the boat afloat might go in the process before the men could be pulled out, or the heavy equipment needed to do the job in a heaving sea might send the boat down. They might tow the boat to shallower water, but this would take a long time while the vessel might swamp and sink during the rough trip. Or, a diver could go in with breathing apparatus and take them out. A diver posed the least risk if a willing, qualified one could be found.

The first two divers flown to the scene studied the conditions and decided they could not do the job. Two commercial salvage divers, Bill Shires and Pat Miller, agreed to have a look, but they lived miles away. A local pilot flew them to Newport (dangerous in itself during the storm). "It was one of those eerie evenings," Shires recalled, "The wind's blowing about forty-five, rainstorms, squalls going back and forth." Everyone knew the importance of speed since the *Odyssey* could sink at any time, but steps had to be taken deliberately. After a quick briefing with the owner of a similar boat, Shires declared that he needed to assess the situation on site. One of the Coast Guard's two helicopters flew Shires and Miller to the scene. They wore wetsuits, ready to go. It was already past midnight.

Later, in the safety and comfort of a warm room, Bill Shires, a thickset man graying at the temples, remembered some of it. "Opened up the helicopter door, we're sitting there with a full set of diving gear on, looking down through the squalls at lights playing on this hull. You'd see the hull drop off the waves and go back up again and bob like a cork. It was frightening, nothing like I'd been into before. The chopper pilot says: 'You going to go?' I said yes, get me down within ten feet of the water. So Pat and I went."

In the dark and cold water, illuminated by searchlight beams from boats and aircraft, Shires discovered that a loose net on deck had encased the furiously surging boat like a bag. They cut through and swam under the deck (which was heaving over their heads). Half of the Dutch door swayed open. Evidently Gary Cutting in his desperation had succeeded. They tugged open the other half and tied back both sections.

Inside, debris tumbled in a chaotic stew—anything loose, from baloney and shirts to chairs. Shires tried to enter and explore, but the flotsam bumped his head and tangled his gear too dangerously. He passed objects item by item to his partner, who carried them to the hole in the net for release. "We got tangled up in a bunch of netting, in gear. I got vertigo because the boat . . . she'd drop off the waves and the hydraulic surge-pressure came up just like a plunger to shove you forward into the boat. Then she'd roll anywhere from sixty to eighty degrees. So I was inside this washing machine goin' around, tryin' to figure what next while I got nauseated, got disoriented, got wrapped three times in my own safety line." After clearing the cabin Shires searched but found no bodies or survivors. Despite a superhuman push by rescuers, more than four hours had elapsed since the young Coast Guardsman had heard the taps from inside. Possibly since then the men had died and been washed away.

Shires returned to the surface, exhausted. After a quick rest he pulled himself together for another try, this time on the exposed hull. He strapped a four-pound hammer to his belt and returned with Miller. "Now remember this thing is an upside down boat, completely slick, in probably fourteen-foot seas. Every time the boat drops off a swell she goes underneath. Pat's about six-one. He grabs the rudder shaft and makes himself a human ladder and I just crawled over his body. I hugged along the keel, tapping on the compartments. And at midships I got this response back. So I did it again. And all of a sudden I could hear this frantic tapping inside."

Inside the boat, crouched and shivering, Terry and Todd had watched the diver's light as it edged the rim of the trap door beneath them, but they found no way to communicate through the barrier of water. They had a curious illumination of their own, caused by phosphorescent plankton that emitted greenish, glowing speckles in the water sloshing against the hull. "That glow," Terry remembered, "it didn't make us feel any better, it was too spooky." A long dearth of action followed the glimpse of the exploring light. "We wondered if the guys outside had given up. When we heard those taps over our head, I guess we banged back like hell."

Shires, outside, returned to the support boat to prepare for a third trip. He had brought with him a load of dive equipment—"I mean I threw in everything, you don't know what you're going to run into." The survivors would be scared and tired, he assumed, and probably had no dive experience. Thus he couldn't risk "buddy breathing"—sharing the mouthpiece to his own regulator by passing it back and forth under water—which required training and discipline. He needed to attach an "octopus," a second breathing line, to his regulator. The only other equipment available to him was Pat Miller's. After Miller had stripped down his own regulator to provide the octopus, he could assist Shires only from the surface.

Shires had tied a down line all the way into the *Odyssey*'s interior, and had attached underwater lights along it every ten feet. "I could watch those lights swing as I worked my way back in." He found the hatch to the engine compartment swollen shut from the water, its handle only a finger-hold lever. "Well, the air had locked and compressed it shut. I placed one finger in the crack of the door. It crushed the finger, but allowed the engine compartment to depressurize. I finally with a real strong sense of urgency, I got it pulled down. I started to work my way up. All of a sudden I saw this hand coming down. It had life, it grabbed me, it scared me. Then I had to work my way through this twenty-two by twenty-two-inch opening in a wetsuit, diving tank, all kinds of regulators. I work my way up. Just as I begin to break water I shine my light up. And I see two sets of eyes."

Up to their chests in water, in a mist of smoke and diesel fumes, the brothers received a brief course in scuba diving. "No mystique, scuba's just basic, a way to get to the work site. So I told these two guys: 'You follow instructions, you live; you don't, you die. Pretty basic course we're goin' to have here today, folks.'" The audience at the Seattle Fish Expo to whom Shires was recounting his experience laughed for the first time. They did it with a relieved heartiness. Most were fishermen, men with muscles bulging from plaid shirts. For the moment they sat agreeably close to food and shelter, but they could project themselves onto the storming dark water.

Shires gave Todd the regulator to demonstrate. "He puts it in his mouth, sucks it, says: 'I can't get no air.' I figured the guy was just stressed out. But he hands it back, and low and behold, I can't get air out of the bottle either!" He had ruptured part of the bulky scuba system trying to come up through the narrow opening. "My *tank's* empty. And now, the guy that's going to make the rescue, he becomes the victim. I'm trapped also inside this boat. Yes, if you're wondering. I felt a sense of real despair."

He did not tell the brothers, but merely said that he needed to go out for more equipment. "I had to make about a forty-five-foot run through the interior of this boat with no air. I'll tell you what, this was one time I prepared. I stripped the gear off, I opened up my knife blade... took three breaths, made a submersion, and started down that line. I can still see those lights swinging." There was a turn to negotiate in the cabin, then a hand-over-hand crossing under the deck to the opening in the fishnet, then a potential snare from cables that had been attached to the boat if he tried to surface before clearing them. He made it, completely exhausted.

Shires recovered himself as quickly as he could. The water in the compartment had risen a rung on the ladder from opening the hatch and time might be running out. Only the bubble of air kept the boat afloat. He decided to return himself since he knew the way in. Carrying individual air bottles and regulators from his stockpile, he faced the brothers again. "Inside there, I know if we lose the bubble we're all gone. I didn't ask who had the most kids or anything like that. I just said: 'You're [Todd] first, you're [Terry] second.'"

He strapped the gear onto Todd and explained how he was to follow the lighted line hand over hand. But, also: "Return to the refuge if anything goes wrong." Todd did panic. "But he made the right decision and went right back. We had a little discussion about get your act together, if you want to get out of here you've got to do what I tell you to. So once again we went down into the interior. I pulled him down by his legs, grabbed his hand." They groped through the net and to the surface.

Shires was sensitive enough to Terry's plight, left alone in the dark, half-submerged in oily water rising around him, to return immediately despite his own fatigue. "Well," Terry admitted a week later, "I don't remember much about that wait. Don't want to, I guess." Strapped into the gear and swimming out, Terry panicked and started groping toward the forepeak: a dead end. "So," said Shires, "I wrassle him back in and turn, made sure that I was in position. I'm prepared to drown him and hope that my topside crew'll be ready to rescue him."

Shires' listeners gasped. He knew he needed to explain. "That's a terrible terrible burden to place on anybody. But in a situation like this where that man's panic might kill you both, you've got to take control of him and hope that your topside crew's prepared." He looked firmly at the faces of fishermen watching him. "I've worked in this ocean. She's an equal opportunity killer." One large man nodded. "I've seen her," Shires continued, "I've seen her kill captains with all kinds of moxie as easily as the guys without brains."

Terry pulled himself together, although he remained disoriented. "Just as he broke the cabin," Shires concluded, "he wanted to go up, and up was upside down and there was the debris. He forgot his instructions, let go the line, and went right into the snare of nets. I pulled him back. After that he saw lights on the surface and headed toward them, hands on the line like I'd told him. You can count on it, the guy's always going to swim toward the light. And he made it."

Later that year the Coast Guard awarded Bill Shires and Pat Miller the Gold Lifesaving Medal, its highest civilian award for valor.

Back home in Newport, people rejoiced at the rescue of the Mason brothers and grieved at the loss of Gary Cutting, whose body was never found. "But you get tired of walking down the street," Terry said a week later. "Everybody wants to know the story, and you've got to tell the whole story." He talked to me the day of Gary's memorial service. After hesitating, he added quietly: "I didn't go. Didn't think I was up to that. You think you're OK, then you get despondent. I couldn't go to sleep last night. . . . But now that the memorial service is over. . . ."

I asked Terry if he felt any guilt and assured him it was natural. His voice came closest to breaking. "Maybe I could have pulled him . . . You know, back there, maybe forced him. . . ."

After the *Odyssey* disaster Terry declared: "Guess I'm just happy to be alive. I've been on a couple of boats when I thought they were going to sink, but nothing like this. Kind of ironical, my thirteen years of fishing, and thirteen hours down there." After a pause: "I don't think I'll go back fishing. I don't want to die that way." But Terry remained a fisherman, whether by choice or circumstance. Four years later his boat went down. This time he drowned.

Bristol Bay, Alaska, 1986: Skipper John Crivello of the *Manhattan Kid,* right, clowns a moment with his longtime crewman and fellow Californian Chris Rivera.

Bristol Bay, Alaska, 1980: The author, left, aboard *Gail T* with a netful of enmeshed sockeyes and hours of picking ahead. Other crew are skipper Dick Nes, center, and Otto Holgersen.

Bristol Bay, Alaska, 1995: Ready to fish, a line of aluminum gillnetters waits at Trident pier in Naknek until the season opens. At low tide, they beach for hours. Other boats anchor to stay mobile. With boat length limited to thirty-two feet, some owners widen beams (note foreground) to increase capacity.

CHAPTER TWENTY-FIVE

Changes—
Count on Nothing

Cordova, Alaska, 1997

"How're you doing?" Jeff Bailey asks Buck Meloy, CB to CB across two miles of rough foggy water. They address each other between the twenty-six-foot *Good Tide* and the twenty-six-foot *Spindrift III* by code names. The radio voices are so reduced and wiry that perhaps eavesdroppers don't recognize them even after years together on the same grounds.

"Got two more than a fat albatross. You?"

"Straw mouse for an hour, she's in Green 38."

"Thin owl and a smiley," reports Kenny Carlson from the luxury liner of the fleet, thirty-one-foot *Tarah Rose.*

It doesn't sound like fishermen keyed for danger, but the Copper River Flats out of Cordova, Alaska, have as dark a reputation for disaster as Grand Bank or the Bering Sea. One recent article called it Alaska's most dangerous fishery. Small boats, fishing on a delta of glacial silt and narrow rivulets, meet twenty-foot tides that rip in from the open Pacific Ocean. It's a foolish place to take a boat, except that the sockeyes pour in here before the Chignik and Bristol Bay runs—thus bringing the highest potential price as first-of-the-season—and these big red-meat salmon are considered by some to be the best of the species in the world.

I've been coming to Cordova since Coast Guard days in 1952. (Indeed, my old ship CGC *Sweetbrier* is now stationed here, a workhorse built in 1944 and still serving.) It's as pure a fisherman's town as there is. No road connects to the outside. You fly in or come by boat. Orca Inlet leads out to Prince William Sound and a wealth of fishing for pink salmon, herring, halibut, and other species, depending on Nature that year and the lingering effects of the 1989 *EXXON Valdez* oil spill. Mountains, white as vanilla ice cream in winter and vibrant green under a summer sun, rise over a storefront main street and frame houses that don't seem to have changed since my earliest visits (compared with Kodiak, which the 1964 tsunami altered beyond recognition). When I drive around with Jeff Bailey or Ken Adams in their pickup trucks, they park for a few hours and leave keys in the ignition.

We leave harbor in calm water. The sun glistens on a colony of cute little otters warming their bellies by an exposed sandbar until, flip, they disappear as we rumble past. They bring memories of oiled creatures in the wake of the *EXXON Valdez* oil spill eight years before, their numbers now recovered, at least on the surface. There weren't many healthy otters around in 1952, and the town's fresh delicacy was razor clams the size of soup bowls. Now the mollusk-eating otters abound, and big clams are history.

Around the bend at Strawberry Point lies the open Pacific. The waves treat Jeff's boat as kindly as a jackhammer would a fly. He braces in the chair by the wheel, and I hug the other, wishing for a seatbelt. In the tight cabin a single bunk laid over the engine fills the stern. The mountain coastline is spectacular, what little we can see through cascading water on the glass. We set our 150-fathom gillnet in the location called Little Softuk.

An ebb tide is pulling from the delta into the ocean, leaving islands of gray mud-sand inches high in the otherwise open water. Lapping waves make the islands disappear for moments. They all have names to those who fish them, as do other bars not visible and channels between: places of anecdote and sometimes catastrophe: Mousetrap, Paulson's Hole, Grass Island, Drug Beach (an echo of hippie days when a bail of pot was found hidden there), Horseshoe, Pumpkin Patch, Straw, Shotgun Gulch, Alaganik Slough, Borsha's Hole, Pete Dahl, Charlie Mohr's Hole, Coffee's Hole, Castle Flats, Cudahay Slough, Katalla.

As Jeff starts the net over the bow something malfunctions on the hydraulic roller. Inside without fuss he moves his sleeping bag and lifts the bunk board. His head disappears inside the engine compartment to search for the trouble. Back at the roller we pick heavy sockeyes from the mesh, snapping each under the gills to bleed it. Soon the salmon lie iced in the hold, handled carefully all the way for a quality product. About thirty fish, an acceptable late-season haul on the Flats: "A fifteen-thousand-pound set in Bristol Bay would be a whole season's fish here," Jeff notes. But coded buddy reports promise better down the line toward Kokinhenik, so that's where we head.

Copper River runs are small compared with other places, and it's a low-investment fishery. Half the boats are still gasoline-powered (cheaper to maintain) in the age of marine diesel. Expectations must focus on quality. Jeff straddles two careers, a walking symbol of the old and new. Ashore he packs the catch of his group and, as chief-every-thing of Prime Select Seafood (office in the basement) sells it air freight to special buyers in the Lower Forty-Eight and Japan. He's on the phone at three in the morning calling the East Coast at wake-up time. A boyish but steadily driving man not yet forty with a new wife, young son, and an infant just born, he seems never to sleep.

I stay most often on the Flats with Kenny Carlson aboard his *Tarah Rose,* where besides good company there's room to lay a panel across his little galley table for a bed. By the time I transfer from Jeff's boat the sky has hazed, taking with it the view of snowy mountains. Sprits of rain pelt off Kenny's oilskins as he drops the buoy end of the net close to a bump of gray sand, then backs the boat straight out, paying net and corks over the bow. He works with one hand on an extended throttle astern. At flood tide now, the water beats in from open ocean against the bar, which seems to sink by the minute. The bar is the only thing visible except the choppy water that tries to drive us toward it. A failed engine would leave us helpless, and we'd be swamped and smashed. Flats fishing is gutsy. Ken risks it on the proven chance that fish swimming in with the tide will cluster here. The wind increases to drive heavier rain.

That night we anchor in the lee of Egg Island, a lump of sandbar high enough to remain permanently exposed, leaving enough line to tide-swing without bumping other boats. Kenny is laid-back, willing to sleep a few hours. Jeff stays outside the bars in the blowing rain to fish all night. Laid-back, perhaps, but during the five hours Kenny allows himself for sleep I wake twice to see him checking our depth and anchor.

These are one-person boats, and flats fishing is self-sufficient and lonely. But it is a community. People stay in touch at least by groups. Among those on the grounds I met three women, as able in their oilskins as the men. Since the grounds are just around the corner from Cordova—about three hours to Softuk at the start of the Flats—it is a commute-fishery compared with Bristol Bay where virtually everyone ships in for a one-month season from somewhere else and then leaves until the following year. Fish and Game usually schedules two Flats openings a week that last twenty-four to forty-eight hours each. The biggest runs start in mid-May, before the mid-June runs of completely different sockeye/red stocks past Cape Igvak to Chignik or the July plug into Bristol Bay.

It is now June and the Copper River run has begun to taper, but it's been the strongest in years. Throughout Alaska, salmon fishermen and processors are watching. One big area return should herald heavy runs in other places. Buyers, led by the Japanese, have already begun to skin down prices they're willing to commit, expecting to be offered all the salmon they can handle. Indeed the year before, 1996, pink salmon poured so heartily into Kodiak waters that by midsummer the ex-vessel price dropped to a devastating five cents a pound; Cordova reds had started the season at $1.75. (An apples-bananas comparison except that both fish are salmon. Copper River reds of seven to eight pounds top the high-priced fresh and frozen market, while pinks of two to four pounds bottom it with many used for canning.) As the 1997 Alaska season progressed, it turned out that even Bristol Bay came in bust, with the catch less than half what was predicted. Only the fishermen of Copper River Flats made out in all of Alaska. Nature had fooled the biologists despite their educated and often successful tabulations.

That's the life of fishing: change. The best survivors are those brave enough to shift targets (new gear money required, often debt) and adapt to new circumstance. To keep track of who's up and who's down is like trying to catch fish with your bare hands. Not just in Alaska. Off California, where sardines once generated an industry on Monterey's Cannery Row (now a tourist layout) but then disappeared, and where the San Pedro–San Diego tuna fleet dispersed when the world needed to be made safe for dolphins, squid and lobster landings have exploded in the past few years to amount to a boom harvest. And Chile, that hotbed of new fishing: In 1996 the *jurel*, jack mackerel, were stuffing the nets off central Chile while the anchoveta up north off Iquique could hardly be found for two years. In 1997 the mackerel turned scarce, but oh what masses of anchovy started pouring into the north! Meanwhile, no one had ever seen such an abundance of swordfish off Coquimbo Province. The shifted winds of El Niño may account for it—at least all credit and blame in the region goes to this phenomenon. Indeed, the El Niño–based warming of the Pacific waters in 1997 may have diverted salmon from Alaska, whatever their homing instincts, to account for the unexpected shortage there.

In other oceans overfishing has turned things around. The great cod masses I helped land and gut during the 1980s off New England and Newfoundland–Labrador have become wistful history (although possibly recovering creepingly under tighter management at last). Taking their place in a reversal of the predator-prey cycle are shrimp, crab, and lobster, good news at least for some. Not all fishermen have the necessary permits on grounds now tightly regulated by alarmed governments.

A steady force of change has governed the way we handle fish. When I first helped pew fish from hold to cannery (Alaska 1952), we drove the pew's hooked prong straight into the body for convenience, with some fish so mushy from long days out of water that they slid down the stick against the hands. The world demand for quality now dictates careful handling that treats the catch as food.

Cowboys' Farewell

Nowhere has change been more dramatic than in the Alaska halibut fishery, which started from large, dory-laden sailing schooners in 1888. In the mid-1970s a mystique of endurance remained about the smaller wooden "schooners," built in the early 1900s, that pitched out for three weeks at a time—the lengths of the openings—to longline for the great fifty- to three-hundred-pound fish. Most aboard were first- or second-generation Norwegians living in the Ballard section of Seattle: big, taciturn "squareheads." When a schooner trip came into Kodiak, the two plants that bought halibut bargained at table with the skipper, usually with a bottle of whiskey to lubricate the negotiation. Once, while I worked below in a crew that slimed halibuts as big as sofa cushions, I watched a skipper, angered at the price offered, storm past us, unmoor his boat, and roar on to a rival plant in Seward.

Sometime in the mid-1980s the halibut stock multiplied, the mystique wore off, and boats that also caught crab and salmon started to compete with the schooners. To manage the fishery, openings were reduced from three weeks to three or fewer days. Each opening became a derby. Crews fished without sleep to take their maximum share regardless of weather. It was exciting. But injuries soared, and gear lost in haste continued to "ghost fish" any creatures trapped and wasted on its hooks.

Derby days ended in 1995 after the North Pacific Council hammered out a system called ITQ or IFQ, individual transferable/fishing quota, a concept started in New Zealand. Those who had fished halibut during 1988, 1989, or 1990 received an annual poundage based on their historic catches since 1984. IFQs provide stability for those who have them, since quotas can be fished at the owner's convenience (that is, on a calm day, or when the price is high). They are expected to give holders a sense of stewardship for the health of the stocks. Those lucky enough to have committed during the grandfathering years have no complaint. Some, in fact, have become rich beyond dreams, since their catch is now guaranteed. Others, even those with a long history on halibut, were left out if they had fished other species exclusively in the years that counted. IFQs now also govern Alaska sablefish, or black cod.

In a corruption of the IFQs' purpose, the Internal Revenue Service has taken to confiscating the IFQs of tax-defaulted fishermen and auctioning them to the highest bidder. It underscores a weakness of IFQs that compromises their strengths: Even though the holders received them for free, they are property, to be sold and traded rather than returned to a common pot for the next in line. The fight has begun over who can amass IFQs: Some owners now sit at home and lease their shares. Shares *are* categorized by boat size to prevent corporations from taking more than partial control, and an owner must be a U.S. citizen. But several brokerage houses now make a living off IFQ sales, and the young of a new generation need thousands of dollars to enter the fishery. "They've done a good job of managing the fish, but not the fishermen," angrily notes one of the losers. The system has enough doubters that Congress, in the most recent version of the Magnuson Act (October 1996), prohibited the creation of any more IFQ fisheries before October 2000, to allow time to study the practice.

Along with bringing order, the assured catch of IFQs has eliminated the boat-to-boat competition that is the zest of fishing among the highliners. "Do we really want a failsafe society?" wonders Bart Eaton, veteran king crab fisherman, fishery council member, and now vice president of Trident Seafoods. "With regulations that tell you where to fish and when, guys feel more and more like they're spare gear in a big bureaucratic machine."

Countering Eaton's concern is Clem Tillion, a red-haired, robustly outspoken Alaskan fishery spokesman who has in his time fished, chaired both the state senate and the North Pacific Council, and served as one governor's "fish czar." A father of the IFQs in Alaska, Tillion asserts that the resource can be saved only by allowing it to be owned privately. "This idea of the commons, it always leads to tragedy. Resources should be owned and traded so you can build a conservation ethic into the owner, because his product is worth more if his stocks are in good shape."

In Alaska, some of the romance and grand foolishness has been lost. "The rodeo days are gone, and there's not much place left for the cowboys," says Chris Blackburn, longtime fishery reporter and data analyst out of Kodiak. She means the heady Alaska decade starting in the mid-1970s, when all the 200-mile seas opened; when profits, abundance, and expectation soared out of sight, prompting banks to float almost unlimited credit for new boats; when, by pushing boldly into the sea and risk be damned, a fisherman could suddenly net enough cash to buy a gold nugget necklace and party on purest Colombian. There have been enough brokers—failed trips—since then, and enough deaths, regulation, and realities, to change the tone of the waterfront. Blackburn sees the change positively. "The industry has grown up. We have good science, good fishing practices, good marketing—a new world. The emphasis is on quality. We're now competing on a worldwide market."

A lot of the cowboys have accepted fences and learned to become businessmen. They keep books, or listen to their wives, who do it for them.

2000: The New Wild West

For nearly two decades, Bering Sea groundfish stocks have remained healthy under the cooperative management of the U.S. and Russia. Suddenly this may change for reasons beyond U.S. control. On the U.S. side, the North Pacific Fishery Council has held to an annual two-million-metric-ton groundfish quota, resisting all attempts to raise it despite pressure from factory trawlers and shoreside plants who say they need more product to stay in business. The protected biomass has remained stable, until recently, while some stocks have actually increased.

So mutually beneficial was Bering Sea cooperation that Russian and American fishery people had started visiting each other at least two years before *glasnost* cleared the way in the early 1980s for open exchanges on official government fronts.

The two great powers stood up to other fishing nations, especially Japan. The Japanese had fished all they could find in an area called the "Donut Hole," surrounded by—but outside—both U.S. and Soviet 200-mile jurisdictions. Donut Hole stocks are part of the whole North Pacific ecosystem, just as the Tail and Nose of Grand Bank are part of this Atlantic system. By 1993 the United States and Russia had combined forces to control the Donut.

It appeared that international and biological politics in the Bering Sea were solved and the decisions reliable. Then in late 1991 the Soviet Union dissolved and so did continuity. According to David Benton, international fisheries commissioner for Alaska, who has been a key liaison with the Russians since Soviet days, "There's no longer a corporate memory of our negotiations in either state department." U.S. officials have retired, and Russian officials have retired or were reassigned.

In the mid-1990s, one of the hottest fishing areas for Americans became the Russian sector of the Bering Sea where the new Russia sold permits to raise hard currency. Dealing with the Russians—not yet sophisticated in the rules of Western business and cavalier about breaking contracts—became a sporty enough course that Americans soon called the area "the Wild West." But there were fish and fortune for those flexible enough to stay on top. Now, however, Russian companies have slapped into shape all the trawlers they could find to harvest the resource themselves. *Fishing News International* reported in March 1997: "Dozens of successful fishing companies have surfaced during the past 18 months in the Russian Far East. Money and effort invested in these small-to-medium-sized businesses by the Primorsky Territory Fisheries Committee in Vladivostok is starting to pay off. Two or three factory motherships, trawlers . . . rebirth of region's ship repair and building industries."

It appears there is now overfishing beyond U.S. control or bargaining clout. A significant amount centers on a narrow triangular area rich in pollock and other groundfish, allotted to the U.S. during a tentative 1967 agreement finally signed in the early 1990s. Russia wants to void the agreement and redraw the sea boundary in its own favor, and in these waters, Russian trawlers—new ships in need of fish—have been testing U.S. resolve, keeping the U.S. Coast Guard busy.

During a 1997 Kodiak meeting of the North Pacific Council, Captain Vince O'Shea, U.S. Coast Guard commander of enforcement activities, reported one of the service's patrol ships in "hot pursuit" of a Russian factory trawler caught fishing in this disputed zone still claimed by the United States. So it has gone since then, with increasing Russian violations and American cat-and-mouse on fishing grounds that had once been stable. The 1998 La Niña exacerbated the problem by apparently diverting into the American zone some of the pollock biomass headed for Russia, leaving hungry Russian ships with less to catch. It came to a head in August 1999 when members of the Coast Guard cutter *Hamilton* boarded Russian trawler *Gissar* fishing illegally inside U.S. waters, and found 37 tons of pollock aboard. As the *Hamilton's* officers prepared to seize the Russian vessel (legally their right), several other Russian trawlers converged and began to place themselves between the American and Russian vessels. The boarding party, thus threatened, returned to their ship, and enforcement was turned over to a Russian patrol while the U.S. State Department lodged a formal complaint. The incident may serve as a wake-up call to both nations, but it sounded like the old times before the two-hundred-mile jurisdictions. The game, always fluid, eases back almost to square one.

China, 1983 to 2000: the Dragon Thumps the Tail

Despite scientific predictions and diplomatic handshakes, fishermen can count on each day's catch only after it comes aboard. Overfishing can tip the balance, or huffy diplomats, or a climate glitch. To foresee the future, ask as easily when the next tanker will ground. In any business that involves politics, technology, chance, Nature, and human nature, change is the constant. One, two, or five centuries ago, the way men caught fish might change dramatically now and then, influenced, say, by the invention of the compass or the marine engine, but generations could pass with one man casting his nets and powering his boat exactly like his grandfather. Now the changes come, not by generations but by the year or quicker.

Japan, the greatest seafood consumer of them all—it imports twice as much seafood as the United States, six times more than any other nation—appears to be slowing. It has begun to lag in its deep-sea and offshore catches, while despite spirited efforts with artificial reefs its coastal fish stocks remain stagnant. Japan's reported 12 million tons landed in 1984 fell to 6.6 million in 1997. (These are its highest and lowest years in the last two decades, as reported by FAO. U.S. figures for these years were 4.8 and 5.4 million tons, respectively.)

The world sleeper of them all is China. In 1984 it reported 5.9 million tons landed, one decade later 23.8 million, including aquaculture, and in 1997 an awesome 35 million. (Peru in 1997 came a far second place with 7.8 million, Japan third with 6.6 million, Chile fourth, the United States fifth.) China held its first big fishery trade show in 1996, and some 350 companies from twenty-eight countries attended. The United States had the largest pavilion, with more than fifty companies. Also represented were all the nations but Indonesia visited in these pages—Japan, Chile, New Zealand, Canada, Norway, Spain, and Russia—as well as others discussed, including Thailand, Australia, Peru, the United Kingdom, even Taiwan. The assemblage recognized a new reality. China's own companies turned out in force, eager for distribution. They are succeeding. From a recent article: "Japan buys more Chinese fresh fish as quality rises."

The companies of China rival even those of Japan for their size and symbiosis with the state. They are the former communes, newly unleashed as collective private enterprise. Some control the whole gamut of the fish business, owning large domestic and international fleets as well as shipyards, processing plants, cold stores, net factories, and seafood marketing operations.

I've glimpsed the commune-to-corporate evolution. In 1983, not long after China opened its doors to the West, and after heavy negotiation for official permission, I arrived at the Hou Hu People's Commune near Wuhan on the Yangtze River. A knot of cautious people waited to greet me. I learned later that I was the first American to come their way. We exchanged first courtesies in a wide, dusty courtyard—more like a parking lot except that the vehicles were bikes—in raised voices among a larger, noisy group. Men and women all wore variations of blue smock-shirts and blue trousers. A band played from the back of a truck, a bright red banner waved from a pole, and some two hundred people of different ages clustered in groups. Forty young members were being given a send-off into the Army.

The head man, Director of the Management Committee, was Mr. Wang You Xing, a man of forty-two with a young face. His close-cropped black hair framed a direct look and a smile both friendly and contained. He appeared tired and wary, and had a day's beard. Inside around a long table Mr. Wang gave formal greetings read and translated, then statistics. The Hou Hu ("Beside the Lake") People's Commune, founded in 1958, attained its present size by merging with two other communes in 1975. It controlled some 7,200 mu (about 1,400 acres) of fields, and 13,000 mu of water surface. Working this were sixteen thousand "laborers" living, with some ten thousand children and old people, in twenty-four brigades.

Within the various brigades, four thousand people worked at fish-farming to raise four species of carp, while another four thousand grew vegetables or raised chickens, ducks, pigs, and milk cows. Another eight thousand worked in eighteen "industrial enterprises" that manufactured such products as wire, electrical instruments, and fertilizer. Each brigade was essentially a separate village. At the Xin Yi fish culture brigade Mr. Tang Dong Ming, its leader, said that his organization consisted of 118 households, population 572, of whom the labor force was 268. (Some family members worked in other brigades.) Mr. Tang himself, a wiry, cheerful man of forty-five with a face the color of cured leather and a pleasantly proud air about him, numbered among his eight-person household a daughter who drove an overhead crane, and three sons who were all commune fishermen. What aspiration had he for his sons? I asked. "That they will all have better educations than me, so that they can raise the level of fish culture."

On the commune road we passed drained ponds where men waded ankle-deep removing muck by bucket line. Tang explained that they were readying the pond for a new school of fish. After a round of tea and sweets in the village at his model two-story concrete house (not all buildings were as grand), we walked across fields and dikes to watch a fish harvest. Near the ponds, the prevailing odor turned sour because of a major fish nutrient: treated sewage from Wuhan City.

In a lake-size pond, some twenty men and women in rubber coveralls waded up to their waists and chests, pulling the two ends of a semicircular beach seine that others in a long skiff held taut in the deep water. The more the enclosure narrowed the more fish flapped to the surface: fat business-like carp with skins of dull brassy silver. A man in the boat grinned and held up one for my camera. As soon as they emptied the net, some men and women packed it away on their shoulders while the rest headed quickly back to the village. The boatmen paddled their load of fish to the opposite shore, where their sons met them to help unload into a truck. The boys handled the boat and the fish eagerly, seriously. I've seen the same kind of lads follow their fathers to the boats in Norway and Newfoundland. These commune sons are now grown, probably part of the same workforce but as employees within a corporate empire, maybe its leaders.

Five years later, in 1988, I visited the Number Two Ocean Fishing Company of Xiamin (pronounced sha-min´), former Amoy, facing Formosa Strait and the South China Sea. The city is seafood-oriented, facing a long quay (and Taiwan-controlled Quemoy in sight but for an intervening smaller island). Live tanks outside sidewalk restaurants offer all manner of local catch from crab to snake, ready at the diner's choice to be chopped and tossed into a spitting wok. Founded as a commune in 1950, Number Two Company converted in 1984. I was greeted not by cautious officials in blue Mao jackets, but by suited businessmen in an office near a harbor typhoon shelter a mile from the city. The Number Two was one of four in the area, explained Mr. Goa Da Chuan, vice-manager, and the largest, with 80 of Xiamin's 158 deep-sea fishing boats. All apartment buildings on the street leading to the harbor were part of the company's "village."

The company did well, Mr. Goa declared. Most of its boats were no more than eight years old. We could hear hammering on a new one under construction at the company's boatyard in the harbor. A company plant I visited later processed shrimp and other quality products for export. In addition to housing, the company maintained a kindergarten, a free eight-doctor clinic, and a "Fishermen's Theatre" for movies, staged shows, and programs for the elderly.

There had been a typhoon warning, and the Number Two's eighty boats lay tied together in a sheltered harbor surrounded by work sheds and warehouses. With the tide out they rested squarely on a black gumbo bottom. Their shark-nosed prows painted auspicious red at the peaks rose above wide-board decks. Most were built of heavy wood, hundred-foot seiners and draggers. A spokesman said six had steel hulls.

Mr. Su Shau-er, a short man with lines beginning to show on his face beneath spikes of youthful black hair, led the way over a dozen sets of rails and across nets on deserted decks to the seiner *Su-Shan,* which he skippered. Several crewmen puttered on deck, probably summoned to receive the visitor. Relaxed and friendly, they seemed as curious about me as I was about their boat. Most wore wristwatches, one of the universal third world signals of Western-aspiring prosperity. (Another is a pen; the ultimate these days, a decade later, is a portable cell phone.) When Mr. Su smiled, which was often, he showed a row of shining metal teeth.

A seine with floats and weights lay on deck, but with no hydraulic power block to bring it in. This was fishing the old labor-intensive way. The net itself was large and heavy: 820 feet around and 525 feet deep, and required a crew of thirty to muscle it aboard assisted only by a long roller on the starboard rail. The Chinese-built engine, in a dark well, had low horsepower; heavy sails provided most propulsion.

We climbed through a trapdoor to the wheelhouse filled mostly by a big wooden spoked wheel. Electronics consisted of a nine-inch radar, which the skipper plugged in to demonstrate, a small loran, and a stylus Fathometer—equipment decades behind that on a standard fishing boat in Taiwan or Japan. Overhead throughout the boat, fitted into grooves, hung varied porcelain wash basins, some decorated, some chipped and plain. Each man had his own, the closest concession to individuality that I saw. The unwalled galley centered around a wood-charcoal stove near the afterdeck. Pots were all big, the thirty-portion variety. The skipper's wife rode aboard to cook, preparing fish from the net, along with thin local noodles served in oil and garlic. Sliding panels revealed berths tucked into the woodwork like cupboards. A center strip in each cubicle separated two bedrolls in a space less than six feet long.

Later I visited the captain at home, an apartment with an airy living room, up three floors in a building bristling with TV antennas. Are more fish caught under the new responsibility system than in the old commune days? I asked through an interpreter. "Oh yes, much more. But the men also work harder now than formerly. We must now put in more effort for efficiency." Has life become more prosperous under the new system? A metal-toothed grin gave the answer.

A robust, overbearing woman accompanied us from the company's union. When I learned that she'd once been a ship's cook I made a joke and she laughed heartily. Then she resumed a watchful demeanor. "The company union has nearly two thousand members," she declared. "All the fishermen of the company belong voluntarily, in fact."

But suppose a fisherman wants to do something else? I wondered.

"Well, under the old commune system he had no choice in the matter. Now, of course, if he wants to leave the boat and work somewhere else, all he must do is make an application and wait for permission to change."

Such core boats and crews now contribute to the massive Chinese fleet expanding into waters beyond its own.

A decade after my 1988 visit, the Number Two Company of Xiamin has become the more grandly titled Xiamin Ocean Industrial Group Share Holding Company Ltd. Its shipyard still turns out heavy wooden boats for large crews working labor-intensive gear. Half its fleet now sails in steel hulls, however, and the company is leaner with thirteen hundred fishermen: seven hundred fewer than before. (Must they still apply to change jobs?) Most vessels carry advanced electronics, including satellite locators, and with more efficiency they require less manpower. Some fish as far afield as Indonesia. The company includes processing and trading subsidiaries, and lists on the Shengzhen Stock Exchange. It still owns apartments—now also some in a new residential area—and still keeps a clinic. But the Fishermen's Theatre for the edification of families and the elderly? It has become a profitable disco pub run jointly with a Hong Kong firm.

Reports show that Chinese vessels now fish the waters of sixty nations and regions. Dominating space at the 1998 China trade fair was the massive China National Fisheries Corporation. Organized only in 1993, it has a fleet of eleven hundred vessels—all but a fraction built domestically—and employs twenty-nine thousand. While many of the boats are still the heavy, wooden, labor-intensive type that fish inland and national waters, about four hundred ships of the fleet are built to fish off Africa, Asia, and the Americas. Within the CNFC complex there are six proprietary enterprises that manage marine fisheries: six for shipbuilding and gear manufacture, six for fish trading, and one for harbor engineering.

China has been the waiting dragon for decades. With the cage now sprung, Chinese boats will change the makeup of the world's fishing fleets and the balance of competition.

Speaking at the inaugural meeting of the International Fisheries Exposition of 1883, British biologist and author T.H. Huxley declared: "In relation to our present method of fishing... I believe that the cod fishery, the herring fishery, the pilchard fishery, the mackerel fishery, and probably all the great sea fisheries are inexhaustible; that is to say that nothing we do seriously affects the number of fish."

This has changed.

CHAPTER TWENTY-SIX

Catching Fish

In late 1999 protestors in Seattle virtually closed down an international meeting of the World Trade Organization. Street theater included people dancing in turtle garb, furiously denouncing the WTO for possibly compromising a U.S. law requiring turtle excluders in shrimp nets. The demonstrators' vehemence dramatized one of the forces with which fishermen today must find accomodation.

Fishermen, the little guys especially, are under seige. So many forces of good intention and pure selfishness are arrayed against them that their's has become an endangered occupation. In the affluent countries food gathering is many steps removed from consumers, and the gatherers can be easily shunted aside, while in poor countries governments often trade off a fisherman's subsistence harvest to the highest outside bidder who waves hard currency.

Throughout this book I've brushed on environmental issues as they have affected fishermen.* My attitude has been occasionally wry. Fishermen are often scapegoats, easy targets in place of elusive industrial polluters, bureaucrats, single-issue environmentalists, and others whose acts can be more expedient than responsible. Especially ready to shrug off the fishing occupation are sport groups competing for the same species who engineer state referendums in the name of conservation (leaving the fish all for themselves), and animal-rights groups intent on saving creatures—especially attractive marine mammals—killed incidentally by nets and hooks at work.

*Note: Encroachers/scofflaws (ch. 5), trawlers (chs. 8, 10, 26), seals (chs. 8, 26), cod shortage (chs. 10, 26), whales (ch. 19), miles-long driftnets (ch. 20), sea birds (chs. 20, 26), dolphin-tuna (ch. 25), by-catch (ch. 26), net bans (ch. 26), sea lions (ch. 26), sea turtles-shrimp (ch. 26), and overfishing in general (throughout).

The goals of the Seattle protestors were mixed across a spectrum of concerns for labor, free trade, and environmental protection. On ocean environments, their focus was the potential compromise of a hard-won U.S. law to protect sea turtles in shrimpers' nets, and by implication, laws protecting dolphins encircled for tuna and other marine mammals. The World Trade Organization has the potential power to override such laws if the U.S. signs, by ruling them prejudicial to free trade when they cut off exports from countries that do not similarly require the same conservation measures. With the WTO's closed-door policy, what if some government swap allowed the U.S. to import fish caught without the restraints required of American fishermen, caught even by such universally condemned practices as miles-long drift nets or dynamiting for fish kill?

Whatever the pressure on American fishermen, and whatever the reality of U.S. laws protecting turtles and dolphins, they are laws that were passed after fights and hard consideration, not to be negated by outside forces. The free trade concept by itself cannot ensure that prosperity will inspire all nations to do right by the environment. The Seattle protests may have been historic in focusing public anger on the despoilers of the environment and all else, and in venting frustration at the helplessness of ordinary people to do anything about it.

Inside the building, one of the agenda items not resolved concerned the fact that some industrialized nations—Canada and Japan among them—subsidize fisheries, giving their fishermen and products a competitive edge over those from other nations, including the poorer ones. As an example, New England fishermen have long chafed at the ability of Canadians to sell fish from their part of Georges Bank to U.S. fast-food chains for less than unsubsidized Americans can afford to do.

There are glitches in the ideal of free trade across the globe. Emerging nations can ill afford the luxury of costly add-on fishing gear that decreases efficiency, even though they desperately need the markets of the affluent. How much can rich nations, who need only make adjustments that compromise a small segment of their society (in this case fishermen), demand of poor ones who must truly sacrifice?

If It Ain't the Partyboats . . .

For sport fishermen, days on the water can have the same mystique as for those catching fish to pay the bills. I went out with lunch box and bait can on Chesapeake Bay with my dad, granddad, and children. Around the Bay, people line bridges, or go out under oar or putput motor and then scale and eat what they catch. It's an option of life not to be scorned. (Many of my net friends sneak days off with a rod or handline.) The threatening power seems to lie in those with heavy money to spend for sport on the water who'd like it all for themselves, who can dine politicians (perhaps at corporate expense), and make campaign contributions.

The recreation argument has its points: Sport lines catch fewer fish per person than nets, and generally (not always) bring up less by-catch, while individual license fees and other money dropped by visiting fishermen bring a state more bucks per fish. Passed over lightly is the fact that, in states without a specific law against it, sportfishermen often sell their catch to pay for their outing, thus competing directly with commercial nets. "We're taking jobs from working people," says Philip Horn of Clark Seafood Company (started by his grandfather) of Pascagoula, Mississippi, "and giving play time to folks who've already got a job and need somewhere to spend their money."

Maryland's Chesapeake Bay watermen almost lost their share of striped bass to sport hooks in the mid-1980s when a governor, said to have friends in the charterboat crowd, tried to push a law that failed in committee. Florida, that haven of retiree wealth, in 1995 banned all commercial gillnets, even small ones, and limited other nets near shore. It was a triumph for the passers-through with their money assured—marching behind the flag of "conservation"—over those who grew up there having to make a living. Texas and Louisiana followed suit with net bans. Oregon voters defeated a similar measure. Washington State almost copied in 1995, and again in 1999, but commercial fishermen left their boats to fight and won each referendum with sixty percent of the vote. The sport lobby in this case joined the aluminum companies, but the environmentalists joined the fishermen, recognizing a less-than-altruistic effort by polluting industries to ease stringent water-purification requirements by simply diminishing fishing and by sport to have it all for themselves. As in the unsuccessful Florida fight the Pentecostal Church sided with commercial fishermen, inveighing against "the spirit of greed." The ultimate battle cry? "Jesus was a gillnetter!"

High Purpose

The protectors of the environment play a constructive watchdog role that has helped bend the ruling portion of the world—the rich and powerful nations—away from pure exploitation. (Less success in underdeveloped nations where the poor need today's sparse food before they can consider setting something aside for the future.) In the process, some protectors have with high purpose manipulated facts and emotions to create hardship in which they do not share, even to generate actions that threaten the overall resource.

I've seen every salmon in Columbia River nets come aboard with its belly torn open, the work of protected and multiplying harbor seals. Protected and multiplying sea lions off California have become so aggressive they storm up stern ramps as they continue eating from hauls of fish coming aboard. In Maine, where seven thousand people hold lobster licenses, one right whale in the past decade has been documented caught in fishing gear. He escaped. Bound by the Marine Mammal Protection Act, which has an important purpose but a narrow focus, Maine lobstermen for a while in 1997 faced a new law requiring them to use breakaway buoys and weak lines that would snap from their traps under the pressure sometimes raised by a strong blow, so that no future endangered right whale might be troubled. The ruling, eventually modified, would have represented a ruinous investment in new gear, and pots lost routinely on the seafloor that would have kept entrapping lobsters. In this case sense prevailed, but the lobstermen had to spend many hours ashore doing battle instead of fishing.

Animal groups cried peril for Canadian harp seals because, they testified while knowing better, sealers killed "ninety percent" of the young. The truth was forty percent to fifty percent, which Canadian fishery people tried urgently to tell blocked ears, including those of the U.S. Congress and the European Union. Jim Winter, a journalist who once worked as a sealer, and as "Berthed Swiler" broadcast his daily impressions on CBC Radio (now on a CD), terms the protests "The imposition of the cultural imperialism of few on the lives of many."

Since the last ship's hunt in 1982 the harp seal population off Canada has doubled and continues to grow. The multiplied seals at 1996 count eat an estimated 6.9 million tons of fish a year—more than that year's total U.S. catch and seven times that of Canadian fishermen—much of it the irreplaceable prespawning stocks of future generations.

Stopping the hunt for harp seal pups exacerbated a new cycle of misfortune. Human overfishing—at least some of it by fishermen who needed to make up the lost sealing part of their income—lowered the cod supply. Hungry seals saved with thousands of warm-hearted donations continued to multiply, and to eat the now-endangered fish voraciously. Attempting to stave off the seal onslaught, most North Atlantic nations, including Russia, Norway, the United Kingdom (a cull off the Hebrides), Iceland, Greenland, and Canada, again authorize limited hunts. They must do it gingerly, forbidding the kill of pups (humane and quick but ugly in photos), wary of retriggering the easy outrage so dear to fund-raisers. Indeed, since 1997 some of the more vociferous groups have run emotional newspaper ads in urban areas where readers have no stake in the disasters of seal overpopulation; one example, using inaccurate information, ran in June 1999 in the *Washington Post*.

Newfoundlanders refer to the animal and environmental activists collectively as "greenpeacers." The namesake organization, Greenpeace, has generally shown reason in its attacks, however dramatized, compared to some of the other groups headed by blatant opportunists. Seal protests aside, I respect much of Greenpeace's work and the gutsy way their members pursue it. Without the greenpeacers making a public fuss, would we now be working as hard as we are to right ecological blunders made through politics, hunger, greed, and stupidity? I wish I could say yes.

But those who sound an alarm loud enough to be heard can lose perspective: Be willing to disrupt a whole system for the perceived good of a single part. While respected for a warrior stance, they should be heard with reservations, and their information scrutinized. So of course should be the defenses their opponents offer.

The Trawler Villains

In August 1997 seven Greenpeace activists suspended themselves from the bridge in Seattle's Lake Union under which trawlers needed to pass, threatening to rappel down and block the ships if they tried to leave. When the climbers returned to safety after forty-five hours, one of them announced with satisfaction (official press release): "We've done more in the last two days and nights to stop overfishing in the North Pacific and protect the Steller sea lion than the Fisheries Service has done in the last five years."

During the late 1990s Greenpeace has been hell-bent on eliminating the American factory trawler fleet in the Bering Sea, presumably a first step toward ending the practice worldwide. In 1996 it
published a persuasively documented booklet titled "Sinking Fast:
How Factory Trawlers Are Destroying U.S. Fisheries and Marine
Ecosystems." One of the booklet's sections concludes: "Factory trawler
fleets are perpetuating the global fisheries crisis today. Their economic
imperatives are leading to the impoverishment of marine ecosystems
and traditional fishing communities everywhere. . . . Mobility, bigger
nets, more horsepower and sophisticated fish-finding gear allow the
world's factory fleets to maintain high catch levels even as fish stocks
are dwindling, but they only temporarily mask the unsustainable
nature of the technology."

The Greenpeace position may be valid for some factory fisheries,
although no longer for their easiest target, the American fleet. Indeed
on some grounds, trawlers overpower other gear methods and overfish. Inshore stocks have often plummeted in the areas of the world
where large trawlers fish unchecked or are inadequately controlled,
leaving empty nets for smaller boats that have worked the waters
for generations. It happened in the 1960s and mid-1970s from New
England to Newfoundland, as well as off the Oregon–Washington
coast, when foreign fleets grabbed too much. Then in the early
1990s, the cycle repeated in the North Atlantic, the fault of overcapitalized hometown fleets. It may be happening again with Russian
and European shrimp trawlers on the Flemish Cap off the Grand
Banks, and certainly with Russians in their own portion of the
Bering Sea.

Whether this condemns trawlers in general is quite another matter.
Trawling is an efficient means of gathering food in a world whose
hungry population keeps expanding, the most practical means to
harvest some midwater and bottom species that school in quantity (just
as seines are practical for the near-surface-schooling anchovy off Chile
or menhaden off the United States.) Even another frequent criticism
of trawlers, that those dragging the bottom destroy the seafloor with
each new pass, has its questioners. In a recent issue of the British magazine *New Scientist*, M. J. Kaiser and J. W. Horwood examined fishing
effort data and concluded, "In a pristine environment, the first ever
passage of a fishing gear will proportionately have the greatest effect
on the community within its path, whether considered in terms of individuals captured or killed. Thereafter, successive passages of the trawl

will cause proportionately fewer changes. Moreover, the first tow may have occurred years or decades ago."

According to Paul MacGregor, executive director of the At-Sea Processors Association that represents the Seattle-based Bering Sea factory trawler fleet, his clients constitute "by far the healthiest, best-managed fishery in the United States, if not the world." He notes that a 1999 report by the National Marine Fisheries Service lists some ninety U.S. species that are overfished or in danger, "Yet not one of those species is associated with the fisheries in which U.S. factory trawlers participate." As for the size of the vessels he represents, he contends anti-trawl activists miss the point "that it is the quality of fishery management and enforcement, not vessel size, which determines the health of the fisheries. The [Bering Sea] fisheries in which factory trawlers participate are healthy because fishery managers, when setting catch limits, select conservative and sustainable harvest rates based on their assessment of population abundance for each groundfish species."

Greenpeace charges that the trawlers are taking the food fish of scarce Steller sea lions and other creatures. On this issue, in a recent British book, *The Last of the Hunter Gatherers*, author Michael Wigan wryly comments, "Greenpeace has moved to the absurdist position of saying that industrial catch should be controlled to provide more food for sea mammals." The trawler people claim that Steller herds began to diminish at a time when the pollock mass—the trawlers' heaviest target—had reached record *high* levels so that there was plenty to go around. By 2000, however, responding to public pressure, the U.S. had closed trawling in several Bering Sea Steller breeding grounds on which American vessels had depended for their catch. Single-issue ecological fights, even those won, don't always constitute victories for the ecology. It appears that some of these protected grounds, unfished, now produce millions of hungry flatfish that eat the sea lions' (and protected walrus') food unmolested by humans.

Greenpeace further charges that the trawlers waste tons of sea life in by-catch. The amount of by-catch reported thrown overboard in some groundfisheries throughout the world is indeed disturbing and is now recognized as a problem that must be addressed. A powerful inducement for Bering Sea trawlers is that all catch, whether retained or discarded, counts toward a ship's (and the Bering Sea's) total quota, while compulsory observers keep reported weights honest. A new U.S. law requires commercial harvesters in the Bering Sea to retain and utilize all their pollock and cod regardless of size or target fishery.

The Bering Sea factory trawler people until recently were fighting more than Greenpeace for survival, while pointing out that the American Bering Sea groundfish industry would not exist without their risks and initiatives during the 1980s. For several years a tug-of-war has raged for allotments of Alaskan pollock between factory ships at sea and shoreside plants.

In Congress, Alaskan senior senator Ted Stevens brought his clout to bear for the shore plants (which incidentally produce more income for his state than the Seattle-based trawlers). Defending the Seattle fleet was fellow Republican senator Slade Gordon from Washington state. Stevens made ownership of the catcher-processors his issue, since despite a fifty-one-percent American share on paper and U.S. flagging, the majority of the ships were foreign dominated. In truth neither side had grass roots. Norwegians controlled most of the factory fleet, while of the four plants in the Dutch Harbor area, two are wholly owned Japanese subsidiaries and only one (Trident) is fully American-owned.

The senators' resultant compromise is expected to control groundfish operations in Alaskan waters well into the twenty-first century, and to set an enlightened example for management in other competing fisheries. The American Fisheries Act of late 1998 that they crafted starts by allotting forty percent of the pollock quota to the factory trawlers, fifty percent to shoreside plants serviced by catcher trawlers, and ten percent to motherships (at-sea factories serviced by catcher vessels, mostly foreign-owned but grandfathered), all this after ten percent is removed from the overall top for Native communities. The new law also raises from fifty-one percent to seventy-five percent the required American ownership of factory trawlers, and provides for the elimination of several vessels, including eight Norwegian-owned already gone for scrap by early 2000.

In exchange for the largest quota, the shoreside plants will help fund the fleet drawdown. The diminished but Americanized at-sea companies in their turn are allowed to form a cooperative. The co-op, now in place under the At-Sea Processors Association, is able to control and assign its quotas. This is expected to reduce expenses and help the environment, reasoned as follows: eliminating the competitive grab for fish among ships will allow the catcher-processors leisure to seek schools of mature fish, thus resulting in less waste from by-catch and undersized fish. Detractors worry that the co-op may become a kind of cartel that shuts out non-members. The pieces are still settling. At this writing the benefits to the health of the resource appear impressive.

Some Light with Other Villains

Under pressure for "dolphin-safe" tuna, an entire American fishery gave up and disappeared from Southern California. Its avatar now operates in the western Pacific with mostly foreign crews chasing lower-valued skipjack tuna that school less with dolphins. In 1986 fishermen killed an estimated 133,000 dolphins in eastern Pacific nets while setting on the desirable yellowfin tuna, according to Dr. Martin Hall, chief scientist of the Inter-American Tropical Tuna Commission. The 1996 kill, reliably tabulated under full observer coverage, was 2,500—a mere 0.04 percent of an estimated ten million population, and by 1998, below 2,000. The kill diminishes further each year "by fishing better rather than fishing less," says Hall, whose work has helped make this happen by analyzing observer data and finding gear techniques least likely to ensnare dolphins.

Hall defends setting on dolphins as ecologically sound. "It catches the optimum-size tuna. There's less than one percent by-catch, while you net very few juveniles of the next generation. When boats fish dolphin-safe, say on floating objects, they don't kill dolphins but they have discards like ten thousand immature tuna per set. Maybe twenty-five percent of the catch is discarded. Very small tuna, sexually imma-ture, five-pounders compared to fifty- or sixty-pounders on dolphin. And there's significant by-catch of other species like sharks and rays and mahi mahi, which are also discarded dead to the ocean. So the question is, what do people prefer? Just save one dolphin and kill a lot of other animals? Or try to make a more intelligent use of the resources."

Meanwhile, with canny or innocent piety, upscale restaurants adver-tise "dolphin-safe" tuna steaks, and those who afford them eat with a warm feeling that something's been done right. A sensible new U.S. law signed in mid-1997 at least redefines "dolphin-safe" to include tuna caught setting on unharmed dolphins: a law supported by Greenpeace but denounced by hardline groups as the "Dolphin Death Act."

Zero by-catch of dolphins, or any other species, is unrealistic. If we allow the human race to keep expanding—as unrealists atop another high plateau demand while they denounce responsible efforts to curb overpopulation—then morally we should do all we can do to provide for everybody at the earth's table. The noble effort has thus far failed. The sentimental protection of attractive creatures not remotely endan-gered—like dolphins, or meat-producing harp seals and minke whales—is arrogance by a people so secure in their own food supply that they can ignore the larger world.

A harder call is that for endangered sea turtles versus endangered shrimpers in the Gulf of Mexico states. These fishermen are more pressured than most because the big browns and whites they harvest come up with masses of small fish by-catch as well as, in some areas, turtles, none of it acceptable these days. All have been legislated to carry awkward grills in their nets called TEDs—turtle exclusion devices. At first, TEDs required on the mud grounds of Louisiana, but designed for sandy Florida bottoms, came up clogged with gumbo rather than shrimp, with web torn by the weight, and decimated fishermen's harvest and income. Blockades and even shootings followed the order among angrily independent Gulf shrimpers, also stressed in the past two decades by the government-assisted import of Vietnamese refugees who now compete in their fishery. Other activities—sport-fishing, for example—also kill the turtles, but commercial fishermen with less political clout became the target. A further law will soon require a second grid that allows small fish to escape. Bureaucrats wisely changed the name of this insert from its original "fish exclusion device," FED, to BRD: "by-catch reduction device."

The issue may be reaching a positive conclusion. Shrimpers, many grudgingly but nevertheless in compliance, have accepted the grids and turned their energies to improving them for the least detriment. In early 1998 *National Fisherman* reported a combined TED-BRD tried in Georgia to be effective without shrimp loss. "A funnel mounted behind the TED directs shrimp into the bag while creating an eddy that allows fish to swim out two escape holes." Fishing people of each generation, when pushed to it, solve problems.

Other Atlantic coast nations also now protect the by-catch that schools with warm-water brown and white shrimp. (There is no need to do this with the smaller cold-water pink shrimp off Alaska, Grand Bank, and Norway, which come up free of by-catch.) A United Nations document of late 1997 reports that Cuba, Venezuela, and Brazil, among others, now require shrimp by-catch excluders or by-catch utilization.

American swordfish driftnetters on the West Coast have worked with environmental groups to avoid entangling whales. The fleet modified its gear to hang at least six fathoms below the surface so that whales could swim over, and attached sonic pingers to warn whales away. Data from federal observers in 1997 showed a seventy-seven percent reduction in whale entanglement. American longline fishermen, faced with seabirds drowned when they peck at bait and hook themselves, must now by law attach weights that immediately sink baited lines beyond the reach of even diving birds. They must also discharge offal on the boat side opposite the hauling station to distract birds from the hooks.

Sometimes neither villains nor rescuers are fishermen. In Cambodia by 1980, following the Khmer Rouge's destruction of boats and nets, the freshwater catch from the Mekong River, and Lake Tonle Sap that it feeds, had fallen from 90,000 to 10,000 tons. Yet, the busy fisheries that I saw in the mid-1990s, on the great Tonle Sap, had been restored. Credit primarily the European Economic Community. To start the recovery, the EEC (now the EU) trucked in traps, gillnets, boats, processing equipment, small ice plants, ovens for smoking, basic tools, outboard engines, and even the bicycles needed for basic intercommunication.

Fish Farms: Not Necessarily

Aquaculture has become a major industry, considered by some the solution to stressed ocean wilds. The practice is certainly here to stay and, when done without harming other parts of the environment, will be an increasingly important world food resource. Fishermen are learning to bend with it, even to join. A day-long seminar on the subject at the Maryland Watermen's Association's annual exposition in January 1998 showed the variety of options. It included sessions on: Oysters, Softcrab Production, Raising Tilapia, Scallop Culture, and New Species for the Future. Fish culture, as practiced in China for centuries, seems to have found a balance with nature. (Or perhaps the Chinese aren't talking.) It may be true for some species like carp. It appears so for oysters. Not, it's turning out, for salmon—big business now in Norway, Canada, Chile, and elsewhere—or for shrimp throughout Asia and in South America.

Farmed salmon has pushed wild salmon from grocery shelves and menus all over America, partly because it is usually cheaper, but also because its production sounds so ecologically neat. Yet salmon raised in pens have proved unecological. They require almost four pounds of low-value fish, reduced to feed meal, for each pound of meat produced. The pens, although located in ambient water, gather concentrated feces and consequent parasites, pollution, and disease. All this requires quantities of antibiotics, vaccines, antifoulants, pesticides, and even flesh colorants. When pen-raised salmon escape into the ocean, as they sometimes do, growing evidence suggests that they carry their contaminants with them to affect wild salmon, even to upsetting genetic homing patterns. In Washington, where in July 1997 some 300,000 transplant-farmed Atlantic salmon escaped in a single accident, the state now by law terms the species (which have different diseases and resistances than do Pacific salmon) to be "living pollutants" subject to control like sewage and other discharges.

According to various 1997 reports: In Chile the bacterium *Piscirickettsia salmonia* has caused a seventy to eighty percent farmed salmon mortality in some areas. In Scotland, salmon farmers now administer the pesticide ivermectin to control sea lice infestations in salmon pens, which inevitably enters the marine environment. In Ireland sea lice floating from the pens have affected wild sea trout. The Norwegians, in controlling an outbreak of furunculosis (oozing sores) originating from salmon pens, poisoned twenty rivers at a cost of $100 million. Sweden has defined salmon farming as an "environmentally dangerous industry."

Catfish farmed in America appear not to pollute, but they are fed on grain meal. As with salmon fed on fish meal, the practice uses much of one protein to make less of another.

Farmed shrimp present a startling ecological record. A virus, called Taura after the river in Ecuador where it was first encountered in 1992, has spread through stocks grown and sold among shrimp farmers, and has caused devastating losses in South America. By 1995 Taura had migrated into some U.S. shrimp farms, which are concentrated in Texas and North Carolina. A recent National Marine Fisheries Service report states that exotic diseases (specifically Taura, White Spot, Yellow Head, and IHHN) are causing "catastrophic" losses on domestic shrimp farms. According to the report: "These outbursts have raised concerns that viruses could spread from aquaculture facilities to the wild shrimp stocks in the U.S. coastal waters with potentially serious implications."

To build tidal ponds for exportable tiger prawns, the Thais have destroyed more than ninety percent of their mangrove swamps, habitat for an ecosystem of creatures including fish and crabs. The disposed feces and chemical-laden muck of the ponds either pollutes the land, or drains back into the ocean to suffocate the sea life caught by fishermen for local consumption. Further, the salt sea, no longer restrained by mangrove swamps, ruins paddies where rice depends on fresh water. Different versions of this ecological mess have been repeated throughout southeast Asia.

At present much of aquaculture offers no panacea to feed the world without harming the precious wilds.

Good Cops: Darkness and Signs of Light

Some seas of the world need always to be protected from industrial efficiency, while all need hard limits on their capacity. In the late 1990s an international riot of boats has converged in southern waters roughly bounded by Argentina and the Republic of South Africa to catch the deep-lying toothfish or sea bass. These creatures have provided a substitute in the Japanese market for species now scarce, and without regulation may themselves be soon depleted. The FAO suggests that boats here are taking seven or eight times more than agreed quotas. On the other hand, Alaskan waters are managed tightly enough that shutting down an entire industry of trawler-processors might give warm righteousness to some with nothing to lose (or in the case of shore plant interests, give tangible product), but would unnecessarily ruin others.

In truth, stocks depleted through poorly regulated overfishing have proved the need for controls to ensure the sea's resources. Only a rare fisherman transcends human nature to sacrifice himself for the common good. I've seen fishdeck subterfuges all over the globe, to beat prevailing law or to outright break it when the cops aren't looking. A grave problem for managers trying to assess the health of ocean stocks is illegal unreported fishing in areas where enforcement is slack or nonexistent, and a multiplication of this makes some data questionable enough to treat it conservatively. "In developing countries," observes economist Michael Geoghegan, "gathering fishery statistics is an art of probability. A twitch of salt over your shoulder will help in the assessment."

Without vigilance, even international commitments can fall short, as with that of a 1992 ban on long driftnets. In July 1996 patrol ships of the United States and Taiwan cooperated to catch a Taiwanese driftnetting in the North Pacific. In June 1997 a U.S. Coast Guard C-130 plane on patrol sighted an illegal driftnetter registered to the Peoples Republic of China, but had no ship on location for chase when it fled. The Chinese government reported the offender's registration invalid, but declared intent to arrest the vessel if it entered Chinese waters. While Japan and other Asian nations have enforced the driftnet ban despite hardships to their fishermen, Italy appears to have trouble with its large, traditional driftnet fleet in the Mediterranean. Under U.S. pressure, Italy in mid-1996 finally signed an agreement to end the practice. But a year later, Humane Society International reported to the United Nations that, during a spot check in the single port of Porticello, "no less than 80 driftnet vessels were found, some with nets clearly exceeding 10 km in length."

The same United Nations document contained reports from several nations on their success (not verified) in complying with the driftnet ban. The list suggests the range of an international effort: Barbados, Mauritius, Latvia, Maldives, Pakistan, Norway, South Korea, the United States, Oman, the Bahamas, Thailand, Turkey, Italy (reports fifty-fifty cost sharing with fishermen to convert gear on 676 driftnet vessels), the European Union, New Zealand, Malta, Kiribati, Fiji, the Philippines, and the states of Micronesia.

Enforcement has given Pacific coast fishermen from California to Washington more than their share of misery. A 1973 federal decision allowed Indian tribes rights to half the Northwest's Pacific salmon, based on old treaties. A 1994 ruling extended this to include other fish as well as crab and shrimp, even though the Indian fishing population is less than ten percent that of others fishing in the region. It put many fishermen out of business, or diverted them heavily to other species. Now, groundfish stocks have suddenly decreased, whether by pressure diverted from salmon, temporarily by El Niño warming that drives out feed plankton, by computer glitches (as charged by one responsible fishing group), or by sheer change of Nature. By early 1998 the National Marine Fisheries Service had imposed drastic quota reductions on all fishermen except Indians, now protected by treaty.

On the East Coast of North America it is generally conceded that the Americans and Canadians who managed the Atlantic cod and other groundfish yielded too often to pressure from fishermen, whatever the latter's need to meet boat payments and pay the bills. Not that the managers didn't agonize, and work sincerely for a balanced solution. They did, often, juggling valid interests while hoping for the best. New England grounds have a stew of species unmatched in the West. A monthly market report in *Commercial Fisheries News* lists not only cod, but haddock, pollock, hake, catfish, redfish, skate, dogfish, scallops, shrimp, loligo squid, monkfish, graysole, lemonsole, blackbacks, yellowtails, plaice, and dabs. Thirteen groundfish species, including cod, haddock, and yellowtail flounder, school together but must be monitored separately within a single management plan. Regulation is not simple.

The late 1990s have seen tighter management off New England: A buyback program to purchase boats and expire their licenses to reduce the groundfish fleet; enforced large mesh size to allow the young of the next generation to escape; areas closed at spawning time, and some closed permanently as marine sanctuaries; and, under the newest plan, a limit on the number of days a year that a boat targeting groundfish can work—eighty-eight since 1997. Stocks are slowly recovering. Boats now bring in some species once wasted or ignored, like dogfish. Each program creates hardship: Limited fishing days mean lowered family incomes. Retired boats leave entire crews jobless, and each represents essentially the close of a small business. Monkfish, which the government urged as a new species, appears now overfished.

On the other side of the Atlantic the amalgam of nations comprising the European Union must deal with competing fishing interests and give-and-take sharing beyond the nightmares of U.S. and Canadian negotiators (who, for example, took from 1969 to 1999 to agree on managing the West Coast salmon that move between Alaska, British Columbia, and Washington). Different mores and cultures, and old animosities, leave a constant potential for aggravation. When Spain joined the EU and received fishing rights, which they now dominate, a worried Ireland sent enforcement agents to train a bit with the Canadians and learn how to handle anticipated trouble. The EU's Common Fisheries Policy, which seeks to lower by forty percent the effort on overfished stocks, has not yet succeeded. Outraged British fishermen are reported illegally landing a "black" catch forty to sixty percent higher than that the new quotas allow: fish they considered their own until their country joined the EU and was required to share.

Yet conservative management has kept some fish stocks in good shape, and restored others. Norway voted in 1994 to remain outside the EU, a decision heavily weighted by fishermen unwilling to give over control of their national grounds. According to Norway's fishery minister, Jan Henry Olsen, in a 1996 interview: "The EU should get a better grip on fisheries management policy in the North Sea. Norway is stricter, our stocks in good shape. We have a stringent regime of short-notice fishery closures, regulations, enforcement, and a multi-species approach to stock management. And a sensible approach to by-catch. We learned our lesson." He meant the cod crisis that hit Norway in the late 1980s and early 1990s.

Cod has indeed returned to Norwegian waters. When the northern stocks shared by Norway and Russia plunged, a joint commission of the two nations in 1990 reduced the entire quota in their 200-mile waters—once an annual 800,000 metric tons—to 160,000 mt (including negotiated shares with EU countries in exchange for other fishing rights). By 1994 there was enough recovery to raise the total allowable catch to 700,000 and in 1997 to 850,000 mt.

Iceland also has positive news. This island country, which lives by the seafood in its adjacent waters, overfished until the mid-1980s, and it cod stocks nearly disappeared. After a decade of harsh boat restrictions, biologists report strong year classes of cod that have built to maturity. The fishery is again strong.

Norway herring is another positive story, a tale of both belated good management and of good luck. In the 1950s and 1960s one of the largest herring stocks in the world straddled the waters off Norway and adjacent countries, but by the late 1960s it had been fished almost to extinction and the fishery collapsed. No Norwegian breakfast table lacks herring, so this was a regional disaster on all fronts. Then in the early 1970s biologists found a pocket of herring stocks hidden in a fjord where no one had fished. The Norwegian government imposed a complete ban: Otherwise boats would have converged. The herring stock, of which this was a segment, spawns on the Norwegian coast, but the larvae drift north to Russia on prevailing currents. To persuade the Russians to leave the juvenile herring alone to grow, the Norwegians negotiated other quotas. "So together we were able to rebuild this stock," according to Stein Owe, fisheries counselor for the Norwegian embassy in Washington. The herring biomass has now recovered. It continues to spawn in Norway but migrates beyond that nation's waters. By agreements between Norway and Russia, Iceland, the Faeroe Islands, and the European Union, the nations again have a herring fishery. The 1997 catch was 1.5 million tons from a biomass of 6 million tons. "Good news as long as it stays," says Owe with Norwegian caution. "But fragile." Overfishing is always a danger if biologists prove wrong in their estimates, or if one party of several breaks the rules.

Any record of farsighted management at near-term sacrifice must include Maryland. In 1985 the legislature imposed a moratorium on catching all striped bass. Rockfish, their local name (the very rock I'd catch by the dozen with my dad and granddad), had gone from abundance to virtual disappearance. Maryland's upper Chesapeake Bay holds the spawning grounds for ninety percent of the entire East Coast stock, from New England to the Carolinas. For a while other states made Marylanders look the suckers by continuing to catch the stripers when they migrated from home water. Eventually a national protective law followed spotty regulations in some states. By the late 1990s rockfish had recovered in healthy enough force to satisfy the needs of both sport and commerce in Maryland and elsewhere.

Fishermen are good at thrashing as they damn regulations and the bureaucrats who make them. Larry Simns, soft-spoken director of the Maryland Watermen's Association who is both a commercial fisherman and charterboat captain (he needs both to make a living), drawls out the strategy that kept sportfishermen from claiming his state's entire striped bass quota. This followed the moratorium, after the stocks had returned enough for the state to allow cautious quotas. "We knew that if we opened the fishery the way we'd closed it, the gamefish people would soon have the ammunition to get rid of us. So we voluntarily put harsh restrictions on the commercial fishery, made sure our restrictions were harsher than the recreational so we could guarantee we didn't go over quota. Like, we tagged every fish, checked at the check-in stations every night. Then when the game people went to the legislature, and said they should make it a gamefish, people said, 'Why? You're not saving *fish* that way. Commercial's staying under their quota, it's recreational's going over.' That saved us."

Simns continued:

"It took a lot to get our fishermen to agree, even with the support of my board. Sometimes they didn't agree, we just done it anyway. Sometimes you put restrictions on yourself to save yourself. That's what didn't happen in Florida, and commercial fishermen got put out of business. Their leaders told me: 'Our people wouldn't let us compromise.' The states that's lost it are the ones that drew a line in the sand and said 'we're not goin' to give you anything.' You can do that for a while, but eventually you lose." The stock now multiplies yearly, but: "We're still catching under quota," says Simns firmly.

In Chesapeake Bay country that drains from New York to Pennsylvania and flows through Maryland and Virginia, rockfish is not the only hopeful story. Two decades ago the health of the great estuary had turned wrong everywhere, but only fishermen and marine scientists seemed to pay attention. In the early 1980s the Environmental Protection Agency generated a report that synthesized existing research to document the conditions of the Bay's decline—plummeted catches, anoxic (without oxygen) water where sea life stifled, disappearing sea grasses that had been habitat for all manner of birds and fish although a damned nuisance in propellers. The report showed that the causes included not only industrial toxics but, to general surprise, an explosion of nutrients from fertilizers and treated sewage that stimulated oxygen-sucking algae into overproduction. The report drew enough attention that politicians, hitherto mainly uninvolved, saw the voter appeal of cleaning the Bay. Many laws, citizen initiatives, and interstate cooperations later, there has been slow, upward progress. While not enough, underwater grasses have increased and anoxic waters declined, some wildlife (eagles but not diving ducks) fly the area again, agricultural runoff from pesticides and fertilizers is better managed, and air pollution has decreased per car (although the number of cars driving the area has quadrupled). The work continues, its importance accepted. As resources recover, planners have begun to consider long-range priorities, since potential users have inevitably started to speak up for future rights to the resources.

Harmful planktons have begun to threaten worldwide coastal fisheries more than ever before. During a few weeks in the summer of 1997 a sinister condition surfaced in the Pocomoke River off Chesapeake Bay following appearances elsewhere in estuarine waters off the U.S. Central Atlantic coast. A microscopic organism called *pfiesteria* chewed lesions into fish, killed them by the thousands, and temporarily affected some humans after direct contact. Will it return? While Bay watermen uneasily first called the thing "hysteria," reflecting its level of local news coverage, pfiesteria is real.

One of a group of phytoplanktons neither plant nor animal called dynoflagellates (which include destructive "red tides" in other waters), pfiesteria generally lives harmless in bottom sediments. It can mutate with dogged survival through twenty-four known life stages, however, and two predatory stages of these were stimulated unexpectedly to produce the fish kills. After doing its damage the pfiesteria reassumed a benign form and settled again to the seafloor. The organism is believed to have existed since prehistoric times: part of the natural environment, neither practical nor advisable to try destroying.

Scientists, just beginning to concentrate on the problem in North Carolina and Chesapeake Bay, tentatively blame excess nitrogen and phosphorus from hog and chicken farm effluent for stimulating the microbe into its harmful forms. Nutrient management to date has focused on excesses of nitrogen. It may be that the focus was too narrow, ignoring the other elements in manure and related runoffs. Actual fish stress may be a related factor, due to pollution, and to other factors that make the fish vulnerable to disease and microbe invasion (as are herring in Prince William Sound following the stressfull oil spill). A deeper cause in Chesapeake Bay may be the decline of oysters, themselves the prey of the natural diseases MSX and Dermo. These bivalves act as natural filters that remove algae and phytoplankton, including pfiesteria, from the water. Six states, from Delaware to North Carolina, have officially begun to share pfiesteria research, a positive way to start facing the problem. The state governments are, with renewed urgency, marking fresh funds for pollution control.

The parasite *Hematodinium* sporadically kills crustaceans in Europe and North America. In 1991 and 1999 it hit crab fisheries along the U.S. East Coast, baffling scientists.

Coming About

Preserving a steady food supply from the sea while juggling competing interests will be a great task of the twenty-first century. Despite pockets of overfishing and depletion, enough whistles have been sounded to scare those able to take hard action into doing so before it is too late. In the United States, the Magnuson Act of 1976 concentrated most of its first two decades on managing the growth of an industry, but with new authorizing language now focuses on conserving the resource. Other countries—not all—are doing the same. The comeabout may be slow, but it has assumed positive direction. There is reason to be optimistic as long as we continue to run intelligently alarmed.

Let this be a plea for perspective and fairness in dealing with an industry of food gatherers as they adapt to change in a livelihood more dangerous and insecure than most.

Appropriate actions, some urgent, include:

- Reduce fishing to a sustainable level.
- Rehabilitate overfished stocks.
- Restore injured marine ecosystems.
- Adjust the size of fishing fleets to a sustainable yield.
- Reduce by-catch, discards, and other waste.
- Develop sustainable but ecological aquaculture.

According to the UN Food and Agriculture Organization (FAO), while some thirty-five percent of the two hundred most important marine fish stocks are overexploited and another twenty-five percent are fully exploited, some forty percent of stocks still have the capacity to be developed. Among those who make it their business to ponder the state of ocean resources, many agree that there is untapped food potential in these sea creatures not yet targeted as well as in the discards and by-catch of nets and hooks.

In a 1999 presentation at a Brussels seafood expo, Dr. Gerd Hubold of the German Federal Research Center declared, citing the FAO figure of the two hundred "most important" marine stocks, that world fisheries are based on not enough stocks from among some twenty-five thousand known. Hubold contended that another twenty million more tons a year could be converted for human consumption if fishing efforts were switched to include other species, and if more by-catch was utilized.

Among ideas: manage fish as a common world resource in order to ensure sustainable use. One of those proposing this is Alexander Fridman, Chairman of Commercial Fisheries at the Moscow Institute for Fishing Industry and Economy. In a 1999 book, *World Fisheries: What Is to Be Done?*, he advocates two main elements; an Advisory Global Fishing Management System, and a World Council of Fishing Ministers.

The UN Agreement on Straddling Stocks (under Law of the Sea) that awaits ratification by thirty nations is the most promising international direction thus far. It has set a new international standard that many nations have begun to observe, whether they have committed or not.

Among imaginative approaches on a selective level are artificial reefs made with sunken objects that attract sea life. The Japanese have fine-tuned the process, tailoring each reef to local currents for maximum sea life generation. However, reefs tear trawls, so they aren't a universal solution. Another approach is marine sanctuaries that forbid or limit all fishing, whether commercial or sport. These work only with cooperation and enforcement. Limited sanctuaries like the eight-hundred-forty-two-square-mile Stellwagen Bank off New England have shown that marine species can regenerate when left alone.

In area management, a positive new example is the U.S. policy hammered out by late 1998 for Bering Sea groundfish. Provisions of the American Fisheries Act of 1998 have reduced the number of factory trawlers that were competing, sometimes recklessly, for a quota kept purposely conservative. The act allows those remaining to form a cooperative that presumably will result in greater stewardship of the resource. Since fish remain to be caught, there seems no reason to fear that the fishing occupation will become obsolete, even though its quality may be endangered. Only that it may become increasingly the work of company employees rather than boatowning independents, a fate like that of small farmers and shopkeepers in first world countries. (Peasant fishing-village economies are more likely to remain the same: at least if their governments protect them.)

Certain massed fish enterprises, like that for surimi groundfish, need company-level organization and investment. But the coastal nation that sells out its fishermen in small and middle-size boats to commercial or sports organizations will indeed lose a resource of seafaring savvy. These are the kinds of men and women whom poets, politicians, and advertisers call for good reason the Backbone of the Nation, precious for maritime defense (as Norway recognizes) in times of military crisis.

A bright spot: In Gloucester I called expansive, eager, work-driven Joey Testaverde, with whom I'd last ridden nearly a decade before aboard an aging wooden dragger in the fleet of a collective second-generation Italian community. I dreaded to hear depressing news, what with New England fishery shortages and Draconian regulations. Instead, it took more than a week to find Joey because he was so busy at sea in his since-acquired steel boat. He and his brothers now fished whiting, and delivered it fresh-iced to their closest port every few days for immediate flight to Spain, not to fluctuating Boston or New York markets. In December he'd start on shrimp closer to home for at least three months. What of the others with whom I'd shared late-afternoon beers after deliveries on days that started at 3 A.M.? All still fishing, though some skippers had sold their boats in the buyback program or lost them at sea, and now crewed with less bookkeeping hassle. While no comfort to hopeful young greenhorn outsiders, the Italian-generation boat community had tightened to accommodate mainly family and buddies, and remained. Like Jack Troake and Don Best in Newfoundland—committed professionals and survivors—Joey and the others still complain freely, roll with the times, and adapt.

Adaptation, indeed, is everything now for a fisherman's survival, whether it be finding imaginative use for former discards, or hanging tough. *National Fisherman* reports regularly on new twists. A recent article tells of two fishermen paralyzed by accidents who, too enamored of their occupation to give it up, have adapted elevated wheelchairs that enable them to continue fishing. (One of them fishes alone!) Among new markets reported: Some Florida fishermen with nets legislated away by sports interests have found Asian buyers for dried "cannonball" jellyfish. On the wilder side (and reported without recommendation) Malaysian fishermen in the state of Sabah suddenly denuded some one thousand pay phones. They had found that the mouthpieces, connected to batteries and lowered into the water, emitted a high-pitched sound that attracted fish to their nets.

There *will* be fewer fishermen on fewer boats. There must be, if those who remain are to make their living on a finite resource. Technology made fishing too efficient, while too many boats and fishermen entered in good times. The hardship of this reality continues in the United States, Canada, the United Kingdom, Spain, Russia, Japan . . . everywhere. But pain to some means that others will keep making it

A wise editorial in *Fishing News International,* the London-based house organ of fisheries worldwide, commented on the UN agreement to rules of international fishery conservation: "What continues to strike us is the sheer abundance offered by the world's marine resources away from the black spots, and the real opportunities which still exist in the industry. If new laws herald managed fisheries which increase catch rates and turn around the economics of fishing ship operations, then this new start can bring real benefits. The UN Straddling Stocks agreement must be applied in the spirit of development rather than constriction to achieve this."

Predicting the Unpredictable

Global distribution has become so routine that diners in the wealthier nations probably need never fear for lack of seafood, and not just from the great marketing centers like Tokyo, New York, and London. Joey Testaverde and his brothers in Gloucester now sell their whiting direct to Spain. Bill Morgan, of three-generation Morgan Seafoods on Virginia's Rappahannock River off Chesapeake Bay, ships in pasteurized crab meat from Vietnam to stay in business, while continuing to buy all the local product he can find. There will always be pockets of crisis. Some will result from causes predicted but ignored, like overfishing or the *EXXON Valdez* oil spill. Others will spring from surprises that might be anticipated but are beyond known control, like El Niño or the pfiesteria microbe. The media can be expected to present each as the end of life as we know it but, to judge from the past, effort and time will mitigate the worst damage. I dare to be optimistic, like Jim Winter's Newfoundlanders.

Here are some apparent trends in the world's waters:

The Indian Ocean and Western Pacific, according to the FAO, are the only seas left with resources yet to tap. All others are being fished to capacity, though not necessarily overfished.

Remote seamounts in the southern hemisphere may yet hold unfished species in deep water. The Republic of South Africa, in part because of this, and with its eastern face to the Indian Ocean, is becoming a world player in the fish business. So also is Argentina. The efforts of other nations will rise and fall. With tight management, the United States and Canada have enough sea wealth off their coasts to recover what has been lost from overfishing—probably. Great Britain is not so endowed. In past centuries London's Billingsgate Fish Market rivaled Japan's present Tsukiji for abundance. Now British trawlers, which once dominated all that nation's surrounding distant waters from Norway to Iceland, no longer stride as far—for the time—under the limitations of the European Union. Spain keeps pushing, determined to remain a fisher of the world's seas. Chile, jump-started by bold entrepreneurs like the Gringos Schmidt, is expected to move into grounds beyond its coasts. China we know is expanding its fleets, Japan perhaps pulling in.

Finding solutions to overfishing has become a world priority, brought home in the most vivid way possible by emptying nets. As responsible governments pass more regulations there will be failures painful to fishermen and investors, eventually fewer boats. And, since fishermen are human, there will be cheating along the way, both malevolent and desperate. Regulations and agreements, however, should come in time to stave off the worst of future crashes. Expect intelligent management—not without sacrifice—to stabilize and even increase some sea stocks now threatened.

Much previous management, as in New England, has focused on the state of individual stocks within an ecosystem. A realistic trend is now to manage an entire ecosystem as a whole, taking into account the effect of one stock on another. Marine biologists have warned that too much fish removed from the lower part of the food chain may create a domino effect of starving creatures higher on the chain.

Despite doomsaying, the world sea harvest continues to grow—one hundred twenty-two million tons in 1997 compared to one hundred million a decade before. A caution not always revealed by the statistics, however, is that much of the volume comes from fish low on the food chain that are rendered into meal and then, for example, into fish farm pellets. Thus, they only contribute to the human food supply in a secondary form. Four pounds of meal fish in this pellet form are required for every pound of farmed salmon they produce.

By-catch, a relatively new concern, will move from an emotional cause begun by environmentalists to practical ecosystem management: assigning value and finding use for what are now considered less desirable species. Aquaculture will grow in importance, but to augment rather than displace fishing direct from nature. Pollution control, at least close to shore, will become a higher priority of local governments.

Some superabundances are probably gone for the remaining days of older fishermen. Jack Troake of Newfoundland thinks so of cod, the Fish to him, when he paints "She's gone, boys, she's gone" on the boat with which he continues to make his living however he can. Concludes old-hand Arthur Nilson of Norway, a traditional coastal fisherman for half a century, who with his bright-tongued, net-pulling wife Sigrun spiced the Lofotens scene when I fished near them in 1980: "When I began, nature alone [e.g. natural forces] was the limiting factor in what man could expect to gather in his nets. Now man has caused the limits by taking too much."

How many of the tales in this book have been a report of overfishing in progress? Definitely that of handlining for bluefin tuna off New Zealand, although ultimately the fault lay with big longliners rather than the small town-based boats. Nor does anyone dispute that over-fishing crashed the cod and flounder from Newfoundland to New England. The work now is to pick up the pieces and learn from experience not to let it happen again. Crab, shrimp, and lobster that have taken Western Atlantic cod's place appear to be holding up, for the time being, under national and international rules that have not allowed fishing to reach the industrial level formerly sanctioned on cod.

In Chile, who can say what happened to the *sardinas* after the huge set aboard Pepe Montt's inefficient little seiner *Elefantes*? Since many fish escaped that night despite the many taken, our bonanza could hardly have wiped out the whole coast without the help of some natural factor. The fish have slowly returned. After Hans Schmidt targeted deepwater Chilean sea bass, he himself saw the finite stocks begin to thin, and backed off into other fisheries. Hans, however, while pointing the way to this target, did not control other boats that followed.

Why king crab and shrimp vanished off Western Alaska has never been settled, except to spread the blame. During the latter years of the 1970s both were fished for all that regulated times and areas allowed, both were abundant beyond dreams, and both abruptly disappeared soon after the 1980 season. Nature played a part here, probably, with a fluctuating sea temperature that might have altered the crustaceans' tolerances or the course of their feed planktons, while the sudden draw-down of foreign groundfishing under the new Magnuson Act at just that time left more predator finfish to feed on baby crabs and shrimp.

Just so, an earlier reversal of these conditions may have created the one-time phenomenon of dreamlike crustacean quantities, since such numbers had not been recorded before.

Overfishing might have played no part. Kodiak bays closed to shrimping by Alaska Fish and Game circa 1976 to 1978, when I helped empty bulging moneybags of the little pandalids and shovel them by the ton, went as dry as those fished heavily. With long-growing king crab, biologists predicted weak recruit stocks on the way, so that the crash surprised only those who didn't read or believe the reports. King crabs are only now returning to the Bering Sea, but in modest numbers that can support only a few boats for a short season. Off Kodiak there has been no commercial fishery for either king crab or shrimp since the collapse.

Some stocks are stressed at this writing, like swordfish and bluefin tuna in possibly parts of the North Atlantic and Southern Pacific, when fished using the most efficient longline technologies. (Harpoon and handline fishing for these species remain selective and ecologically OK.) So, soon, will probably be the newly popular toothfish in the South Atlantic as all nations converge, including expansion-hungry China. These are far-ranging creatures not so easily regulated by individual nations.

Many of the fisheries of my tales, however, are roaringly healthy despite the warnings of some doomsayers who imply that all modern fishermen hazard the stocks of the ocean wilds. Plentiful are Alaska sockeye salmon in Bristol Bay, Chignik, and Copper River Flats, although runs in some years are big and in others thin. Minke whales and big neon flying squid have never been endangered, and now with the halt of most whaling and the ban of all long driftnets they are free to multiply, as are harp seals under other protection. The striped bass/rockfish husbanded back into numbers enough for both sport and commercial fishermen along the U.S. Atlantic coast are now so abundant that they threaten to gobble the young of other species. In Chile and Pery nothing seems to stem the flow, at any given time, of at least one of sardines, anchovy, or jack mackerel, all fished by the same means for the same ultimate fish meal product, although off different parts of the coast.

Jack Troake, who lost cod but now fishes a living on snow crab as far from land as 150 miles, reports with pleasure the 1997 reappearance of whales, dolphins, and birds in his part of the water, a sign that the small fish and planktons they feed on have also returned. "Haven't seen that since just before the fishery failed. For the past five, six years, haven't seen life on the ocean, just a dead sea. When we see things coming back, we know the environment is turning right again, see?"

The vitality of the world's waters to heal themselves when given the chance is awesome. But pollution of our oceans is a terrible danger for all living creatures, overfishing can tip the balance, and any complacency is stupid if it makes us drop our guard. An eternal truth is that nature has programmed everything living to need fuel. The sad fact for the year 2000 and beyond is that the Earth's root environmental threat is overpopulation. If we cannot, or will not, curb human reproduction, then we cannot—however painful—protect every single attractive creature that competes for the Earth's limited production of nourishment. What we can do is seek every possible means of balance to preserve humans and other creatures alike—all of us. The Seattle protestors, at their best, were seeking some means to do this.

In world waters, the United Nations' initiative awaiting ratifications offers one of the best hopes, but only if all nations enforce it. China, with its exploding fleet, will be a growing problem. All fisheries will need controls. The wisdom of the controls is what will count. There is no easy solution, only a direction in which to work.

To Fish

One Fourth of July in Kodiak my son, Wynn, and I start the day hearing the names called for those lost at sea. Then we watch the parade led by marching sailors from the nearby Coast Guard Air Station. The Coasties in their trim dress blues receive cheers as they pass. Some of the watchers owe their lives to rescues at sea. In the afternoon everyone crowds around a raised boxing ring erected in the harbor. Comers sign to put on the gloves for three rounds. Buddies swagger up as shipmates gleefully bet their greenbacks, fellows with a dockside grudge darkly climb the steps, and random adventurers square off against others their weight and size. Butch, a short, quiet man with a gold earring, a plugger on deck, turns out to be a driving tiger in the ring. During the afternoon some blood spills, but not as much blood as beer from the nearby Legion and other bars. This is an Alaskan fisherman's Fourth—at least it was in 1976. No more boxing nowadays. In an America become litigious, some injured bravo might decide to sue the city.

Things continue noisily, even when a light rain moves in. Eventually the part of Kodiak goes home that runs garages and supermarkets and law offices, as do the fishermen who have children to put to bed. The remaining celebrants, some like Butch with random purple bruises on his face and a peaceful expression, move into the bars. By eleven, however, the harbor lies deserted. Wynn and I, each yearning for a berth while supporting ourselves otherwise, have 5 A.M. cannery timeclocks to punch. But with Tom Casey we stroll the quay, too restless to give up the night. Only an occasional *whoop* alters the quiet. Lights glow sparsely from the canneries along the shore beyond town. They silhouette the masts of a hundred-odd fishing boats moored on the floats below the quay where we stand. Bulbs burn dim and yellow from a few cabin windows. A raw deck beam shines aboard a single boat. Figures pass seabags and cartons over its rail, a sure sign the crew is putting to sea. The engine starts with a few putts and a chug. A dark figure tosses mooring lines, calls "OK," and thuds aboard. The boat backs from its slip and the deck light snaps off, leaving the glow from a cabin window, the red point of the port running light, and a white running light atop the mast. To a quiet throb the boat traverses the passage among other hulls and masts, moving as a little package of lights. Out in the harbor buoys flash, inviting her on.

Beyond the breakwater enough sea takes over to make the mastlight swoop. The boat comes alive, entering its element. Wynn and I watch. We want to be aboard with boots bracing the wet deck rather than here with brogans kicking gravel. "Shit . . . " mutters Tom wistfully. He's experienced his share of harsh fishing aboard halibut longliners. All three of us know why boats, even the scruffiest, can find men to take them to sea. Tom has firecrackers. Each packet explodes into multiple rat-a-tats when we light and toss it. We light and toss.

Many fish because it is still the thing they want most in the world to do. Out of adeptness at a multitude of skills comes a pride in self-sufficiency. To fish requires working outdoors, which many prefer, and it combines the spice of gamble with that of the chase. Unique among ways to make a living, it depends on the pursuit and harvest of a product that remains invisible, inaccessible, until its capture. And then—call this appeal atavistic, in the way it can reach the animal subconscious—fishing sometimes requires the facing of primal forces as no other occupation.

For all their diversification the fishermen of the world have a commonality of outlook and experience that sometimes makes them more brothers around the world than with others of their own countrymen. You can see it in the way they visit on fishing grounds from Norway to Alaska to Chile to New Zealand, boat beside boat, to swap tales, pass messages, discuss weather, and generally complain about how hard times are, while scanning the other deck for clues of good catches and hedging on any of their own bonanzas.

You can see it in the way fishermen, even in a laid-back Bali village, compete for the largest catch and to be the first boat to deliver. "I am village head-man," explained Embli Astara as we fingered a cold curried rice concoction from a banana leaf after having carried our fish ashore in baskets balanced shoulder-high, wading chest-deep from the boat anchored just beyond the surf. "How will it look if I deliver late with only little?" Or, far distant from Bali in the icy Bering Sea, as spray cascades down the wheelhouse window, we gun harder than necessary toward the plants in Dutch Harbor a hundred miles away with our tanks full of crab. We want to be first in from the opening. "Then we don't wait in any goddamned line," rationalizes skipper Jack, but it really means that all of us want to be the crew and the boat that fished tough enough to fill our holds first.

You can see the commonality in the way a fisherman drops work in the middle of hauling gear, sometimes at loss of catch, to aid a fellow boat in distress even though it may be a rival—knowing of course that some day his own engine might die as wind carries him helpless toward a shoal.

You know it in the way coping with pain becomes part of the everyday. I felt it routinely with the sleep-robbing scorch of carpal tunnel syndrome from endlessly pushing the same wrist muscles to stack web, cull crabs, ice down shrimp, or gut cod. Backs, knees, feet, shoulders, neck, elbows: Fishermen all hurt eventually and most live in later years with arthritis.

Among themselves, you find community in the hearty manner most fishermen have toward the world—especially at delivery in fisheries that bring them together at the end of a hard trip. (Compare this to a farmer's weed-chewing taciturnity.) Fishermen are also known for straight talk—although sometimes they lace it with yarn and metaphor close to downright lying. Conversation dockside, wheelhouse, or in a fisherman's house, anywhere, seldom strays beyond: "Finally set in twenty fathom, and . . ." "Coming around nor'ly, I don't know . . ." "Needs overhaul . . ." "Gets you four cents a pound more over to . . ." "Three-and-a-quarter-inch mesh, that's what . . ." Fishermen's wives, incidentally, must accommodate to this obsession, wrapping their own lives around it in traditional fishing communities, often these days suing for divorce in more mobile communities. But that is another story.

The work itself is repetitive, but you find the unexpected every-where: in squalls, sunrises, empty nets and full ones, sudden towering seas or flat calm, breakdowns that challenge the ingenuity. There are terrible icy days when hours of working nets or lines with numb hands bring nothing but ripped web or hooks dangling rotten bait—nothing anywhere in the sea to pay even fuel and grub much less bills at home. Then there are days, now and then, when the gear comes in exploding with life. Legs on deck can barely move for the abundance. Scuppers must be blocked to keep fish from flapping out. You shout, laugh, dance, throw things—all the while knowing that now, instead of rest for a sore back between sets, you'll pick, mend, ice, shovel, bait, gut, strap, and haul for hours, even days, before your next stretch in a bunk. You may be near-dead with good fortune, but you're also alive, with every nerve and muscle blasting signals as seldom on land.

Down East in Maine I ride bundled in wool and oilskins against a brisk chill with a lobsterman as he works his pots. In a distance hazy rocks and spruce line the shore. Choppy gray water stings our faces with zips of spray. The odors on deck combine the stenchy bait barrel, the brine of fresh catch, and sickening engine exhaust. Suddenly the sun appears for a moment, to sparkle and glisten on everything wet. "Wish I could fish a thousand years, like this," he says.

Chignik, Alaska, 1986.

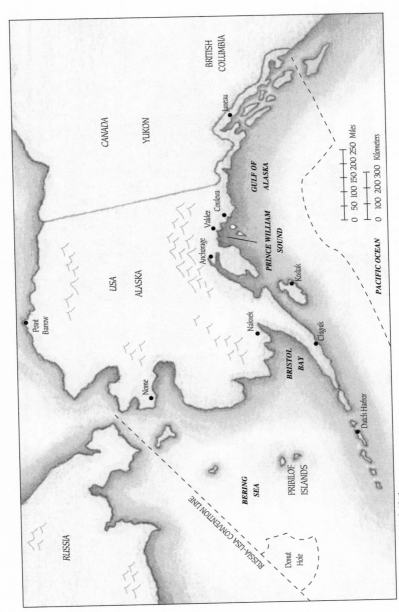

Bering Sea and Gulf of Alaska

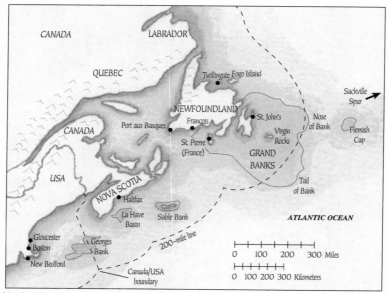

North Atlantic

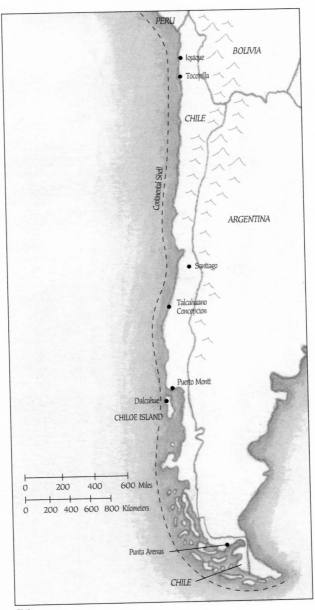

Chile

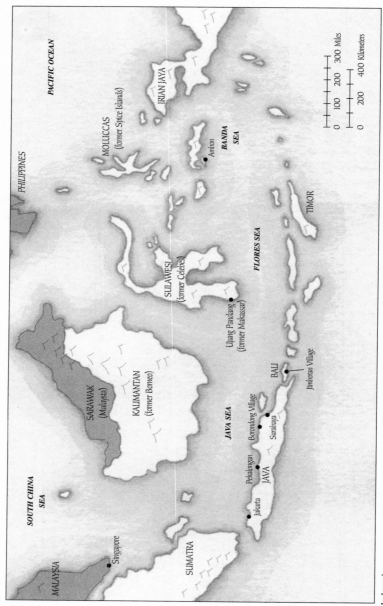

Indonesia

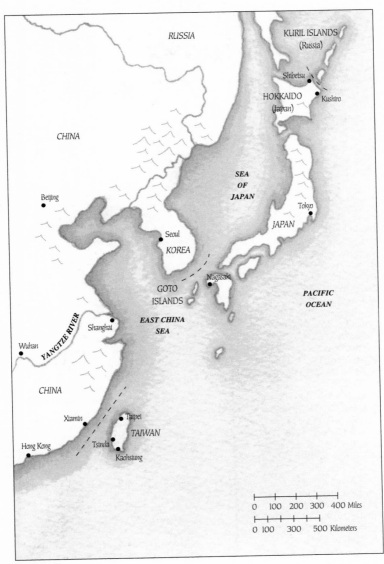

North Pacific

Index

photo by Wynn McCloskey

William McCloskey is a retired member of the Johns Hopkins University Applied Physics Laboratory. A former merchant seaman and Coast Guard officer, he returned to the sea as a peripatetic commercial fisherman in 1975 and has worked with crews all over the world. He is a keen observer of the politics as well as the practice of fishing, and his accounts, written from firsthand experience, interviews, and research, have appeared in *The New York Times*, *Atlantic Monthly*, *Smithsonian*, *National Fisherman*, and *International Wildlife*. His most recent book is *Breakers*, a sequel to his highly praised 1979 novel, *Highliners*.

"*Their Fathers' Work* is a rich, deeply rewarding text for anyone who has a love—or even a curiosity—about one of the world's oldest and hardest professions."

—*San Diego Log*

"McCloskey evokes vividly the strenuous but exhilarating life of men against the implacable ocean."

—*Library Journal*

"An eloquent statement about the poor health of the world's fisheries, as well as the lives of the world's fishermen. Few recent books have told their story in such epic proportions."

—*The Telegram*, St. John's, Newfoundland

"A gritty, evocative account of commerical fishermen at work in a hard profession."

—Peter Mathiessen, author of *In the Spirit of Crazy Horse*, *The Snow Leopard*, and *Bone by Bone*

"For twenty years, Bill McCloskey has been living and working with Alaskan fishermen; he knows us and writes about us better than anyone else. Some of the fleet's top highliners took him out on their seiners because they judged him to be a straight-shooter and a good shipmate. Reading the Alaska chapters will put you in the shoes of the fishermen who work Alaskan waters daily, trying to squeeze a living out of elusive fish and shellfish stocks, rough seas, high winds, and cold temperatures."

—Tom Casey, Bering Sea crab fishermen's representative

"No one writing today can match William McCloskey's knowledge of fishing or the breadth of his experience at sea. He is the writer of record on world fishing."

—William Warner, Pulitzer Prize winner, author of *Beautiful Swimmers* and *Distant Waters*